plished their goal. This book is simple yet profound and is chock-full of
al examples and illustrations. Interpreting the Bible correctly is not just
k of pastors or Bible teachers. It is the responsibility of every Christian,
ductive Bible Study provides the basic tools needed to make that possible."
—**Benjamin L. Merkle,** professor of New Testament and Greek,
e Southeastern Baptist Theological Seminary, Wake Forest, NC

npossible to study the Word of God too deeply or too well. These eternal
deserve the best we have to offer. It is exciting to see this work that blends
uctive method with the historical disciplines. To observe well on our part
dig well into the background behind the text has inestimable worth. Our
anks for this invaluable resource for quality Bible study."
—**Grant R. Osborne,** professor emeritus,
inity Evangelical Divinity School, Deerfield, IL

nd Köstenberger's new book will help a new generation of students dis-
e joy of studying the Bible for themselves. Here you will find a hermeneu-
ound and accessible guide to studying the Bible inductively."
—**Robert L. Plummer,** professor of New Testament interpretation,
e Southern Baptist Theological Seminary, Louisville, KY, and host
www.DailyDoseOfGreek.com

ny, engaging in Bible study can be overwhelming and complicated. Fuhr
stenberger have written a work that equips anyone to engage, investigate,
out the promises and truths of Scripture. If you are a small-group leader,
k will equip your small group to dig deeper into the Scriptures and ignite
to become lifelong students of God's Word."
—**Matt Purdom,** Kairos discipleship minister,
ntwood Baptist Church, Brentwood, TN

berger and Fuhr combine earlier work on the hermeneutical triad—the
l, literary, and theological context of a passage—with the traditional
of inductive Bible study. The result is not only a sound academic
to Scripture, but practical handles for observing, interpreting, and
the Scriptures. This book is a tremendous gift to the serious student of
. Highly recommended!"
—**Roger Severino,** adult minister of leadership,
ntwood Baptist Church, Brentwood, TN

RICHARD ALAN FUHR JR.
ANDREAS J. KÖSTENBERGER

INDUCTIVE
BIBLE
STUDY

OBSERVATION, INTERPRETATION, AND APPLICATION
through the Lenses of
HISTORY, LITERATURE, AND THEOLOGY

ACADEMIC
NASHVILLE, TENNESSEE

Inductive Bible Study
Copyright © 2016 by Richard Alan Fuhr and Andreas J. Köstenberger
Published by B&H Publishing Group
Nashville, Tennessee
All rights reserved.
ISBN: 978-1-4336-8414-2

Dewey Decimal Classification: 220.6
Subject Heading: BIBLE—STUDY AND TEACHING / BIBLE—CRITICISM /
BIBLE—EVIDENCES, AUTHORITY, ETC.

Printed in the United States of America
6 7 8 9 10   BP   25 24 23 22 21

Dedication

Contents

Authors' Preface

Why another book on inductive Bible study? Since the 1952 work *Methodical Bible Study* by Robert A. Traina, dozens of books, ranging from popular-level works to academic textbooks, have presented a methodical, inductive approach to the study of the Scriptures.[1] Another book is needed for the following two reasons. First, as evangelical scholarship of the Bible continues to bring greater insight to the field of hermeneutics, there's an ever-present need to incorporate those advances into a usable, applied guide for the study of the Bible. Second, as practitioners in teaching the next generation of students, we understand that there's always room for improvement in developing an academically sound yet practically manageable presentation for learning how to do Bible study. This text assimilates a hermeneutically viable model into a step-by-step methodical approach to Bible study. We trust that the next generation of students, pastors, and all who desire to know God's Word will be enriched by its insights and practical layout.

With the 2011 publication of *Invitation to Biblical Interpretation: Exploring the Hermeneutical Triad of History, Literature, and Theology*, I (Al) began incorporating the figure of the hermeneutical triad into my inductive Bible study courses.[2] By laying a foundation for what the Bible is as history, literature, and theology, I discovered that the traditional model of inductive study was not only compatible with the hermeneutical

---

1. Robert A. Traina, *Methodical Bible Study* (1952; repr., Grand Rapids: Zondervan, 2002).
2. Andreas J. Köstenberger and Richard D. Patterson, *Invitation to Biblical Interpretation: Exploring the Hermeneutical Triad of History, Literature, and Theology* (Grand Rapids: Kregel, 2011).

triad but was enhanced by it.[3] This textbook is the product of the vision to assimilate the hermeneutical-triad concept with a step-by-step, inductive methodology for the study of the Bible. It is borne out of the collaborative efforts between two individuals who have taught in the field of hermeneutics and inductive Bible study for a combined forty years. I (Andreas) have greatly appreciated my co-author's congenial partnership on this project. Having written a previous hermeneutics text, I was excited about the vision of incorporating the hermeneutical triad into the tried-and-true inductive Bible study method. I believe I can speak for both us in saying that blending the two approaches has worked out even better than either of us could have imagined.

In *Inductive Bible Study: Observation, Interpretation, and Application through the Lenses of History, Literature, and Theology*, the hermeneutical triad is the foundation upon which the inductive method is based. Building upward from the premise that the Bible is historical, literary, and theological and should be studied in terms of these three dimensions, the inductive method builds a framework for methodical, step-by-step study that embraces all facets of the hermeneutical triad. Following the framework of step-by-step progression, you might visualize the steps of the inductive method as moving upward from the historically grounded text to arrive at the pinnacle of theology, the natural result of an inductive study of Scripture. Our approach is to present individual, specific steps for applied study through the primary steps of observation, interpretation, and application. Within this framework, there are specific and unique steps of observation, interpretation, and application, all of which contribute to the development of biblical theology. Following the model of working upward from the triad base, each inductive step reflects an awareness of the Bible's historical, literary, and theological traits.

Our textbook is divided into four units. The first unit introduces inductive study with an overview of the challenges set before the modern reader. Tasked with the study of an ancient book, the modern reader is on a quest to discover its relevance for his or her life today. Through an

---

3. The hermeneutical triad approach proposes that the Bible should be studied in terms of its historical, literary, and theological dimensions.

awareness of basic hermeneutical principles and equipped with a step-by-step method for Bible study, we lay the foundation for a confident reception of God's Word in the twenty-first century.

The second unit of the textbook presents five steps of observation. These steps equip you to read the Bible as a book but to do so carefully, observing intently and asking proper questions of what lies before them through the written word. In the unit on observation, we explore the value of comparing translations as tools for observation (chapter 3), learning to ask the right questions of the text as an active listener (chapter 4), and reading with discernment (chapter 5). In addition, as further steps of observation, we explore miscellaneous features in prose and poetic literature (chapter 6) and learn to determine literary units through basic discourse analysis (chapter 7).

Our third unit involves the reader in exploring the second primary step of the inductive method: interpretation. Here we begin to analyze and interpret the data by considering historical, literary, and theological kinds of context (chapter 8), by performing interpretive correlation (chapter 9), and by focusing these efforts on examining the meaning of individual words and phrases within literary units (chapter 10). Beyond the expositional study of the text, we also explore the case for topical study within an inductive framework (chapter 11) and cap this off with an overview of the role of consultation and research within the inductive method (chapter 12).

In the fourth and final unit, we unpack the various steps and concerns involved with applying the ancient biblical text as the relevant Word of God for today. This involves important hermeneutical considerations in the practice of establishing relevance and legitimacy in applying an ancient text in the modern world (chapter 13). Our concerns, however, don't end with the theoretical. We also examine practical ways in which the biblical text may appropriately speak to us in our own individual circumstances (chapter 14). Finally, we close our unit on application by exploring the place of theology as the natural outflow of inductive study, the culmination of a step-by-step process of drawing the whole meaning of Scripture upward from the observation, interpretation, and application of Scripture's many individual parts (chapter 15).

We trust that our hermeneutically sensitive, step-by-step approach to inductive Bible study will bring insight and practical benefit to many who endeavor to know God through the depths and riches of his Word, the Bible. In this we offer our gratitude and acknowledgments to those who have contributed to this volume. Included among these are hundreds of students who have shaped and developed our thinking through their questions, interaction, and feedback. We also thank those graduate assistants and student workers, most notably Alex Kocman, Wesley Walker, and Josh Alley, who have assisted with this volume and the courses associated with its development. And most of all, we thank our families, who have allowed us extended hours in writing so that we might share our love for studying God's Word with you.

UNIT I

INTRODUCTION
Sizing Up the Task

1

The Task
of Bible Interpretation
Bridging the Gaps

Studying the Bible is extremely, even eternally, rewarding. Those who devote their lives to the study of this one book—which, unlike any other work, is the divinely inspired Word of God with the power to transform our hearts and lives—will never be the same. God's Word is living and active (Heb 4:12), and while written centuries ago, Scripture has the ability still to speak to us today, because ultimately God himself is the author through the Holy Spirit (2 Pet 1:21). In fact, Scripture is indispensable for equipping us to do God's work: "All Scripture is inspired by God and is profitable for teaching, for rebuking, for correcting, for training in righteousness, so that the man of God may be complete, equipped for every good work" (2 Tim 3:16–17). Truly, like the man who found a priceless pearl and sold everything he had so he could buy it, we are right to focus all our attention on God's great love letter to humanity.

And yet, the Bible is not an easy book to study. In its pages we are confronted with a history that is not our own, cultural norms that are often different from contemporary practices, literature that communicates through a complex array of genres and subgenres, and theology that defies simplistic categorization. And while it's proper to speak of the Bible as a unified work, we nonetheless find ourselves challenged by a collection of sixty-six books, each reflecting its own unique history, literature, and theology.[1] If the Bible were just any collection of books from antiquity, its study most likely would be the exclusive domain of scholars, its mysteries researched and unraveled for a select community in the halls of academia. Yet the Bible is anything but exclusive in reach, its pages open to all who seek to know the truth in faith.

Paradoxically, the Bible is a deep well whose waters lie close to the surface. There is profound irony in the fact that students earn PhDs writing learned tomes on narrow areas of biblical research (for no one person could possibly master all the fields related to the study of Scripture), while a five-year-old can understand the basic message of the gospel and be saved. A plethora of volumes have been published surrounding the study of the Bible, from children's Bibles to scholarly monographs and treatises. The Scriptures have been translated into countless languages and dialects, all to make possible the comprehension of God's Word. Year after year, the Bible and the tools that aid in its study are the best-selling books on the market. People want to dig into that deep well of God's Word, even though they begin at the surface.

As mentioned, the challenges to understanding the particulars of any given portion of Scripture are formidable. And yet, timeless truths await in the pages of Scripture, intended by God to be appropriated by all those who have placed their trust in Jesus Christ and what he's done for them on the cross. This is the challenge of Bible study: its particulars are often complex but never vexing; its message is simple but not simplistic; the study of Scripture requires hard work—in fact, it entails a lifelong journey—and yet along that pathway of discovery you'll find enrichment and growth from day one. God uses his Word wherever you and I may be in our journey of biblical literacy, often in spite of our ignorance and limitations. At the same time, Scripture encourages us to move to maturity in many different realms of spiritual experience, not

---

1. In the remainder of this book, we'll refer to history, literature, and theology as the "hermeneutical triad," the three dimensions of the biblical text requiring careful study. See Andreas J. Köstenberger and Richard D. Patterson, *Invitation to Biblical Interpretation: The Hermeneutical Triad of History, Literature, and Theology* (Grand Rapids: Kregel, 2011); abridged as *For the Love of God's Word: An Introduction to Biblical Interpretation* (Grand Rapids: Kregel, 2015).

the least of which involves developing greater skills in handling God's Word (Heb 5:11–14; 2 Tim 2:15).

To a large degree, the challenges involved in studying the Bible stem from the fact that it is an ancient, human book rooted in events far removed from contemporary experience. Its antiquity notwithstanding, Scripture is read by believers as eternally relevant, the Word of God written to them and meant to be applied directly to their everyday lives.[2] Rather than dictating a set of laws and propositions unclouded by the tapestry of human history, God chose to reveal his Word in and through human affairs. He did this by inspiring the work of authors where they lived in the timeline of history, reflecting their experiences, displaying their distinctive style and vocabulary, and writing to an audience as far removed from the twenty-first century as the authors were themselves.

In this chapter we'll embark on our journey of discovery by introducing you to several gaps to understanding the Bible. Yet we don't want you to be unduly concerned or even discouraged. While those barriers are real and should be squarely faced, we can surmount each of them with the right approach and attitude. It's like building a shed in your backyard. The most important thing is to count the cost before you start. Then you need to get the right tools and buy the proper supplies. Finally, you need to follow the instructions of someone who's done it before. While the process of building your shed may involve a certain amount of trial and error, if you persist in your effort you'll eventually succeed. When it comes to Bible interpretation, believers have the Holy Spirit guiding and equipping them every step of the way. So as we introduce you to a series of challenges to Bible study, remain undaunted: you can get the job done!

Bridging the Gaps:
Facing the Challenges to Understanding

Did you know that in the ancient world girls often got married and had children in their early teens? The same cycle repeated in the lives of

---

2. On the phrase "eternal relevance" and its tension with historical particularity, see Gordon D. Fee and Douglas Stuart, *How to Read the Bible for All Its Worth*, 4th ed. (Grand Rapids: Zondervan, 2014), 25.

their children (even though many infants and their mothers died during childbirth). This meant that many women became grandmothers in their early thirties! While this may happen on rare occasions today, it's certainly uncommon. This is just one of many illustrations we could give of a gap between contemporary culture and Bible times. In fact, when interpreting the Bible, we encounter significant challenges, or gaps, in understanding.[3] These gaps create distance we can bridge only through hard work and study, but they can be bridged.[4]

What's more, these gaps aren't limited to the Bible's human dimension. That Scripture is inspired by God creates a challenging dynamic unique to the study of the Bible, one that includes theological demands placed on the interpreter. Recognizing these challenges to the study of Scripture, both human and divine, is an essential first step to bridging the gaps that cause distance in understanding the Word of God. Although variations exist within each of the following categories, there are several historical, literary, and theological gaps that exist between the ancient text of Scripture and the modern reader seeking to understand it.

Table 1.1 — Historical Challenges to Understanding the Bible	
Gap	**Meaning**
The Time Gap	The events depicted in Scripture occurred in a historical context far removed from the twenty-first century.
The Geographical Gap	The events recorded in the Bible took place in lands far removed from that of most Bible students.
The Cultural Gap	The cultures reflected in the Bible are drastically different than our own.

---

3. On the presentation of gaps that cause distance in understanding, see Roy Zuck, *Basic Bible Interpretation* (Colorado Springs: Chariot Victor, 1991), 15–18.

4. We recognize that we may not be able to bridge the historical gaps perfectly (we cannot step back in time), but we maintain that we can bridge them satisfactorily.

Gaps Related to History

The Time Gap

Truth is, we're far removed historically from the events taking place in the pages of the Bible. The history reflected in Scripture ranges from creation to the first decades following the birth of Christ, a vast range of material at a considerable distance from our own experience. The narratives in Scripture reflect a complex socio-political matrix of events, movements, and figures that for many of us may seem rather daunting. In addition, students of the Bible must also study the circumstances that gave rise to the writing of these documents.

The time gap can be illustrated through examples in more recent history. For instance, if you were to pick up a newspaper from London, England, dated to the fall of 1940, certain key names and events would invariably populate the front page. You should expect to read about Winston Churchill, Adolf Hitler, the *Luftwaffe*, and the RAF (Royal Air Force). What was taking place on the British Isles in the summer and fall of 1940? The Battle of Britain, one of the key events of World War II.

For the Londoner living under the constant threat of aerial raids and impending invasion, the Battle of Britain was very real, and most would be familiar with the key persons and events. However, fast-forwarding to the twenty-first century, you'd find that an increasingly large number picking up that newspaper won't grasp the details due to historical distance. While some will still recognize names such as Churchill, the details of the Battle of Britain would be lost on many if not most.

What's the point of this illustration? For the Londoner living in the fall of 1940, there'd be no time gap to speak of when picking up that same newspaper. The American living in the twenty-first century, however, faces greater challenges to understanding the details. Applying this illustration to Scripture, how many today are familiar with Sennacherib or Nebuchadnezzar, Cyrus or Herod? The distance is palpable. Yet these and many other characters play key roles in the unfolding of God's historical program revealed in the pages of the Bible.

If you could step into a time machine and travel back in time, experiencing for yourself the events recorded in Scripture, the perspective you'd bring to reading the text would change dramatically. This is true for all the books of the Bible, but especially for the Old Testament prophets whose message was often tied to the socio-political events of their day. Certainly you'll be able to grasp the meaning of the Old Testament narratives more readily if you're conversant with ancient Near Eastern history, just as you'll understand the Gospels and Acts with greater precision if you know something about Roman history.

This, it's worth pointing out, isn't merely a matter of cognitive understanding; it affects our ability to relate emotionally as well. The words of Jeremiah in the book of Lamentations certainly had greater emotional impact on those who experienced the traumatic siege and captivity of Jerusalem by the armies of Nebuchadnezzar than on those of us who read about these incidents today, at a time far removed from the actual events.

If we could step into a time machine and walk alongside Moses, Jeremiah, or Paul, doubtless the pages of Scripture would come alive in a manner beyond our wildest imaginations. While we can't do this literally, as we open the pages of Scripture we are in fact invited to walk alongside these figures, to step into their shoes and experience the challenges they faced with them, with historical imagination and emotional empathy. To make those shoes fit, and to bridge the time gap, we must study the multifaceted history of the Bible.[5]

The Geographical Gap

We are far removed geographically from the places of the Bible. The events transpiring in the pages of Scripture take place in a myriad of locations throughout the Middle East, Persia, Egypt, and the Mediterranean, but the primary focus is on the land of Israel. For those living in various parts of the world today, the lands of the Bible may seem rather foreign. The geographical awareness assumed by the writers of Scripture is often

---

5. See on this especially chapter 2, "History," in Köstenberger and Patterson, *Invitation to Biblical Interpretation*, where you can find helpful charts on Old Testament and Second Temple history and on the chronologies of Jesus and Paul.

unwarranted in the case of modern readers who need a map to locate the various sites. Thus we're called to bridge the geographical gap that opens up between us and a particular biblical text, especially if theological significance is attached to a given geographical location, but also to give us a sense of perspective in terms of distance, topography, or general geography.

Examples include nations large and small, the locations of thousands of cities and villages throughout the Bible, and the challenges involved in travel between those places. For instance, many a Coloradan would be shocked to discover that the grade and elevation change between Jerusalem and the Dead Sea is more severe than that between Denver and the Summit Country ski resorts, even though the hills of Jerusalem do not compare visually to the Rocky Mountains. And many a Californian would be surprised to find out that the Sea of Galilee is lower in elevation than Death Valley.[6] In a very practical way, an awareness of such features will impact the way we follow the travels of Old Testament patriarchs, kings and armies, or the movement of Jesus and his followers as depicted in the Gospels.

In fact, when I (Andreas) first studied the Gospel of John more seriously, I spent several hours going through the entire Gospel, carefully noting any movement by Jesus and his followers. Then, on a map of the Holy Land, I traced their movement from Galilee to Judea, or Samaria, and back to Galilee, and so on in order to get a sense of proportion when it comes to geographical movement and location. This helped me to appreciate the distance Jesus and his followers traveled. Taking some time to study biblical geography proved to be a valuable aid in bridging the geographical gap that every interpreter of Scripture must strive to overcome.

Just a century ago, North American and European believers had very limited opportunity to bridge the geographical gap. Today, Bible students enjoy full-color atlases, computer software, and internet sources that bring the geographical outlay of Scripture to all corners of the globe. Moreover, the opportunities for travel to the lands of the Bible have never been greater, and as any pilgrim will testify, a trip to the Holy Land will bring the black-and-white pages of the Bible into full living color.

But to have a map in hand is a poor substitute for local knowledge, and a walk through modern Israel, Turkey, or Greece will not replicate the setting of ancient boundaries, walls, and villages. Modern cities have been built over ancient sites, and geographical characteristics change

---

6. Death Valley, the lowest point in North America, bottoms out at 282 feet below sea level, but the shores of the Sea of Galilee, where so much of the Gospel narratives take place, is 686 feet below sea level.

over time. Regions once forested now lie barren, and coastal harbors, through centuries of siltation, are now fields harvested for crops.[7] Like the time gap, the geographical gap is impossible to bridge completely, but with careful study, some imagination, and the proper resources, it is possible to "see" what we read in the pages of the Bible.[8]

The Cultural Gap

Though the cultural gap in many ways derives from the time and historical gaps, the distinctions between them are sufficiently clear. The impact of cultural distance on the modern reader demands that special recognition be given to this challenge to the accurate interpretation and application of Scripture. The cultures reflected in various parts of the Bible are rather different than our own, and the danger of misinterpretation due to cultural distance is very real.

There are hundreds, if not thousands, of examples throughout the Bible where we're confronted with cultural norms whose significance is anything but self-evident today. Sifting through the pages of Scripture, there's a temptation to read too much into cultural particulars while at other times it's quite easy to miss the point altogether when confronted with a unique cultural feature. Even when we understand how a particular cultural practice might have functioned in the ancient world, transferring that practice to today presents a whole new set of challenges.

For example, five times the New Testament letters conclude with the admonition to "greet one another with a holy kiss."[9] From our perspective it's hard to know what such a kiss entailed, how and to whom it would have been properly given, and what meaning would have been conveyed through the practice. What's more, even if this could be determined with a high degree of confidence, it'd be yet another thing for

---

7. A great example of a silted harbor is the ancient city of Ephesus, which in the day of Paul was a harbor city. However, once the city was abandoned and dredging operations ceased, the ancient harbor filled in and is today dry land. The Aegean coast is now six miles from the site of ancient Ephesus, a city in and out of which the apostle Paul once sailed.

8. There are several excellent Bible atlases available, among them John D. Currid, *The Crossway ESV Bible Atlas* (Wheaton: Crossway, 2010), not to mention maps at the end of most Study Bibles. See further chapter 12.

9. Rom 16:16; see also 1 Cor 16:20; 2 Cor 13:12; 1 Thess 5:26; 1 Pet 5:14.

us to discern how to apply it in our own setting, where "greeting one another with a kiss" may land you in jail, divorce court, or the unemployment line!

Can we bridge the cultural gap? Yes, but only with some effort. After all, even in a modern setting, moving from one culture to another is hardly ever easy and free from potential misunderstanding. How can we expect to understand the many cultures represented in the pages of Scripture through the mere study of books? Experts will admit that literature and archeology can only bring us so close to understanding ancient cultures. With a healthy dose of humility, we can nonetheless attain a better understanding of the cultural dimension of Scripture as we immerse ourselves in the study of the customs and practices encountered in the Bible.

Table 1.2 — Literary Challenges to Understanding the Bible	
Gap	**Meaning**
The Language Gap	The languages of the Bible are far different than English. The Old Testament was primarily written in Hebrew with small segments in Aramaic. The New Testament was written in *Koine* (common) Greek.
The Literary Gap	There are many genres and subgenres utilized by the biblical authors. To properly handle the text, we have to learn to navigate the diverse literary genres represented in Scripture.

Gaps Related to Literature[10]

The Language Gap

Language is human convention, and in the case of the Bible—a millennia-old book—ancient languages are the means by which the

---

10. Köstenberger and Patterson, in *Invitation to Biblical Interpretation*, do not merely distinguish between the triad of history, literature, and theology but further distinguish in the literary realm between canon, genre, and language, and in the linguistic realm also between syntax (word relationships), semantics (word meanings), and figurative language. Gaps are present in each of these realms that must be overcome by getting acquainted with the linguistic and literary features of Scripture.

message is communicated. For the Old Testament, the primary language is Hebrew, with small segments written in Aramaic, a language quite similar to Hebrew. For the New Testament, it is *Koine* (pronounced *coy-nay*) Greek, the language commonly spoken in the first century. While it is the premise of this book that quality Bible study can be performed through modern translations, it's nonetheless important to understand that some facets of meaning or subtle nuances may at times be lost when students of Scripture don't engage with the original languages of the Bible.

Language is a very complex phenomenon that cannot be defined by alphabet, vocabulary, grammar, and syntax alone. It's intricately tied to culture and the people who speak a given idiom. Linguistic conventions are dynamic, ever developing along with those who use them, or, conversely, dying when people cease to do so. Words can be translated from one language into another, but often only imperfectly, for no two languages can fully convey all aspects of meaning tied to its particulars. This reality poses the challenge of studying a book written in languages that most of us don't understand. There's a language gap between the text of the Bible and the modern reader of that text. For this reason, almost all believers today depend on translations for their Bible reading. Even those trained in the original languages will often read the Bible in translation, for it's only natural to be most comfortable reading in your native language. And yet you must recognize that translations, while bridging the language gap, do so imperfectly. In short, the original languages of the Bible should rightly take precedence over any given translation.

In the twenty-first century, American readers are blessed to have available many high-quality English translations; the breadth and quality of translations in other modern languages continues to expand as well. You'll be able to bridge the language gap as you read and compare translations, engage in original-language word study through the use of various reference tools, and follow exegetical conversations in the better commentaries. Some will take this a step further, studying the original languages, eventually reading and translating biblical passages on their own. But most will never achieve a level of aptitude and confidence in the original languages at which they cease to use translations. This is understandable, and to read Scripture in translation is certainly acceptable. Later we'll discuss how to bridge the language gap through the use of various study tools and how to use translations themselves in our study of Scripture.

The Literary Gap

The literary gap stems from the fact that the Bible is an ancient human book written by dozens of authors in a variety of literary genres. As such, we should expect the text of Scripture to have been written in styles unique to ancient literary culture and language. What places the Bible in a class of its own, however, is the variety of literary techniques found in Scripture. Because the Bible was written by so many authors over such a long period of time reflecting such variety in purpose and origin, the outcome is a text representing a dozen or so primary genres and many more subgenres. God could have revealed to his people a list of laws, a procedural manual on how to do church, a theology textbook, or an apologetics guide answering difficult questions. To some extent, we find a bit of each of these features in the pages of Scripture. However, the Bible is so much more, a multifaceted masterpiece of unparalleled quality and diversity. God could have chosen to reveal a less complex Word, but he didn't. And while this presents us with certain challenges, these pale in comparison with the rich benefits conveyed through the variegated literature of the Bible.

The literary gap recognizes that most readers will not inherently know the rules of engagement appropriate to the respective literary genre at hand. Yet knowing these rules is absolutely essential in gaining a more informed and accurate interpretation of a given portion of Scripture. Just as you shouldn't read an opinion page the same way you read actual news, so different rules apply to the interpretation of law code, historical narrative, prophetic oracle, proverbial wisdom, epistolary discourse, and apocalyptic vision. The mention of rules of interpretation for different types of literature may sound daunting, but as we grow in biblical literacy, the genres and subgenres in the Bible become less foreign and the literary gap closes more and more. With training in the special skills required for the study of biblical literature, we'll be well on our way to traversing the distance that arises from the literary diversity of Scripture.

Table 1.3 — Theological Challenges to Understanding the Bible	
Gap	**Meaning**
The Supernatural Gap	The Bible presents supernatural realities and miraculous events, things not normally experienced in the natural world.
The Theological Gap	The Bible is God's self-revelation in his Word and must be read with the expectation that it communicates truth to humankind.
The Appropriation Gap	Even once we bridge the gaps to interpretation, we still must transfer the message from interpretation to application. This is often a greater challenge than interpretation, but absolutely necessary.

Gaps Related to Theology

It may sound paradoxical, but properly understood, the Bible is a divine, contemporary book. By "divine" we mean that the Bible is inspired by God and reflects the perspective of divine authorship. By "contemporary" we mean that the Bible is eternally relevant for every generation of God's people, even as a given generation is far removed from the time at which the events of Scripture originally transpired. This feature of dual authorship is the basis for additional gaps in understanding that are truly unique to the Bible. The collection of books comprising Holy Scripture is in fact the Word of God, revealed by God to all of humanity. As a message from God, it's meant to be applied; without the appropriation of its message, the Bible ceases to function as the eternally relevant Word of God. What's more, the Bible reveals supernatural realities unlike any merely human book; in the pages of Scripture we peer into the realm of God's dealings with humanity. It's this divine engagement that permeates the text of Scripture and binds the sixty-six books of the Bible together historically and thematically. In fact, many of the challenges we face when reading Scripture aren't historical or literary but theological.[11]

The Supernatural Gap

In a book about God, we should expect to find supernatural truths. The Bible nowhere defends the existence of God; it assumes it. Likewise, God's interaction with humankind pervades Scripture from beginning to end. For modern readers who are steeped in naturalistic thinking, a supernatural gap opens up when they discover that they can't replicate the miracles of the Bible in a modern, scientific setting. Miracles can't be repeated in a test tube, nor should we expect them to be. The very point of a miracle is that God is intervening in human history in a supernatural way that is non-normative and non-recurring. Conversely, others expect that God will act today in exactly the same way as he has done in the past. This, too, can be misleading and result in frustration and disappointment.

For the ancient recipients of Scripture, the expectation of supernatural activity was quite different from that of most modern readers. In the world of the Bible, God's immanence was assumed, and the question was not *whether* God would intervene in the affairs of human history, but *how*. In our modern world, bridging the supernatural gap is ultimately a matter of faith, and believers certainly should approach the Bible with certain expectations that are different from those of unbelievers.[12] However, it's also important to realize that the Bible won't defend itself against misguided modern expectations and that the goal of interpretation is not to sift through the Bible in order to distinguish between fact and fiction. Modern critical approaches to the study of Scripture are doomed to frustration, for they inadequately fail to recognize that the Bible is a spiritual book revealing supernatural realities and thus must be approached through a lens of corresponding expectations.

---

11. See Köstenberger and Patterson, *Invitation to Biblical Interpretation*, who break down the interpretive task into studying the historical background, literary context, and theological message of a given passage in each respective genre.

12. On viewing certain presuppositions in a positive, foundational light, see J. Daniel Hays and J. Scott Duvall, *Grasping God's Word*, 3rd ed. (Grand Rapids: Zondervan, 2012), 146.

The Theological Gap

Ultimately, the Bible is God's revelation about himself. Yet in Scripture we find that God reveals himself in the context of human history. To some extent, the theological gap is tied to the supernatural gap, but it implies more. To bridge the supernatural gap, we must read with the expectation of divine activity, accepting that God is immanent in human *history*. The theological gap, however, is based on the premise of God's self-revelation in his *Word*. It is one thing to expect the miraculous in the Bible, but it's another to read Scripture with an eye trained to discern the self-revelation of God through the history, literature, and theological message of the Bible. It's not that God is merely active in the pages of the Bible. Through Scripture, he is actually revealing to us truths about himself and his relation to creation, whether explicit or implicit, propositional or circumstantial.

Reading the Bible is unlike reading any other book. In this collection of sixty-six books, from Genesis to Revelation, we detect an unparalleled continuity of story, thought, and message. The theological truths expressed in Scripture progressively unfold through its pages but never in such a way that they contradict each other. At times there may be a certain amount of tension in the way in which the Bible communicates complex supernatural truths, yet the fundamental teachings embedded in Scripture are consistent and clear.

While you can find nuggets of truth in the smallest portions of text, your study of Scripture pays the richest theological dividends when you're able to correlate a given truth throughout Scripture from beginning to end. This requires a certain amount of biblical literacy, a mind trained to "connect the dots," and, of course, time. Reading the Bible theologically is a lifelong pursuit. At the same time, students of the Bible will begin building upon their knowledge of God from the very first day that they open the pages of Scripture.

And so we find that the reader faces a set of challenges related to this most important dimension of Scripture. Although we read the Bible in a quest for God, we don't attain to a comprehensive understanding of God's revelation of himself all at once. Rather, the multifaceted nature of God is revealed in Scripture, and in this sense a gap exists between the reader who seeks after God daily through studying the parts and God who reveals himself through the whole canon of Scripture over the course of time.

How do we come to discover God in a book that requires such a breadth of expertise and experience? Again, we return to the premise that the Bible is a deep well whose waters lie close to the surface. A new believer can pick up the Bible and God will use it mightily, but our knowledge of God derived from our reading of Scripture is only partial. At every stage in our spiritual journey, as we study portions of the Bible, like Pilgrim in John Bunyan's famous work *Pilgrim's Progress*, we're gradually progressing in our knowledge of God. Even those who devote a lifetime to the study of Scripture will never be able to "master" God or his Word (despite the fact that we call a theological degree a "master of divinity"). Although God reveals himself through Scripture, there will always be a gap between the human and the divine. Similar to the other gaps we've discussed, we can bridge this theological gap increasingly, but never completely.

In these various ways, we face formidable challenges in our study of Scripture because we're not merely trying to interpret the meaning of a given text but seeking to discern spiritual truth. This, in turn, is predicated upon the new birth that results from genuine repentance and conversion to Christ and trust in his finished work on the cross for us. Even as Spirit-born and Spirit-filled believers, however, interpreting Scripture isn't always easy; much less do we arrive at an accurate interpretation automatically! In spite of the various challenges to understanding God's Word, however, the Holy Spirit uses Scripture to "teach, rebuke, correct, and train [us] in righteousness" (2 Tim 3:16).[13] Through his Word, God convicts the heart of the unbeliever, trains the mind of the believer, and encourages those who are discouraged with words of comfort, peace, and reassurance.

---

13. See further the discussion of the role of the Holy Spirit in interpretation in chapter 14.

The Appropriation Gap

So now you know about the gaps related to the Bible's nature as history, literature, and theology. One more gap remains for us to overcome as we strive to apply the biblical teaching: the appropriation gap. Although Christians generally understand that the Bible is a book to be applied, Scripture doesn't always specify exactly *how* something should be applied, or even *whether* it should be applied at all. Thus one of the primary challenges facing us today is not correct interpretation but appropriate application. Even once we bridge historical, cultural, linguistic, and literary gaps in the interpretation of the text, we're still faced with transferring the message from the "then and there" to the "here and now."[14]

How do you apply culturally relative commandments such as the earlier-cited "greet one another with a holy kiss" example? Does Jeremiah 29:11 ("For I know the plans I have for you ... to give you a future and a hope") apply to today's high school or college graduating class, and if so, how? Should we seek to emulate all characters in biblical narrative, and are all instructions in Scripture normative? As you contemplate the absurdity of always doing exactly what the original recipient of a past portion of Scripture did, the answer becomes an obvious "no," but working through examples case by case still poses a considerable challenge. Some commandments, exhortations, examples, and instructions in Scripture are directly transferable, while others are historically or theologically constrained and don't apply to us directly. Between these options, many degrees of application are possible, including finding cultural equivalents and drawing principles from the text, both practical and spiritual. But this is a nuanced art that requires not only interpretive skill but also spiritual seasoning and maturity.

Additionally, we shouldn't overlook the fact that interpreting and applying Scripture to our lives as sinful men and women presents a challenge all its own. The Holy Spirit is certainly instrumental in bridging this aspect of the appropriation gap, and it's our firm conviction that the Bible will mean something different to the believer than it does to the unbeliever. In fact, the Holy Spirit will use God's Word in the life

14. See Fee and Stuart, *How to Read the Bible for All Its Worth*, 27–35.

of the Spirit-filled believer in spite of his or her misunderstanding and even misinterpretation. Yet as students of the Bible we always ought to approach the text with reverence and humility, recognizing that we're seeking to interpret and apply the revealed Word of God with sinful, finite minds. Hard work and study alone will never bridge the appropriation gap. Only the Spirit of God working effectively in the life of the believer will transfer the message of the text from the mind to the heart.[15]

An Invitation

God is more intent on revealing himself to you than you are to get to know him. For this reason you can be confident that you can come to know God in and through his Word and that you can grow in your understanding of his character and his will for your life. You can also learn to understand your place in the story of God's plan of salvation in history and how you can be part of his mission in this world.[16] While interpreting the Bible may be challenging at times, the rewards are literally out of this world. Not only are we convinced that the Bible *can* be understood, we can say with confidence that it was *meant* to be understood. Bridging the gaps mentioned in this chapter requires a certain amount of effort, but by following proper interpretive principles and a methodology that applies these principles practically, everyone who desires to understand the Word of God can come to know its meaning and significance for his or her life. The aim of this book is to provide you with the capacity to approach the Scriptures with humble confidence and to give you the tools you need for a lifetime of fruitful Bible study.

---

15. On application, see chapters 13, 14, and 15 in Unit IV: Application: Acting on the Text.

16. See on this Andreas Köstenberger, "What Is Life's Purpose? Why Are We Here?" *Biblical Foundations* (blog), http://www.biblicalfoundations.org/what-is-lifes-purpose-why-are-we-here, accessed September 15, 2015.

2

Inductive Bible Study

A Step-by-Step Approach

Hermeneutics, in its most basic form, is the science and art of Bible interpretation. Obviously we could give more sophisticated descriptions. Nevertheless, on the basis of this simple definition, two essential aspects of Bible interpretation are clear. First, as a *science*, hermeneutics provides the interpreter of Scripture with sensible principles to guide and direct his or her thinking with regard to interpreting the Bible. These principles are sometimes virtually self-evident while at other times they may require a little more conscious thought and effort. Some principles are rooted in the fact that the Bible is an ancient book, following certain cultural conventions of written communication, while others are based on the unique quality of the Bible as the divinely revealed and inspired Word of God.

Second, as an *art* or *skill*, hermeneutics provides the interpreter of Scripture with a methodical process that, with practice, may be applied to the biblical text and result in an accurate understanding of the Bible. While hermeneutical principles may help in guiding the reader of Scripture, most students find it necessary to follow a methodical process in pursuing the task of Bible study. The procedure presented in this book is the *inductive method*, a task-oriented, step-by-step process that has been widely accepted in Bible-believing circles as the most popular and most effective approach to the study of Scripture.[1] We trust that our

---

1. The classic treatment is Robert A. Traina, *Methodical Bible Study* (1952; repr., Grand Rapids: Zondervan, 2002). The sequel by David R. Bauer and Robert A. Traina, *Inductive Bible Study: A Comprehensive Guide to the Practice of Hermeneutics* (Grand Rapids: Baker, 2011), is not as accessible as one might like.

presentation of the inductive method will be sufficiently thorough while remaining simple and clear so that it will inspire and equip you to a lifetime of fruitful Bible study.

The term "hermeneutics" can mean different things to different people (yes, there is some irony in this). Many works have appeared in recent years covering different aspects of interpretation. Some books have focused on the philosophical side of hermeneutics, where conversations can become quite dense, while others have dealt with the hands-on dimension pertaining to the process of "rightly dividing the word of truth" (2 Tim 2:15 KJV). For those who treasure the Word of God and seek to interpret it accurately, both aspects are essential. With that said, this book is concerned primarily with method and is unapologetically practical in orientation. Our goal is to equip you with a method that will help you interpret Scripture accurately. This goal, however, requires guiding principles. Thus we begin by presenting the basic hermeneutical principles behind our method of Bible study.

Table 2.1 — Seven Sensible Principles for Thinking through Scripture		
	Principle	**Meaning**
1.	The Literal Principle	Take the words of the Bible at face value. Avoid reading into the text what is not there.
2.	The Contextual Principle	Always strive to understand the text within the confines of its historical, literary, and theological context.
3.	The One-Meaning Principle	There will normally only be one correct interpretation of a text, although there may be multiple applications.
4.	The Exegetical Principle	The meaning of any biblical text must be drawn from the text rather than be ascribed to the text.

	Principle	Meaning
5.	The Linguistic Principle	The original languages of the Bible always take precedence over any given translation.
6.	The Progressive Principle	Later revelation may clarify, complete, or supersede earlier revelation.
7.	The Harmony Principle	Any given portion of the Bible can have only that meaning which harmonizes with the doctrine of the Bible as a whole. There will be continuity between books of the Bible.

Table 2.1 — Continued

Seven Sensible Principles to Guide Our Thinking through Scripture

Any method used for the study of Scripture must be based on sound hermeneutical principles. While most of the following principles are universal and pertain to all forms of written communication, some are in force only in view of the Bible's unique character as the inspired, inerrant Word of God. On the basis of the inerrancy and inspiration of Scripture, following these principles will provide a sure hermeneutical foundation that will guide our thinking throughout the practice of inductive Bible study.

#1 *The Literal Principle*

The literal principle acknowledges that the Bible should normally be understood in a literal fashion, with the words of the text being taken at face value. This means that the Bible interpreter shouldn't allegorize the text or look for hidden meanings, nor should he or she assume that the Bible must be decoded in order to be understood. This principle doesn't negate the intentional use of rhetorical devices and literary imagery but acknowledges that, as with other forms of written communication, the

Bible was written in ordinary languages and was meant to be understood. The literal principle acknowledges the legitimate feature of figurative language found throughout the Bible, and clearly figures of speech such as metaphor, metonymy, hyperbole, and anthropomorphism are found literally (pun intended) thousands of times throughout the Bible.[2] In addition, the literal principle acknowledges the legitimate use of symbolism and typology as reflected in the intentions of the human authors and the divine author.

Though all sorts of literary devices are evident, readers of Scripture ought to exercise restraint. It is notoriously easy to read symbolism into the text of Scripture where there's little justification for its presence. Intentional symbolism is present in the Bible, but it isn't as widespread as some might expect. What is more, whenever figures of speech are recognized in the Bible, you should always look for the literal intent behind the non-literal terminology. For instance, if on a hot and humid day we say that it's "soupy" outside, our intended audience should understand that we're referring to the oppressive humidity in the air, and we as communicators expect that *intended* response. We'd be quite surprised if people thought we were referring to clam chowder or chicken noodles floating around the atmosphere, and we certainly wouldn't want to be accused of being misleading through the use of our non-literal terminology! Likewise, the authors of the Bible frequently use non-literal terminology to convey literal intention, and in most cases this intended meaning is quite obvious. So the literal principle acknowledges rhetorical imagery and figurative language but understands that these are based in literal intent.

It should also be noted that the literal principle assumes the preeminence of authorial intent in the interpretation and application of any given text of Scripture. As to interpretation, this suggests that *the meaning of the text must be the meaning intended by the original human author by the words he used to communicate to his original recipients.* As to application, this means that *the text cannot mean today what was never intended by the original author.* Obviously, the issue of meaning is much

---

2. A sampling of various kinds of figures of speech will be covered in chapter 5.

more complicated than we can discuss here.[3] It's worth noting, though, that when we speak of an author's intention in the unique case of the Bible, we're dealing with the dynamic of dual authorship between a human and the divine author, a dynamic that shouldn't be ignored in discussions of the intended meaning of Scripture.

#2 The Contextual Principle

Concerning accurate interpretation, perhaps the most important principle to remember is the contextual principle. The contextual principle simply affirms that the text of any portion of Scripture must always be understood within the confines of its historical-cultural, literary, and theological-canonical context.

The Historical-Cultural Context. The historical-cultural context of any given portion of Scripture relates directly to its position as a historical document rooted within the drama of human history. Some may refer to this kind of context as "background context," but this terminology is unnecessarily vague. We find that it's better to specify the two primary aspects in view here: the historical and the cultural background of the text, noting, of course, that these often function in tandem.

Because the Bible was written by real human authors in the context of history, most of the Bible is set within the context of historical events. This may involve the chronological context of events described in narrative or the socio-political context in which the prophets spoke their oracles from God. In many cases, specific books of the Bible can be labeled as "occasional documents," meaning that their composition was required by an event or situation set in history.[4] Of particular importance is the fact that the purpose for which an author wrote was usually dictated by

---

3. For a thorough treatment, see Appendices 1 and 2 in Grant R. Osborne, *The Hermeneutical Spiral: A Comprehensive Introduction to Biblical Interpretation*, rev. ed. (Downers Grove: InterVarsity, 2006).

4. Fee and Stuart label the New Testament epistles as "occasional documents," although to varying degrees this "occasional" nature can be seen in the origin and composition of virtually all the books of the Bible. See Gordon D. Fee and Douglas Stuart, *How to Read the Bible for All Its Worth*, 4th ed. (Grand Rapids: Zondervan, 2014), 60.

events set in the context of history, and grasping this purpose involves the interpreter in the discovery of essential historical facts.

Historical context functions on two levels: the events described in Scripture and the origin of the text itself, including author and audience. This two-level dynamic with regard to historical context can be tricky for those new to reading the Bible, but it's an important aspect of understanding the Bible contextually.[5]

Culture is influenced by many variables, not the least of which is historical timeframe, which is why we combine cultural with historical context. That said, cultural context is a distinct aspect of background and presents some of the more egregious opportunities for misinterpreting Scripture. As noted in chapter 1, the events portrayed in the Bible represent cultural contexts far removed from our own. The reader of Scripture is exposed to a broad array of ancient cultures, and cultural mores and expressions vary throughout the Bible. Nevertheless, in spite of the challenge of cultural particularities, accurate interpretation and appropriate application can ensue when we immerse ourselves in the study of the culture of the biblical text.

The Literary Context. There are two primary facets of literary context, both involving the form and function of written communication. The first facet of literary context has been variously described as "surrounding context," "grammatical/syntactical context," or "co-text." Whatever term you use, this facet of literary context deals with the meaning of words and phrases and is what most people think of when they hear the word "context." Simply put, words, phrases, sentences, and even paragraphs may have multiple meanings, and these are almost always determined by what precedes and follows. *The ideas that precede and follow any given portion of Scripture constitute the context of that unit.* Because thoughts are typically expressed in association rather than isolation, the context of a passage always determines the meaning of a given word. Practically speaking, when studying the meaning of a particular word in the Bible, *contextual* meaning (i.e., what a word means

---

5. The significance of this insight, along with other features pertaining to historical context, will be addressed in greater detail in chapter 8, "Considering the Context."

in conjunction with adjacent words and phrases) will always take precedence over *lexical* meaning (i.e., a mere dictionary definition of a word apart from a specific context).[6]

The second facet of literary context pertains to the *literary genre* or *subgenre* of any given portion of Scripture. The Bible is a rather complex book, not only in its content but also with regard to the form in which its contents are conveyed. God chose to inspire his Word as a literary masterpiece containing a great variety of literary styles. In order to interpret and apply the Bible accurately, we must learn to recognize the various forms of literature in the Bible and become conversant with the genre-specific interpretive principles related to each. As a sampling, in the Old Testament we encounter narrative discourse, law code, poetic stanzas, proverbs and sayings, prophetic oracles, and apocalyptic visions. In the New Testament we find gospel narratives, personal and corporate letters (epistles), and the apocalypse of Revelation.[7]

To further heighten the challenge of reading the Bible contextually, each literary genre (macro-level) contains several subgenres (micro-level). For instance, in a prophetic book you might encounter apocalyptic visions, autobiographical narrative, historical narrative, prophetic drama, hymns, allegory, judgment speeches, woe speeches, salvation oracles, lamentation, or instructional discourse. In the New Testament Gospels you might find narrative discourse, commentary, genealogies, hymns, parables, sermons, woe speeches, or allegory. Virtually every book of the Bible exhibits a diverse array of literary subgenres, and reading contextually requires an ability to discern the form and features distinguishing each literary unit while appreciating the unique message distinct literary subgenres may convey.

The Theological-Canonical Context. A form of context that is often misunderstood, or simply ignored, by readers of the Bible is the theological-canonical context of a given portion of Scripture. Again, we're

6. An understanding of this principle applied to word studies is absolutely essential and will govern our treatment of word studies in chapter 10.

7. For detailed discussions of the interpretation of various subgenres in Scripture, see Andreas J. Köstenberger and Richard D. Patterson, *Invitation to Biblical Interpretation: Exploring the Hermeneutical Triad of History, Literature, and Theology* (Grand Rapids: Kregel, 2011).

combining two distinct but related aspects of context, the theological and the canonical context of Scripture. *Theological* context tends to emphasize the covenant relationship that God has with his people and the representation of that relationship in the progression of salvation history. Of primary concern are the expectations and requirements presented in Scripture as distinguished by various covenants, including the Abrahamic, Mosaic, Davidic, and new covenants. We should expect that activities, commandments, and prophetic promises in Scripture are aligned with the covenant to which they are related.

To provide but one example, reading the Mosaic law code you should recognize that the law functioned quite differently for the ancient Israelite than it does for the New Testament Christian and that this is based not simply on ethnic, cultural, and chronological distinctions but, more importantly, on distinctions between the respective covenant. Simply put, it's not just that we aren't ancient Israelites living in an ancient Near Eastern context. More significantly, we live under a different *covenant,* complete with expectations and promises that are different from theirs. For this reason, as those who interpret and apply Scripture, we must always be mindful of the underlying covenant anchors that form the theological context of a given portion of Scripture.

Canonical context concerns not just the place in the timetable of revelation in which a biblical writer lived or wrote but also the way in which individual books of the Bible function together to form one comprehensive book. The cohesion of Scripture is a matter that we'll address particularly in chapters 11 and 15, as well as the implications of reading the sixty-six books of the Bible as a single book. For now, suffice it to say that surrounding context is not limited to words, phrases, sentences, and paragraphs. In a different sense, in a way that is unique to the Bible, we must *consider the context of a book of Scripture within the entire scope of God's revelation,* that is, its canonical context.

The contextual principle is obviously complex yet utterly essential. As we learn to observe, interpret, apply, and systematize the teaching of Scripture, we'll refer to the various kinds of context again and again. We'll provide many examples in the chapters to come as we seek to implement this principle in the steps of the inductive method. For now, let's continue with our survey of guiding principles.

#3 The One-Meaning Principle

The one-meaning principle is a general guideline teaching that any given portion of Scripture in any given context can have only one correct interpretation, although it may have multiple (yet not unlimited) applications. In other words, if faced with a choice between potential interpretations of a specific text, the one-meaning principle would suggest that multiple options, especially if mutually exclusive, cannot all be correct. For instance, regarding the interpretation of the "perfect" in 1 Corinthians 13:10, there are three or four common approaches. Some suggest that Paul was referring to the completion of the New Testament or the recognition of the completed canon. Others (especially those with a postmillennial perspective) conclude that Paul had in mind the second coming of Christ or the perfection of the church leading up to that point. Still others believe that "perfect" refers to the culmination of human history in the new heavens and new earth. The one-meaning principle suggests that Paul couldn't have meant *all* of these things when anticipating the coming of the "perfect." Either *one* of these options is *correct*, and the *others* are *wrong*, or they're *all incorrect*, but they *can't all be correct at the same time*. Paul could have nuanced intentions, especially given his use of a rather vague term in this case, but he most likely had one event, or one future reality, in mind. Thus the one-meaning principle is predicated upon a certain amount of evidence-orientation in interpretation. You can't simply "will" the Bible to mean whatever you want it to mean, and interpretations can, and often will, be incorrect.

The one-meaning principle, like many others, has its basis in authorial intent.[8] It should be noted, however, that because of the dual nature of inspired authorship (human and divine), there may be exceptions to this rule. Some texts, especially those of a prophetic nature, are pregnant

---

8. See here especially the classic work by E. D. Hirsch, *Validity in Interpretation* (New Haven, CT: Yale University Press, 1967). Hirsch rightly argues that apart from authorial intent validity in interpretation proves elusive.

with meaning, and many scholars recognize the phenomenon of *sensus plenior*, or "fuller sense," in prophetic fulfillment.[9] In fact, as Old Testament prophecy is cited as "fulfilled" by New Testament writers, the fulfillment often seems quite distant from the Old Testament context of the prophecy. In the realm of hermeneutics, one of the most challenging subjects for modern interpreters is the role of apostolic exegesis as the biblical writers quoted the Old Testament in the New Testament Gospels and Epistles.[10] What we're stressing at this point is one potential shortcoming of the one-meaning principle. Again, this is a general rule, not an irrefutable law.

A second potential shortcoming of the one-meaning principle comes as the byproduct of the inherent flexibility of metaphor. In this case, a human author can intend to convey multiple, often overlapping concepts through the use of metaphor.[11] For instance, when the psalmist describes God as a "rock," we understand that the intention is not to describe God as a literal rock or geological structure of any kind but to highlight some aspect of God's character that is "rock-like." Thus the psalmist may highlight God as a strong and sure foundation, as a stable and everlasting entity.[12] But at the same time, you should exercise caution, as it's quite unlikely that the psalmist intended to describe God as dense, heavy, or abrasive. Metaphor is a complex aspect of human language that has the capacity to communicate multiple strains of thought. This capacity is evidenced throughout Scripture, and in some cases an

---

9. For a sensible assessment, see Douglas J. Moo, "The Problem of Sensus Plenior," in *Hermeneutics, Authority, Canon*, ed. D. A. Carson and John D. Woodbridge (Grand Rapids: Zondervan, 1986), 175–211.

10. To examine this topic adequately would require a volume of its own; we'll briefly discuss this topic in chapter 6 and cite resources for further study there. The standard reference work is G. K. Beale and D. A. Carson, eds., *Commentary on the New Testament Use of the Old Testament* (Grand Rapids: Baker, 2007).

11. On the inherent, intentional flexibility of metaphor to communicate multiple ideas with singular concision, see D. Brent Sandy, *Plowshares and Pruning Hooks: Rethinking the Language of Biblical Prophecy and Apocalyptic* (Downers Grove: InterVarsity, 2002).

12. See also the conundrum of 1 Cor 10:4, where Paul depicts Jesus as the rock in the wilderness during Israel's exodus wanderings.

appreciation of such nuances is critical to accurate interpretation.[13] That said, it's nonetheless wise to embrace the guidance of the one-meaning principle while remaining open to possible exceptions such as those just described.

#4 The Exegetical Principle

The exegetical principle teaches that the meaning of any biblical text must be drawn *from* the text rather than be ascribed *to* the text. In other words, the reader is responsible to discover the intent of the author *in* the text rather than imposing her understanding *onto* the text. Often readers approach the Bible with an agenda, using it to support various doctrines (whether orthodox or heretical), proof texting along the way. Others will use the Bible as a springboard for various points of interest, focusing on an aspect of the text without asking what the author was really trying to say in the original context. The exegetical principle suggests that a better way to read Scripture is to approach it on its own terms and to allow it to speak for itself. It's this exegetical principle that provides the proper foundation for the inductive method of Bible study.

The reader of the Bible will always bring a certain prior understanding (also called "preunderstanding") and set of presuppositions to the text. While this is inevitable, the interpreter of Scripture must constantly be on guard against allowing preunderstanding to dictate her understanding of the text. Preunderstanding refers to "all of our preconceived notions and understandings that we bring to the text, which have been formulated, both consciously and subconsciously, before we actually

---

13. An example of intentional multivalence is the use of the key Hebrew word *hevel* in the book of Ecclesiastes. This word occurs some 38 times and is critical in understanding the problem, and ultimately the message, of the book. The word literally means "mist" or "vapor" but is used metaphorically throughout the book to describe various aspects of life experienced in a fallen world. Translations will often use a single English gloss to translate the word throughout the book, but this approach fails to recognize the breadth of meaning conveyed through this symbol. The NET Bible does an admirable job in translating the word through a variety of associated glosses that best capture the aspect of meaning that is highlighted passage by passage throughout the book. For more on this example, and multivalence in general, see Douglas B. Miller, *Symbol and Rhetoric in Ecclesiastes: The Place of Hebel in Qohelet's Work* (Atlanta: Society of Biblical Literature, 2002); and Richard Alan Fuhr Jr., *An Analysis of the Inter-Dependency of the Prominent Motifs within the Book of Qohelet*, Studies in Biblical Literature 151 (New York: Peter Lang, 2013), 29–63.

study the text in detail."[14] Preunderstanding won't always lead you astray, but it certainly has the potential to skew your understanding of the text and can at times lead to grievous examples of misinterpretation. Following the exegetical principle doesn't demand the elimination of all preunderstanding but encourages *awareness* of preunderstanding to help ensure that it doesn't unduly influence our interpretation of the biblical text.

Presuppositions, as distinguished from preunderstanding, relate to our view of the Bible as a whole. In other words, presuppositions such as the inerrancy, infallibility, and authority of Scripture provide a needed foundation for the whole process of Bible study and thus are a positive influence on our understanding of the text. Obviously, all of us will approach the Bible with certain presuppositions, whether faith-based or critical. We'd encourage you toward a faith-based approach; in fact, this is the approach we take in this text. We believe in the integrity of the biblical text and approach it as the Word of God. Faith-based presuppositions do not need to be suppressed in your study of Scripture. Rather, we suggest you embrace them.

#5 The Linguistic Principle

The linguistic principle teaches that the original languages of the Bible must take precedence over any given translation. While today's English translations are both accurate and readable, some facets are nonetheless difficult to capture and retain in the translation process. No two languages are alike in terms of grammar, syntax, and vocabulary, and thus the most precise exegetical interpretation of any given text will be drawn from the text in its original language. For example, the phrase "husband of one wife" in 1 Timothy 3:2 means most likely "faithful husband," that is, "one-woman-kind-of-man." This is an example where

---

14. J. Scott Duvall and J. Daniel Hays, *Grasping God's Word: A Hands-on Approach to Reading, Interpreting, and Applying the Bible*, 3rd ed. (Grand Rapids: Zondervan, 2012), 139. We're using the terminology adopted by Duvall and Hays in distinguishing between preunderstanding and presuppositions.

a given idiom in the original Greek cannot be brought over into the English language in a formally equivalent way.

What is more, all translations will inevitably demonstrate exegetical decision making as part of the translation process. This is not a matter of bias but of necessity. Translation invariably crosses into interpretation as translators are faced again and again with decisions regarding what the original language meant as they seek to convey equivalent meaning into the receptor language (in our case, English). Many incorrectly assume that this can be resolved by sticking to a literal theory of translation, but even a literal or word-for-word approach to translation will by necessity face interpretive decisions, as no two languages align precisely in terms of vocabulary, grammar, or syntax.

The interpretive nature of translation will be thoroughly illustrated in the next chapter, where we will set forth guidelines that will help you discern exegetical decision making in the translations you use. At this point, we're simply stressing the fact that translations may at times be unable to convey certain nuances found in the original languages. You should therefore be aware that when you read the Bible in translation some aspect of meaning may be lost or potentially distorted over against the original wording.

#6 The Progressive Principle

This principle deals with the progressive nature of revelation.[15] God didn't reveal his Word to humanity all at once, nor has he set forth the same conditions for humankind throughout history. Therefore, some of his later revelation may supersede former stipulations, as later information may complete or clarify what was given earlier. It should be noted, however, that a change or progression in Scripture doesn't imply that a contradiction is present. Rather, as you examine the audience, circumstances, and covenantal context of two allegedly contradictory

---

15. By using the term "progressive," we are not intending to convey linear, progressive trajectory culminating in an ideal conclusion. God's revelatory interaction with humankind is often characterized by cyclical movement, as demonstrated by recurring yet unique dietary restrictions in the example relating to food laws.

commandments or statements in Scripture, you'll find that God isn't obligated to work in static fashion as he engages with humanity through an ever-changing set of circumstances.

Examples of the progressive principle are abundant in Scripture, especially between the Testaments but sometimes within the same Testament. For instance, relating to food laws, in Genesis 1:29 it appears that mankind was created vegetarian. Then, after Noah's flood, humanity is given "every living creature" as food to eat, in addition to "green plants" (Gen 9:3). With the institution of the Mosaic law, God gave ancient Israel stringent regulations forbidding them from eating certain foods (Leviticus 11), while Jesus rescinded these food laws for his followers (Mark 7:19; Acts 10:9–16). Some may claim that we aren't comparing apples with apples here and that the contexts are quite distinct, but that is exactly the point: the progressive nature of Scripture demands that we be aware of contextual movement in the pages of the Bible.

The progressive principle has clear similarities to theological and canonical context as described above. The difference is that here we're concerned not only with movement between different covenants (theological context) and individual books within a broader corpus (canonical context) but also with revelation history. The biblical text comes out of the interface of God and humanity, which took place over time. We shouldn't read Scripture as if it was revealed apart from the progression of history.

#7 The Harmony Principle

The harmony principle teaches that any given portion of the Bible can have only that meaning which harmonizes with the doctrine of the Bible as a whole. This is a safeguard and thus presupposes that the Bible won't contradict itself. We wouldn't surmise that a single author would contradict himself in one and the same book. However, the harmony principle extends to the whole corpus of Scripture based on the premise that ultimately God is its single author. The harmony principle suggests that there will be continuity *between* individual books of the Bible, even as these books may in some cases be quite distant in terms of origin, context, content, and genre.

This underlying notion of harmony or unity allows for a certain amount of diversity in the way in which the various authors of Scripture express themselves. The human side of Scripture displays the unique vocabulary, style, and perspective of a given biblical author. For example, while the four Evangelists (especially Matthew, Mark, and Luke) record many of the same events, how they tell a particular story may vary. Likewise, what Paul and James say about the role of works in the Christian life reveals a certain amount of diversity of outlook. At the same time, such diversity, as mentioned, should be understood against the backdrop of the Bible's underlying unity.[16]

This brings us to a second aspect of the harmony principle: the fact that the individual parts of the Bible can and should be understood in light of the whole. The harmony principle provides the philosophical basis for interpretive correlation, which we'll examine in greater detail in chapter 9. Comparing Scripture with Scripture is especially useful when conducted within the same book, but given divine authorship and the resulting unity of Scripture, you should expect continuity *between* books of the Bible, not just *within* them.[17] For this reason you can expect to gain insight as to the parts by comparing them to the whole, and in this way the Bible functions as its own best commentary.

While the seven principles stated above provide sure guidance for the reading of Scripture, there remains a need for a methodical approach to studying the Bible that those with varying levels of expertise and experience can embrace and utilize. This brings us to the place of examining method, which represents our core interest in this book. Rather than examining methods (in the plural) of Bible study, whether rhetorical,

---

16. For an example of such underlying unity in the face of diversity, see Andreas J. Köstenberger, "Does the Bible Ever Get It Wrong? Facing Scripture's Difficult Passages," *Canon Fodder* (blog), September 15, 2014, http://michaeljkruger.com/does-the-bible-ever-get-it-wrong-facing-scriptures-difficult-passages-4-andreas-kostenberger. See also idem, "Diversity and Unity in the New Testament," in *Biblical Theology: Retrospect and Prospect*, ed. Scott J. Hafemann (Downers Grove: InterVarsity, 2002), 200–23.

17. As we will examine in chapter 9, the benefits of interpretive correlation diminish with literary and canonical distance, but the general continuity of the inspired Word of God does help in maintaining the integrity of this practice throughout both Testaments.

critical, topical, or devotional, we're interested in examining and presenting a comprehensive method (in the singular) comprised of logical steps and linear progression toward the goal of understanding Scripture. This is the *inductive method* of Bible study.

Induction v. Deduction

Without getting bogged down in the theoretical, it's important at this point to consider the merits of *inductive*, or evidence-based, study vis-à-vis *deductive*, or assumption-based, study. In so doing, it's vital to understand that we're weighing the merits of a system appropriate for Bible study, not other fields such as logic or mathematics. In other words, certain closed-system fields are appropriate to deductive reasoning because one begins with absolute premises and from these moves on to equally certain conclusions. However, in the study of the Bible, as with the study of history and literature, we're faced with open options for interpretation and appropriation.

As those who accept the Bible as communication authored by human intent under divine oversight, we make it our goal to discover what the *author intended* to say through the text we read. Deduction is not inferior or negative in and of itself, but for those who seek to discover what the Bible means, an assumption-oriented approach to the meaning of individual texts is counterproductive and impedes discovery. Induction, on the other hand, is more suitable to the study of the Bible because you compile the evidence and then, proceeding from your analysis of the evidence, reach probable, albeit at times tentative, conclusions.

With an *inductive* approach to Bible study, you explore the Bible and arrive at conclusions only once you've compiled all the evidence. The process of compiling evidence, ascertaining the significance of strains of evidence, and arriving at conclusions comprises the essence of the inductive method. Induction is discovery, and we believe that approaching the Bible with an attitude of seeking to discover the meaning of the text is most compatible with the Bible as intentional communication from God to us. Thus an attitude of discovery, coupled with a process for implementing the discovery of meaning, drives us toward the inductive method for Bible study.

With a *deductive* approach to Bible study, on the other hand, you begin with certain assumptions or beliefs and allow the Bible only room to support those assumptions or beliefs. What's more, for some taking a more active role in proof texting, a deductive approach facilitates turning to the Bible only to find support for their own belief system. This, in turn, leads to a tendency to read into the text affirmations never intended by the original author. A deductive approach often presupposes conclusions before the evidence is gathered and fails to ask the critical questions pertaining to what the author intended to say through the text being studied.

Table 2.2 — Understanding the Differences between Deduction and Induction	
Deduction	**Induction**
Assumption based	Evidence based
Moves from universals to particulars	Moves from particulars to universals
Begins with absolute premises and derives certain conclusions	Pieces the data together to derive meaning

Three additional considerations apply as we weigh the merits of induction over deduction and set out to assess the viability of the inductive method. First, as we pointed out in our discussion of the exegetical principle, all of us will invariably carry *preunderstanding* with us as we study the Bible.[18] The goal, however, is not to eliminate all preunderstanding, which would be impossible, and even if possible would ultimately be counterproductive. In fact, an inductive approach will benefit from prior study, utilizing biblical and theological literacy as an aid to enhance and inform current research. However, while benefiting from prior knowledge, an inductive approach doesn't allow assumptions based

---

18. For a helpful treatment of preunderstanding, see "Chapter 5: The Interpreter" in William W. Klein, Craig L. Blomberg, and Robert L. Hubbard Jr., *Introduction to Biblical Interpretation*, rev. ed. (Nashville: Thomas Nelson, 2004).

on *prior* conclusions to dictate the results of *present and future* study. Induction, therefore, encourages awareness of the potential impact of preunderstanding but doesn't compel you to eliminate it altogether.

Second, realize that the conclusions reached through an inductive approach are by nature *probable* and not absolute. Even so, we believe that you can reach firm interpretive conclusions, and that you can approach the text with confidence, expecting to be able to understand its meaning. After all, as we affirmed in chapter 1, the Bible is *meant* to be understood. The Bible can be understood in reference to individual segments as well as regarding its message as a whole. Nevertheless, in an open-ended system of communication where authors can't be interviewed as to their actual intentions, we're of necessity dealing with probable, rather than proven, conclusions.

This principle of probability, however, shouldn't be cause for concern or discouragement.[19] Supported by sound principles of hermeneutics and a methodical approach for study, you'll be able to reach most interpretive conclusions with a *high degree* of certainty, and those findings that are more tentative tend to be the exception rather than the rule. We trust that practitioners of the inductive method will be able to approach Scripture with confidence, knowing that they've taken measures to study the text with informed guidance and a thorough process while at the same time remaining humble, knowing that induction by its very nature demands that we remain open to wherever the evidence may lead.

Finally, let's clarify (or perhaps confess) that while we believe that the inductive method is the best comprehensive approach for the study of the Bible, this is not to suggest that we're purists and never apply deductive reasoning to our study of Scripture. Certainly, as we develop and teach systematic theology, deduction is often evident in the presentation, if not the development, of our theological system. And as we trace our own personal histories of preaching, teaching, and writing, we're quite certain that there are cases where we, too, have not allowed the Bible to speak for itself, where we have imposed our own understanding upon the text before discovering its meaning through the process of inductive

---

19. Bauer and Traina, *Inductive Bible Study*, 26.

study. Nevertheless, we're convinced that induction, as a driving force in Bible study, is superior to deduction and can produce more accurate and reliable results.[20]

What Does the Inductive Method Look Like?

Although the inductive method has taken on different forms and representations in recent years, we're presenting a traditional three-step framework: observation, interpretation, and application.[21] This basic framework is strikingly simple yet has the capacity to integrate very complex procedures for those more advanced in their studies. This is part of the beauty and utility of the inductive method. At its core, it is a very simple procedure that all interpreters can adopt. Even so, scholars will employ the same methodology to conduct the most advanced exegetical work. Our presentation aims somewhere in the middle, with enough solid food to keep advanced students fed while encouraging those new to inductive study with simple, step-by-step procedures that provide a workable platform for future development.

The inductive method begins with *observation*, transitions to *interpretation*, and concludes with *application*. Within each of these primary steps of induction are distinct activities (or steps within steps) that conduct the implementation and control the process of moving from observation through interpretation and finally onto application. There will inevitably be movement back and forth between these steps, but the general flow will be linear, moving from observation to interpretation and then on to application. Implicit in interpretation and application is *correlation*, the comparison of an interpreted text with other related texts. That's why we conclude our presentation of the inductive method by teaching students how to go about *doing theology*. Following is an outline of the three basic steps of the inductive method, along with

---

20. Proof texting of this kind often lies behind the theology of groups such as the Jehovah's Witnesses. However, deductive proof texting has been used to support many strains of theology, both good and bad. Evangelicals should carefully consider examples of proof texting in their own circles, not just from those with whom they disagree.

21. Alternative approaches include that of the "interpretive journey" in Duvall and Hays, *Grasping God's Word*.

subcategories (or steps within steps) that we'll detail in the remaining chapters of this book.

Figure 2.1: The Inductive Method

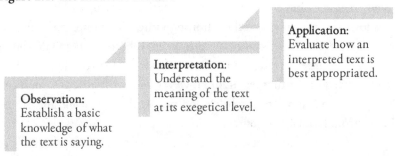

Observation

Observation seeks to establish a foundational knowledge of what the text is saying and to discern those issues that may warrant focused study. Good observation is by nature inquisitive and will result in the right questions being asked of the text. When performed thoroughly, observation will ensure that all the pieces of the text are laid out on the table before the reader. Observation may not put all the pieces together, but that is not the goal of observation. Simply put, good observation will ensure that all the pieces are available.

Observation includes methodical, step-by-step activities such as comparing translations (a helpful tool even for those capable of working with the original languages, chapter 3), distinguishing significant or nonroutine terms from self-evident or routine ones (identifying words and phrases that warrant word study, chapter 5), observing miscellaneous features in prose and poetic literature (chapter 6), and discerning special structural and literary relationships in the text (chapter 7). Permeating all steps of observation is an inquisitive agenda, extracting and developing those questions which form the basis for the interpretation of the text (chapter 4).

Interpretation

Interpretation seeks to understand the meaning of the text at its exegetical level, that is, what the text was intended to convey by its original author to his original audience. Interpretation develops as interpretive questions are answered, and thus thorough interpretation is possible only once the process of observation is completed. Observation will doubtless contribute to interpretation, sometimes answering interpretive questions without need for further research. However, many interpretive questions do require additional research, sometimes in the text itself and sometimes through outside resources.

The steps of interpretation can be summarized by the three Cs of interpretation: considering the *context* (chapter 8), conducting interpretive and thematic *correlation* (chapters 9 and 11), and doing commentary *consultation* (chapter 12). In considering the *context,* multiple aspects are in play, including those presented earlier under the "contextual principle." In our case, we'll utilize the hermeneutical triad of history, literature, and theology to establish aspects of context that reflect these three areas of biblical interpretation.

Interpretive *correlation* involves allowing the Bible to function as its own best commentary through linguistic, grammatical, literary, and topical parallels. Also, in reference to significant, nonroutine terms, word studies may be warranted as a further step of interpretation. Conducting word studies allows students to analyze and interpret specific word meaning through the assimilation of context and interpretive correlation (chapter 10). Finally, as an interpreter you'll take advantage of prior scholarship and research by *consulting* Bible study tools and resources, including commentaries. However, in an inductive approach, we don't simply rely on commentaries but rather engage with them to gain relevant insights and find answers to questions which would otherwise be left unanswered.

Application

Application is a multifaceted step based on the idea that the Word of God is eternally relevant, speaking not just to an ancient audience but to a contemporary one as well. However, the contemporary audience is quite different from the original one and is itself quite varied. Thus application is more involved than simply putting knowledge into practice. Application must evaluate *how* an interpreted text is best appropriated, and sometimes the distance between interpretation in the "then and there" and application in the "here and now" requires careful nuancing and keen discernment.[22]

Application is not merely subjective, as valid application must have its basis in an accurate interpretation of the text. Nevertheless, some of the more significant challenges in Bible study pertain not to interpretation but rather to application. To use an earlier example, it's one thing to figure out what Paul meant when he told the church at Corinth to "greet one another with a holy kiss" (1 Cor 16:20), but it's quite another to determine how this should be applied today, and determining this relies significantly upon a good dose of "sanctified common sense."[23]

Application begins by finding sensible parallels between interpretation and application, and thus interpretation must precede application. (This may seem obvious, but how often does the tail wag the dog and we start with application?) Usually we can frame sensible parallels around teaching points and from them apply Scripture. However, in the process of developing such teaching points, whether for personal or public presentation, application must be processed through two levels of reading Scripture as the Word of God for today.

First, we must determine what the text might mean to *us* today as the people of God. This form of application is critical, as theological distance may affect how we should apply the text today. At this stage

---

22. Fee and Stuart have an excellent discussion on the distance between the "then and there" and the "here and now" in application. However, they apply their discussion to the New Testament epistles, and we would suggest that these challenges apply just as well to the rest of the Bible. See Fee and Stuart, *How to Read the Bible for All Its Worth*, 27, 74–90.

23. Fee and Stuart (ibid., 75–76) refer to a "commonsense hermeneutics" and the role of "common sense" in the task of application. We would suggest a better term is "sanctified common sense," considering the role of the Holy Spirit in the appropriation of God's Word.

we must evaluate the text's relevance for application in the "here and now," considering issues of cultural relativity and normalcy, along with literary dimension and theological discontinuity. These matters are often ignored by purely devotional approaches to application, but are vitally important.

Second, as believers seeking to appropriate Scripture personally and individually, we must determine what the text means for *me* today, applying Scripture in an introspective, devotional way. It's at this point that the role of the Holy Spirit is seen in application, as the Word of God speaks directly to the heart of the individual (Heb 4:12).

Finally, correlation seeks to systematize the teachings of the Bible based an accurate interpretation of the parts. This is essentially what it means to "do" theology, whether biblical or systematic.[24] Correlation also involves distilling themes and motifs for topical study, resulting in a practical theology for the church. Correlation is ultimately what helps us understand Scripture as part of a lifelong course of study.

Five Reasons for Inductive Bible Study

We've provided a rationale for why induction is a more desirable approach to Bible study than deduction. We've also sought to describe, in summary form, the basic steps of the inductive method. However, we'd like to conclude this chapter by highlighting five reasons why the inductive method has inherent value and practical benefit for those who learn it and put it into practice.

First, the inductive method is a process for Bible study that finds its basis in principle, namely, the *exegetical principle*. While there's a pragmatic element to certain aspects of the inductive method, it is not devoid of principle. The inductive *method* begins with an inductive *attitude*, one driven to discover the intended meaning of the Word of God.[25] In principle, there's no higher calling in the world of communication. The inductive method is a process born out of principle.

---

24. Although we will argue in chapter 15 that an inductive approach better supports biblical theology.

25. Bauer and Traina refer to this as the "inductive spirit" (*Inductive Bible Study*, 18).

Second, the inductive method is a process that benefits from *order* yet also encourages *flexibility* and recognizes the dynamic integration between steps. While the inductive method is typically presented in terms of sequential steps, these steps are integrated in a cyclical fashion as well as a linear one. In other words, while it's important to compile the evidence inductively through observation before moving to interpretation, one can't help but draw interpretive inferences during the process of observation. In addition, asking interpretive questions breeds an inquisitive spirit even before research ensues. Also, as we move through the various steps of interpretation, it's only natural to continue to observe the text, and application sometimes poses new questions that have a bearing on the interpretation of the text. Correlation, for its part, can be oriented toward the interpretation of individual texts, as Scripture functions as its own best commentary. At the same time, correlation can also develop out of the comparative analysis of interpreted parts. The balance between order and flexibility is helpful, providing direction and movement toward a goal while allowing for revision and refinement throughout the process.

Third, the inductive method is a *personal* approach that can be adapted to fit the student of Scripture wherever she is in her pursuit of biblical literacy. Whether she is completely new to the Bible or seasoned by decades of exposure, she can implement the inductive method at any stage in the journey. Some of you reading this book will find that you've been practicing aspects of the inductive method all along, while others may find that it's completely revolutionary to your reading of Scripture. Wherever you may fit into that equation, we're sure that the inductive method will take you to the next level in your personal Bible study.

Fourth, such an approach is *practical*, allowing shortcuts as time constraints may demand. The inductive method is more than just a set of principles guiding our thinking through Scripture; it's also a flexible and adaptable process. You'll be able to perform many of the steps described in the following chapters in abbreviated form, especially once you've grasped the essentials. So whether reading a devotion at the breakfast table or preparing next week's sermon at the office, you'll be able to adapt the steps of the inductive method to fit your specific needs and time constraints.

Fifth, the inductive method is *beneficial* in that it encourages the development of your own Bible study skills. The inductive method truly prepares you to study the Bible on your own. But this is not to suggest that you abandon all forms of consultation in practicing the inductive method. In fact, the inductive method encourages consultation while also equipping you to be more discerning in how to use sources. It even prepares you to disagree with the conclusions of others when the evidence doesn't support those conclusions.

Evangelical Christianity touts the merits of *sola scriptura* (Scripture alone), and in fact, given the history of the church over the past 2,000 years, the opportunity for individual Christians to study the Bible for themselves and to arrive at their own conclusions is something we should never take for granted. However, while affirming the opportunity for self-directed study and individual conclusions, most evangelical churches haven't done particularly well in equipping God's people to study his Word. It's our hope and prayer that this text will find a welcome home with college students, seminarians, pastors, and laypeople alike who would like to learn to study the Bible for themselves.

Finally, while methodology, outlined in the principles in the previous pages, is very important, we're not just developing a *method*; we're developing a *person*. Bible study is more than simply following a series of steps; it involves growth on the part of the interpreter in developing certain interpretive habits, or virtues, such as historical-cultural awareness, canonical consciousness, linguistic and literary competence, sensitivity to genre, a growing grasp of biblical theology, and an ability to apply the insights gained from the inductive study of Scripture to one's own life and to share them with others.[26] If we master the essence of the inductive method and in so doing grow in our pursuit of these interpretive virtues, we'll be well on our way to hearing God's "Well done, good and faithful servant," with regard to our study of Scripture.

---

26. See Köstenberger and Patterson, *Invitation to Biblical Interpretation*, 80.

UNIT II

OBSERVATION
Engaging the Text

Five Steps of Observation

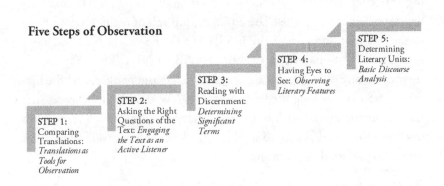

STEP 1:
Comparing
Translations:
*Translations as
Tools for
Observation*

STEP 2:
Asking the Right
Questions of the
Text: *Engaging
the Text as an
Active Listener*

STEP 3:
Reading with
Discernment:
*Determining
Significant
Terms*

STEP 4:
Having Eyes to
See: *Observing
Literary Features*

STEP 5:
Determining
Literary Units:
*Basic Discourse
Analysis*

3

Comparing Bible Translations

Translations as Tools of Observation

I n the English-speaking church, today's Bible reader is faced with dozens of translations. While for some 300 years the King James Version was the Bible of the English-speaking world, this has significantly changed since the late twentieth century. Most of you who are reading this chapter right now are likely using any variety of translations developed since the 1970s. These translations might include revisions to former translations such as the NASB, NKJV, ESV, and NLT[1] or independent translations such as the NIV, HCSB, or NET Bible.[2] Of course, there are many other significant translations on the market, and the history of translation long predates the 1970s.[3] With so many choices, the Bible student is faced with quite a quandary deciding which translation to choose, and perhaps more significantly, knowing why one translation might be preferred over another.[4]

---

1. The New American Standard Bible (NASB; 1971, 1995) is a revision of the American Standard Version (ASV; 1901); the New King James Version (NKJV; 1979) is a revision of the King James Version (KJV; 1611, 1769); the English Standard Version (ESV; 2001) is a revision of the Revised Standard Version (RSV; 1952); and the New Living Translation (NLT; 1996, 2004) is a revision of the Living Bible (LB; 1971).

2. The New International Version (NIV; 1978, 2004) was developed by a committee of over 100 scholars and underwent significant revision in 2011. The Holman Christian Standard Bible (HCSB; 2003, 2009) was also a committee project comprised of roughly 100 scholars, and the New English Translation (NET; 2001) was completed by approximately 25 scholars and is perhaps best known for its very extensive translator's notes.

3. For a concise survey of the history of English Bible translations, see Andreas J. Köstenberger and David A. Croteau, eds., *Which Bible Translation Should I Use? A Comparison of 4 Major Recent Versions* (Nashville: B&H, 2012), 6–21. For a comprehensive history of English translations, especially in the process of revision, see Bruce M. Metzger, *The Bible in Translation* (Grand Rapids: Baker, 2001), 55–190.

4. To help with this is the purpose of Köstenberger and Croteau, *Which Bible Translation Should I Use?*

Because most believers in the English-speaking church don't read Greek or Hebrew, they'll depend on one or more of these translations in their reading and study of God's Word. To study the Word in translation is nothing new; even Jesus and the apostles utilized the Greek Septuagint in their reading of the Old Testament.[5] What is more, the Gospel writers were actually involved in some level of translation as they composed their inspired texts, as Jesus and his disciples were likely speaking Aramaic, yet their words are presented in the Gospels in common, everyday Greek. In the early stages of Christianity, the Bible was translated into a variety of languages,[6] and for over 1,000 years the Western church recognized the Latin Vulgate as the received Word of God.

For today's Bible student, the most basic tool is a good translation of the Bible in his or her own language. You should realize, however, that there's no such thing as a perfect translation, and thus the diligent student of the Bible should utilize a variety of versions. To study using a variety of translations is simply one step among many in the observation stage of inductive Bible study and doesn't diminish the importance of specific word studies in the original languages. However, on a practical level, with so many quality translations available, why wouldn't the English Bible reader utilize a variety of translations in their Bible study? This is especially important at the level of observation, where differences between translations often act as "red flags," indicating difficult exegetical or textual issues that warrant further investigation.

There's almost always a good reason why translations may differ on any particular passage, and to discover the reason behind a difference in translation will always lead to a more informed interpretation of the text. When differences are observed between translations, students should endeavor to discover the reason behind the difference and should allow observed differences to prompt at least some of their interpretive

---

5. The Septuagint (LXX) is the Greek translation of the Hebrew Scriptures originating some 250 years before Christ. Many of the New Testament quotations of the Old Testament reflect familiarity with or direct quotation of the Septuagint.

6. For a survey of ancient translations, including Syriac, Old Latin, Coptic, and Arabic versions, see Metzger, *Bible in Translation*, 25–54.

questions.[7] Through inductive study, most English Bible students can discover the reason behind a difference in translations and in so doing gain a better understanding of the interpretive issues involved in the passage they're studying.

Most English Bible translations come as the result of years of painstaking committee-based research and debate. Translation committees are typically comprised of experts in the original languages (Greek, Hebrew, and to a lesser degree, Aramaic), textual criticism, translation theory, and modern English style and composition. While translators will inevitably be involved in interpretive decision making, there is a hedge of protection from theological prejudice as Bible translation committees typically represent a variety of ecclesiastical traditions and theological positions.

Bible translators also know their grammar and syntax and are fully aware of the influence of context on meaning. In other words, when opinions differ between translators, and ultimately between translations, there's rarely, if ever, any malicious intent to tamper with the original intent of the authors or to undermine the integrity of the Word of God. Nor is incompetence an issue. Rather, differences occur due to legitimate points of view that come into play in the process of translation. Therefore, knowing that there are places where challenges exist in the translation process, it's always to the benefit of the reader to understand as much as possible *why* a difference between translations exists.

In comparing translations, you'll observe that differences typically result from one of the following four reasons.

Exegetical Decision Making

A basic fact of translation is that whenever translation occurs, interpretation occurs, at least at some level. This can't be avoided and will happen even without any intentional bias. Many questions of translation are relatively straightforward, but at other times scholarly opinion can be quite varied. Because of the flexible nature of Greek and Hebrew vocabulary,

---

7. The art of asking interpretive questions will be dealt with in chapter 4. Asking interpretive questions based on observed differences between translations is simply one track to take as students learn to ask quality interpretive questions.

grammar, and syntax, translations will at times differ based on the exegetical choices translators have made. What is more, how words function in a given context must always be discerned by the reader, or in the case of translation, by the translator.

Interpretation is invariably part of translation because much of the translator's work involves making exegetical and syntactical choices regarding the meaning of a given word or phrase as it is found in a particular context. Fortunately, in most cases the vocabulary, grammar, and syntax of the text in the original language is sufficiently clear, and translations reflect little variance in the conveyance of meaning.

There are, of course, instances where this is not the case, and the exegetical decisions that translators make become the basis for significant differences between translations. If, in observing differences between translations, a student has reason to suspect that an exegetical issue is in play, he or she should strive to discover the basis for the exegetical decision translators are making. In turn, through the steps of interpretation, the diligent student will then seek to answer the interpretive issue on his or her own (stay tuned; there is more on this to come!).

Examples of Exegetical Decision Making Affecting Translation

Perhaps the best way to explain the very real issue of exegetical decision making in translation is to illustrate it through a variety of examples. There are quite literally hundreds of examples of exegetical decision making in the Bible, each reflecting different lexical, contextual, historical, and literary considerations that come to affect the decisions relating to interpretation (and thus translation). Knowing that the variety of potential examples is beyond the scope of this chapter, we'll try to look at a sampling of texts that reflect a few of the kinds of issues that translators face as they interpret the text as translators.[8]

---

8. For additional examples, see Köstenberger and Croteau, *Which Bible Translation Should I Use?* For examples from John's Gospel, see Andreas J. Köstenberger, "Translating John's Gospel: Opportunities and Challenges," in *The Challenge of Bible Translation. In Honor of Ronald Youngblood*, ed. Glen G. Scorgie, Mark L. Strauss, and Steven Voth (Grand Rapids: Zondervan, 2003), 347–64.

Psalm 8:5. Our first example reflects an exegetical decision involving a single common word based in a somewhat ambiguous context:

Table 3.1 — Psalm 8:5		
"You made him little less than **God** and crowned him with glory and honor."		
"God"	**"Heavenly Beings"**	**"Angels"**
HCSB	ESV	KJV
NRSV	NET	NKJV
NASB	NIV 1984	LXX
NLT		NIV 2011

The most significant difference in this example is obvious: "God," "angels," or "heavenly beings"? The Hebrew word behind these varying renderings is *elohim*, one of the most common names for God in the Old Testament. While this word is most often translated "God" in the Old Testament, it can be translated in other ways depending on the context.[9] Typically in a situation where the word might mean something other than the standard reference to God, the context is sufficiently clear to warrant this. However, in Psalm 8:5 the context is rather ambiguous, and translators are thus confronted with a rather difficult exegetical decision. This ambiguity is reflected in the way in which versions differ in how they render *elohim* in this verse of Scripture. The HCSB, NASB, NRSV, and NLT translate *elohim* as "God," while the KJV, NKJV, and NIV 2011 translate it as "angels." The ESV, NET, and NIV 1984 take a less distinct approach by translating *elohim* as "heavenly beings," perhaps reflecting the whole host of available options.[10]

---

9. Most often, when not in reference to God, the term functions as a plural reference to the generic "gods" of the nations. Only rarely will the term be used of "angels," most particularly in the book of Job. For more on the term, see Terence E. Fretheim "אלהים," in Willem A. VanGemeren, gen. ed., *New International Dictionary of Old Testament Theology and Exegesis*, vol. 1 (Grand Rapids: Zondervan, 1997), 405–6.

10. In addition, note that the translators of the NIV changed their rendering from the more general "heavenly beings" in 1984 to the more specific "angels" in 2011!

While footnotes may reflect alternative glosses,[11] each translation must make a choice; transliteration is not a viable option in this case.[12] *Elohim* most often is translated "God" in the Old Testament, but in this context such a translation is somewhat awkward: "You [God] made him [man or humanity] a little less than God" (HCSB). Conversely, while "angels" is rarely attested as the meaning of *elohim* in the Old Testament, the context seems to favor this reading: "You [God] have made them [humankind] a little lower than the angels" (NIV 2011). Lexically, "God" seems superior, but "angels" makes better sense of the context. In addition, *elohim* here could mean "heavenly beings": "Yet you [God] have made him [the man or the human being] a little lower than the heavenly beings" (ESV), presumably including the whole heavenly realm, perhaps even God himself.

The context describes the exalted nature and favored role of humankind as the crown of creation (Ps 8:5b–8) and recalls the language of Genesis 1:26–27, where man and woman are created in the image of God. Yet the psalm also exalts God as Creator over humankind, worthy of all praise and worship (Ps 8:1, 3, 8). So verse 5a acts as a hinge, describing humanity's lowly position as earthly rather than heavenly while also evoking the idea of humankind's exalted position as made in the image of God and as having been given dominion over creation. The earthbound state of humankind is certainly a little lower than that of the angels, yet made in the image of God humanity is in some sense made only a "little lower than God."

Clearly, any of the three translation choices could work, and a good argument can be made lexically and contextually for any of them. This brief case study helps us understand the differences in translation for this verse: choosing an English gloss here is quite a challenge![13] In cases such

---

11. The HCSB footnote states the following: "or gods, or a god, or heavenly beings; lit. Elohim."

12. In some cases, transliteration is a viable option. For instance, it has become common for more recent translations to transliterate the Hebrew *Sheol* rather than attempt to make an exegetical distinction between "grave" or any other potential aspects of the Hebrew word.

13. It is worth noting that Hebrews 2:7 quotes Psalm 8:5 as part of an argument demonstrating the superiority of Christ over the angels, even as seen in the incarnation of Christ and his post-resurrection exaltation. The quotation of Psalm 8:5 is from the Greek Septuagint, which translates *elohim* with the Greek word *angelos* or "angels." For some, by quoting from the Septuagint, the inspired writer of Hebrews is in some sense validating the translation "angels" in this particular text.

as these, it's highly beneficial to use multiple translations. The perusal of, say, the HCSB, ESV, and NIV will surface all three major translation options and alert the discerning Bible student to the choice the translator and interpreter face in coming to terms with the contextual meaning of this important passage.

Amos 4:4. Sometimes exegetical decision making is required of translators who (like any Bible student) must read with literary discernment and an awareness of related biblical texts. In our second example, we observe that translations of Amos 4:4 take quite distinct approaches to the translation of the Hebrew word *yom* into either "days" (HCSB, NASB, NKJV, NLT, ESV, NET) or "years" (KJV, NIV).

Table 3.2 — Amos 4:4	
" . . . Bring your sacrifices every morning, your tenths every three **days**."	
"Days"	**"Years"**
HCSB	KJV
ESV	NIV 1984
NASB	NIV 2011
NKJV	
NLT	
NET	

Typically, the Hebrew word *yom* ought to be translated "day" (or "days" in the plural), especially as qualified numerically, but the word can be understood to depict other units of time.[14] In Amos 4:4 the prophet calls for tenths (or tithes) to be brought every three *yom*. The problem here is that there was no law in Israel requiring a tithe every three days. However, there was a "year of tithing" every three *years*, when a special tithe was given to the Levite and to the poor (Deut 14:28; 26:12).

---

14. See P. A. Verhoef, "יוֹם," in Willem A. VanGemeren, gen. ed., *New International Dictionary of Old Testament Theology and Exegesis*, vol. 1 (Grand Rapids: Zondervan, 1997), 419–24.

Correlation alone might favor a less typical translation of *yom* in Amos 4:4. Certainly, as mentioned, there was no tithe brought every three days in ancient Israel. However, the very point of Amos 4:4 may in fact require the absurd instruction to bring a tithe every three days. Amos 4:1–5 simply drips with sarcasm. Because the first class citizenry of Israel had come to place so much confidence in their religious rituals and offerings, even as they maligned the poor of the land, Amos has come to invite them to "up the ante," to "rebel even more" (Amos 4:4a). Instead of tithing for the poor every three *years*, according to their logic, why not do it every three *days*? After all, this "is what you Israelites love to do" (v. 5b)! The irony here is quite striking; those who were guilty of oppressing the poor, yet who trusted in their rituals to garner God's favor, were now being told to take their misguided thinking to the point of absurdity—go ahead and take the very offering that was meant for the poor and multiply it hundreds of times over—see if this brings you God's favor!

We could go on with our analysis of the text of Amos, but this short commentary should bring home the point. Some translations, perhaps missing the sarcasm and choosing to align *yom* with the tithe given to the Levite and the poor, have therefore translated Amos 4:4 with "every three years" rather than "every three days." Whether you agree or disagree with a given rendering, knowing the underlying issues helps you make sense of the translation differences and enables you to make your own informed decision as to what you think a given verse means.

1 Corinthians 7:1. Our third example reflects the significant difference that punctuation can make in determining the meaning of written communication. This is illustrated in 1 Corinthians 7:1, where the use of quotation marks in the HCSB, ESV, NET, and NIV 2011 suggest that Paul is citing a statement made by some in the church at Corinth, while those translations that leave the statement, "It is good for a man not to have relations with a woman," without quotation marks infer that this is Paul's own proposition.

Table 3.3 — 1 Corinthians 7:1		
Now in response to the matters you wrote about: "It is good for a man not to have relations with a woman."		
Quotation Marks	**No Quotation Marks**	**"Yes, it is good"**
HCSB	KJV (colon)	NLT
ESV	NKJV (colon)	
NET	NASB (comma)	
NIV 2011	NIV 1984 (colon)	

The distinction between translations using and not using quotation marks is significant in driving the reader one direction or the other in how they ought to understand Paul's teaching in this text. On the one hand, the HCSB, ESV, NET, and NIV 2011 suggest by their use of quotation marks that this statement in 1 Corinthians 7:1b is a summary of an ascetic teaching circulating among some in the church at Corinth. Paul is now in his letter addressing this particular issue of sexual abstinence and ascetic teaching with which the Corinthian church is struggling. Evidently, as absurd as this might appear, there was a faction in Corinth that was teaching a brand of asceticism forbidding sexual relations even between married couples. In the rest of chapter 7 Paul speaks to this issue as an apostle, correcting the false teaching of the ascetic faction.

On the other hand, without quotation marks translations infer that these words are a summary proposition of Paul, a thesis that drives his teachings throughout the chapter. The New Living Translation even takes this one step further, stating in the affirmative, "Yes, it is good to abstain from sexual relations" (1 Cor 7:1b). And so the reader using the NLT, KJV, NKJV, NASB, or NIV 1984 will see these words as apostolic admonition, with verse 2 stating a concession that represents less than God's ideal ("Nevertheless, but . . .").

The Greek text itself does not indicate with clarity whether to take these words as a quotation or not (the original Greek has no punctuation). Thus translators must make an exegetical decision as to how to frame the statement with proper English punctuation. It's interesting that recent translations have tended to side with the opinion of most modern commentators, viewing the statement as a quotation (this is especially clear in the movement between the 1984 and 2011 editions of the NIV). However, this is ultimately an exegetical decision that each translation must make, and the reader should be aware of how quotation marks will affect the meaning of the text. Again, note that unless you are using multiple translations, you may not even be aware that an important interpretive decision must be made, and depending on which translation you are using, you may well end up being directed down the wrong path (depending, of course, on which translations got it right!). In any case, this example, too, illustrates the importance of using multiple translations in one's study of Scripture.

Exegetical decision making is inevitable in translating the Bible. Translators may seek neutrality in their work, but this is often impossible. In many cases, the ambiguity inherent in vocabulary and syntax will lead to very different options in translation. Translators can't avoid this, and many would argue that they shouldn't. Knowing this, English Bible readers should be aware of how often exegetical decision making is reflected in the Bibles they're using in their study. To restate the obvious, readers of any given translation will inevitably subject themselves to the exegetical choices made by translation committees and thus should conduct their study with a variety of translations on hand.

Translation Theory

Generally speaking, differences that occur as a result of translation philosophy are more issues of style than substance, but these differences are evident when translations are compared. Because no translation can be completely literal, all translations will employ a certain degree of dynamic equivalence (i.e., free translation or paraphrase) in the process of translation from the original language (Hebrew, Greek, or Aramaic) to the receptor language (in our case, English). Generally speaking, a so-called literal (or formal, word-by-word) approach to translation will attempt to translate any given passage by staying as close as possible to the words and phrasing of the original language. This approach to translation will tend not to bridge differences between languages in areas of idiom, grammar, syntax, and culture. However, because no two languages are equal in terms of vocabulary, grammar, and syntax, a truly literal approach to translation will result in a virtually unreadable English translation of the Bible. This can be seen in modern interlinear Bibles or in other attempts at a fully literal translation (such as Young's Literal Translation, YLT Bible, 1898).

As translators attempt to convert an accurate translation of the Bible into a readable text, they're inevitably involved in some degree of dynamic equivalence, translating words, phrases, and idioms from the original language into their proper English equivalents. When a Bible translation attempts to use dynamic equivalence as a driving, structural norm, then it might be labeled as a "thought-for-thought" translation. Since its inception, the NIV has taken the mantle as representing excellence in this approach to translation. When a version seeks as much as possible to render the text in a literal manner, it might be labeled a "word-for-word" translation. The NASB has traditionally been accepted as representing the best of "word-for-word" translation, although more recently the ESV has laid some claim to this distinction as well.

Again, it's important to realize that all translation involves a degree of dynamic equivalence, and thus there's no such thing as a perfectly literal translation (at least among commonly used translations). Also, "literal" doesn't necessarily mean "accurate." Certainly a word-by-word translation can be accurate in many cases, but a dynamic translation can also accurately represent the meaning of the original language text in certain instances where a literal translation is not possible due to differences between the original and receptor languages. In fact, in some cases a more dynamic translation may cut through potential misrepresentation in original-language vocabulary, grammar, syntax, and idiom, and thus be more accurate in conveying the actual intended meaning. Some have called this "optimal equivalence."[15]

---

15. See E. Ray Clendenen's defense of "optimal equivalence" in reference to the Holman Christian Standard Bible (HCSB) in Köstenberger and Croteau, *Which Bible Translation Should I Use?*, 117–21.

The extent or degree to which a given translation will tend to veer from the literal will determine where on the scale a given translation might fall. However, remember that the following scale merely represents overall tendencies. You can find examples where a more literal translation in a certain case is quite dynamic, and other examples where a more dynamic translation elects in a given place to render a passage quite literally (perhaps even more so than the typically literal translations).[16]

Figure 3.1: Bible Translations from "Word-for-Word" to "Thought-for-Thought"

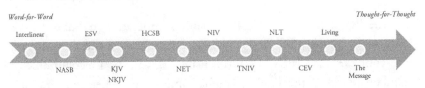

The key is to understand that translation theory is actually a rather neutral, yet necessary aspect of the translation process. The degree to which a translation embraces equivalence in any given part may affect the wording of its English-language product. As various English translations are compared, differences may reflect various issues involving translation theory. For instance, distinctions between "word-for-word" and "thought-for-thought" translation are most obvious in reference to idiomatic language in the Bible.

Examples of Translation Theory Affecting Translation

Luke 9:44. In the following example, an idiom that may misrepresent meaning or simply read poorly in English is translated into a thought-for-thought equivalent by the more typically dynamic translations.

---

16. For an excellent overview of translation theory, especially regarding inconsistency in the application of literal versus dynamic translation theory, see Dave Brunn, *One Bible, Many Versions: Are All Translations Created Equal?* (Downers Grove: InterVarsity, 2013), 19–98.

Table 3.4 — Luke 9:44		
"Let these words sink in: The Son of Man is about to be betrayed into the hands of men."		
Literal	**Dynamic**	**Idiomatic**
KJV	HCSB	NET
NKJV	NIV	
NASB		
ESV		

The literal translation of the opening imperative in Luke 9:44 is represented by the KJV, NKJV, NASB, and ESV: "Let these words sink into your ears . . ." (ESV). While sensible, this is not a recognizable or standard idiom in the English language but rather reflects an original-language idiom. The more dynamic translations will tend to translate the words of the text into an equivalent meaning, as seen in the NIV: "Listen carefully to what I am about to tell you. . . ." The NIV is not incorrect in conveying the meaning of these words, although this is certainly not a literal translation. Some might consider this a matter of preference, although some admittedly have a strong opinion on such matters.

The important thing to keep in mind is that translations will differ due to translation theory, and a comparison of translations will often reveal the nuanced meaning behind a given idiom. It's interesting to note how the HCSB has retained a degree of literalness by only partially translating the idiom and in effect has expressed the wording in a more acceptable English-language formulation, "Let these words sink in. . . ." An even more interesting (and perhaps most satisfying) approach is found in the NET Bible, where the translators have chosen an English-language idiomatic equivalent to communicate the meaning of the text: "Take these words to heart."

Galatians 3:24. While matters of idiom, culture, and simple phraseology are usually easy to recognize and matter little in conveying accurate meaning, sometimes this is not the case. An interesting example where cultural terms wrapped in language may miscommunicate meaning is found in Galatians 3:24. Here, the Greek word *paidagōgos* is variously translated as "schoolmaster" (KJV), "tutor" (NKJV, NASB), "disciplinarian" (NRSV), or "guardian" (HCSB, ESV, NIV 2011). In the original context, the Greek word *paidagōgos* actually refers to a slave whose duty was to transport a child to and from the place of education. Paul's argument in Galatians 3:24 is that the law is like a *paidagōgos*; it essentially is like this particular slave whose duty was to supervise the child when moving from one place to another.

Table 3.5 — Galatians 3:24		
"The law, then, was our **guardian** until Christ . . ."		
"Guardian"	**"Tutor"**	**"Schoolmaster"**
HCSB	NASB	KJV
ESV	NKJV	
NET		
NLT		
NIV 2011		
NCV		

Obviously, we don't have slaves today who take our children to school, watching over them on their daily journey. However, in Paul's day, the role of the *paidagōgos* was familiar enough that he was able to use it as an illustration without needing to provide any background explanation or linguistic clarification. The Galatian believers knew who a *paidagōgos* was; they saw those people on a regular basis, and some of the recipients of this letter may have even owned a *paidagōgos*. Paul's point was not that the law was in every way like the *paidagōgos*, but he was assuming a particular point of reference, and this analogy should be inferred from the context. Perhaps the 1984 NIV hits the mark with its rather dynamic, interpretive translation, "So the law was put in charge to lead us to Christ. . . ."

However, if a translation seeks to keep some sense of the illustrative nature of Paul's point, an approximate equivalent in our contemporary setting is needed. To simply translate *paidagōgos* as "slave" would be far too misleading, as a contemporary American reader would assume the slavery of the antebellum South. The KJV has "schoolmaster," which elicits in the mind of American readers the picture of a one-room schoolhouse overseen by a strict disciplinarian wearing a hair bun with a ruler in her hand! The word "tutor" evokes the idea of a graduate assistant or off-duty teacher who is doing "one-on-one" tutoring to assist a struggling student and perhaps to earn a little extra cash, while "guardian" conveys the idea of a parental substitute.

What this illustrates is that finding an adequate dynamic equivalent is not always an easy task, and often translations, while helpful, cannot communicate every linguistic and cultural particularity with clarity and precision. What is more, dynamic equivalence to some degree involves exegetical decision making; this is true with regard to grammar, syntax, idiom, and vocabulary, and the student should be aware that exegetical decision making and translation theory are virtually inseparable.[17] There is ultimately no substitute for digging into the historical, cultural, and linguistic backgrounds of the text, and at least in some cases, a comparative study of translations will assist in taking the first steps of that journey.

A Note on Paraphrases

Before turning to our next reason why translations might differ from place to place, and while on the subject of translation theory, we'll make a few suggestions concerning the use of paraphrases. While dynamic translation is inevitable, some have attempted to translate in a truly paraphrastic manner, departing in large scale from the vocabulary and grammar of the original text. Notable paraphrases include Eugene Peterson's *The Message* and, to a lesser degree, the original (1996) edition of the New Living Translation (NLT). While these may be helpful supplements for Bible study, you shouldn't use them as primary translations for study

---

17. See David Dewey, *A User's Guide to Bible Translations: Making the Most of Different Versions* (Downers Grove: InterVarsity, 2004), 29–89.

or regular reading of God's Word. All translations reflect exegetical decision making and dynamic equivalence, but a paraphrase does this more than necessary, and you will subject yourself extensively to the exegetical opinions of the translator(s) when reading a paraphrase. Therefore, if you consult a paraphrase, treat it as you would a commentary.[18] Beyond this, we'd caution you against using paraphrases as primary tools in Bible study or daily reading.

Textual Basis behind a Translation

Bible students often confuse the translation of the Bible with the transmission (copying and preservation) of the Bible. One infamous example of this mistake is found in the Eighth Article of Faith of the Church of Jesus Christ of Latter-Day Saints (the Mormon Church), which reads in part: "We believe the Bible to be the word of God as far as it is translated correctly. . . ." What Joseph Smith (the founder of the Latter-Day Saints) meant by this was, "We believe the Bible so far as it is *transmitted* correctly." Of course, Mormons don't believe that the Bible was transmitted correctly. As a matter of fact, they believe the Bible is so full of corruptions and errors in the transmission process that it is thoroughly unreliable (a point with which we would adamantly disagree) and in need of additional revelation (in their view, the Book of Mormon). The point of this is to illustrate how easy it is to confuse transmission with translation. Many English Bible readers don't realize that transmission precedes translation, and the two are quite distinct. Nevertheless, issues in the transmission of the biblical text are reflected in the eventual translation of the Bible, which brings us to our third reason why translations may differ: textual issues behind a translation.

Establishing a standard Greek or Hebrew text for translation is the work of textual criticism, a necessary science that seeks to reproduce the

---

18. To illustrate the utility of a paraphrase, note the rendering of *paidagōgos* in Galatians 3:24 (our last example) from *The Message*: "The law was like those Greek tutors, with which you are familiar, who escort children to school and protect them from danger or distraction, making sure the children will really get to the place they set out for." While this is a helpful interpretive gloss, it certainly stretches the meaning of "translation."

most accurate text possible based upon available manuscript evidence. The term "criticism" is often misunderstood but the term is used in the sense of being *discerning*, not necessarily *critical* in a negative sense. In any case, in order to begin to translate the Bible into English, one needs to first determine the most accurate Greek and Hebrew texts of the Bible that will form the basis for any given translation. Only then can translation begin.

You might wonder why determining a standard Greek and Hebrew text of the Bible is even necessary. After all, wouldn't the same God who inspired the written Word also choose to preserve it?[19] The answer to this is "yes," but it's not as simple as God taking the original autographs of individual books of the Bible and simply preserving them in a glass case. As a matter of fact, there are no autographs of any portion of the Bible in existence today. What we do have is copies ("manuscripts"), and these frequently contain differences between them ("variants"). But don't be dismayed; variants are usually exegetically insignificant, and no area of Christian doctrine rests upon a textual variant. However, this is not to suggest that variants are rare or irrelevant. On the contrary, they're quite common and in a few cases exegetically significant. Nevertheless, through the work of textual criticism, comparative analysis can determine with a high degree of certainty how a textual variant came to be and, in most cases, how the original text would've read.[20]

The variants existing within the manuscript pool are actually quite a positive reality. In the transmission of the Bible, God, for reasons about which we can only speculate, allowed variants to develop, and so we must analyze the text to determine the most accurate representation of the original text. Ironically, however, the best safeguard for the preservation of the Bible rests in the fact that textual variants exist among biblical

---

19. For a helpful response to these and other questions, see Andreas J. Köstenberger, Darrell L. Bock, and Josh Chatraw, *Truth Matters* (Nashville: B&H, 2014); and even more in depth the work by the same authors, *Truth in a Culture of Doubt* (Nashville: B&H, 2014). In addition, various study tools are available in conjunction with these volumes.

20. See especially Paul D. Wegner, *The Journey from Texts to Translations: The Origin and Development of the Bible* (Grand Rapids: Baker, 2005). For a brief introduction to New Testament textual criticism, see Andreas J. Köstenberger, Benjamin L. Merkle, and Robert L. Plummer, *Going Deeper with New Testament Greek: An Intermediate Study of the Grammar and Syntax of the New Testament* (Nashville: B&H Academic, 2016), chapter 1.

manuscripts and that through the science of textual criticism we have the means and the opportunity to engage in fair-minded analysis of the text.

Old and New Testament textual criticism are quite distinct fields, working with different elements in very diverse developmental contexts, yet the outcome for translation is quite similar. Most modern translations utilize critical (in the sense of "thoroughly analyzed") editions of the Greek and Hebrew texts which represent the best scholarly consensus regarding the wording of the original autographs. For the Old Testament, this text is the *Biblia Hebraica Stuttgartensia* (BHS), and for the New Testament typically the latest edition of the United Bible Societies' Greek New Testament or Nestle-Aland's *Novum Testamentum Graece*. Each of these texts includes a critical apparatus that informs the reader of text-critical issues that may be involved in any given verse. Although most English-Bible readers will be unable to read in detail the textual commentary in the standard Greek and Hebrew Bibles, modern English translations often utilize some form of textual footnoting, and these notes often reflect in summary fashion the more complex apparatus found in the original-language texts.

Most text-based issues in translation involve the Old Testament, where the nature of the Hebrew language (a consonantal alphabet, letters that often look alike, and tightly spaced script in the manuscripts) often leads to textual ambiguities. Although translators typically adhere to the BHS, they will in the process of translation make informed textual decisions, and there are numerous cases where the BHS, following the Masoretic manuscript tradition (the Masoretes were very careful Jewish scribes), is not supported by other key elements in Old Testament textual history, including the Greek Septuagint and the Dead Sea Scrolls.[21] In

---

21. The Masoretic text of the Hebrew Old Testament was developed between AD 600 and 1000 by the Masoretes, Jewish scribes who were largely responsible for the written symbols representing the vowels that had previously only been vocalized. The Septuagint is the Greek translation of the Hebrew Old Testament and is the Bible commonly used during the New Testament era. The Dead Sea Scrolls represent a large collection of Hebrew scrolls discovered near the shores of the Dead Sea in the late 1940s. These scrolls represent the earliest extant Hebrew manuscript tradition, dating back to about 100 years before Christ. Together, most Old Testament textual criticism revolves around the comparison of these three collections, although other ancient translations and commentaries are also considered in doing Old Testament textual criticism. For an introduction to Old Testament textual criticism and source material, see Wegner, *Journey from Texts to Translations*, 165–205.

Old Testament textual analysis, the Masoretic text typically forms the basis for the Hebrew text, unless challenged by ancient translations (the primary among these being the Septuagint) or the Dead Sea Scrolls. A great example of this that is not often reflected in English translations but illustrates the point well concerns the height of Goliath in 1 Samuel 17:4.

The Masoretic text forms the basis for the popular acceptance of a 9 ½-foot-tall Goliath. The Hebrew of the Masoretic text (and the BHS) literally places Goliath's height at 6 cubits and a span (KJV, ESV, NASB). With a cubit being roughly 18 inches (an arm length), and a span 9 inches (a hand span), the conversion would put Goliath somewhere over 9 feet tall (HCSB, NIV, NLT). However, the Dead Sea Scrolls and the Septuagint describe Goliath at 4 cubits and a span, which would equate roughly to a 7-foot-tall Goliath (NET). While many translations include a footnote with the alternative reading, few have ventured to incorporate this textual alternative in their main text translation.[22] Nevertheless, it's worth noting that a textual discrepancy does exist that may be reflected in English translations. Perhaps if not such a sensitive subject (a lot of "Goliaths of your life" sermons need a 9 ½-foot-tall Goliath), more translations would reflect the textual alternative.[23]

Examples of Text-Critical Challenges Affecting Translation

Hosea 7:14. An example of Old Testament textual ambiguity that is more evenly reflected in English translations is Hosea 7:14. In the second half of verse 14, the key distinction observed between translations pertains to the phrase "they assembled themselves" (KJV, NKJV, NASB, NIV 1984) or "they slashed themselves" (HCSB, ESV, NET, NLT, NIV 2011).

---

22. For instance, the HCSB includes a footnote reading, "DSS, LXX read *four cubits and a span.*" See also the fascinating study by J. Daniel Hays, "Reconsidering the Height of Goliath," *JETS* 48 (2005): 701–14, who favors "four cubits and a span."

23. Old Testament scholarship tackles textual discrepancies between the Masoretic text, the Dead Sea Scrolls, and the Septuagint on a case by case basis. For an excellent review of the textual and literary arguments for the alternative (DSS and LXX) reading, see Hays, "Reconsidering the Height of Goliath," 701–14.

Table 3.6 — Hosea 7:14	
"... They **slash** themselves for grain and new wine ..."	
"to sojourn/assemble"	**"to cut/slash/gash"**
KJV	HCSB
NKJV	ESV
NASB	NLT
NIV 1984	NET
	NIV 2011

While not theologically significant, the variance between "they assembled themselves" and "they slashed themselves" does convey a distinct meaning. The Masoretic text reflects a verb meaning "to sojourn" or "to assemble," while the Septuagint indicates (through the Greek translation) a Hebrew verb meaning "to cut" or "to slash." In written script, both Hebrew verbs look very much alike, and one can imagine that scribes could easily mistake one verb for the other. Understanding the textual discrepancy, translators are forced to follow either the Masoretic rendering or the Hebrew rendering that presumably stands behind the Greek Septuagint. In most cases where there's a discrepancy, translators follow the Masoretic text over the Septuagint, but in this case many would argue that the context better supports the alternative reading found in the Septuagint.[24] Whatever approach translators take, their rendering is in part reflective of a *textual* choice that they have decided to follow (textual decisions are always in part exegetical decisions).

In the case of the New Testament, most modern translations will use a Greek version that reflects an eclectic text tradition, meaning that textual variants and discrepancies in the manuscript pool are weighed case by case throughout the New Testament and no one family of manuscripts

24. The thematic context of Hosea reflects condemnation over the practice of rebellion through idolatrous practices, as does the last line of verse 14, "they turn away from Me" (HCSB). Hosea repeatedly condemns the Israelites for their involvement in Baalism, which practiced cultic "cutting" as a means to elicit the favor of the fertility god Baal (cf. 1 Kgs 18:28). That the Israelites would rebel by "slashing themselves" to elicit the favor of Baal for grain and new wine fits well into the context of Hosea (cf. Hos 2:8).

holds significant precedence over others.[25] New Testament textual criticism (or analysis) is a complex science, but the results are such that we can affirm with confidence that the Greek New Testament we hold today is an accurate reflection of what was written in the original autographs.[26] The available manuscript pool supporting the Greek New Testament is varied and continually growing as new manuscript fragments are discovered and research is refined.[27] This reality provides a firm foundation for the translation of the New Testament, and relatively few significant textual differences are apparent in the New Testament between modern translations.[28] However, you'll notice in comparing the King James or New King James Bibles to most other modern translations that differences in the New Testament often do involve textual discrepancies. This is because the KJV and NKJV New Testaments are based on a different Greek text than most other modern translations. The Greek text used as the basis for the King James Version, the *Textus Receptus* (Latin for "Received Text"), is considered by most scholars to be less reliable on the whole than most recently discovered Greek texts, especially the early papyri, yet the *Textus Receptus* continues to hold considerable sway in popular circles.[29]

There's a great deal of misinformation concerning the *Textus Receptus*, no doubt in part due to the implication of divine endorsement suggested by its name, "Received Text."[30] In reality, this name has nothing

---

25. A "family" of manuscripts designates those Greek manuscripts representing a common historical time period, geographical location, or ecclesiastical tradition.

26. For an overview of New Testament textual criticism, see Wegner, *Journey from Texts to Translations*, 207–40.

27. See Daniel B. Wallace, "Challenges in New Testament Textual Criticism for the Twenty-first Century," *JETS* 52 (2009): 79–100.

28. Even though there are numerous variants among Greek New Testament manuscripts, these are typically resolved through the process of textual analysis, meaning that translators do not often face uncertainty regarding the text of the New Testament.

29. The quality of the *Textus Receptus* compared with more recently discovered Greek texts, especially papyri, is a matter of scholarly debate. However, while affirming the general quality of the *Textus Receptus*, it should be noted that it was developed from a rather limited number of manuscripts, representing one family of manuscript tradition, and without the benefit of modern tools for research and analysis.

30. The *Textus Receptus*, in turn, is based on the so-called "Majority Text" which is found in the largest number (though not the oldest) manuscripts. The Majority Text, for its part, exhibits the Byzantine text type which is often written in minuscule (lower-case) letters. Most modern English versions (though not the NKJV) are based on an eclectic text which more closely follows the Alexandrian text type.

to do with revelation, inspiration, or divine endorsement. Rather, it was simply the standard (or "received") Greek text at the time when King James I commissioned a new translation of the Bible for the common use of the church in England in the sixteenth century. Modern advances in New Testament textual criticism, including discoveries of literally thousands of Greek manuscripts that were unknown at the time of the King James translation, as well as computer technology used in the study of the Greek manuscripts, demands that modern translations carefully consider all available manuscript evidence in determining the Greek text that most accurately represents the originals. For this reason, there are points of departure from the *Textus Receptus* in most modern translations.

Colossians 1:14. This can be easily illustrated by one of the better known examples, the "blood of Christ" phrase in Colossians 1:14.

Table 3.7 — Colossians 1:14	
"We have redemption, the forgiveness of sins, in Him."	
Includes "blood of Christ"	**Does not include "blood of Christ"**
KJV	HCSB
NKJV	ESV
	NASB
	NIV
	NLT
	NET

The fact that most modern translations don't include the phrase "through His blood" has led to numerous accusations, including the notion that the NIV, among other modern translations, equates to some form of a "bloodless Bible," having maliciously removed the blood of Christ from Scripture. The truth is that this is not a malicious ploy to remove the blood of Christ from the Bible but rather a classic example of a textual variant in the New Testament. The phrase "through His blood" is found in only a few late New Testament manuscripts yet is represented in the *Textus Receptus*. Therefore the phrase is included in the KJV and was adopted by the NKJV and a few not as widely known modern translations.[31] However, the vast majority of modern translations, utilizing the modern eclectic text of the New Testament and recognizing the weak textual support for this phrase in Colossians 1:14, don't include it in translation.

You might wonder how this textual variant came to be, and if this variant affects or jeopardizes any vital New Testament doctrines? The parallel phraseology is found in Ephesians 1:7, "We have redemption in Him through His blood, the forgiveness of our trespasses, according to the riches of His grace" (HCSB). The textual support for "through His blood" in Ephesians 1:7 is very strong, and most scholars believe that "through his blood" was inserted into some late manuscripts of Colossians 1:14 due to the similarity between Colossians 1:14 and Ephesians 1:7. Perhaps a later copyist made an assumption based on familiarity with the Ephesians verse or initially made a marginal notation that was later inserted (rather smoothly) into the Colossians text. Whatever the history behind the variant, clearly the New Testament doctrines relating to the blood of Christ don't depend on the variant in Colossians 1:14. Although Ephesians 1:7 is the closest in wording to Colossians 1:14 and is likely the origin of the added phrase in Colossians, the blood of Christ and the doctrinal implications related to its efficacy are well attested throughout the New Testament, including in passages such as Romans 3:23–25, Ephesians 2:13, and Colossians 1:20.[32]

---

31. Interestingly, the 1996 New Living Translation included the phrase ("with his blood"), but the more recent revisions (2004, 2007) do not include it.

32. The broad representation of references citing the blood of Christ can even be attested in "bloodless Bibles" such as the NIV. For more on textual differences and the impact that this has when comparing modern translations to the KJV, see James R. White, *The King James Only Controversy: Can You Trust the Modern Translations?* (Minneapolis: Bethany House, 1995), 149–91. See also D. A. Carson, *The King James Version Debate: A Plea for Realism* (Grand Rapids: Baker, 1979).

The Dynamic Nature of Living Languages

Our final reason translations might differ from place to place relates not to the translation process but to the dynamic nature of living languages. Because all languages, including English, change slowly over time, you may find that differences occur between translations simply due to changes that have taken place in the receptor language. While using a modern translation alleviates much concern over this issue, there are those who prefer to use older translations, particularly the King James Version. When studying from an older English translation, you should be aware of anachronistic and obsolete terms as well as archaic spelling and sentence construction.

Examples of English-Language Changes Affecting Translation

James 2:3. A clear example of language whose meaning has changed over time is seen in James 2:3: "And ye have respect to him that weareth the gay clothing . . ." (KJV). A few generations ago, the word "gay" could be used to refer to someone who was happy or glad, and centuries ago it was used to refer to something that was fine or precious. Today the word almost exclusively refers to someone who is homosexual. In context, James is obviously not referring to the man who walks into an assembly wearing "homosexual" clothing, whatever that may entail. He is referring to the rich man wearing fine clothes and is addressing the problem of favoritism frequently shown to the rich in the first century (and we would dare say the same does happen today). Any confusion is easily resolved by consulting modern translations such as the HCSB: "If you look with favor on the man wearing the fine clothes . . ." (see also the NKJV, ESV, or NIV).

1 Peter 2:12. While most examples of differences incurred through the dynamic nature of the English language are insignificant and easily recognized, there are a few that can be quite problematic. For instance, consider the word "conversation" in 1 Peter 2:12.

Table 3.8 — 1 Peter 2:12		
"**Conduct** yourselves honorably among the Gentiles . . ."		
"conversation"	"conduct/behavior"	"live good lives"
KJV	HCSB	NIV
	ESV	NLT
	NASB	
	NET	

When most people read the word "conversation," they think of verbal communication between individuals. In 1 Peter 2:12, the KJV admonishes the reader to have "conversation honest among the Gentiles." This certainly makes sense in the English language, and this even makes sense in the context of 1 Peter 2:12. The problem is that the word "conversation" means something today that is quite different from what it meant a few hundred years ago.[33] In fact, the Greek word behind "conversation," *anastrophē*, does not infer verbal communication, but rather the broader elements of human conduct and behavior.[34] Therefore, modern translations use words such as "conduct" or "behavior" to translate the word literally, while others such as the NIV choose a more dynamic approach to convey the meaning: "Live such good lives among the pagans. . . ." Obviously, this example has no striking theological implications, but it's one that could easily be misleading for those who use only the KJV in study. There's certainly nothing wrong with preferring the style of the KJV, and there are many who will use the KJV as their preferred translation. However, note that even the King James translators encouraged the comparison of translations, as you

---

33. Although many assume that the KJV they read today is the same as was originally published in 1611, this is not usually the case. The KJV has undergone many revisions since it was first published, and most readers today are using either the Oxford or the Cambridge edition of the KJV. These were both released in 1769. For sources on the history of the King James Version, including its revisions, see Metzger, *Bible in Translation*, 70–80; and Wegner, *Journey from Texts to Translations*, 307–40.

34. See also 1 Pet 3:1: "Likewise, ye wives, be in subjection to your own husbands; that, if any obey not the word, they also may without the word be won by the *conversation* of the wives," where the phrase "without the word" in the immediate context removes all doubt whether or not "conversation" refers to verbal communication (cf. v. 2: "while they behold your chaste *conversation* coupled with fear").

can see in the preface to their work: "Therefore, as S. Augustine saith, that variety of Translations is profitable for the finding out of the sense of the Scriptures."[35] This bit of wisdom is perfectly in line with the premise of this chapter, and we'd dare say that many who use the KJV in an exclusive manner would do well to read the preface to that translation.[36]

2 Corinthians 8:1. For those who are accustomed to reading the KJV, most examples of archaic syntax, word choice, and spelling will not cause too much confusion. However, there are examples where just about any modern reader will be unable to understand the wording of the text. For example, consider 2 Corinthians 8:1: "Moreover, brethren, we do you to wit of the grace of God bestowed on the churches of Macedonia" (KJV). We're not sure if anyone without consulting other translations could know exactly what Paul is saying in this verse. However, the NKJV, along with all modern translations, makes the meaning quite clear: "Moreover, brethren, we make known to you the grace of God bestowed on the churches of Macedonia." This, of course, isn't to indict the KJV as a poor translation of the Bible. Rather, it's simply to point out that the English language has changed over time. The reader of the KJV or other older translations must be aware of this fact, knowing that a comparison of translations will in most cases clarify the difficulties presented in reading from an older English version.

Final Thoughts

On a practical level, what should the English Bible student do with all this information? Is there a sensible process for comparing translations as a step of observation? Certainly, as explained above, it's helpful to know why translations might differ from place to place, but should we

---

35. As quoted from the KJV preface in Köstenberger and Croteau, *Which Bible Translation Should I Use?*, 12.
36. While most publications of the King James Version don't include the preface titled, "*The Translators to the Reader*," the Holman KJV Study Bible does. For this reason, in addition to the excellent study notes and full-color maps, we'd recommend this Study Bible to those who would like to read from the KJV.

not begin by simply observing when and where differences *do* take place among translations?

The answer to this is a resounding "yes." At the level of observation, the starting point must be learning to read with eyes trained to look for significant differences in translation. Of course, knowing something about *why* translations vary helps you discern between significant and insignificant differences. If you understand that minor word variation might occur as a result of English style or translation theory, then these observations may not warrant further attention as we move from observation into interpretation.

However, when translations represent the communication of opposite concepts, or even nuanced variation is observed that affects meaning, then this may warrant additional attention during the interpretation stage. If an entire phrase or clause is missing or if the wording of a sentence reflects little similarity between translations, most likely because of text-critical issues, then these are matters worth investigating.

Therefore, when observing any significant translation difference, ask yourself the question: Is the difference the result of (1) differing interpretations (the *same* text being translated differently), (2) differences in translation theory (still the same text being translated), (3) an underlying text-critical issue (*different* texts being translated and thus the translation being different), or some combination of these? Essentially, whenever meaning is substantively affected, our observation of differences becomes the basis for interpretive questions, and in turn, as our questions are answered, we'll be interpreting the text in a more informed and conclusive manner.

So how do you implement a translation comparison in doing inductive Bible study? And are there available shortcuts given our limited time and resources? Obviously the process begins with gathering sources and comparative tools. The first and most obvious place to go will be the Bible translations on your book shelf (or computer or smart phone!). During times of personal study, biblical studies research, lesson preparation, or sermon preparation, we'd recommend you always have at least four or five reliable Bible translations open on your desk (or screen).

In the electronic age in which we live today this is more easily accomplished than at any other previous time in history. Students can quickly access multiple translations of the Bible online, and virtually all Bible software programs have features for the comparative analysis of English translations, including graphs and charts illustrating the degree to which translations differ in any given passage.

However, even with the advances of technology, there's no substitute for experience and discernment when comparing translations. This is why we spent so much time in this chapter detailing the primary reasons why translations might differ. When you understand the translation process, even just through the observation of English Bible versions, you'll more likely be able to read your Bible with an awareness of the differences in translation. With intentional effort to compare translations, and the experience to discern significant differences (and even why they might be occurring), you've taken an important first step in the observation stage of inductive Bible study. The observation of the text will certainly involve more than comparing Bible translations, but this step will often raise the most significant red flags as you survey the horizon of interpretation.

As a final point, we want to assure you that there's nothing wrong with having a preferred translation of the Bible for devotional reading, teaching, or preaching. However, having a *preferred* translation of the Bible doesn't demand an *exclusive* use of that translation. What is more, if you have a preferred translation, we'd highly encourage you to know something about the translation you're using and to have a good reason *why* you prefer that translation over others. Read the preface and the translator's notes, as they will reveal the underlying translation theory and textual base behind that translation. You'll also learn about the history behind the translation, whether it is a revision of older versions, and if there was a historical event or context precipitating the development of that translation. The reasons for preferring one translation over another will vary from person to person, but for all readers of the Bible this should be a matter for sustained and intelligent reflection.[37]

---

37. We recommend Köstenberger and Croteau, *Which Bible Translation Should I Use?* as a useful aid for choosing a Bible translation.

4

Asking the Right Questions
of the Text

Listening Actively to the Text

A key factor in facilitating the Bible student's inductive thought process is the ability to ask well-informed questions of the text. To quote Fee and Stuart, "The key to good exegesis, and therefore to a more intelligent reading of the Bible, is to learn to read the text carefully and to ask the right questions of the text."[1] In terms of the inductive method, reading the text carefully is done by following the steps of observation while asking the right questions of the text means formulating interpretive questions. In the overall course of the inductive method, interpretive questions primarily function as a bridge between observation and interpretation, although questions can play a role throughout the entire inductive process. Essentially, this means that observations prompt interpretive questions (observation having revealed the interpretive issues inherent in the text), and as those questions are answered, the interpretation of the text will naturally ensue. The quality of interpretation will often depend on the quality of interpretive questions, and thus we turn to the task of learning to ask the right questions of the text.

As simple as this may sound, the ability to ask well-informed questions doesn't come easily or automatically. In fact, this is an art that develops over a lifetime of inquisitive study. Even the concept of a "well-informed question" is an oxymoron of sorts—if we're so well informed,

---

1. Gordon D. Fee and Douglas Stuart, *How to Read the Bible for All Its Worth*, 4th ed. (Grand Rapids: Zondervan, 2014), 30.

then why should we have the need to ask or answer any questions of the text? One of the paradoxical aspects of education is that the more you learn, the more you realize how much more there is to learn. In the same way, as your level of biblical literacy rises, you learn to ask more detailed interpretive questions that have a bearing on the issues of historical background, word meaning, literary function, and theological implication.[2]

Although the task may seem daunting, you should be encouraged to know that the ability to ask good interpretive questions becomes easier with practice, almost to the point of being habitual or natural. However, we've found that for many students, asking quality interpretive questions represents quite a challenge and is a skill requiring guidance, practice, and commitment. In the present chapter we therefore provide step-by-step instructions and principled recommendations for the development of informed and relevant interpretive questions.[3]

You may ask why we're presenting a chapter on interpretive questions before detailing the primary steps of observation. The simple reason is that interpretive questions develop *throughout* the process of observation, not simply after observation has been completed. Students should train their eyes to see the text with an awareness of features that may not be readily apparent to the casual observer. This training takes place through the process of learning to observe the text with comprehensive precision. While observing the text to see what is there, the reader must also confront the text with an inquisitive mind, setting the stage to understand what is seen even as the layers unfold. Therefore, you should approach observation with a mind primed for discovery, developing expectant questions through the process of observation.

This should come as no surprise. After all, an inquisitive mind provides the fuel for inductive study, as there's a certain inductive virtue in

---

2. Essentially, interpretive questions run the gamut of categories illustrated by the hermeneutical triad of history, literature, and theology.

3. While interpretive questions primarily function as a means to bridge the gap between observation and interpretation, many of the more difficult questions arise in the transition between interpretation and application. Therefore, inquiry and the framing of guiding questions play a necessary part in the whole process of inductive study.

approaching the Bible with "holy curiosity."[4] Curiosity drives us to the Bible and keeps us returning to the Bible again and again throughout our lives. Without a curiosity to know the truth with increasing depth and a fresh perspective, the motivation to study God's Word would quickly evaporate, and Bible study would become a lifeless burden without expectation and joy. However, curiosity must be harnessed to provide real benefit in Bible study, and inquiry must work in concert with the inductive method if the engine of the mind is to run with efficiency and power.

The other essential quality for successful observation is *perceptiveness*.[5] By nature some of us may be more perceptive than others, but when it comes to observation, all of us must seek to cultivate perceptiveness because without perceptiveness, our observations will be dull or even run dry. Those of us who are "observationally challenged" and lack perceptiveness or listening skills must work extra hard at stepping outside of ourselves to enter empathetically into the world of the text. This will in turn help us overcome the various gaps discussed in chapter 1 of this volume. The good news is that while some of us may be naturally more observant than others, perceptiveness is a skill that can be honed over time and a quality in which all of us can improve if we earnestly strive to develop it.

Quality interpretive questions must first and foremost stem from the text itself. Following the exegetical principle and the theoretical basis for induction, interpretive questions are naturally drawn *from* the text rather than applied *to* the text. In this sense, observation functions as a safeguard, keeping the focus of inquiry on the elements present in the text rather than on side issues unrelated to the text. What is more, interpretive questions are transitional, moving *through* the steps of the inductive method. Even while making initial observations, interpreters will inevitably begin asking questions of interpretation and application. This is only natural and should be viewed as positive, but we ought to also be patient, asking questions in proper sequence. As we harness the

---

4. For the phrase "holy curiosity," see the subtitle by that name in Lindsay Olesberg, *The Bible Study Handbook: A Comprehensive Guide to an Essential Practice* (Downers Grove: InterVarsity, 2012), 133.

5. Perceptiveness in the sense of simply "seeing what is there" in the text was the hallmark of the hermeneutic of the Swiss-German interpreter Adolf Schlatter (1852–1938). See further the discussions of reading Scripture attentively in chapters 5 and 6.

inductive spirit of curiosity, there will be time to ask increasingly detailed questions of interpretation *and* application as the process unfolds.

Digging in a little deeper, interpretive questions will prompt you to move from the obvious to the less obvious, asking questions of context and relationship and exploring rhetorical strategies used to convey meaning. Continuing beyond interpretation, asking the right questions of the text will drive you toward an exploration of its meaning for today. Interpretive questions facilitate the transition between interpretation and application. Finally, questions of implication arise throughout the process, steering the student of Scripture toward an understanding of theological ramifications arising from the text and their significance in terms of theology and worldview perspective.

Noting the transitional nature of inquiry throughout the inductive process, there are various *kinds of questions* that facilitate different aspects and stages of the inductive method. We've divided these kinds of questions into four categories: questions of content, relationship, intention, and implication. Useful inquiry ought to represent each of these four categories of interpretive questions, moving the student of Scripture toward the goal of correct interpretation and application. To illustrate the distinctions between these kinds of questions, we'll use as an example potential questions that may be asked when studying Jeremiah 29:11: "For I know the plans I have for you—this is the LORD's declaration—plans for your welfare, not for disaster, to give you a future and a hope" (HCSB).

Table 4.1 — Four Kinds of Interpretive Questions	
Questions of Content	These questions seek to understand the substance of the text and the significance of its content.
Questions of Relationship	These questions probe the relationship of words, phrases, and concepts within and between literary units.
Questions of Intention	These questions probe authorial intention.
Questions of Implication	These questions explore the implications and ramifications of interpretation.

Questions of Content

Questions of content draw upon the most basic aspects of observation, even if the answers to these questions aren't always simple. In this sense they tend to involve defining what one sees in the text before striving to understand the significance of that content. However, questions of content aren't limited to observation; they are simply based there. Any question that explores the interpretation of (or definition) of terms, seeks to understand a theological concept of motif in a passage, or drives the reader toward a better understanding of the historical past may be considered a question of content. Even though questions of content typically begin within the realm of language, dealing with the meaning of words and phrases in Scripture, they also explore questions of historical and theological interest, thus drawing from all aspects of the hermeneutical triad.[6] Using Jeremiah 29:11 as an example, potential questions of content may include the following:

- What is the historical context of this declaration? When did Jeremiah receive it (or write it), and when was it delivered to the original recipients?
- Who were the original recipients of this declaration? Was it Nebuchadnezzar or the captives living in Babylon?
- What circumstances were the recipients experiencing at the time, and, from their perspective, what kind of "hope and future" would they have expected (as an alternative to "disaster")?
- What literary genre is this declaration set within? Is it a salvation oracle or a letter?

Note that this is not a comprehensive list of questions, but just a sampling. Focusing just on Jeremiah 29:11, these questions relate to historical and literary content issues.

---

6. Thinking in terms of theology, questions of content relate primarily to defining themes and motifs within specific texts.

Questions of Relationship

Questions of relationship involve thinking outside the perimeters of a specific unit and concern the relationship of words, phrases, and concepts to that which precedes and follows. In other words, questions of relationship are those that drive you to consider the context of what you're studying. As such, a question of relationship may pertain to a relatively narrow relationship within a passage of Scripture (such as how two words relate to one another in a passage), or a broader relationship, such as how a concept in a particular passage relates to the passages that precede and follow. Therefore, questions of relationship aren't confined to context; they also involve thinking through intertextual connections to other portions of Scripture, driving the reader toward the practice of interpretive correlation (that is, comparing Scripture with Scripture to allow the Bible to function as its own best commentary).[7]

As implied above, questions of relationship revolve primarily around interpretation, probing beyond the confines of basic content and into the realm of related meaning. However, it's equally clear that questions of relationship involve other aspects of the inductive method, even asking those questions that relate to the development of theology.[8]

Potential questions of relationship involving Jeremiah 29:11 include the following:

- The declaration in verse 11 is clearly part of a broader declaration that begins in verse 10 (vv. 10–14). However, where does the complete prophetic letter begin and where does it end?
- Verse 10 states that these blessings will be realized "after seventy years are completed." When did these seventy years begin, and when did they end?

---

7. The practice of interpretive correlation is explored in detail in chapter 9.

8. Questions of relationship are relevant to all three points of the hermeneutical triad. The timeline of history flows throughout the pages of Scripture, yet the Bible does not follow a perfectly chronological arrangement. Therefore, the reader is challenged to correlate and coordinate between the pages of Scripture and the *history* behind those pages. Questions of relationship also facilitate all aspects of *literature* and provide the core basis behind the development of *theology*. Thus questions of relationship play an integral role in facilitating the whole spectrum of the inductive process.

- Are the details of what a "future and hope" entail specified in the verses that precede or follow? Are there other portions of Jeremiah that speak of seventy years as the duration of captivity? Is there a prophetic basis within Jeremiah that provides the reason why the recipients of this letter should be promised a "future and a hope" while others are not promised such a blessing (noting the contrast of fortunes between 29:10–14 and 29:15–20)? How does the contrast function in relation to promises of cursing, such as those found in Jeremiah 44:27?

Questions of Intention

Questions of intention assume that there is a logical and purposeful intention by the author to communicate meaning through *what* he says, what he does *not* say, and *how* he says it. Questions of intention therefore probe into the nuanced features of the text and ponder *why* something is said the way it is said. A question of content may ask what something means in a definitive manner, but a question of intention will probe meaning on a logical level. In other words, through questions of intention the reader ponders the rationale behind the text, assuming authorial purpose and knowing the significance of intention in the communication of meaning. Questions of intention may therefore be quite narrow, asking why a particular word is used rather than another,[9] or broad, asking why the author is focusing on one motif or excluding another in the development of the book as a whole.

Questions of intention tend to move beyond the mere observation of what is said and involve intentional meaning, the very heart of interpretation. This doesn't mean that application is separate from intentionality, for appropriation of the text is certainly based upon an understanding of the author's purpose in writing. However, readers must learn to ask questions of intention in order to understand what the *author* intended to say through the words of the text. Moreover, whatever stage of the inductive method is involved, the relevance of questions of intention are

---

9. This is a primary question asked in semantic field word studies, explored in detail in chapter 10.

significant in pressing toward a more penetrating reading and appropriation of the biblical text.[10]

For Jeremiah 29:11, suggested questions of intention might include the following:

- Why did Jeremiah write this letter to Nebuchadnezzar (or the captives) in regard to the duration of captivity? Was it meant to provide hope for the captives or to instruct the King of Babylon regarding his treatment of those captives?
- Through this letter, was Jeremiah simply communicating the fulfillment of the vision he received in chapter 24 (the vision of the good and bad figs)? Was this a message of hope to some and a message of warning to others?
- Is the promise in verse 11 universal in scope or does it apply only to a select and historical group? Did Jeremiah intend it as an unqualified promise or is it contingent upon select circumstances and recipients? To what extent is the new covenant a fulfillment of this promise?

Questions of Implication

Questions of implication probe beyond content meaning, moving beyond relational and intentional meaning into the arena of implications. In other words, questions of implication explore the possible ramifications of interpretation on the broader teachings of Scripture.[11] Often these questions will surmise an inference and explore how it may affect the interpretation of a specific text, its application, and especially how this may relate to the whole of Scripture. Questions of implication often demonstrate proficiency in theology; however, this is not a

10. Considering the hermeneutical triad once again, we note that questions of intention explore history primarily in the arena of historical situation, understanding that there's always a direct link between the occasion precipitating the writing of a biblical document and its content. In reference to literature, the very manner in which a text is framed, including elements of selectivity and arrangement, reflects directly on the intention of the author in writing what he wrote. Finally, theological emphasis is clearly at the core of authorial intention (authors sought to communicate *something*).

11. In reference to the hermeneutical triad, questions of implication most naturally function as a means to aid in the understanding of theological message.

requirement for asking questions of implication. The primary requirement is that the reader thinks outside the box of content and questions what the interpretive options might mean in relation to the testimony of Scripture. The question of implication will often begin with an "if" premise and follow through with potential ramifications.

As we've presented the four kinds of interpretive questions, a loose progression is evident between content, relationship, intention, and implication. Questions of content often form a *basis* for questions of relationship and intention, and questions of implication most naturally *follow* questions of relationship and intention.[12] In the scheme of the inductive method, questions of implication often relate to the last step of induction, the development of theology.[13]

Questions of implication in Jeremiah 29:11 include:

- If verse 11 is historically and thematically particular, referring to the captives taken in 597 BC (the "good figs" of Jeremiah 24), then can it or should it be received as a universal, unqualified promise of good fortune to all?

- Is the fulfillment of verse 11 contingent upon a new covenant relationship as implied in verses 12–14?

- If the promise of good fortune can be appropriated by believers today (even by way of general principle), then does the warning of disaster in verses 15–20 apply as well?

- Are there modern-day equivalents to the "good figs" (Jer 24:4–7; 29:10–14) and the "bad figs" (Jer 24:8–10; 29:15–20) in the book of Jeremiah? In what way does this affect our theology of God and our expectation of universal and unqualified blessing?

---

12. Bauer and Traina suggest that there is an order in asking different kinds of interpretive questions, and we'd agree. As they present primary kinds of questions, they divide these into three categories: definitive/explanatory questions, rational questions, and implicational questions. Their definitive/explanatory questions are approximate to our questions of content, their rational questions are similar to our questions of intention, and their implicational questions are nearly identical to our questions of implication. Arguing for order in attending to these different kinds of questions, they state, "In our examination of the interpretation phase, we will see that normally one must attend to the definitive/explanatory question(s) before one can adequately address the rational question(s), and one must always answer the definitive/explanatory and rational questions before addressing the implications of the answers to these questions." See David R. Bauer and Robert A. Traina, *Inductive Bible Study: A Comprehensive Guide to the Practice of Hermeneutics* (Grand Rapids: Baker, 2011), 130.

13. See chapter 15.

Obviously, the questions used as examples from Jeremiah 29:11 are only representative, and we could (and should) ask many other similar questions throughout the process of studying this verse and associated portions of Scripture. Also, questions will often flow from content to relationship to intention and on to implication around issues within a passage of Scripture. Therefore, dividing questions of different kinds into set categories may be awkward at times. Nevertheless, we trust that the examples listed above help to distinguish between the different kinds of questions that comprise a well-rounded investigation of the text.

Ten Suggestions for Asking the Right Questions of the Text

Perhaps more than anything else that we present in this book, the practice of asking interpretive questions is better caught than taught, and there's certainly no substitute for practice. Honing one's ability to ask quality interpretive questions that represent the four kinds of questions noted earlier comes with time and practice, but every reader of the Bible can begin where they are to start asking better questions of the text. In fact, all readers are either consciously or subconsciously asking questions of the text every time they read Scripture. The goal is to intentionally develop the questions that we're already asking to better facilitate the process of interpretation (or inductive study) and to improve the quality of these questions along the guidelines taught in this chapter.

So far we've given only a few examples of interpretive questions. In concluding this chapter, we'll offer possible questions that one might ask involving two portions of Scripture, James 1:1–8 and 1 Timothy 2:8–15. However, before turning to these examples, we make ten suggestions for asking quality interpretive questions (you'll see these implemented in the examples that follow). As you engage the text as an active listener, asking questions of the text, consider each of these suggestions along the way. As you do so, you'll ask better interpretive questions, the kind of questions that penetrate into the text while avoiding tangential distractions.

1. Allow your observations to be a springboard for your interpretive questions. Perhaps you've observed a difference between translations, encountered a particularly difficult or important word, or observed an illustration whose point needs clarification. Maybe you've noticed an Old Testament verse being quoted in the New Testament or a difficult grammatical structure or a figure of speech whose function is unclear. As you observe the text, be sure to take note of relevant questions as they come to light.

2. When asking interpretive questions, don't limit yourself to general issues of content. Quality interpretive questions will penetrate deeper, moving the reader beyond the observation of structural form and on to the communication of functional meaning. Quality interpretive questions will help to facilitate this transition and thus shouldn't revolve only around the *content* of what one sees in the text but rather should inquire as to the *meaning* of what one sees.

3. Simple questions of who, why, where, what, and how may be a good starting point, but the serious student will ask more detailed questions that are particular to the text at hand. Effective interpretive questions must be specific yet will often require complex and compound sentences in order to fully engage the student in a contextually particular understanding of the text. In addition, the student should develop "question sets," or groups of related interpretive questions that effectively and comprehensively probe the text for potential answers.

4. Interpretive questions should be both broad (questions of intent and purpose) and narrow (questions pertaining to word meaning). In other words, interpretive questions will involve inquisitive thinking on multiple levels (questions of content, relationship, intention, and implication) and will consider portions of the Bible outside of the specific text that is the focus of one's study.

5. An interpretive question can and often should speculate regarding possible answers, and speculative questions ought to be a hallmark of any inquiry that probes deep into the text. As one develops a set of questions, there ought to be room to frame possible and probable answers within the questions themselves. Interpretive questions are "leading" questions; they are not formulated out of informational vacuums. As a matter of fact, thorough observation, coupled with biblical and theological literacy, will almost demand that speculation ensues. Students should learn to speculate when asking interpretive questions, using this as an opportunity to lay the interpretive options out on the table.

6. Allow your knowledge of biblical and theological issues to influence you in the question-asking process. The beginning student will have less of a framework of knowledge to work with, yet with time his breadth of knowledge will expand and he'll ask more informed questions with better speculative tendencies. While an inductive approach favors an open mind toward interpretive possibilities, there's merit in having an awareness of the interpretive options, issues, and pitfalls when asking interpretive questions. A direct observation of the text will ideally draw out the most relevant issues that should be explored at an interpretive level. However, there's simply no substitute for biblical and theological literacy when it comes to asking the appropriate questions of a specific text in matters of history, literature, and theology. Serious students of the Bible will embrace their own biblical and theological literacy when asking interpretive questions, utilizing this past knowledge to facilitate a fresh reading of the text.[14]

7. Remember, the process of asking interpretive questions will begin with observation but may be further enhanced and expanded during the interpretive process. As one implements the steps of interpretation and engages in the research necessary to answer interpretive questions, invariably new questions will arise that were missed in the initial stages of observation. Flexibility must be allowed within the framework of moving from observation to interpretation, and questions should be augmented along the

---

14. A new believer who picks up the Bible and begins to read the text won't be asking the same penetrating questions as the seasoned student of Scripture. In part, this can be remedied by learning to ask appropriate questions of the text, but there's also a necessary amount of background knowledge that precedes informed interpretive questions.

journey so as to drive the reader toward an increasingly precise and ultimately more valid interpretation of the text.

8. Some questions aren't interpretive questions at all but rather pertain to application (what the text means to us today) rather than interpretation (what the text meant to the original readers). Therefore, in the same manner that asking the right questions of the text aids in moving between observation and interpretation, questions will again be enlisted in assisting the reader through the transition from interpretation to application.

9. Questions shouldn't be asked simply for the sake of asking questions! A commandment didn't come off of the mountain proclaiming, "Thou must ask interpretive questions!" Nor is there any merit in asking *more* interpretive questions. Rather, we suggest that a student strive to ask *better* questions of the text, questions that will ultimately facilitate not only a detailed interpretation of the text but a relevant one as well.[15]

10. Finally, remember that asking interpretive questions is simply that— asking questions—and one shouldn't feel compelled to answer interpretive questions prematurely. While the answer to some interpretive questions may be rather obvious based upon preliminary observations, it's better to avoid haste in moving from observation to interpretation and to allow sufficient time to answer interpretive questions through the prism of methodical interpretation.

---

15. Tangential questions draw the reader away from the text rather than into it. While curiosity may lead the reader on tangents, these are ultimately counterproductive in facilitating interpretation. Olesberg uses the example of John the Baptist's diet of honey and locusts to illustrate the tangential question. Curiosity may lead a reader to ask, "What do locusts taste like?" but such a question will benefit little in the interpretation of Mark 1. See Olesberg, *Bible Study Handbook*, 138.

Table 4.2 — Ten Suggestions for Asking the Right Questions of the Text	
1.	Observations should be a springboard for interpretive questions.
2.	When asking interpretive questions, don't limit yourself to general questions of content.
3.	Seek questions deeper than just "Who?" "Why?" "Where?" "What?" and "How?" More elaborate questions are preferable.
4.	Ask both broad (questions of intent and purpose) and narrow (questions pertaining to word meaning, etc.) questions.
5.	Speculate regarding possible answers to your interpretive questions.
6.	Allow your knowledge of biblical and theological issues to influence your questions.
7.	The question-asking process begins with observation but may continue throughout the process of interpretation and into application.
8.	Some questions relate more to application than to interpretation.
9.	Do not be asking questions simply for the sake of asking questions! Quality is better than quantity.
10.	Do not feel compelled to answer interpretive questions prematurely.

Sample Interpretive Questions

The following sample questions aren't meant to be comprehensive but they do illustrate the diverse nature of interpretive questions. They're framed around individual verses (or sets of verses), although we offer a few questions that pertain to the unit as a whole.[16] As you explore these passages, you may ask additional questions or augment our questions to suit your own inquiry. Although we argue the case for asking the *right* questions of the text, we also understand that there's a degree of subjectivity in asking interpretive questions.

In addition, you'll find that we ask questions representing each of the kinds of questions offered earlier (content, relationship, intention,

---

16. All sample questions are based upon the HCSB translation of the Bible.

and implication), generally adhering to order and movement in how these are arranged. Finally, notice that questions are often grouped in "sets" that focus on a related group of issues, often built around speculation as the issue is interrogatively probed.

Interpretive Questions: James 1:1–8

[1] James, a slave of God and of the Lord Jesus Christ: To the 12 tribes in the Dispersion. Greetings.

Questions related to James and the historical setting:

- Who is James? Is this James the half-brother of Jesus (Gal 1:9; Acts 12:17; 15:13) or the martyred brother of John (Acts 12:2)?
- What evidence exists to support one choice or the other?
- Are there literary or thematic clues in the book that might suggest that this is James, the half-brother of Jesus?
- If this is James the brother of John, then could the book have been written prior to his martyrdom in Acts 12:2?
- If this is James the half-brother of Jesus, then when was this book written—before or after the Jerusalem Council (Acts 15)?
- What difference would it make whether the book was written before or after the Jerusalem Council?

Questions related to the recipients:

- To whom is James writing? Is "brothers" in this context referring just to men or to men and women?
- Is the author writing to Christians (brothers in the faith), Jews (ethnic brothers), or Jewish Christians?
- Would the distinct address to the "12 tribes in the Dispersion" suggest any of the above-stated choices (perhaps disqualifying Gentile believers)?
- Is "12 tribes in the Dispersion" a metaphorical title? If so, what is the referent?

- What impact might the question regarding the identity of the recipients have on the purpose and message of the book as a whole?
- Are there other clues to the identity of the recipients in the book itself?
- If the reference to the 12 tribes is in some manner related to the church, then does this imply some form of replacement theology?

With regard to James describing himself as a "slave of God":

- With regard to James describing himself as a "slave" in the HCSB, a "bondservant" in the NKJV and NASB, and a "servant" in the ESV and NIV, what is the Greek word behind these translations, and how is the word used elsewhere in the New Testament?
- Does the word carry a different connotation in New Testament usage beyond the standard usage in first-century Greco-Roman culture?
- Based on the lexical evidence, what English gloss best represents the Greek term for "slave" (*doulos*)? Does the English language have a precise equivalent to the Greek *doulos*?
- In the English language, what is the difference between a "slave," a "bondservant," and a "servant"? What term best reflects the term *doulos*?
- Why did James refer to himself as a *doulos*? Was this a title reserved for the apostolic community or was this term meant to describe all believers?
- Is James seeking to lead by example?
- Do the teachings within the book of James relate to or describe practical ways in which one may be a *doulos*?
- What are the practical implications of being a *doulos*? Is this an equivalent to "discipleship" in the Gospels or to "taking up one's cross" in the teachings of Jesus? Does this imply that I, too, am a *doulos*?

² Consider it a great joy, my brothers, whenever you experience various trials, ³ knowing that the testing of your faith produces endurance.

Regarding trials and temptations:

- Is verse 2 referring to "trials" or "temptations" (as in the KJV)?
- In the English language, what's the difference between trials and temptations, and what is reflected by the Greek word?
- Does this word (and concept) in some manner describe the same word and concept as encountered later in James 1:12–15?
- If these are trials, then do they refer to everyday problems or specifically to persecutions for the faith? In other words, are these trials the result of living in a fallen world (such as a car breaking down) or specifically the result of living for Christ?
- Is there an implied temptation (perhaps to forsake Christ) that comes as a result of trials?
- Are these trials brought on by God with a specific purpose or are they random in purpose but profitable as to result?
- With regard to the occasional situation described here that relates directly to the intended audience, would the identity of these recipients (the "12 tribes in the Dispersion") argue in favor of these trials being based in persecution? If so, can these persecutions be linked to any specific accounts of persecution in the book of Acts?
- Does the grammar suggest an active or passive "experience" in trials, and what implications would the voice of the verb have in interpretation and application?

Regarding specific terminology:

- Are terms such as "considering" and "knowing," which seem to work in tandem in this context, used elsewhere in James (or in other New Testament books) to teach active, attitudinal solutions to life's experiences?

- To what does "faith" refer? Does it in this context refer to the body of Christian doctrine, one's faith in God's control over individual circumstances, or belief in God's existence?
- Does "endurance" refer to a proper godly response to a given trial while the trial is taking place (the endurance not to "crack" under pressure and respond sinfully)? Or does it refer to an enduring character trait that develops over time?

[4] But endurance must do its complete work, so that you may be mature and complete, lacking nothing.

- Does the connective "so that" suggest purpose or result? In other words, does God bring trials into our lives with the purpose of using these to bring us to maturity (implying design and purpose), or is maturity simply the resulting byproduct of trials received with the proper attitude and response?
- What does it mean in this context to "lack nothing"? Does this mean that one has all the right spiritual "equipment" to respond properly to trials? Or does this refer to God's supply of grace to get through trials, whatever these might entail? Or is something else in view?
- Are there other New Testament passages that speak to the issue of developing maturity through the experience of trials? If so, in what manner does correlation aid in understanding the message of James 1:2–4?

[5] Now if any of you lacks wisdom, he should ask God, who gives to all generously and without criticizing, and it will be given to him.

- To what does wisdom refer: wisdom in general, wisdom in how to respond properly to trials, or wisdom in how to discern the endurance producing aspect or lesson of the trial?
- Can this promise of God's granting wisdom be applied outside of the context of trials? In other words, would the experience of Solomon in some way be normative for all New Testament believers (1 Kgs 3:6–14)?

- For the promise to be granted (whatever wisdom might entail), must the one who asks be a believer?
- For wisdom to be granted, must one be going through trials, or must one be at the point of maturity and "completeness"?
- Is wisdom simply a characteristic of maturity and completeness (v. 4)?
- What does it mean that God gives wisdom "without criticizing"?

[6] But let him ask in faith without doubting. For the doubter is like the surging sea, driven and tossed by the wind. [7] That person should not expect to receive anything from the Lord. [8] An indecisive man is unstable in all his ways.

- Does the requirement regarding how one asks (in faith) apply only to the context of asking for wisdom or does it apply to all prayers of petition?
- Does the reference to an "indecisive" man have theological implications regarding his soteriological position (could this kind of man not even be saved)?
- How does "faith" in verse 3 compare to "faith" in verse 6? Are they the same or completely different kinds of faith?
- How does this segment (vv. 6–8) relate back to the issue of trials, endurance, and the development of maturity? Is the doubter in effect the opposite of the mature and complete trial-bearer?

Questions for the whole unit (vv. 1–8):

- In what manner does this unit (pertaining to trials, maturity, and wisdom) relate to the following unit (vv. 9–11; pertaining to the rich and the poor)?
- There seems to be little direct connection between the two units, yet verses 1–8 seem better connected with verses 12–18 (on enduring trials), and 9–11 seems best connected with 2:13. Is there a unifying theme in the first two chapters of James?
- Could it relate to the "law of freedom" in 1:25 and 2:12?

- Could the emphasis on trials and the oppression of the poor allude to the situation of the original recipients, the "12 tribes in the Dispersion"?
- Is there any discernible progression of thought or structural framework that James is following in the opening of this letter?

Interpretive Questions: 1 Timothy 2:8–15

[8] Therefore, I want the men in every place to pray, lifting up holy hands without anger or argument. [9] Also, the women are to dress themselves in modest clothing, with decency and good sense, not with elaborate hairstyles, gold, pearls, or expensive apparel, [10] but with good works, as is proper for women who affirm that they worship God.

Regarding men:

- What would the historical practice of "lifting up holy hands" have entailed? What would it have looked like?
- Is this a culturally relative practice, or does this imply the endorsement of a normative practice (a posture of prayer for men)?
- Are women excluded from this posture of prayer?
- What is the logical connection between the action of lifting up holy hands and doing so "without anger and argument"?
- Might this better imply the desired attitude of prayer (as suggested by the punctuation in the NKJV)?

Regarding women:

- What was the historical norm for women's dress in the first-century world of Paul and Timothy?
- Does this exhortation regarding dress imply that there was a problem with immodesty in the church in which Timothy served?
- Which church was this (location and correlation to Acts)?

- Does the description of dress deal with the adornment of fine clothing and aspects of beautification or with promiscuous or revealing clothing, or a combination of both?
- What are the implications of this passage on modern views of modesty, and how does this affect the way women dress and wear makeup and jewelry today, especially in church?

Comparison:

- Which parallels exist in this passage between Paul's instructions regarding men and those regarding women?
- Is there a parallel between "without anger and argument," "with decency and good sense," and "with good works"?

[11] A woman should learn in silence with full submission. [12] I do not allow a woman to teach or to have authority over a man; instead, she is to be silent.

- What is the historical situation that led to this set of commands addressed to the women in the church?
- Does Paul provide general instructions for men's and women's conduct in the church, especially with regard to the exercise of leadership, or is he giving these instructions because women were actively usurping men's authority in the church, or both?
- If dealing with women's misconduct, did the issue involve women teaching falsely or interrupting the teaching that was taking place in the church? Were the women countering the men and arguing against their teaching in the church?
- When Paul said, "learn in silence or quietness," does this mean that women weren't permitted to talk at all, perhaps not even to ask questions, or that they were supposed to be in proper submission to the male leaders of the church?
- The issue of silence or quietness is twice related to submission and authority. Was the primary issue that of women engaging in teaching and public speaking, or was it women occupying roles and positions of authority in the church, perhaps revolving around the oversight of doctrine?

Application-related questions:[17]

- To what extent does culture impact our interpretation of this passage?

- Was it normal for women to learn in silence in the first century (even outside the church)?

- Would women speaking or teaching in a mixed assembly made up of men and women have been a social taboo in the first century?

- How much does cultural relativism (i.e., an emphasis on the occasional nature of Paul's letters) impact the way in which we apply this passage today?

- Are the principles enunciated in these instructions rooted in first-century cultural expectations?

- If so, in what way should women today apply the principle in a way that is culturally appropriate? Or are the underlying principle and its application inextricably linked?

- It seems that women are instructed in these verses to (1) learn in silence or quietness, (2) not to teach, and (3) not to have or exercise authority over a man. What justification is there for applying any of these injunctions today while dismissing other points as culturally relative? Conversely, what justification is there for dismissing any of these injunctions today as culturally relative while applying others as normative?

- Can women today talk in gathered assemblies of men and women but not teach or hold positions of authority over men? Or can they both speak and teach as long as they don't hold positions of authority over the men of the church? What's the bottom line here?

- Do these instructions apply outside of the church or only in particular settings within the church? If the latter, in which

---

17. For an excellent resource for studying and applying 1 Tim 2:9–15, see Andreas J. Köstenberger and Thomas R. Schreiner, eds., *Women in the Church: An Analysis and Application of 1 Timothy 2:9–15*, 3rd ed. (Wheaton: Crossway, 2016).

settings do the instructions apply? What about women teaching Sunday School or home Bible studies for men and women?

^{13} For Adam was created first, then Eve. ^{14} And Adam was not deceived, but the woman was deceived and transgressed.

- Paul is clearly referring to Genesis 2:18–25 and 3:1–7 to support his instructions in verses 11–12. What precisely is the point of the illustration, and is the focal point teaching or authority (or, in Paul's mind, do these go hand in hand)?
- If the primary point is authority, which is rooted in creation (given the illustration here), does this imply that teaching is less of an issue?
- Would the argument based on creation rule out the idea that role relationships (the authority of men over women in the church) are culturally relative (and thus would only apply to Paul's first-century context)?
- It appears that Paul's argument for male authority is based first in the order of creation (v. 13). However, Paul furthers the argument by alluding to the deception of Eve. What is his point? Is he saying that women are by nature more apt to deception? This would provide strong rationale for women not to teach in the church or having doctrinal authority over the men, but this seems rather chauvinistic. Is that okay or am I misreading this?
- If not alluding to women's greater vulnerability to deception, what is Paul's point here? Is he perhaps referring to the role reversal at the fall where Satan tempted the woman, and the woman led the man into sin, rather than the man serving as the leader as God intended?

^{15} But she will be saved through childbearing, if she continues in faith, love, and holiness, with good judgment.

- How does verse 15 relate back to the preceding verses? Does the ESV better nuance the connection with "yet" (implying concession), or is the relationship contrastive ("but")?

- Who is "she" referring to? Does "she" refer to women in the plural (as in the NIV) or is it singular? If singular, could it be referring back to Eve?
- Does "saved" in this context refer to salvation from the penalty of sin which is death, does it refer to deliverance from physical danger in childbearing, or does it refer to spiritual preservation from Satan's deception?
- Could "saved" in this context refer to the woman's fulfillment and satisfaction in finding her appropriate feminine role?
- Or could "saved" in this context refer to women being released from the stigma of having brought sin into the world (v. 14) through the role of motherhood?
- Might the relationship to verse 14 infer that the curse of Genesis 3:16, at least as it involves women, is somehow lessened through the role of women bringing up children in godliness (i.e., women experience pain in childbearing because of the fall, yet in God's grace they experience the joy of childbearing through the generation of godly offspring)?
- Depending on what "saved" means in this context, how does it relate to "through childbearing"? Is it that women are saved by means of childbearing or saved from the childbearing process or perhaps saved in spite of childbearing? Could childbearing be a synecdoche for childrearing, with the role of godly womanhood devoted to the bearing *and* raising of children (implied by the second half of v. 15)?
- If this is a universal ideal for women, then what does this imply for women who aren't married or who can't have children? Is there any sense in which this ideal role in motherhood, along with the instructions in verses 11–12 on speaking, teaching, and having authority over men, is culturally relative or does the grounding in creation (vv. 13–14) mitigate against this?
- How should the condition "if she continues in faith, love, and holiness, with good judgment" be understood? Does the woman's "salvation," whatever this entails, depend on the attitude

toward her role, or her performance in raising her children? Is
there a shift from singular to plural between the first and second
"she" in verse 15? If so, what is the significance of this shift? Is
there a parallel between "good judgment" in verse 15 and "good
sense" in verse 9? If so, then what is the significance of this
parallel?

Questions for the whole unit (vv. 8–15):

- How does the "therefore" function in connecting this unit
(2:8–15) back to the preceding unit (2:1–7)? Is the connection
back to the resulting statement in verse 2 ("so that we may lead a
tranquil and quiet life in all godliness and dignity")? This seems
a rather obscure statement in the preceding unit but does seem
to complement the content in verses 8–12. Was this a practical
issue that Paul emphasized in his instructions to Timothy (perhaps seen elsewhere in the letter)?

- How does verse 15 relate to the next unit in 1 Timothy? It is
interesting that Paul now gives qualifications for overseers,
having just instructed Timothy on gender roles in relation to
authority and doctrinal oversight (teaching) in the church.
Does this transition into qualifications for overseers (3:1–7) and
deacons (3:8–13) impact how we view his instructions to men
and women in 2:8–15?

Final Thoughts

For some, the concept of interpretive questions may seem rather laborious, and for others it may seem an unnecessary sideshow to interpretation.
However, our experience indicates that we're already asking questions
as we read. Our goal is to intentionally develop that inquisitive spirit and
to methodically instruct students to harness those questions into a more
detailed, focused, and accurate study of Scripture.

Interpretive questions should be viewed in light of the goal, which is
a more accurate and thorough interpretation of the text, an interpretation

that speaks to the issues in the text that really matter. Intentionally crafted interpretive questions are meant to aid in facilitating interpretation, and we trust that you will frame them with this goal in mind.

Finally, while asking interpretive questions is a skill that requires practice over time, we've found that the learning curve is rather high, and once practiced students find that asking better questions comes quite naturally. Therefore jump right in and put your curiosity to good use. And remember: never allow the challenge of asking the right questions of the text to overshadow the goal of inductive Bible study, which is an informed and engaging encounter with the living Word of God.

5

Reading with Discernment
Determining Significant Terms

Careful observation requires more than a casual reading of the biblical text. In the previous two chapters we've laid a foundation for observation by the *comparative* reading of various translations (chapter 3), and the *inquisitive* reading that prompts the formulation of interpretive questions (chapter 4). We now turn to yet another aspect of reading the text carefully: reading with *discernment*.[1]

As inerrantists, we believe that every word of the Bible is inspired and that all the words in the Bible represent the Word of God.[2] However, it would be impractical and potentially counterproductive to study each word or phrase in a passage of Scripture with the same amount of detail. Some words and phrases are peripheral to the primary content of a passage, while other words and phrases are central, carrying the weight of meaning that is integral to the message of the text. In yet other cases, the meaning of a word is obvious and doesn't require further study. Simply stated, there will always be some inspired words that are more significant for interpretation than others, and learning to distinguish between these

---

1. Perhaps it is more accurate to say that we are learning to read the text with "discrimination," learning to choose to emphasize in study certain words and phrases over others. However, given the pejorative sense of that word, we have chosen to title this chapter "Reading with Discernment."

2. We consider inerrancy a foundational belief that provides the general framework for inductive Bible study. Support for inerrancy, as well as distinctions within the inerrancy debate, fall within the purview of apologetics and theology. On views of biblical inerrancy, see J. Merrick and Stephen M. Garrett, gen. eds., *Five Views on Biblical Inerrancy* (Grand Rapids: Zondervan, 2013). Regarding the term "foundational belief," see J. Scott Duvall and J. Daniel Hays, *Grasping God's Word*, 3rd ed. (Grand Rapids: Zondervan, 2012), 145.

is a matter of discernment that leads to a more focused and efficient process for interpreting the text.

At the point of observation, the reader should begin to distinguish between those words that warrant special attention and those that don't. This isn't to imply a kind of literary discrimination against inerrancy but rather to suggest that in the interest of time and energy, some words and phrases, more than others, warrant greater attention at the level of interpretation. These words and phrases should be recognized as "nonroutine," or "significant," and will require additional lexical, contextual, and historical study as we move from observation to interpretation.[3]

The recognition of nonroutine terms is in part a matter of opinion and may be influenced by the background and subjective reasoning of the interpreter.[4] However, this is not to suggest that there's nothing objective in discerning between routine and nonroutine words and phrases.[5] Careful observation will provide a "feel" for those words and phrases that are primary in carrying out the message of the text. What's more, as we'll see in just a moment, many nonroutine terms follow rather objective categorical distinctions and, even when you understand them, should be designated as nonroutine for the sake of the argument (or in the case of preachers and teachers, for the sake of the audience). Through the recognition of the following kinds of nonroutine terms, we trust that you'll read with heightened discernment and increasingly focus your interpretive efforts on the specific points in a passage that really matter.[6]

---

3. We used the word "significant" to refer to that which is "nonroutine" in the chapter subtitle. This was to eliminate confusion regarding the general subject matter of the chapter.

4. Bauer and Traina distinguish between routine and nonroutine "observations" rather than "terms." This is helpful in that there are cases where a clause or even a concept may better represent that which is "nonroutine" (rather than a word or a phrase). However, in the interest of keeping our observations concrete and discernible, we have elected to retain the terminology "terms." See David Bauer and Robert Traina, *Inductive Bible Study* (Grand Rapids: Baker, 2011), 163.

5. Bauer and Traina (*Inductive Bible Study*, 164) include a "fourth class" of nonroutine observation: "things of personal interest." While this may be valid at some level, there's a sense in which this bucks against the very notion of induction, i.e., allowing the text to speak on its own terms and to emphasize its own points of interest.

6. Traina distinguishes between "banal" routine terms whose meaning is immediately obvious and nonroutine terms that either carry special significance or are difficult to understand. He further classifies nonroutine terms into three categories: difficult to understand terms, crucial terms, and profound terms. He also distinguishes between literal and figurative terms. See Robert A. Traina, *Methodical Bible Study* (Grand Rapids: Zondervan, 1952), 34–35.

Table 5.1 — Six Kinds of Nonroutine Terms	
Term	**Definition**
1. Contextually Crucial Terms	Words and phrases that in a particular context convey the primary argument or meaning of a passage
2. Theologically Profound Terms	Words and phrases that infer theological significance
3. Historically Particular Terms	Culturally, geographically, or historically particular terms that may not be understood outside of the world of the Bible
4. Exegetically/Textually Uncertain Terms	Words that are exegetically or textually uncertain in their context
5. Figurative Terms	Words and phrases that convey figures of speech
6. Symbolic Terms	Words and phrases that convey symbolic significance in a given context

Contextually Crucial Terms

Contextually nonroutine terms are the words or phrases that in a particular context convey the primary argument or meaning of a passage. In a sense, these are the terms that carry the weight of meaning in a given passage of Scripture. That said, context always determines whether a word in a particular segment of Scripture is crucial or not. Contextually crucial terms don't have inherent critical characteristics but rather take on critical significance in a particular context to support an argument or statement. In other contexts, these same words or phrases may simply play a support role and be designated "routine." However, in *this* context, *these* words and phrases carry special significance, for the primary thrust of meaning is communicated through *these* terms. Simply stated, *if one were to summarize the passage, these are the words and phrases that would be indispensable to that summation.*

Discerning contextually crucial terms in a given passage involves personal discernment, and two readers may very well disagree on what is, or is not, crucial. However, by reading and rereading the text of Scripture and by asking the simple question, "What terms are critical to the central idea in this passage?" most readers can discern between what is crucial and what is not. Sanctified common sense may be the greatest asset in discerning crucial terms, but there are additional criteria that may indicate that a term has a critical function in a particular context.

If a word or phrase is repeated throughout the passage, or if words or phrases are used in a comparative or contrastive relationship in that passage, they may in fact be crucial to that passage. What is more, if a word or phrase is used in introducing or concluding a unit of Scripture, then it may function as a crucial term. In some cases, crucial terms are positioned prominently at the end of a climactic progression or as the pivot point in a particular inversion pattern. But there isn't always a structurally based observation that objectively determines the function of a term. Therefore contextual awareness, even at the observational level, is necessary in determining crucial terms.

The primary corrective in determining crucial terms is the ability of the reader to state *why* a crucial term is crucial in a given context. If you can't state why a term is crucial, then it probably is not. Remember, the goal is not to find more or less crucial terms but to determine which terms really stand out as crucial to the text and thus warrant more interpretive attention. As a step of observation, the goal should be to find the terms that are truly crucial—that is, the terms that are nonroutine in some way or another. This is perhaps best taught through illustration, so let's take a discerning look at 1 Corinthians 8:1–13 as an example:

1 Corinthians 8:1–13 (HCSB)

About food offered to idols: We <u>know</u> that "we all have <u>knowledge</u>." <u>Knowledge</u> inflates with pride, but love <u>builds up</u>. If anyone thinks he <u>knows</u> anything, he does not yet <u>know</u> it as he ought to <u>know</u> it. But if anyone loves God, he is <u>known</u> by Him.

About eating food offered to idols, then, we <u>know</u> that "an idol is nothing in the world," and that "there is no God but one." For even if there are so-called gods, whether in heaven or on earth—as there are many "gods" and many "lords"—

yet for us there is one God, the Father.
All things are from Him,
and we exist for Him.
And there is one Lord, Jesus Christ.
All things are through Him,
and we exist through Him.

However, not everyone has this <u>knowledge</u>. In fact, some have been so used to idolatry up until now that when they eat food offered to an idol, their <u>conscience</u>, being <u>weak</u>, is defiled. Food will not make us acceptable to God. We are not inferior if we don't eat, and we are not better if we do eat. But be careful that this right of yours in no way becomes a <u>stumbling block</u> to the <u>weak</u>. For if someone sees you, the one who has this <u>knowledge</u>, dining in an idol's temple, won't his <u>weak conscience</u> be encouraged to eat food offered to idols? Then the <u>weak person</u>, the brother for whom Christ died, is ruined by your <u>knowledge</u>. Now when you sin like this against the brothers and wound their <u>weak conscience</u>, you are sinning against Christ. Therefore, if food <u>causes my brother to fall</u>, I will never again eat meat, so that I won't <u>cause my brother to fall</u>.

This passage provides an excellent test case for crucial terms that have special, contextually driven significance. For instance, the word "knowledge" clearly refers to specific knowledge about food offered to idols, and having this knowledge seems to separate two groups of individuals in the Corinthian church. What is more, Paul is writing to address certain actions and attitudes in the church that came as a result of this knowledge. Whatever the actual meaning of the term and its impact on the message of the passage, it's quite certain that the term "knowledge" plays a critical role in conveying that message, and thus in this context is clearly a crucial term.[7]

In addition to the word "knowledge," there are other contextually crucial terms in this passage (the reader may be tipped off to these by repetition). Paul uses the related terms "know" and "known" in the beginning of the unit, perhaps to play off of the main issue of knowledge. In addition, there is an emphasis on the "weak conscience," and by extension, the "weak person." This appears to be a contextually particular use of the term "weak," relating back to the issue of knowledge. To think that this is describing physical, emotional, or even spiritual weakness or immaturity in this context may be quite misleading (note that Paul never exhorts the weak brother to become strong). Again, in this context, the term "weak" appears to be crucial, and its meaning is not immediately obvious, nor is it based primarily on its lexical meaning.

Finally, note that the particular practice of "eating meat" conducted by Paul's recipients (based on "knowledge") was in essence a "stumbling block" to the "weak," and as such had the capacity to cause a brother "to fall." In the designation of crucial terms, it may be helpful to also include "stumbling block" along with the concept related in the phrase "cause my brother to fall," as this seems to play a significant role in piecing together the issue and argument Paul is making throughout 1 Corinthians 8.

Could other terms in this passage be designated as contextually crucial? Most certainly an argument could be made for including words such as "food," "eating," "idols," or "meat." However, the theological argument Paul is making doesn't depend on these terms. Conversely, Paul's argument demonstrably depends on terms such as "knowledge," "weak conscience," or "stumbling block." If you come to understand the meaning and relationship of these crucial terms to the passage, a full understanding of the text is not far behind.

---

7. It is worth noting that this "knowledge" is not what is typically perceived of as "knowledge" by modern readers—in other words, it has nothing to do with "book smarts," "academia," or the pursuit of higher education.

Theologically Profound Terms

Theologically profound terms are significant words or phrases that tend to be particular to biblical or systematic theology. These terms wouldn't typically be understood by the general public, and even Bible students may not be familiar with their technical definition. Certainly, as you become more theologically literate you'll tend to better understand these terms, but designating them as "nonroutine" isn't simply a matter of personal understanding. If a term is theologically profound, then it is likely to carry special interpretive significance in a particular context, perhaps even in all contexts in which it is found. What is more, preachers and teachers will often find it helpful to define and explain theologically profound terms in the text for their audience rather than assuming that all their listeners understand such terminology.

While most theologically profound terms are inherently nonroutine, there are situations in which theological profundity is entirely context driven. For instance, in the famous *kenosis* (self-emptying) passage of Philippians 2:6–11, Paul uses (or quotes) certain terms that carry tremendous Christological significance in the context of Paul's letter.[8] Words and phrases such as "form of God" (v. 6), "equality with God" (v. 6), and "emptied Himself" (v. 7) all carry theological significance in *this* context, even though there's nothing inherently theological about these words in the English ("form," "equality," "emptied") or the Greek language (*morphē, isos, kenoō*). Therefore, as a step of observation, the careful reader should designate these terms as "theologically profound," understanding that the interpretive attention given to defining and understanding these terms in this context is absolutely essential to "rightly dividing *these* words of truth."[9]

---

8. Most modern commentators consider the text of Philippians 2:6–11 to be a quotation of an ancient Christian hymn or creed. Thus the terms found within this quotation have deep Christological significance in the hymn itself along with the context of Paul's use of the hymn in supporting his line of argument in the letter.

9. For a helpful commentary on this passage, see Peter T. O'Brien, *Commentary on Philippians*, NIGTC (Grand Rapids: Eerdmans, 1991), 203–32, esp. 218 (on the Kenotic view, holding that Christ emptied himself of attributes of his deity such as omniscience, omnipresence, and omnipotence, which O'Brien calls "impossible" to maintain exegetically) and 223–24 (summary evaluation, focusing on the status of slaves in the first century as devoid of all rights; thus Jesus emptied himself in stages, first in the incarnation, then by becoming like a slave, and finally by submitting to the inhumane death on a cross).

In most cases, theologically profound terms can be discerned with a fairly quick reading of a biblical text (although some of the more dynamic translations will often attempt to simplify these terms, and in some cases eliminate them). To consider a few examples, let's look at the following passages of Scripture.

Romans 3:24–26 (HCSB)

They are <u>justified</u> freely by His <u>grace</u> through the <u>redemption</u> that is in Christ Jesus. God presented Him as a <u>propitiation</u> through faith in His blood, to demonstrate His <u>righteousness</u>, because in His restraint God <u>passed over</u> the sins previously committed. God presented Him to demonstrate His <u>righteousness</u> at the present time, so that He would be <u>righteous</u> and declare <u>righteous</u> the one who has <u>faith</u> in Jesus.

Even at a quick glance, certain terms jump out at the reader as "theologically profound." We would never expect that the man or woman on the street, even if educated, would understand the term "propitiation," much less the deep theological significance this term carries in context. Perhaps equally technical is the term "redemption," especially when describing the work of Christ. Although less technical in general usage, the term "justified," when noted in the broader context of Paul's writings, has tremendous theological significance as well. In addition, you could make a case for designating terms such as "grace," "righteous," "righteousness," "faith," and even "passed over" as theologically profound (and thus crucial) in this context, although at some point it's best to stress only the more truly profound terms in this exercise.

2 Corinthians 5:17–21(HCSB)

Therefore, if anyone is in Christ, he is a new creation; old things have passed away, and look, new things have come. Everything is from God, who <u>reconciled</u> us to Himself through Christ and gave us the ministry of <u>reconciliation</u>: That is, in Christ,

God was <u>reconciling</u> the world to Himself, not counting their trespasses against them, and He has committed the message of <u>reconciliation</u> to us. Therefore, we are ambassadors for Christ, certain that God is appealing through us. We plead on Christ's behalf, "Be <u>reconciled</u> to God." He made the One who did not know sin to be sin for us, so that we might become the righteousness of God in Him.

The term that should stick out as most theologically profound in this passage is "reconciliation" or "reconciled." However, there are a few other phrases that may count as theologically profound. Consider, for instance, "new creation," along with the contrastive comparison between "old things" and "new things." In the context of this passage, along with the broader thematic context of Pauline theology, these phrases do carry theological implications that far exceed the standard lexical meaning of these words.

As noted, the recognition of theologically profound terms is rather straightforward. However, you may at this point be wondering if contextually crucial and theologically profound terms can ever overlap. Should the term "reconciliation" in 2 Corinthians 5:17–21 be viewed as crucial? In short, the answer is "yes," and the designation of a kind of nonroutine term is never exclusive. When it comes to designating *kinds* of nonroutine terms, don't feel constrained to take an either/or approach but understand that a both/and approach is perfectly valid.

Historically Particular Terms

These terms include culturally, geographically, or historically particular words and phrases that may not be understood outside of the world of the Bible. Because the Bible is an ancient book written by real people in the context of human history, it is naturally saturated with words and phrases associated with culturally particular items and activities, geographically particular places, and historically particular people and events. These terms can be found throughout the Bible in all literary genres and represent a broad cross-section of geopolitical movements and cultural understanding. While they wouldn't have posed a signifi-cant challenge to the original readers of the various books of the Bible, they do present obstacles for us today.

For instance, how many people today understand the political and religious distinctions between the Sadducees and the Pharisees? Or how many modern American readers immediately identify appropriate value when they read about ancient currencies (talents, denarii, etc.) or mea-surements (cubits, homers, etc.)?[10] How many Bible readers today can identify the location of eighth-century Jerusalem or Samaria on a map? What about Beth Aphrah, Shaphir, Zaanan, Beth Ezel, Maroth, and Lachish? Certainly the original recipients of Micah's prophecies knew the locations of these cities and villages, along with their geographical, political, and social particulars (which Micah addresses through master-ful word-play; cf. Mic 1:10–16).

To give an even more poignant example, how many modern readers resonate with the shame of a Roman cross? After all, most first-century recipients of Paul's letters had likely seen victims hanging upon crosses—something no modern reader has thankfully experienced! There are lit-erally thousands of terms in the Bible that carry historical nuance or meaning, and these terms should be designated by modern readers as nonroutine, requiring further study into the details of background and situation for a fuller, more accurate understanding of the biblical text.

Observing and designating historically particular terms is rather straightforward, although those better educated in Bible backgrounds should nonetheless stay consistent in designating such terms as non-routine even when they themselves are familiar with them (this is to the benefit of the audiences of preachers and teachers). What is more, careful observation will consider the way in which the original audience may have understood a term differently than modern readers, and thus designate such terms as nonroutine.

Noting again the example of the Roman cross, first-century readers of the New Testament would have understood the ramifications of a

---

10. Though note that in most cases modern English translations have done the work for us by substituting the English equivalent for the ancient currency or measurement.

cross in society and would have felt emotions related to their experiences having seen Roman crosses that modern readers simply can't comprehend. Indeed, you wonder what a first-century Roman citizen would have thought of modern Christians wearing the cross on a necklace. Have the purveyors of such jewelry ever considered that the cross was for early Christians a sign of shame, death, and execution? To some degree, we'll need to think outside the box about what terms might be historically particular even when they're quite common in modern vernacular.

Hosea 11:1–5 (HCSB)

As an example, let's consider a passage from one of the Old Testament prophets:

> When Israel was a child, I loved him, and out of Egypt I called My son. The more they called them, the more they departed from Me. They kept sacrificing to the Baals and burning offerings to idols. It was I who taught Ephraim to walk, taking them in My arms, but they never knew that I healed them. I led them with human cords, with ropes of love. To them I was like one who eases the yoke from their jaws; I bent down to give them food. Israel will not return to the land of Egypt and Assyria will be his king, because they refused to repent.

Hosea is noted for his prophetic analogies and historical reflection, and certainly both of these are seen in Hosea 11:1–5. In this text, there are numerous terms that carry special historical, geographical, political, and cultural significance. For instance, throughout Hosea the terms "Israel" and Ephraim" are essentially synonymous, with Ephraim, the most significant tribe of the Northern Kingdom, coming to represent Israel.[11] The term "Egypt" has historical and theological significance, and the context of Hosea 11:1 suggests that the historical exodus event establishes a pattern that has prophetic significance for the future (Hos

---

11. This is an example of synecdoche, a figure of speech in which the part (Ephraim) represents the whole (Israel).

11:8–11; cf. Matt 2:15). In addition, "Assyria" plays a significant historical and political role in Old Testament prophecy and history, but the full scope of this isn't readily apparent to the casual reader of Hosea 11.[12] At the very least, the reader should know about the events involving the Assyrian oppression and eventual destruction of the Northern Kingdom in 722 BC (an event fulfilled in the "near" future following Hosea's prophecies).

What is more, there's a set of terms in this passage alluding to the pagan religious cult of the day, Baalism. Understanding Baalism is a virtual necessity for understanding the book of Hosea, but most readers today will not understand Baalism and its practices so terms revolving around the rites of Baalism should certainly be included as nonroutine.

Finally, in drawing the picture of God's relationship to his child Israel, Hosea refers to human "cords," "ropes" of love, and perhaps shifting the metaphor from a child to an animal, "yokes" from their jaws. These terms are culturally particular, probably understood with a full range of nuance by the eighth-century recipients of Hosea's prophecies but not by the modern reader. The point isn't that we understand all the historical and cultural implications embedded in these terms at first glance but that we give special attention to the background issues of the terms that warrant such study.

Exegetically or Textually Uncertain Terms

These are words that are typically discovered by English Bible readers through the comparison of English translations. In some situations, these terms are crucial, but fortunately most of these terms don't carry the primary weight of meaning in a verse or passage. These are simply

---

12. Both the theological and historical significance of Egypt and Assyria in the eighth-century prophets is quite profound and establishes multiple patterns throughout Scripture. From a historical vantage point, a parallel may exist in Poland during the 1930s, set between Nazi Germany and Soviet Russia. Poland was between a rock and a hard place and suffered greatly between her more powerful neighbors. Israel also found itself between two powerful neighbors often at war with one another, Egypt and Assyria. The point is that most modern readers identify at least in part with the historical, geographical, and political significance of World War II Poland, Germany, and the Soviet Union but fail to understand the significance of Egypt and Assyria in ancient Near Eastern history.

words and phrases that are difficult to interpret (and thus to translate) due to exegetical ambiguity, lexical difficulty, or textual uncertainty.

Exegetical ambiguity occurs when the context doesn't reveal how a certain word should be translated. At the observational level, this can be seen when translations differ in how they translate a given word. For instance, in Hosea 11:12 the Hebrew verb *rud*, "to roam about freely," can be understood with either positive or negative connotations, depending on how the reader (or translator) understands the preposition *im* ("with," or in an adversative sense, "against"). A quick comparison of English translations makes clear that something is going on here. Some translations, such as the ESV, understand the relationship of Judah roaming with God in a positive light: "but Judah still walks with God and is faithful to the Holy One," while others, such as the NIV, understand the relationship in a decidedly negative manner: "And Judah is unruly against God, even against the faithful Holy One." The point is that terms translating *rud* and *im* ("still walks with," ESV; "unruly against," NIV) ought to be deemed nonroutine simply based on the exegetical ambiguity of their meaning in this particular context.

In some cases, especially in the Hebrew Old Testament, exegetical challenges derive not from contextual ambiguity but rather from *lexical difficulties* stemming from the limited use of a given word in the Bible. This is especially taxing when a word isn't found in extrabiblical literature and is used only once in the Bible (this is called a *hapax legomenon*, lit. "once said"). Because we don't have ancient Hebrew and Greek lexicons handed down through the centuries, nor modern lexicons that fell out of heaven inspired, the only way we know what a Hebrew or Greek word means in the Bible is through observing its use in various contexts. This presents little difficulty when a word is used frequently, but when used only a few times, or even just once, this can make lexical certainty a challenge.

As English Bible readers are made aware of lexically challenging words through differences observed between translations or through translation footnotes (an especially helpful feature in many modern translations), these words should be noted as nonroutine. An example of this is found in the latter half of Ecclesiastes 2:8, "I gathered male and female singers for myself, and many concubines, the delights of men" (HCSB). The Hebrew term *shiddah* is translated by most modern translations as either "harem" (NIV) or "concubines" (HCSB, ESV), but this is a *hapax legomenon* found only here in the Bible, and its meaning is only understood through this context and associated words from related languages. The difficulty here is highlighted by such alternate translations as "musical instruments" (KJV, NKJV) and "treasure chests" (CEB). Technical commentaries explain the rationale behind alternate translations, but the point here is that because the meaning of the word is uncertain it's by default a nonroutine term.

Another subset of this kind of nonroutine term is those terms (words and phrases) that are uncertain due to *textual issues* within the original language. As noted in chapter 3, one major reason why translations reflect differences is because of the textual decisions that translators must make in doing the work of translation. In cases where a word or phrase is based on a disputed textual reading or where alternate readings are available, the word or phrase should be designated as nonroutine. A good example of this is John 6:47 ("Verily, verily, I say unto you, He that believeth on me hath everlasting life," KJV), where the KJV and NKJV, following the *Textus Receptus*, specify the object of belief ("on Me" or "in Me"). Modern translations, following more recently discovered Greek texts, don't specify the object of belief ("I assure you: Anyone who believes has eternal life" HCSB). The context is quite clear regarding the object of belief in this verse, and elsewhere in John's Gospel belief in Christ ("in Me") is made explicit.[13] Not only is this phrase theologically significant,[14] it is also nonroutine on the basis of its textual uncertainty.

Figurative Terms

Enhancing the rhetorical strategies that accompany literary genres and subgenres, the Bible contains thousands of individual, discernible

---

13. John 7:38; 11:25–26; 12:44, 46.

14. This is not to suggest that the object of faith in New Testament theology rests on the textual variant in John 6:47. Clearly, both the context of John 6:47 and the testimony of many other verses in John's Gospel specify Jesus as the object of saving faith.

figures of speech. While the interpretation of figurative language is an important aspect of hermeneutics affecting all literary genres, it's beyond the scope of this chapter to detail the function of figurative language and the special hermeneutics associated with its interpretation. For now, we simply encourage you to be on the lookout for figures of speech and to designate them as nonroutine. Most can quickly identify distinct figures of speech even when they don't fully understand what kinds of figures of speech they see. While knowing at least a few of the common figures of speech in Scripture is helpful in distinguishing between figurative and non-figurative language, even when you can't identify what kind of figure of speech is in a text, you can usually state with confidence *that* a figure of speech is being used. Whenever words or phrases are used in a figurative manner, these terms should be designated as nonroutine, indicating that further attention is needed to discover the kind of figure of speech and the literal intent behind it (which is the essence of interpreting figurative terminology).

In the next chapter, we'll present and define various kinds of figures of speech that will enable you to recognize figures of speech and to understand their rhetorical function. At this point, our interest is to discern between the routine, literal use of language and the nonroutine, figurative use.

Psalm 22:12–15

To demonstrate the basic recognition of figurative language in Scripture, let's consider a well-known portion from the Psalter, Psalm 22:12–15.

> [12] Many <u>bulls</u> surround me;
> strong ones of Bashan encircle me.
> [13] They open their mouths against me—
> <u>lions</u>, mauling and roaring.
> [14] I am <u>poured out like water</u>,
> and all my bones are disjointed;
> my <u>heart is like wax</u>,
> <u>melting</u> within me.

^{15} My strength is <u>dried up like baked clay</u>;
my tongue sticks to the roof of my mouth.
You put me into the <u>dust of death</u>.

To some degree, there are more figurative terms in this passage than literal ones, which can make designating specific words as nonroutine rather challenging (in many cases, the entire verse or stanza comprises the figure of speech). Even so, it's helpful to recognize that literal bulls and lions aren't attacking David, and that he isn't literally poured out like water. His heart isn't literally wax or melting like heated wax, and his strength isn't literally dried up. Through the use of simile, metaphor, and hypocatastasis (a point of comparison through direct naming; e.g., bulls and lions), the psalm describes a rich sense of emotion that can't be conveyed through standard, literal terminology. What's more, the intensity of despair is heightened by hyperbole as David's "bones are disjointed" and "his tongue sticks to the roof of his mouth."[15] The phrase "dust of death" is perhaps an idiomatic way of describing the common grave, combining for intensity the locus of the grave ("dust") with the actual condition of dying. In any case, at this point we're simply concerned with recognizing what may be figurative and designating these terms for further study.

Symbolic Terms

Symbols are either literal or figurative terms that carry a normally expected and frequently repeated pattern of meaning in specific contexts (whether literary or cultural).[16] Symbols are often more easily discernible as single words and phrases than figures of speech (whereas a figure of speech might comprise an entire sentence of prose or line of poetry), and tend to followed expected patterns throughout Scripture. Apocalyptic

---

15. Certainly these could be describing David's literal and historical condition. However, in the context of this lament, these phrases appear to describe the extent of David's despair rather than his actual physical condition. Of course, in fulfilling the typological pattern expressed through this psalm, these figurative descriptions take on a very literal sense of fulfillment experienced in the physical sufferings of Christ on the cross.

16. Symbolism is often contained in literal terms. For instance, a name, place, or number may have symbolic significance yet not technically constitute a figure of speech.

and prophetic literature contains many examples of symbols, but you can find symbols in every portion of the Bible. Symbols are found in visions (Jer 24:3–8; Ezekiel 37), discourse (John 3:5–8), poetry (Song 8:4–8) and prophetic drama (Jer 27:1–12; Ezek 5:1–4). Moreover, symbolism attaches to names (Abram to Abraham), numbers (3, 7, 40), and colors (white and purple).

Obviously you should exercise caution in determining the extent of symbolic intention, but you shouldn't ignore the often explicit and pervasive way in which terms are assigned symbolic value throughout Scripture.[17] The Gospels contain many of these examples, and Jesus was quite fond of using symbols in his teaching. John is well known for his extensive use of symbolism.[18] For example, note the prominence of polar opposites in John's writing, such as light and darkness, sight and blindness, or life and death. A quick survey of John also reveals the symbolic use of terms relating to sustenance (bread and water), agriculture (vineyards and sheep), and the human body (blood and birth). Citing just one passage from the Gospel of John, note the variety of symbols and the importance of recognizing them as symbolic terms.

John 6:53–59

So Jesus said to them, "I assure you: Unless you <u>eat the flesh</u> of the Son of Man and <u>drink His blood</u>, you do not have <u>life</u> in yourselves. Anyone who <u>eats My flesh</u> and <u>drinks My blood</u> has eternal life, and I will raise him up on the last day, because <u>My flesh is real food</u> and <u>My blood is real drink</u>. The one who eats <u>My flesh</u> and drinks <u>My blood</u> lives in Me, and I in him. Just as the living Father sent Me and I live because of the Father, so the one who <u>feeds on Me</u> will live because of Me. This is the

---

17. For a helpful discussion of interpreting figurative language in Scripture, see Köstenberger and Patterson, *Invitation to Biblical Interpretation*, chapter 14. For a concise survey of symbols in Scripture, along with interpretive principles for interpreting symbols, see Roy Zuck, *Basic Bible Interpretation* (Colorado Springs: Chariot Victor, 1991), 184–93. See also Leland Ryken, James C. Wilhoit, and Tremper Longman III, eds., *Dictionary of Biblical Imagery* (Downers Grove: InterVarsity, 1998) for a comprehensive resource on symbols and imagery in the Bible.

18. See Andreas J. Köstenberger, *A Theology of John's Gospel and Letters*, BTNT (Grand Rapids: Zondervan, 2009), 155–67.

<u>bread</u> that came down from heaven; it is not like the manna your fathers ate—and they died. The one who eats this <u>bread</u> will live forever."

Determining the significance of these symbols in John 6:53–59, and throughout John's Gospel, is the work of interpretation and correlation (in this case, understanding John's theology), but one can certainly see the need for recognizing these expressions as symbolic, even at the level of observation (Jesus was certainly not teaching cannibalism!). While special hermeneutics are involved in the interpretation of symbols in Scripture, the general principle of authorial intent remains: a symbol's meaning is that intended by the author, and thus we must apply the basic procedures of considering the context, noting the point of resemblance, and tracing the pattern of symbolic usage as a means of interpreting its intended sense. However, at this stage of observation our primary concern is to recognize symbolic terms as such, allowing for more precise interpretive conclusions to come.

Thinking Conceptually

Although we've kept the focus of reading with discernment on words and phrases, there are instances when *ideas* are in view, and the interpretation of the text depends in part on the accurate understanding of implied concepts where the word isn't found in the text but the idea is. When this is the case, the same general categories as with words or phrases apply, but you may need to suggest terms to aid in thinking through what is conceptually significant. A great example of this is found in 2 Corinthians 5:21, cited in an earlier example of theologically profound terms.

While the primary theological term repeated in the passage is "reconciliation" or "reconciled," the astute observer can't help but notice that verse 21 contains a theologically profound *concept* that is never related as a single word or phrase in the passage: that of substitutionary atonement. Although not referred to as a phrase in the passage, the concept is clearly functioning as both a contextually crucial and a theologically profound element in the passage. The keen observer would be remiss to ignore this just because the term is not found in the passage.

Mix and Match

When it comes to designating nonroutine terms, you are not constrained to take an either/or approach to determining *kinds* of nonroutine terms. Rather, a both/and approach to determining kinds of nonroutine terms is perfectly valid. In other words, in many cases a theologically profound term will also be contextually crucial, or a historically particular term might also be theologically profound.[19]

It's quite common that an exegetically uncertain term is also crucial, perhaps profound, or historically particular (or a combination thereof). Many symbolic terms are based on a specific kind of figure of speech and thus can be labeled both figurative and symbolic.[20] In other words, feel free to recognize the different ways in which one term may function as nonroutine; just know that you should be able to explain *why* a certain term is nonroutine in a variety of ways.

Final Thoughts

As with any step of observation, determining nonroutine terms is simply one element among many in reaching the goal of knowing God's Word. We certainly don't suggest that a commandment came down from heaven instructing the reader to discern between routine and nonroutine terms. This step of observation is meant to help you, not hinder you or place unnecessary constraints on you as you study the Bible.

However, knowing the amount of effort involved in "rightly dividing the Word of truth," we believe that taking the time to distinguish

---

19. Consider the example of the cross cited earlier; cf. 1 Cor 1:18–25.

20. It should be noted that not all symbols are based in figures of speech. For instance, if the number 40 carries symbolic significance in Scripture, this isn't rooted in a particular kind of figure of speech. Likewise, symbols in visions and apocalyptic literature are not usually framed around a particular figure of speech, although there may be some distant representative relationship (e.g., the horn came to be representative of political and military power, perhaps based off of the strength embodied in male oxen). See the entry "Horn" in *Dictionary of Biblical Imagery*, 400.

between terms that require more attention and those that don't is a wise stewardship of time and effort in Bible study. Our experience is that the time spent in observation discerning between nonroutine terms is richly rewarded by providing a sharper focus during the process of interpretation.

6

Having Eyes to See

Observing Literary Features

The noted Swiss-German theologian Adolf Schlatter simply but poignantly described the task of hermeneutics as "seeing what is there."[1] At this point in our survey of the steps of observation, we've learned to read the Bible *comparatively* (chapter 3), *inquisitively* (chapter 4), and *discerningly* (chapter 5), but now we've arrived at the core of observation: reading the Bible *attentively*. Just as a distinction can be drawn between *hearing* and *listening*, when we read the Bible, there's a difference between *seeing* and *perceiving*. We've all had the experience of reading while day-dreaming, only to come to our senses after a few paragraphs and think, "What was I just reading?" (We trust that this does not describe you right now!) Obviously, comprehension requires more than just seeing the words on a page and tracing them across a series of sentences and paragraphs. The attentive reader must focus his mind along with his vision in order to see with accuracy and precision all that lies before him in the biblical text. It's our goal in this chapter to provide a set of "observational lenses" to aid in reading attentively—categories and suggestions that help the reader both see and perceive.

Attentive reading requires persistence—the pursuit of discovering what really lies before us through a careful reading and rereading of the biblical text. However, simply reading the same text over and over by itself will constitute little progress toward perception. The attentive

---

1. See Andreas Köstenberger, "Adolf Schlatter: A Model of Scholarship," *Biblical Foundations* (blog), http://www.biblicalfoundations.org/adolf-schlatter, accessed September 6, 2015, and the resources for further study cited at the end of this entry.

reader should have some idea of the kind of things that she is searching out—certain rhetorical features and strategies employed by the biblical writers that recur throughout the sixty-six books of the Bible. We agree with Bauer and Traina when they suggest that "One of the primary ways in which one can nurture exactness and precision in observation is to give specific labels to what one observes. Indeed, one is more likely to observe the various elements present in the text if one has labels or categories at hand."[2] In this chapter we label a variety of features and strategies in discrete categories and survey them as a means of facilitating attentive observation.

The Bible communicates meaning not only by *what* it says but also by *how* it says it. Therefore it's important to be aware of at least some of the strategies employed by the authors of Scripture. Most of the features that we highlight in this chapter are simple and straightforward, yet the recognition of these often factors into the eventual interpretation of the biblical text. They do more than just produce an enlightened appreciation for the literary form of the text; for the attentive reader they assist in tracking with the very Word of God.

The following features are meant as guideposts for the attentive observation of Scripture. This survey is by no means comprehensive, yet we believe that these features form the core of observation, the essential "bread and butter" of attentive reading. The arrangement of these categorical observations may appear random. To some degree, this is due to the broad representation of features throughout all genres of Scripture. However, we do recognize that certain features are better represented in certain genres and subgenres than others. For instance, while irony is used throughout Scripture, its function in narrative literature is quite different from its function in prophetic judgment speeches. And while irony features prominently in the prophets, it's hardly found in the Old Testament legal code. Similar genre-specific considerations are appropriate to all of the points we survey in the pages ahead. The more significant of these are noted as examples are drawn from those genres that best represent each literary feature.

---

2. David R. Bauer and Robert A. Traina, *Inductive Bible Study: A Comprehensive Guide to the Practice of Hermeneutics* (Grand Rapids: Baker, 2011), 76.

Table 6.1 — Literary Features for Observation		
Literary Feature	**Definition**	**Biblical Examples**
Repetition	When a word, phrase, or concept is used more than once in a passage.	Jonah 4:1; Romans 11:28–32
Escalation	When a line of argument builds towards a climax.	Ecclesiastes 2:24–25; 3:12–13, 22; 5:18–20; 8:15; 9:7–10; 11:9; Amos 6:17; Zephaniah 1:14–16; Romans 8:31–39; and 1 Corinthians 15:50–58
Contrast and Comparison	When words, phrases, concepts, or figures are juxtaposed against something else as a means of further explanation.	Joshua 2–7; Proverbs 1–9; John 5; 9; Romans 14:1–15:6; Galatians 5:16–25
Association	When words, phrases, or motifs relate to one another in association.	Spiritual Gifts/Love Passages: 1 Corinthians 12–14; Romans 12:6–8; and Ephesians 4:11–12; 1 Corinthians 13; Romans 12:9–20; Ephesians 4:13–16
Question and Answer	When questions are used to frame an argument.	Luke 18:18; Romans 6:1–2a; 8:31–35; Galatians 3:19
Conjunctions	Words that direct the flow of a discourse.	Ephesians 4:17; Titus 4:7
Conditional Clauses	Clauses that contain a statement of condition.	Galatians 1:10; Colossians 3:1; 1 John 2:1
Illustration	An example of some kind which serves to clarify a point.	Philippians 2:1–11; 2 Timothy 2:3–7; James 2:14–26
Quotation	Echoes, allusions, and quotations of previous material, most notably, the Old Testament in the New.	Philippians 2:6–11; Colossians 1:15–20; 1 Thessalonians 5:16–22; 1 Timothy 2:5–6; 3:16; 2 Timothy 2:11–13; Jude 14–15
Irony	A figure of speech in which words express opposite meaning from what is intended, or where plot outcomes are the opposite of what is expected.	Joshua 2–7; Esther; Job; John 3:4; 1 Corinthians 1:18–31; Galatians 6:2

Repetition

Be on the alert for the use of repetition in Scripture. The repetition of a word, phrase, or concept will often provide clues regarding the author's purpose in a passage or at the very least will highlight the key point(s) of interest. Sometimes repetition simply reflects the interests of the writer, while at other times repetition is an intentional device used to heighten the impact of a word or concept in the text. Although repetition has no universal function in Scripture, its impact is significant across all literary genres, and attentive reading that captures the repetition of words, phrases, and concepts will prove valuable on multiple levels.

Romans 11:28–32

Consider as an example the repetition of the word "mercy" in Romans 11:28–32:

> Regarding the gospel, they are enemies for your advantage, but regarding election, they are loved because of the patriarchs, since God's gracious gifts and calling are irrevocable. As you once disobeyed God, but now have received <u>mercy</u> through their disobedience, so they too have now disobeyed, resulting in <u>mercy</u> to you, so that they also now may receive <u>mercy</u>. For God has imprisoned all in disobedience, so that He may have <u>mercy</u> on all.

The word "mercy" is used four times in this paragraph and carries significant weight in bringing Paul's line of argument to a conclusion (a cohesive line of argument beginning in chapter 9 and concluding in chapter 11). With such an emphasis on "mercy," it should come as no surprise that after a concluding hymn of praise (Rom 11:33–36; functioning as a literary capstone to the entire section beginning with chapter 9), the next segment of Romans begins with an inferred imperative based on the "mercies of God": "Therefore, brothers, by the mercies of God, I urge you to present your bodies as a living sacrifice, holy and pleasing to

God; this is your spiritual worship" (Rom 12:1).[3] Although the concept of God's mercy is certainly found throughout the first eleven chapters of Romans, the repetition of the term in 11:28–32 prepares the reader to embrace the injunction to service in 12:1–2. An attentive reading will see the repetition in 11:28–32, make a connection to 12:1, and ponder the significance of this relationship.

Jonah 4:1

The prophets frequently repeat words and variations of words as a means of drawing attention to their message. This is one aspect of prophetic wordplay as demonstrated through the repetition of key Hebrew words in the book of Jonah. For instance, in the movement between God's response to the repentance of the king of Nineveh in Jonah 3:10 and Jonah's response to that response in 4:1, note the repetition of the Hebrew word *raah*:

> Then God saw their actions—that they had turned from their evil [*raah*] ways—so God relented from the disaster [*raah*]. He had threatened to do to them. And He did not do it. But Jonah was greatly displeased [*raah* x2; the intensification "greatly" is communicated through the repetition of the word in Hebrew] and became furious.

The semantic flexibility of the Hebrew term *raah* provides Jonah the opportunity for wordplay, but, depending on the specific translation, this repetition may be lost to the English Bible reader. However, repetition and wordplay is such a significant feature of the book of Jonah that even in English translation many examples of repetition can be found.[4] Train your eyes to find repeated words and phrases throughout the book of Jonah; you will be astonished by what you find!

---

3. Consider as well the implied connection between the "hymn of praise" that concludes chapter 11 and the reference to "spiritual worship" that begins chapter 12.

4. For a more complete survey of wordplay and repetition in Jonah, see J. Daniel Hays, *The Message of the Prophets: A Survey of the Prophetic and Apocalyptic Books of the Old Testament* (Grand Rapids: Zondervan, 2010), 302–7.

In some books repeated words and phrases convey recurring themes. Perhaps there's no better example of this than in the book of Ecclesiastes. An attentive reading of Ecclesiastes will reveal repeated words such as *hevel*, variously translated as "vanity" (KJV), "futility" (HCSB), or "meaningless" (NIV), repeated phrases such as "under the sun" and "pursuit of the wind," and repeated refrains such as "enjoy life," accompanied by the recurring phrase "there is nothing better."[5] Concepts such as the inevitability of death, the enjoyment of life, and the fear of God are recognized motifs that recur through a variety of "catch words" in the book. These words and phrases "carry" the message of Ecclesiastes, and their repetition frames the foundation for advanced study of the book.[6]

Repeated phrases and clauses may additionally act as a cohesive measure in Hebrew poetry and prophetic oracles. For instance, consider the repetition of the concluding statement, "Yet you did not return to Me," in the stanzas comprising Amos 4:6–11. As each stanza concludes with this statement, the sense of Israel's guilt builds, preparing the reader for the climactic pronouncement of judgment in 4:12: "Israel, prepare to meet your God!" Repetition links each stanza between verses 6 through 11 together while serving to heighten the sense of Israel's guilt in the process.

There are hundreds of examples where repetition affects how the message of Scripture is communicated. The next time you open the pages of Scripture, focus your eyes on repetition, and you, too, will find that the examples multiply many times over.

Escalation

Escalation generally involves a line of argument that builds toward a climax of some kind. Observing escalation involves a certain feel for the

---

5. The "enjoy life" refrain is repeated seven times in the book, perhaps having some bearing on the significance of this motif. Also, it has representation throughout the broad scope of the book of Ecclesiastes (2:24; 3:12–13; 3:22; 5:18; 8:15; 9:7–10; 11:8–10).

6. While most modern commentaries on Ecclesiastes pay special attention to recurring words, phrases, and themes in the book, perhaps the two studies that best reflect the importance of repetition as the cornerstone of interpretation for Ecclesiastes are Doug Ingram, *Ambiguity in Ecclesiastes* (New York: T&T Clark, 2006) and Richard Alan Fuhr Jr, *An Analysis of the Inter-Dependency of the Prominent Motifs in the Book of Qohelet* (New York: Peter Lang, 2013).

movement of the text that requires especially attentive reading. Often coupled with repetition, escalation functions to heighten the impact of the message of the text. Escalation is found among a variety of literary genres and can be broad (developing through a book) or narrow (confined to a particular unit of thought) in scope.

Building off repetition (and our prior example of repeated motifs in Ecclesiastes), one might observe escalation occurring through the movement in the "enjoy life" refrains in Ecclesiastes (2:24–25; 3:12–13, 22; 5:18–20; 8:15; 9:7–10; 11:9).[7] The manner by which each successive refrain is introduced demonstrates escalation, even if the essential content remains consistent. The first four refrains (2:24–25; 3:12–13, 22; 5:18–20) simply assert an understanding of the value of joy while the fifth refrain (8:15) commends enjoyment to the reader. However, the last two refrains clearly *command* the enjoyment of life. The introductions to each refrain successively build from reflection to affirmation to imperative. Failure to see the escalation in these refrains may lead one to miss an essential aspect of the message of the book.[8]

Examples of escalation in narrow contexts are abundant; virtually all examples of parallelism in Hebrew poetry involve a degree of escalation.[9] In addition, escalation in the judgment speeches of the prophets is a standard literary technique, heightening the effect of God's impending judgment. Consider Zephaniah's description of the day of the Lord (Zeph 1:14–16) or Amos's indictment of the "notable people" of the "first of the nations" who "anoint themselves with the finest of oils"—and who therefore go out as "the first of the captives" (Amos 6:1–7).[10] The prophets also heighten the effect of rejoicing through escalating rhetoric. Who hasn't read Isaiah 40 with growing expectation, led along by rhetorical

---

7. The "enjoy life" refrains were cited as an example of repetition; escalation often is developed through repetition. On the recognition of escalation through these refrains, see R. N. Whybray, "Qohelet, Preacher of Joy," *JSOT* 23 (1982): 87–98.

8. On the significance of the enjoyment of life in the wisdom of Ecclesiastes, see Fuhr, *Analysis of the Inter-Dependency of the Prominent Motifs in the Book of Qohelet*, 137–59; and Eunny Lee, *The Vitality of Enjoyment in Qohelet's Theological Rhetoric* (Berlin: de Gruyter, 2005).

9. See our examples later in this chapter.

10. The escalation and repetition in this text is coupled with wordplay. The "first class" citizens of the "first" (*reshit*) nation who use the "finest" (*reshit*) oils will be the "first" (*rosh*, derived from the same root as *reshit*) to go into captivity (v. 7).

questions and a building case for God's salvation culminating to the poetic crescendo of verse 31: "they will soar on wings like eagles"?

A clear example of escalation in the New Testament epistles is found in 1 Corinthians 15:50–58. A similar example is Romans 8:31–39. Read these passages out loud and see if you can retain an even pitch through your reading—we bet you can't! That is because there's escalation in the line of argument in each of these texts, culminating in a climax at the end. If written communication involves more than lexical definition and grammatical form (and it does), then the observation of escalation plays an integral part in both understanding and *feeling* the power of the Word of God.

Contrast and Comparison

An attentive reader should be alert to words, phrases, concepts, and figures that are contrasted or compared within or between passages of Scripture. Various points of contrast and comparison may provide the backbone of content in a particular context, and the primary point of a passage is often encapsulated in the relationship between these parts. Contrast and comparison is found in all genres of Scripture and may be *concrete* (identified by words) or *conceptual* (reflected in themes and motifs).

The primary difference between contrast and comparison is that contrast focuses on *differences* while comparison tends to highlight some aspect of *similarity*.[11] For instance, note how the differences are emphasized between "light and darkness" and "love and hate" in John's rhetoric. Likewise, Paul contrasts law and grace throughout Galatians, and "walking in the Spirit" and "walking in the flesh" in Galatians 5:16–25. However, there are also points of comparison among these contrastive relationships. For instance, "walking in the Spirit" has a comparative relationship to grace, while "walking in the flesh" corresponds to life under the law. Observing these relationships requires recognition of

---

11. J. Scott Duvall and J. Daniel Hays, *Grasping God's Word*, 3rd ed. (Grand Rapids: Zondervan, 2012), 56.

contrasting terms and phrases but also of the conceptual themes that relate to these terms.

Usually, contrast and comparison are quickly identified through repeated terms, but there are exceptions. For example, note the contrast between "the weak" and "the strong" in Romans 14:1–15:6. In most English translations, the term "weak" is found only in 14:1–2, while "strong" occurs only in 15:1. And yet these two groups are identified in numerous ways throughout the passage, with distinct instructions given to both. In observation, the reader should note the descriptions of "the strong" along with those of "the weak." How are these two groups contrasted (noting differences), and how are they compared (noting similarities)? What instructions does Paul give to the weak, and how does he instruct the strong? How do these two groups relate to one another? A reader looking for contrast and comparison will observe these relationships in a manner that discerns the line of argument and, ultimately, the message of this passage.

Perhaps the greatest number of individual examples of contrast and comparison in the Bible is found in the book of Proverbs, where the point of the proverb is typically communicated through contrastive relationships between lines of poetry (antithetical parallelism) or comparative relationships between corresponding lines (synonymous parallelism).[12] However, contrast and comparison in Proverbs goes beyond the form of the proverb. There is a continual contrast between wisdom and folly throughout the book, and many of the standard topics in Proverbs reflect this relationship (the sluggard is a fool while the diligent is wise; the proud man is a fool while the humble man is wise; etc.). In the instructive discourses (Proverbs 1–9), the reader is implored to consider the merits of wisdom compared to the pitfalls of folly, and even in metaphor the contrast between "lady wisdom" and "the woman folly" is fundamental to the message of the book.

Biblical narrative often highlights contrast and comparison between people, places, and events and this, coupled with irony, forms much of the literary strategy found in narrative writing. For instance, consider

---

12. See the treatment on parallelism that concludes this chapter.

the narratives introducing the conquest of Canaan (Joshua 2–7). Eyes trained to find elements of contrast and comparison will notice some fascinating points of correlation between the figures of Rahab and Achan. Some of these are primary (Rahab is a Canaanite woman while Achan is a Hebrew man), while others are secondary (Rahab hides the spies on the roof and her family is spared; Achan hides the spoils of war under his tent and his family is destroyed). However, the many points of contrast and comparison between these narratives are strikingly profound. Rahab is a Canaanite prostitute, condemned to perish. Achan is a member of the tribe of Judah (Josh 7:18), the tribe through whom all nations would be blessed. Yet through her act of faith Rahab is incorporated into the messianic line (Matt 1:5)[13] while Achan is effectively eliminated from among God's people. The very first narrative about the conquest of Canaan is an exception to the plan, highlighting God's grace and the incorporation of believing Gentiles into his program.

Read the narratives of Joshua 2–7 for yourself and see how many points of contrast and comparison you can find.[14] Do the same for other collections of narratives, especially those in the Gospels. Particularly fruitful examples are the narratives in John 5 and 9 featuring a lame man and a blind man, both of whom were healed by Jesus. As you'll discover, while both of these men were made well by Jesus, they didn't respond to him in exactly the same way, and to make the reader reflect on these contrasting responses is precisely John's authorial intent. Perhaps even more significantly, note the way in which John juxtaposes his accounts of Nicodemus, the Jewish teacher, and the nameless Samaritan woman in chapters 3 and 4 of his Gospel.[15] Again, an eye attuned to discovering contrasts will be richly rewarded by careful study. Now that you know what you should be looking for, you'll be amazed at what you will find!

---

13. See John Nolland, *Matthew*, NIGTC (Grand Rapids: Eerdmans, 2005), 78 for support that the Rahab of Matt 1:5 is the same as the one of Joshua 2 and 6.

14. Hays and Duvall provide an excellent treatment of contrast and comparison between these figures. See *Grasping God's Word*, 336–38.

15. If, after having inductively studied these contrasts, you want to check what you've found, you may want to consult Andreas J. Köstenberger, *John*, BECNT (Grand Rapids: Baker, 2004), 112.

Association

Although most cases of contrast and comparison infer association, not all associations in Scripture are born out of contrastive or comparative relationships. This is especially true when motifs relate to one another in the Bible. As an example, notice that the three primary Pauline passages on spiritual gifts (1 Corinthians 12–14; Rom 12:6–8; Eph 4:11–12) correspond directly to the three primary Pauline passages on love (1 Corinthians 13; Rom 12:9–20; Eph 4:13–16). What is more, Paul's emphasis on Christian unity (described through the metaphor of the body) is prominent in these same three texts. Obviously, these motifs relate to one another in a significant manner. When reading Scripture, consider how ideas might develop out of an association of words or themes. Sometimes to understand the whole we must first see how the parts associate, relate, and depend on one another.

Question and Answer

A common feature throughout the Bible is the use of question and answer, often employed to build arguments and to frame discourse. This is common in the Pauline Epistles (especially the book of Romans; see below) but occurs in other books and genres as well. In many cases questions in Scripture are actually rhetorical questions—questions that are meant to state a point and therefore do not require a response.[16] However, there are also examples of interrogative questions in the Bible that are used to frame an issue or pose a problem.[17] Both should be pursued in attentive observation.

Question and answer may be easy enough to spot, but the use of this device can vary in both form and function. For example, in Romans 6:1 Paul asks, "Shall we continue in sin, that grace may abound?" only

---

16. The "God speech" in Job 38–41 contains over seventy rhetorical questions, all to drive home one single point.

17. Consider how questions in Ecclesiastes are used to navigate through the issues pondered in the book. Many of these are real questions, not rhetorical statements. The entire book may in fact be "programmed" by the question posed at the beginning of the book, "What does a man gain for all his efforts that he labors at under the sun?" (Eccl 1:3).

to immediately answer in the next breath, "God forbid" (v. 2a, KJV). This technique of anticipating and rebutting potential objections continues throughout the discourse of Romans 6–7, only to shift in Romans 8:31–35 to a series of escalating rhetorical questions, bringing the entire argument to a climax in the concluding jubilation of Romans 8:38–39.

One should also note examples of interrogative questions, as they often provide a programmatic clue for the context of the attendant passage. Interrogative questions can appear in a variety of genres. How would we have understood Christ's words differently if they hadn't followed the rich young ruler's interrogative question, "Good Teacher, what shall I do to inherit eternal life?" (Luke 18:18)? What is more, it's interesting that the interrogative question is followed in Jesus's response with a rhetorical question—you can see how questions are used in various ways.[18] A capable observer will note where questions appear in narrative literature and how they function in the surrounding context.

Interrogative questions, however, aren't limited to narrative dialogue. Paul often uses non-rhetorical questions to indicate the flow of his arguments in the epistles. In Galatians 3:19, for example, Paul poses the question of why the law was given if the prior covenant with Abraham was based on faith. The answer is then made explicit; Paul anticipates that his readers won't know the answer, so he provides it in the ensuing passage. Thus the question serves as a programmatic cue for the resulting content. Even outside of dialogue, non-rhetorical questions should pique the interest of the capable observer.

Conjunctions

We're taught basic conjunctions, or words that conjoin—"and," "yet," "or," "but"—from an early age. But the keen observer shouldn't ignore such innocuous words. Beyond basic functions such as forming lists,

---

18. Jehovah's Witnesses have notoriously used Jesus's rhetorical question in Luke 18:19 (NKJV: "Why do you call Me good? No one is good but One, that is, God") as proof he didn't claim divinity, seeing the implied answer as "no." But in verse 18 we see that Jesus's rhetorical question is framed by the rich young ruler's claim that Jesus was a "good teacher" (that is, a good teacher and perhaps nothing more). In this case, careful observation of the context of question and answer is vital to an accurate interpretation of the passage.

establishing parallel thoughts, or dictating basic contrast, conjunctions also relay causal relationships, explain reasons, facilitate inference, and perhaps most significantly, link together independent clauses.[19] Conjunctions thus act as signposts in the text, assisting in the development of the line of argument and directing the flow of thought in a passage of Scripture. Reading Scripture without giving attention to conjunctions is like driving on an unfamiliar street without reading the road signs—we'll almost certainly get lost!

Conjunctions such as "because," "since," "so that," and "in order that" tend to direct relationships between statements in Scripture, often with nuanced distinction. For instance, in Titus 3:4–7 Paul explains that God justifies by grace *so that* believers might become "heirs with the hope of eternal life" (v. 7). Is Paul indicating that the purpose of God's grace is to bring believers to the place of eternal life (this is God's design), or is he simply encouraging believers with the expected result of God's grace (namely, eternal life)? Certainly the distinction is a nuanced one, but these are the kinds of questions borne from the careful observation of conjunctions.

Perhaps most vital to the observation process is when conjunctions indicate an inference on the part of the writer. "Therefore" and "for" are prime examples, although other words function similarly ("so," "thus," "wherefore," and "accordingly"). These words are contingent upon their preceding and possibly their following context for their meaning. If your favorite pastor or preacher has ever come to a passage in Scripture and said something like, "Whenever you see a 'therefore,' you have go see what it's *there for*," then you have first-hand experience with pinpointing these conjunctions.

When, for instance, Paul begins Ephesians 4 with "Therefore I, the prisoner of the Lord, urge you to walk worthy of the calling you have received," you should recognize this and the following verses as

---

19. That is, clauses that can grammatically function as full sentences on their own, containing a subject and a predicate. For an advanced treatment of conjunctions that are significant for understanding the flow of a given discourse in Scripture, see Steven E. Runge, *Discourse Grammar of the Greek New Testament: A Practical Introduction for Teaching and Exegesis* (Peabody, MA: Hendrickson, 2010), chapter 2.

applications contingent on the passages preceding it. Paul in fact climbs quite a hefty theological mountain in the first three chapters of Ephesians, and many have observed the shift from the theological in chapters 1–3 to the practical in chapters 4–6. The "therefore" in 4:1 seems to function as a major point of inference ("based upon, or in light of the theological realities that I have just explained, this is the logical, practical outcome that is expected . . ."). However, not every example of "therefore" coordinates major segments of the text. For instance, is the "therefore" in Ephesians 4:17 contingent upon the prior argument beginning in chapter 1 or simply upon the material in the immediately preceding context (4:11–16)? Again, the observation of conjunctions lends itself to important questions of content *and* relationship.[20]

Conditional Clauses

Conditional clauses are typically framed around an "if/then" relationship, although variation to this structure does occur. Any statement of condition is worth noting in observation because the relationship between the condition (usually introduced by "if") and the result (often introduced by "then") carries interpretive significance. Students of New Testament Greek know that this language provides greater clarity to the function of a conditional clause by way of sentence construction and form. However, in English translation, the function of a conditional clause won't be seen by grammatical form but rather by context.

The standard classifications for Greek conditional clauses illustrate the variety of ways conditional clauses function in Scripture.[21] The first-class condition *assumes the condition as true for the sake of argument* and thus clearly has a rhetorical function. This assumed reality is illustrated

---

20. Watching for conjunctions such as "therefore" or "for" in much of the New Testament will help the reader spot patterns of indicative statements (passages elaborating on certain truths) followed by imperative statements (lists of commands and applications of those truths), which in some way inform the structure of almost every epistle. Likewise, such conjunctions will also help the observer learn where to demarcate boundaries for what "passage" he is isolating in a given text.

21. For the classification of Greek conditional clauses, see Daniel B. Wallace, *Greek Grammar Beyond the Basics: An Exegetical Syntax of the New Testament* (Grand Rapids: Zondervan, 1996), 687–701.

by Colossians 3:1, "So if you have been raised with the Messiah, seek what is above, where the Messiah is, seated at the right hand of God." Paul is assuming that the Colossian readers have been "raised with the Messiah," but for the sake of argument, and perhaps to encourage reflection, he frames his statement in the form of a first-class condition.

The second-class condition *assumes that something is not true*. For instance, in Galatians 1:10 Paul follows two rhetorical questions with a second-class conditional statement: "If I were still trying to please people, I would not be a slave of Christ." Paul is obviously not a people-pleaser—that's the whole point of what he's saying! But through the use of the second-class condition, he brings his argument to a climax, perhaps even adding some rhetorical "sass" for good measure!

The third-class condition *suggests an uncertain yet probable future fulfillment*. A classic example of this is 1 John 2:1: "And if anyone does sin, we have an advocate with the Father—Jesus Christ the Righteous One." John is not limiting the likelihood of this "sinning" coming true—but he's also not encouraging it or stating it as an established fact. In using the conditional clause, he distances his readers from the negative reality of sin yet cleverly reinforces the positive advocacy of Christ.

There are a little over 600 conditional clauses in the New Testament. While the first step of observing a conditional clause is simply to see it as such, it's an invigorating exercise to try to discern between the various kinds of conditional clauses (even if by context in English translation), bearing in mind that not all conditional clauses fall as neatly into categories as the examples above.[22] So please don't be turned off or discouraged by the technical jargon in this section (first-class condition, etc.) and set your eyes on the interpretive rewards that come from this kind of attentive reading of the biblical text.

---

22. Hebrew does not have the precision of Greek in distinguishing the function of conditional clauses. However, conditional clauses are found in the Old Testament, even though they are not as prominent as in the New Testament.

Illustration

Illustrations are found throughout all portions of the Bible, serving to elucidate what is unclear and to enrich the rhetoric of the biblical writer. While many examples of illustration in Scripture are rather straight-forward, some are less obvious to the casual reader. Attentive observation requires intentional effort to see illustration in the text.

Once illustration is perceived in the text, it naturally follows that the reader will begin asking "What's the point?" behind this illustration.[23] Often illustrations in Scripture function much like sermon illustrations in modern preaching—there's one primary point in the illustration, and the goal of the reader is to draw that singular point from the text. However, not all illustrations in Scripture are confined to singular points of reference. In many cases there are multiple referents in an illustration, and you must detect the connections between referents as a prerequisite to understanding their meaning. But, at least to begin with, the recognition of illustration in observation is essential; beyond that, you enter into the task of interpretation, grappling with intended meaning.

To demonstrate the importance of observing illustration in the text, consider the relationship of Philippians 2:1–4 to 2:6–11. Through a first-class condition (vv. 1–2) followed by contrastive imperatives (vv. 3–4), Paul builds an argument instructing the Philippian believers to live with one another in a spirit of humility. While his point is quite clear in verses 1–4, he brings the argument to a climax (can you see escalation here?) by pointing the reader to the ultimate example of humility, the incarnate Christ (v. 5). As theologically rich as Paul's rhetoric (or quotation?) in verses 6–11 is,[24] the primary function of this text is to illustrate the attitude of humility he's calling the Philippians to emulate. Paul is making a very practical point of exhortation to the church, and he illustrates his point by drawing his readers' attention to Jesus, the ultimate example of

---

23. As a general rule, whenever an illustration in Scripture is observed, you should ask, "What is the point of this illustration and how does it relate to the context as a whole?"

24. There is some debate among scholars as to whether Phil 2:6–11 constitutes elevated prose on the part of Paul or a quotation of an ancient Christian hymn or creed. To some extent, the observation of structure is foundational to the debate and highlights the need for the careful observation of structural features (see chap. 8).

looking to "the interests of others" (v. 4).[25] To miss this relationship is to miss the very point Paul is trying to make in the passage!

Sometimes illustration is rooted in past events or figures in Scripture. For instance, in his epistle James makes the case for a relationship between faith and works in which faith is vindicated through works (2:14–26). To strengthen his point, he concludes his argument with two illustrations from the Old Testament and another from metaphysics. In the first illustration, James draws his readers to the narrative of Abraham offering his son Isaac on the altar (v. 21; Genesis 22),[26] and in the second, he points to Rahab's protection of the Hebrew spies (v. 25; Joshua 2). In both of these illustrations James uses historical examples to strengthen his argument that faith is shown to be true only by the actions that follow. In the third example he illustrates the same point from the metaphysical realm; "just as the body without the spirit is dead, so also faith without works is dead" (v. 26). This time he appeals to logic and experience rather than to history, but the effect is similar—his argument is strengthened, even to the point of reaching a climax, through the validity of his illustration. Seeing these three illustrations and their function within the line of argument is essential to the interpretation of the text. Again, we see that thorough observation leads to accurate and informed interpretation.

Illustrations, much like proverbs, parables, and allegories, have an inherent capacity to elicit reflection. For example, note the three-tiered illustration in 2 Timothy 2:3–7. Following his exhortation to "be strong in the grace that is in Christ Jesus" (v. 1) and his instructions to take "what you have heard from me" and commit these things "to faithful men who will be able to teach others also" (v. 2), Paul uses three illustrations from ordinary life—the soldier, the athlete, and the farmer—to

---

25. Fee and Stuart make the excellent point that "much of the theology in the Epistles is task oriented and therefore is not systematically presented." We would consider this a classic example of such "task theology," noting that Paul was not setting out with a primary goal of teaching Christology to the church at Philippi. Gordon Fee and Douglas Stuart, *How to Read the Bible for all Its Worth*, 4th ed. (Grand Rapids: Zondervan, 2014), 90.

26. To further heighten the effect of the illustration, James quotes Gen 15:6 as fulfilled after Abraham offered Isaac up on the altar, even though the "cutting" of the covenant in Genesis 15 occurs some 30 years prior to the events of Genesis 22. To understand the chronology behind the historical illustration makes the point theologically: while Abraham was justified by his faith in Gen 15:6, the vindication of that faith followed later (Genesis 22) through works (when Abraham acted on his faith).

strengthen or clarify what he has commanded in verses 1 and 2. However, the points Paul is making in each of the three illustrations don't seem to be identical, nor are they immediately clear. The reader must reflect on the point—and Paul seems quite intentional in challenging his readers to reflection through these illustrations—as verse 7 suggests ("Consider what I say, for the Lord will give you understanding in everything").

All illustrations aren't created equal; they are drawn from a multitude of sources and convey a variety of purposes. Some are concise, and others are extended. Nevertheless, half the battle is simply recognizing an illustration as such. Once the reader sees that an illustration is in play, she can ask the proper questions that lead to an understanding of the author's point—which, of course, is precisely the point!

Quotation

One of the more fascinating features of the New Testament is its colorful use of the Old Testament. The New Testament writers quote the Old Testament over 250 times, using the text of the Old Testament for a variety of reasons. In quoting the Old Testament, the New Testament writers selectively adapted the text to meet a variety of purposes. Moreover, the New Testament writers often recognize truth apart from the historical and literary context of the Old Testament setting. All things considered, the study of New Testament's use of the Old Testament is one of the more challenging areas in biblical studies.

Space doesn't allow for a thorough treatment of the fascinating and at times complex hermeneutical issues involved in the New Testament's use of the Old. There are many excellent resources are available on this topic, and we'd recommend that you take the time to explore the hermeneutical implications and interpretive approaches pertaining to this field of study.[27] At this point we're simply encouraging you to train your eyes

27. Recommended sources include G. K. Beale, *Handbook on the New Testament Use of the Old Testament* (Grand Rapids: Baker, 2012); G. K. Beale and D. A. Carson, eds., *Commentary on the New Testament Use of the Old Testament* (Grand Rapids: Baker, 2007); and Andreas J. Köstenberger and Richard D. Patterson, *Invitation to Biblical Interpretation* (Grand Rapids: Kregel, 2011), 703–8. Note also the parallel passages indicated in good study Bibles (though be aware that there are a variety of reasons why a given passage may be cited as a parallel other than the use of the Old Testament in the New).

to recognize the use of quotation as such and to observe a few key features in the way in which New Testament writers use the Old Testament.

Quotations are often indicated by introductory phrases such as "It is written," "It is said," and "The Scripture says," along with language revolving around the concept of fulfillment. However, not all quotations from the Old Testament are introduced as such, and often quotations are strung together from different sources but presented as one. Nevertheless, even in the absence of introductory phrases, recognizing Old Testament quotations in the New Testament is usually not difficult. Modern translations typically frame quotations on the page by using a combination of quotation marks, italics, bold lettering, and special indentation, so it's quite easy to notice a quotation visually on the page. The real challenge in observing quotations involves the *way* in which the New Testament quotes the Old, not the simple *fact* that it does.[28]

At the observation level, the most striking feature of Old Testament quotations is often the variation in wording between the Old Testament text and the New Testament quotation. Such variations should be noted, especially in cases where major segments are omitted and where the wording is changed to convey ideas not represented in the wording of the Old Testament text.[29] Of course, minor variations should be expected as a result of translation, whether by New Testament authors translating the Hebrew into Greek themselves or by quoting from the established Greek translation of the day, the Septuagint. In either case, you should take note of the differences in wording between the Testaments, especially differences significant enough to demonstrate intentional selectivity and adaptation.

On a final note, not all quotations in Scripture involve New Testament writers quoting the Old. In some cases, the New Testament authors quote sources other than the Old Testament Scriptures,[30] and sometimes the Old Testament authors quote (or borrow) from other Old Testament

---

28. However, when one accounts for paraphrase and allusion, even recognizing a quotation as such can be quite challenging.

29. Variations may include grammatical shifts, omission of wording, and significant paraphrasing.

30. For instance, consider the possibility of quoted material in the following texts: Phil 2:6–11; Col 1:15–20; 1 Thess 5:16–22; 1 Tim 2:5–6, 3:16; 2 Tim 2:11–13; and Jude 14–15. In each of these examples, the possible quotation is not derived from the Old Testament but rather from other sources.

books.[31] The authors of Scripture were clearly comfortable incorporating preexistent material into their work, and attentive reading should distinguish quotations accordingly.

Irony

As we said earlier, the message of the biblical text isn't simply communicated by *what* the writers said but also *how* they said it. This dynamic is perhaps best seen in the rich use of irony throughout Scripture. Irony is not so much something funny as a joke would be; it is rather akin to paradox in that it strikes one as unusual or out of the ordinary, perhaps because it involves double entendre or a person speaking or acting better than they know. Irony is used across the spectrum of genres in the Bible, saturating biblical narrative, enhancing prophetic oracles, and adding texture to the New Testament letters. Irony, however, can be missed, resulting in misinterpretation and a lack of appreciation for what the writer is really trying to communicate. The attentive reader will keep his or her eyes peeled for irony in Scripture.

As briefly touched on previously, irony is often framed through paradox and flavored by sarcasm. For instance, note the irony and sarcasm in Paul's argument regarding the "foolishness of God" in relationship to the "wisdom of man" (1 Cor 1:18–31). Paul clearly doesn't believe that God is foolish while people are wise; nor does he encourage anyone to become "foolish" in a standard sense (1 Cor 3:18). Rather, he uses the terminology of naysayers (Jews and Gentiles) to enhance his argument; the "foolishness" of God is indeed wiser than the wisdom of people (1 Cor 1:25), and God has chosen what is "foolish" in the world to shame the wise (1 Cor 1:27). To miss the sense of irony throughout this passage is to miss the point altogether.

Sometimes irony isn't so obvious. Throughout the book of Galatians, Paul blasts the Judaizers (Jews who refuse to allow Gentiles into the church without becoming "Jews" first) for burdening the church

---

31. Consider the quote of Mic 3:12 in Jer 26:16–19, or the presumed borrowing between Mic 4:1–3 and Isa 2:2–4 (who borrowed from whom is unclear—the two prophets were contemporaries).

with the demands of the law. Then, as he brings his letter to a close, he exhorts his readers to "carry one another's burdens; in this way you will fulfill the law of Christ" (Gal 6:2). The irony shouldn't be missed: Paul has vigorously argued that justification by the law is incompatible with justification by faith in Christ, yet now he refers to the "law of Christ." What is more, rather than bearing the burden of the Judaizers' "law," Paul exhorts his readers to carry the burden of others and *in this way* fulfill the "law of *Christ.*" The irony is palpable, but without careful observation you could easily miss it.

A wonderful example of broad-based irony is found in the book of Job. Throughout the dialogue between Job and his three friends (Job 4–31), Job regularly envisions a time when he will put God on the stand and question him; Job is quite confident that God will answer by affirming Job's innocence and admitting his own "accounting" error. Adding to this, one of the vexing frustrations for Job is that although he desires to argue his case before God, God is nowhere to be found. Yet striking irony occurs in chapter 38—when God finally does speak, he asks all the questions—in fact, more than seventy rhetorical questions that altogether silence Job (40:4–5)! In the end, it is God who asks the questions, not Job.

In portions of narrative we often find instances where characters, events, and settings are contrasted with a flare of irony. Consider again the example of Rahab and Achan in Joshua 2–7. How ironic it is that the first encounter with a Canaanite proves to be an exception to the commandment to exterminate the people of Canaan! And how ironic is it that the first person exterminated is an Israelite from the tribe of Judah? How much more is the irony enhanced when we find that this Canaanite prostitute is incorporated into the very line of the Messiah, the line to which the family of Achan belonged! If you miss the irony embedded in these narratives, you may also miss the theological message laying a foundation for what God is doing by grace through faith.

Examples could be multiplied. The entire book of Esther is dripping with irony.[32] In the end the villain of the story, Haman, is hanged

---

32. See the excellent introduction by Tremper Longman III and Raymond B. Dillard, *An Introduction to the Old Testament*, 2nd ed. (Grand Rapids: Zondervan, 2006), 213–23.

on the gallows he himself prepared for his archenemy, Mordecai. In this way the entire plotline, carried along by several banquet scenes, hinges on the building irony. The Gospels, too, are replete with misunderstandings conveying a sense of irony. Mark, in particular, shows how not only Jesus's antagonists, the Jewish authorities, are susceptible to misunderstanding, but even his own followers are.[33] John, likewise, regularly exposes misunderstanding on the part of a variety of characters, encompassing a wide range of individuals.[34] For example, Nicodemus misunderstands Jesus's saying that he must be born again and asks how he can literally enter his mother's womb a second time and be reborn (John 3:4), a manifest absurdity. You get the idea—irony in Scripture is rather common, but like the biblical characters, the contemporary reader of Scripture must discern the true spiritual reality of things or run the risk of misconstruing what Scripture is actually saying.

Tone

Anyone with "ears to hear" knows how important tone is in verbal communication. However, many neglect to see the significance of tone in written communication. Knowing that Scripture was written in the context of real human history and understanding the emotional depth reflected by the content and literature of Scripture, the attentive reader should strive to "hear" the tone of the text. Scripture is saturated with emotive language and reflects the full range of human feelings. However, tone is not limited to emotional reflection. Books such as Job and Song of Songs convey an array of deep emotional overtones (everything from despair to erotic love), while other writings convey tone with very little emotion. For instance, the instructive discourses of Proverbs 1–9 exude a serious, reflective, personal, and instructive tone. The legal code in Leviticus is also serious and instructive, but generally not reflective and personal. Galatians conveys a sense of urgency in light of the Judaizing heresy. Paul's first letter to the Corinthians communicates an aura

---

33. See, e.g., Mark 6:52: "they did not understand about the loaves, but their hearts were hardened."

34. See Andreas J. Köstenberger, *A Theology of John's Gospel and Letters*, BTNT (Grand Rapids: Zondervan, 2009), 141–45.

of methodical patience, even though the content addresses divisions, moral abuses, misguided thinking, and the misuse of spiritual gifts in the church. In the second letter to the Corinthians, one might sense that Paul's patience is running out. Every book of the Bible contains tone—in fact, every book of the Bible reflects multiple moods and types of atmosphere that attentive reading will capture.

Tone is especially relevant in written texts that reflect an oral event or history. For instance, the oracles of the prophets were once preached, the psalms were once prayed and/or sung, and one would presume that the Song of Songs was once sung as well. The New Testament letters were often read in the churches. In each of these, tone is almost as important as content (OK, this may be a slight exaggeration, but you get the point). Narratives draw the reader into the setting, and the epistles were written in place of apostolic presence. Certainly, if Paul had been in Galatia, those in his presence would have heard the scolding tone of Galatians 3:1–4 in his preaching. Why should we think that we can't "hear" it in the written letter? Thus "hearing" and discerning tone is one aspect of "seeing" the text and perceiving its significance.

Tone is particularly important in dialogues and personal encounters recorded in the Gospels.[35] Take Jesus's interaction with Nicodemus, the Jewish rabbi, for example, which you can find in John 3. We're told that Nicodemus came to Jesus at night (perhaps to avoid attracting undue attention) and that he said to him, "Rabbi, we know that You have come from God as a teacher, for no one could perform these signs You do unless God were with him" (John 3:2). On the face of it, it appears that Nicodemus understood who Jesus was: a teacher come from God, performing miraculous signs. But, perhaps surprisingly, Jesus retorts, "I assure you: Unless someone is born again, he cannot see the kingdom of God" (John 3:3). In the ensuing conversation it becomes gradually clear that Nicodemus doesn't truly grasp Jesus's identity and is in dire need of spiritual rebirth. How are we to account for the surprising nature of Jesus's response? Did Jesus not appreciate Nicodemus's compliments and

---

35. Peter Cotterell and Max Turner, *Linguistics and Biblical Interpretation* (Downers Grove: Inter-Varsity, 1989), calls this "The Special Case of Conversation." See chapter 8 and the case study of Nicodemus on pp. 278–87.

respond in an unduly harsh manner? This is where it's important to read between the lines, in keeping with ancient Near Eastern cultural norms where it was common to start a given conversation with an opening pleasantry or even flattery.[36] Obviously Jesus saw right through this (he knew what was in people and so didn't entrust himself to anyone [John 2:25]) and addressed Nicodemus on the level of his true need, not on the surface cultural level. It's also interesting that by changing the topic of conversation, Jesus asserted his authority over Nicodemus, because it was customary for the more important person to set the topic.[37]

Developing a list of kinds of tone might include dozens of distinct and nuanced options. As a reader, simply seek to describe the tone of the passage at every juncture. Attentive reading will usually bear this out with little technical analysis needed. As you read Scripture, if the tone isn't obvious, try to read the text out loud in order to hear the tone. It's almost impossible not to inflect your voice in concert with the perceived tone of the written text. Finally, as you read, note any change in tone that occurs. A shift in tone can be quite significant in highlighting points of contrast and recognizing the structural breakdown of the words you're reading (or perhaps better, "hearing").

Figures of Speech

In chapter 5, we introduced the idea of observing figures of speech as nonroutine terms. Now we revisit figures of speech as one of the more significant rhetorical features to observe in attentive reading. Although figurative language is most often associated with poetry, an observant eye will catch figures of speech throughout all genres and books of the Bible (did you find any figures of speech in this sentence?). Figures of speech are so pervasive in Scripture that readers don't even blink an eye at their use (see how difficult it is to avoid imagery in communication?). And yet without attentive reading, many fail to see figurative language for what it

---

36. See, e.g., a certain Tertullus when addressing Felix the governor in Acts 24:2–8.
37. Cotterell and Turner, *Linguistics & Biblical Interpretation*, 284.

is and thereby limit themselves to reading the Bible in "black and white" rather than in "literary color."

Understanding how the words of Scripture function requires an appreciation for figurative language, and this begins with the ability to discern between different kinds of figures of speech. Although context and common sense will usually distinguish figurative from non-figurative language, it's quite helpful to learn at least a dozen of the most common figures of speech. At the level of observation, seeing a figure of speech and knowing what kind it is will assist you in appreciating the full impact of language as an interpreter. In fact, reading the Bible without an awareness of the presence of figurative language will inevitably lead to a failure to appreciate the function of figurative language. Put another way, "The *function* of statements in the Bible can be as important for understanding their meaning as the *content* of the statements."[38] Understanding the function of language begins with seeing a figure of speech for what it is, and this is within the purview of observation.

Although specialists will discern many more distinct kinds of figures of speech than we do here, the ones listed in the following chart are sufficient in getting started. When observing figurative language, always make an effort to define the kind of figure of speech that you see. This can be challenging, especially when figures of speech are stacked and intertwined together (there are times, especially in poetry, where three or four discernible figures of speech can be found in one verse of Scripture!). Engaging in this exercise will enhance your ability to discern between figurative and non-figurative language and in the end will lend itself to a better understanding of the specific function of the figure of speech and the literal intention behind the non-literal terminology.

---

38. D. Brent Sandy, *Plowshares and Pruning Hooks: Rethinking the Language of Biblical Prophecy and Apocalyptic* (Downers Grove: InterVarsity, 2002), 82.

Table 6.2 — Biblical Figures of Speech

Figure of Speech	Definition	Biblical Examples (HCSB)	Additional Examples
Simile	A comparative figure of speech in which one thing resembles another through the use of "like" or "as."	**Psalm 1:4**: The wicked are not like this; instead, they are <u>like chaff</u> that the wind blows away.	Psalm 22:14 Isaiah 40:22 Micah 1:4
Metaphor	A comparative figure of speech in which resemblance is communicated by a form of the "to be" verb.	**Psalm 31:3**: For You <u>are my rock and my fortress</u>; You lead and guide me because of Your name.	Psalm 22:6 Psalm 46:7, 11 Isaiah 40:6–8
Hypocatastasis	A comparative figure of speech in which resemblance is communicated through direct naming.	**Psalm 22:12–16**: <u>Many bulls surround me</u>; strong ones of Bashan encircle me. They <u>open their mouths against me—lions, mauling and roaring</u>. I am poured out like water, and all my bones are disjointed; my heart is like wax, melting within me. My strength is dried up like baked clay; my tongue sticks to the roof of my mouth. You put me into the dust of death. <u>For dogs have surrounded me</u>; a gang of evildoers has closed in on me; they pierced my hands and my feet.	Job 13:25 Amos 4:2 John 21:15–17
Metonymy	The substitution of one word for another (inferring some point of comparison or relationship).	**Proverbs 12:18b**: . . . but the <u>tongue</u> of the wise brings healing.	Song of Songs 2:15 Jeremiah 2:15
Synecdoche	The substitution of a part for the whole.	**Proverbs 1:15–16**: My son, don't travel that road with them or set foot on their path, because their <u>feet run</u> toward trouble and they hurry to commit murder.	Romans 16:4 1 Corinthians 1:17

Table 6.2 — Continued

Figure of Speech	Definition	Biblical Examples (HCSB)	Additional Examples
Personification	Ascribing human characteristics to inanimate objects or animals.	Isaiah 55:12: You will indeed go out with joy and be peacefully guided; the mountains and the hills will break into singing before you, and all the trees of the field will clap their hands.	Job 38:8–11 Psalm 98:8 Hosea 10:8
Anthropomorphism	Ascribing human characteristics to God.	Psalm 8:3: When I observe Your heavens, the work of Your fingers, the moon and the stars, which You set in place.	Job 36:32–33 Isaiah 64:8
Zoomorphism	Ascribing animal characteristics to God.	Psalm 91:4 He will cover you with His feathers; you will take refuge under His wings. His faithfulness will be a protective shield.	Hosea 5:14–15 Hosea 11:10
Euphemism	The substitution of an inoffensive word for a more offensive one.	Luke 8:52: Everyone was crying and mourning for her. But He said, "Stop crying, for she is not dead but asleep."	Genesis 4:1 1 Thessalonians 4:13–15
Hyperbole	A deliberate exaggeration used to communicate a point.	Matthew 18:9a: And if your eye causes your downfall, gouge it out and throw it away.	Isaiah 34:8–10 Jeremiah 17:3–4
Sarcasm	An indirect form of a ridicule expressed as a compliment.	Job 12:1–4: Then Job answered: "No doubt you are the people, and wisdom will die with you! But I also have a mind; I am not inferior to you. Who doesn't know the things you are talking about? I am a laughingstock to my friends, by calling on God, who answers me. The righteous and upright man is a laughingstock."	Job 13:1–5 Job 38:5 Amos 4:1–5
Rhetorical Question	The use of a question to make a statement (where a response is never intended).	Job 38:2: Who is this who obscures My counsel with ignorant words?	Job 6:5–6 Job 15:2–3 Galatians 1:10

Parallelism

Parallelism is the practice of balancing lines of poetry through a correspondence of words or ideas. For instance, consider Psalm 19:1:

> The heavens / declare / the glory of God,
> and the sky / proclaims / the work of His hands.

There's a clear correspondence of ideas between these lines of poetry, made all the more discernible by breaking the lines up into units. Essentially, both lines are working together to communicate a single, contextually unified idea. This is the essence of parallelism. The second line isn't saying anything that wasn't essentially stated in the first; in all cases of parallelism, the second line corresponds to the first. In some cases (such as this one), the first line could even act independently without the second line. But the point is that the two lines *do* function together. Through the technique of parallelism, the second line enhances the first line, heightening the effect, resulting in a one-two punch; and in some cases, providing a literary knockout blow! Such is the impact of parallelism in Scripture, and thus it's critical that attentive readers see parallelism in the text and ultimately understand its function in enhancing and heightening the message of Scripture.

Most verses of Hebrew poetry exhibit some adherence to this practice, and thus parallelism is common in Scripture.[39] Many readers of Scripture, however, have never considered, through no fault of their own, just how pervasive and significant this literary feature is in the Word of God. And like figures of speech, there are different kinds of parallelism that exhibit distinct ways in which correspondence between lines takes place. Learning to observe parallelism will benefit the reader far beyond aesthetic appreciation. The way one thinks contextually in poetry is driven by the recognition of parallelism, and thus it is a critical component of reading the Bible attentively. Although scholars use a variety of terms to distinguish between kinds of parallelism, consider the

---

39. It should be noted that elements of parallelism are also found in prose literature, although with less frequency and structural clarity.

following five types of parallelism as representative of how parallelism works in Scripture:

1. Synonymous parallelism. The thoughts in each line correspond synonymously, saying the same thing with different words. The degree of similarity may vary between examples, noted in the contrastive element between "day" and "night" in Psalm 19:2:

> Day after day / they pour out / speech;
> night after night / they communicate / knowledge.

2. Antithetical parallelism. The thoughts in each line correspond through a contrastive relationship. The conjunction "but" is an important clue in recognizing this type of parallelism. Antithetical parallelism is frequent among the "sayings" within the book of Proverbs, where opposites correspond to make a single point. This is clearly illustrated in Proverbs 14:28:

> A large population / is a king's / splendor,
> but a shortage of people / is a ruler's / devastation.

3. Synthetic parallelism. The primary thought in the first line is developed and enriched by the corresponding second line. With synthetic parallelism, the correspondence of ideas is intact, although the structural arrangement lacks formal congruence. The manner in which the second line develops the first varies within this broad category. For instance, in Proverbs 20:4, the second line highlights the *result* of the action expressed by the first line:

> The slacker does not plow during planting season;
> at harvest time he looks, and there is nothing.

In Proverbs 22:9, the second line specifies *how* the person is generous, and *why* he is blessed:

> A generous person will be blessed,
> for he shares his food with the poor.

In Proverbs 20:24, the rhetorical question in the second line simply reflects upon and reinforces the idea expressed in the first line:

A man's steps are determined by the LORD,
so how can anyone understand his own way?

These are just a few of the ways in which two lines may correspond to complete one primary thought. Consider the development and completion of a single point through corresponding lines as the critical characteristic of synthetic parallelism.

4. Emblematic parallelism. The corresponding lines of poetry relate in a comparative sense. Emblematic parallelism functions in a manner similar to metaphor or simile, revealing the referent in one line and the point of comparison in the alternate line. Words such as "is" and "like" are a ready clue to emblematic parallelism. A clear example is Proverbs 11:22:

A beautiful woman who rejects good sense
is like a gold ring in a pig's snout.

5. Climactic parallelism. Through successive lines corresponding thoughts build in detail and descriptive force, conveying the impression of escalation. This technique is often found in prophetic oracles and frequently involves stanzas with multiple lines. In formal examples, a portion of the opening line may be repeated in successive lines within the stanza. For an example of this technique in the prophets, consider Amos 3:15:

I will demolish the winter house
and the summer house;
the houses inlaid with ivory will be destroyed,
and the great houses will come to an end.

Table 6.3 — Types of Parallelism in the Bible			
Type of Parallelism	Definition	Example (HCSB)	Additional Examples
Synonymous	The thoughts in each line correspond by similarity.	**Psalm 19:1**: The heavens declare the glory of God, and the sky proclaims the work of His hands.	Proverbs 19:5 Proverbs 22:1
Antithetical	The thoughts in each line correspond by contrast.	**Proverbs 15:1**: A gentle answer turns away anger, but a harsh word stirs up wrath.	Proverbs 11:12 Proverbs 20:8 Proverbs 30:5
Synthetic	The first line is developed and enriched by the corresponding second line.	**Proverbs 20:4**: The slacker does not plow during planting season; at harvest time he looks, and there is nothing.	Proverbs 22:9 Proverbs 20:24
Emblematic	The second line reveals the referent of the metaphor used in the first line.	**Proverbs 11:22**: A beautiful woman who rejects good sense is like a gold ring in a pig's snout.	Proverbs 26:11
Climactic	A portion of the first line is used in the second line, and the second line adds to it.	**Psalm 29:1, 8, 10**: Ascribe to Yahweh, you heavenly beings, ascribe to the LORD glory and strength. The voice of the LORD shakes the wilderness; the LORD shakes the wilderness of Kadesh. The LORD sat enthroned at the flood; the LORD sits enthroned, King forever.	Isaiah 1:8 Amos 3:15

Final Thoughts

The items for observation listed in this chapter are not comprehensive, but they do represent the most significant, and we believe the most helpful, observations that an attentive reader will pursue. Additional items to look for may include word lists, pairings, prepositions, pronouns, cause and effect, and imperative. However, as suggested in the introduction to this chapter, attentive reading must do more than simply underline appointed observations. Attentive reading is perceptive reading, and perception tends to connect the dots, to make sense out of relationships, and to build upon the significance of the basic observations introduced in this chapter. The observation of the text leads to an awareness of the text that fosters better interpretive questions and ultimately speaks to the interpretation of God's Word.

7

Determining Literary Units
Basic Discourse Analysis

Over the past century Bible study at the technical, exegetical level has been virtually synonymous with the detailed analysis of words, phrases, and sentences. This involves the necessary study of grammar, vocabulary, and syntax, ideally in the original languages, but often in translation. And while there certainly is benefit in parsing verbs and declining nouns, it's our conviction that "the primary locus of discourse meaning resides above the sentence level."[1] In other words, an *analytical* reading of Scripture must consider structural form and function—even beyond the sentence level—as an integral aspect to the communication of meaning in Scripture. With this in mind, we come to our last chapter on observation—the observation of structural form in written discourse.

Besides garnering an appreciation of the aesthetic form and communicative function of a highly structured text (and it should be noted from the outset that all Scripture is highly structured), the observation of structural boundaries is critical in doing inductive Bible study. This is actually quite pragmatic, for without observing the structural breakdown of the biblical text, the reader loses all bearing on *what* portion of Scripture to study. Versification and chapter breaks aren't a part of the original, inspired text of Scripture, yet many readers allow these to determine the units and segments of the text they study. Certainly chapters and verses are helpful for referencing Scripture, but they may at times be less than 100 percent accurate in breaking down a text in its

---

1. George H. Guthrie, "Discourse Analysis," in *Interpreting the New Testament*, ed. David Alan Black and David S. Dockery (Nashville: B&H, 2001), 256.

constituent subunits.[2] At the level of observation, it's therefore important to learn basic elements of structural analysis as a means of organizing the text according to its own rules. A reading of Scripture free from versification, chapter breaks, and subheadings (from study Bibles) will inevitably require you to observe the text analytically, discovering the organizational clues that the text itself delivers. Moreover, as you observe structural units within the text, there's a natural sense in which contextual units are determined. It's therefore necessary to observe Scripture *analytically*, noting the way in which thoughts are organized within the text as a lead into interpreting Scripture according to its appropriate surrounding context.

Structure and Genre

The broadest area of literary and structural distinction in Scripture is between biblical prose and biblical poetry. Through translation, prose literature is framed by sentences and paragraphs, while poetry is framed around parallel lines and stanzas (have you noticed that in most Bibles you can tell the difference between poetry and prose at a glance?). While this may be an oversimplification of the structure of the text, it suggests an important point: for the reader of Scripture, the most basic structural observations entail the *recognition of prose literature versus poetic literature*. While many of the categorical observations surveyed in this chapter apply to both, there are certain rhetorical strategies that lie primarily in the domain of poetry and others that are featured primarily in prose literature. Our approach is to survey all of these observations together but to highlight those categories that are more likely found in prose genres and those that are common within poetic genres.

What is more, typical structural formulas and the means to recognizing structure are necessarily determined by genre. This is often obvious, but sometimes subtle. For instance, narrative literature is characterized by structural devices not typical in the Psalter (this should be obvious), but

---

2. Note, for example, how John 2:23–25 serves as the introduction to the Nicodemus pericope in John 3:1–15, which makes it appropriate to delineate the unit as 2:23–3:15 rather than 3:1–15. We'll discuss this passage in greater detail later in this chapter.

Old Testament narrative may exhibit traits somewhat different than those found in Gospel narrative (this is less obvious). And while it's clear that all poetry isn't the same, there are distinctions between lyrical poetry (such as found in Psalms and Song of Songs), poetic oracles (Isaiah 40–66), and the poetry of wisdom literature (such as found in Proverbs and Ecclesiastes). In addition, there are distinct structural characteristics pertaining to subgenres in books of the Bible. Even a quick analytical reading of Proverbs suggests that there are distinct subgenres within the book of Proverbs that reflect different structural techniques (and perhaps conventional "rules"). The first nine chapters flow together as a homogeneous discourse, while chapters 10–29 are comprised of individual, pithy sayings arranged in a seemingly haphazard manner.[3] The book concludes with a highly structured, acrostic poem on the virtuous wife (Prov 31:10–31).[4] You don't expect to find the same structural techniques in the instructive discourse (1–9) as you find in the collection of proverbs (10–29), and the poem on the virtuous wife has its own distinct acrostic structure. Yet all of these sections—indeed the whole book of Proverbs—is rightly considered poetic, proverbial wisdom literature, typified by parallel lines and stanzas.

Perhaps more important, genre will dictate the kind of units that you find within books of the Bible. For instance, it's common to use a term such as "pericope" to describe a self-contained literary unit in narrative, but in the Psalter a self-contained unit is the psalm itself.[5] In the Prophets we might expect to find oracles, in apocalyptic literature you'll find visions, and the book of Proverbs will contain individual proverbs or a series of proverbs that are arranged topically. Genealogies are often part of historical books (including the Gospels), but you'd hardly expect

---

3. This is not to suggest that there are no distinct structural patterns among and between the individual proverbs within the collection. See Duane A. Garrett, *Proverbs, Ecclesiastes, Song of Songs*, NAC (Nashville: Broadman, 1993), 33–48, for an excellent summary of structured patterns among the proverbs and structured collections between the proverbs.

4. An acrostic occurs when each line of poetry begins with a successive letter of the alphabet. While (Hebrew) acrostics are found throughout the Old Testament, they are lost to the English reader in translation, though some versions include separate headings for successive letters of the alphabet.

5. Fee and Stuart rightly observe that a key hermeneutical principle in interpreting the Psalms is to read a psalm as a complete unit. Each psalm itself is an individual, complete literary unit. See Gordon D. Fee and Douglas Stuart, *How to Read the Bible for All Its Worth*, 4th ed. (Grand Rapids: Zondervan, 1993), 217–18.

to find a genealogy in the Song of Songs (although you might encounter a chorus or a refrain). The Gospels contain parables, the Epistles contain greetings, and the Pentateuch contains law code. Obviously not all books of the Bible will contain the same kinds of literary units.

Before we tackle the four primary aspects in which discourses are structured, it should be noted that each book of the Bible will employ its own unique structural techniques. These may be determined by the conventions of style or they may be borne out of the unique and sometimes complex circumstances of the book itself.[6] For instance, prophetic books such as Jeremiah are basically anthologies, "best of" collections from the oracles of the prophets. This is not to suggest that broader arrangement is absent, but logical and chronological flow is not the guiding principle in how most of the prophetic books are arranged. By contrast, the Gospels exhibit traits of both chronological and logical structure between units (though each of the four Gospels displays its own distinctive structural arrangement and criteria of selectivity).[7]

Structural distinctions between books are sometimes a matter of authorial preference, some reflecting situation, others conveying the nuance of genre. A quick survey of the New Testament epistles reveals that they don't all reflect the same structural patterns, not even among those written by the same author. And some of the letters exhibit rather unique characteristics. For instance, while considered an epistle, the book of Hebrews reflects many traits of a sermon or series of messages that were first preached and then later combined and compiled to form a written piece. It should therefore come as no surprise that the "letter" opens with a very oral feature—alliteration—with Hebrews 1:1 containing five words begins with the Greek letter π.[8]

---

6. "Situation" refers to the real life-setting underlying a given passage of Scripture, comprising the larger relational web of relationships which, in turn, is firmly embedded in a historical, social, political, economic, and general cultural framework. The recognition of the importance and relevance of situation is an important safeguard against reading a given text in an abstract fashion or merely in light of one's own contemporary situation.

7. See Andreas J. Köstenberger and Richard D. Patterson, *Invitation to Biblical Interpretation: Exploring the Hermeneutical Triad of History, Literature, and Theology* (Grand Rapids: Kregel, 2011), 397–407.

8. See ibid., chapter 10.

A great example of historical situation influencing literary structure is the Old Testament book of Lamentations. The book itself is highly structured in the form of seven acrostics.[9] The Hebrew alphabet has 22 letters, and one can see at a glance that chapter 1 is a complete acrostic, containing 22 verses (versification was accurately arranged around the acrostic). Chapter 2 also has 22 verses, chapter 3 has 66 verses (actually comprised of three acrostics), chapter 4 has 22 verses (our sixth acrostic in the book), and chapter 5 has 22 verses (what we would expect to be the final, seventh acrostic in the book). However, quite surprisingly, the seventh expected acrostic is no acrostic at all—the formal acrostic completely breaks down, even with 22 verses! Was this accidental, or did Jeremiah simply run out of "creative juices"? Perhaps a better explanation is found when you consider the weighty, dire content of the book. Lamentations is a lament over the destruction of Jerusalem that occurred in 586 BC. When writing so that later generations may *remember* the siege and destruction of Jerusalem, Jeremiah uses acrostics as an aid to memorization. When writing so that later generations may *feel* the *destruction* of the city (through his words), he illustrates this through the *breakdown* of his own literary edifice!

One might also observe that each of the Gospels, as well as the book of Acts, is structured in its own unique way to convey theological message of the book. Matthew arranges his material around five discourses of Jesus: the Sermon on the Mount (chaps. 5–7), the sending of the Twelve (chap. 10), parables of the kingdom (chaps. 13 and 18), and Jesus's end-time discourse (also called "Olivet Discourse," chaps. 24–25). In this way, Matthew presents Jesus as the new Moses and Teacher imparting a law and righteousness greater than Moses, presenting, as it were, the "five books of Jesus," mirroring the five books of Moses (or Pentateuch).[10]

Mark essentially features Jesus's movement from Galilee to Judea (Jerusalem) following a geographical pattern, with Peter's confession of Jesus as the Messiah at the midway point of his narrative as a pivot

---

9. See the earlier footnote defining "acrostic."
10. See Andreas J. Köstenberger, L. Scott Kellum, and Charles L. Quarles, *The Cradle, the Cross, and the Crown: An Introduction to the New Testament*, 2nd ed. (Nashville: B&H Academic, 2016), chapter 4.

(Mark 8:26/27). It's possible, if not likely, that Mark's simple linear pattern of presentation provided the blueprint for other Gospels, including those of Matthew and Luke (cf., Luke 1:1–4). Particularly important is the designation of Jesus as the powerful, miracle-working Son of God, which spans the Gospel from beginning to end, culminating in the confession of a Roman centurion, no less (the Gospel was addressed to Rome), that Jesus was in fact the Son of God (Mark 15:39).[11]

Luke, similar to Matthew, opens up with Jesus's birth narrative and genealogy (albeit in reverse order) and then roughly follows the same kind of geographical pattern as Mark. However, Luke includes an extended ten-chapter unit, the so-called Travel Narrative (Luke 9:51–19:27), that features Jesus on his lengthy approach to the Holy City, Jerusalem, where he would eventually be crucified. In this way Luke presents Jesus's ministry and mission against the backdrop of his sacrificial death on the cross. In the book of Acts, the sequel to Luke's Gospel, Luke continues the geographical pattern, narrating the gradual spread of the gospel from Jerusalem to Judea, Samaria, and ultimately the capital of the empire, Rome (see esp. Acts 1:8).[12]

John, finally, organizes his presentation of Jesus around his performance of a series of messianic signs demonstrating that Jesus is the Messiah and Son of God (20:30–31). As such, John narrates, first, Jesus's mission to the Jews which ends in rejection (12:36–40). This is followed, second, by Jesus's mission to the world accomplished through Jesus's own commissioned representatives, the Twelve (John 20:21; cf. 17:18). In this way, John holistically presents in his one Gospel the missions of Jesus and the early church, which Luke covers in his two volumes.[13] A comparison of the Gospels demonstrates the vital need for analytical observation of literary structure. With that, let's now move on to discuss the essential features and implementation of structural analysis as a step of inductive study.

---

11. See ibid., chapter 5.
12. See ibid., chapters 6 and 8.
13. See ibid., chapter 7.

Figure 7.1: Two Goals of Structural Analysis

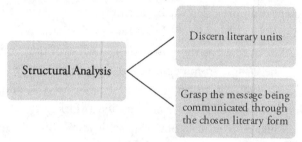

Two Goals of Structural Analysis

The first goal in analytical observation is simply to discern literary units. As noted earlier, the Bible wasn't inspired in the form of chapters and verses, yet many readers structure their study along these boundaries. Doing so is akin to driving with blinders that block out peripheral vision; one can see what is straight in front, but there may be significant features all around that one misses (perhaps a beautiful mountain vista on one side of the road and a thousand-foot drop-off on the other side!). The parallel to reading Scripture is obvious. By seeing the text all around and by noting its structural apparatus (including boundaries), one gets a broader perspective on context, becoming aware of the structure intended by the author. In some sense, analyzing structure at the level of observation helps to keep us on the road, knowing what text to study and why this is contextually important.

A notable example of this is John's account of Jesus's encounter with Nicodemus. While the chapter division occurs at 3:1, there are several links between 2:23–25 and 3:1–2 that suggest that John, the author, intentionally used 2:23–25 as a bridge from the previous pericope (the clearing of the temple, 2:13–22) to the Nicodemus narrative. For example, in 2:25 the evangelist points out that Jesus knew what was "in man." Then, in 3:1 the introduction reads, with obvious redundancy, "Now there was *a man* of the Pharisees . . ." Why "*man* of the Pharisees"? In the original Greek as in English, "Now there was *a Pharisee*" would have been perfectly acceptable and stylistically more elegant. Yet John, by repeating the word "man" (Greek *anthrōpos*), wanted to stress that Nicodemus was one of these people, mentioned in 2:25, to whom Jesus did not entrust himself because they didn't truly understand who he was (i.e., the Messiah and Son of God). The evangelist even repeats the word "signs" in both 2:23 and 3:2, drawing attention to the fact that the signs Jesus performed in Jerusalem before people's very eyes were the same signs for which Nicodemus commended Jesus in 3:2. Yet, as Jesus's response to Nicodemus shows, Jesus didn't trust the rabbi's flattery and opening pleasantries. He instructed the "Teacher of Israel" (3:10) about his need for spiritual rebirth (3:3, 5).

The second goal in analyzing structure is to grasp "the authorially intended vehicles for communicating meaning and a particular theological message."[14] This, of course, suggests a link between observation and interpretation, as should be expected. After all, while ideally sequential, observation and interpretation often work in tandem, with observation influencing accurate interpretation *through* the inductive process. Consider the interpretation of "time" in Ecclesiastes chapter 3. The concept is prevalent from 3:1 until 3:17, with 3:2–8 comprising the famous poem on time,[15] 3:11 stating that "He has made everything appropriate in its time" (inferring either actual time or appropriate time), and 3:15 citing the repetition of events on the time/space continuum.[16] Interpreting the poem on time is notoriously difficult because of the semantic flexibility of the term (in English *and* in Hebrew). Time can refer to *actual* time (a point on the time/space continuum) or *appropriate* time (the right time to plant, the right time to harvest). The emphasis on God's sovereignty in the chapter may infer *determined* time, but the aura of wisdom in the book might suggest *ideal* time (the ability to make choices according to *appropriate* time). However, another motif in the chapter (and the book as a whole) is God's judgment (3:16–17a). When you recognize the structural link between 3:1

---

14. Köstenberger and Patterson, *Invitation to Biblical Interpretation*, 603.

15. This poem is often referred to by commentators as the "catalog of times."

16. The final line of verse 15 may infer determined time (as per the HCSB: "God repeats what has passed") or appointed time (a "day of reckoning," as per the NIV 1984: "and God will call the past to account").

and 3:17 (*inclusio*; the language pertaining to a "time for everything" is repeated between 3:1 and 3:17), then it's natural to include all of these concepts into the writer's musings on time (the *inclusio* infers that the meaning of "time" in Ecclesiastes chapter 3 isn't limited to either determined time, appropriate time, or appointed time, but encompasses all three). While this is a rather complex example, it does speak to the impact structural observations can have on interpretation.

By including a chapter on structural analysis among the steps of observation, we aren't trying to teach elaborate analytical techniques but rather to provide general awareness of those structural features that you ought to be looking for as a means of discerning literary units and structural function. In reality, an analytical reading of Scripture beyond the observation level often does entail techniques for diagramming (in exegesis) and outlining (in homiletics). However, such an approach tends to get bogged down in the details of proper format, and students often lose sight of the goal set before them (discerning the structure of the text, natural literary units, and their significance in written communication). Therefore, our approach in this chapter is simply to draw attention to and create awareness of the four primary aspects of structural analysis that provide an inductive advantage in the observation of Scripture.

Table 7.1 — Four Primary Aspects of Structural Analysis	
Aspect	**Definition**
1. Boundary Features	Markers which help the reader determine where one unit in a larger text begins and ends.
2. Structural Formulas	The way a text is intentionally constructed to portray the author's intended message.
3. Cohesion	The basic qualities which unify a literary unit.
4. Relationship	The connection(s) within and between literary units.

Four Primary Aspects of Structural Analysis

Boundary Features

In discerning the separation of one literary unit from another, there's simply nothing more important than learning to see boundary features in the text. This is in fact a very practical measure, as the proper delineation of a text is critical for inductive Bible study.[17] But ask ten individuals where to begin and where to end their study of a portion of a book of the Bible, and you'll likely get several answers (often dictated by the subheadings in the various study Bibles those individuals are using). That said, we trust that an eye trained to see boundary features in the text will be capable of discerning where to begin and where to end a particular study of Scripture in keeping with authorial intent.

At the very outset, we can't state emphatically enough that what we're after in inductive Bible study is not the interpreter's *own* creative structural outline but a discerning, perceptive approximation of the *biblical author's* way of structuring his material. Let us say it again in case anyone missed it: discerning the literary structure of a given book or unit of the Bible isn't about *us*; it's about determining in what way the biblical authors *themselves* organized and presented their narrative, discourse, or poetry. This calls for perceptiveness, and a certain amount of knowledge of ancient literary conventions, more than it calls for creativity or clever homiletical moves on our part.

Here we survey the three most basic kinds of boundary features: (1) initial markers that begin a new unit; (2) final markers that close a unit; and (3) *inclusio*, a literary means to "wrap" a unit with parallel "bookends," thus indicating the beginning and the end of a unit. As you would expect, among these three there's a vast array of literary means by which boundaries are marked, often dictated by genre. The examples listed on the following pages are merely representative—but enough to indicate the kind of phrases that you should be looking for.

---

17. Ultimately, the proper delineation of a text is also critical for preaching and teaching the Bible. See Köstenberger and Patterson, *Invitation to Biblical Interpretation*, 595.

(1) *Initial markers* indicate that a new literary unit has begun. Common markers in the Epistles include vocative address ("Dear children," 1 John 2:1, 12; "brethren," Jas 1:2; 2:1; 3:1; 1 Cor 14:6, 20, 26, 39), rhetorical question (Jas 2:14; 3:13; 4:1; 1 Cor 15:12, 35), conjunctions of inference ("therefore," Rom 12:1; Eph 4:1, 17; Heb 12:1, 12), adverbial indicators ("finally," (Eph 6:10; Phil 3:1; 4:8), and topic statements ("Now concerning . . . ," 1 Cor 7:1; 8:1; 12:1). In narrative, initial markers are typically phrases that indicate changes in time, setting, character, or situation ("In the spring when kings march out to war . . . ," 2 Sam 11:1; "There was a man in Caesarea named Cornelius . . . ," Acts 10:1; "About that time King Herod cruelly attacked . . . ," Acts 12:1). Prophetic literature will often employ markers to indicate new oracles. Many are external to the oracle ("This is the word that came to Jeremiah from the LORD," Jer 11:1), while others comprise the opening statement in the oracle ("Now it shall come to pass in the later days," Mic 4:4 NKJV).

(2) *Final markers* indicate that a literary unit has come to a conclusion. The Epistles often include formal markers such as doxologies (Eph 3:20–21) and benedictions (Eph 6:23–24). Narratives frequently provide summary statements (Matt 4:23–25; John 4:54) or formulaic conclusions (2 Kgs 20:20–21; 21:7–18; 21:25–26). Narratives will occasionally conclude a pericope (narrative unit) with commentary (John 3:16–21, 31–36) or extended theological summation (2 Kgs 17:7–23). It is common for the prophets to conclude an oracle with confirmation of divine authority ("The LORD has spoken," Amos 5:17) or intent ("Then they shall know that I am Yahweh," Ezek 36:38; common and distinctive to Ezekiel).

(3) *Inclusio* provides the means of marking the beginning and the ending of a literary unit, often through parallel phraseology or subject matter. A classic example of this technique is seen in Ecclesiastes 1:2 and 12:8 with the proclamation, "Vanity of vanities, all is vanity" (NKJV; Heb. *hevel* in the superlative). Between these "bookend" statements, the idea of life lived in a *hevel* ("vain," "absurd," or "fleeting") world is

examined inside and out.[18] Or consider a less obvious example in Ecclesiastes, the programmatic search for gain (Heb. *yitron*) that drives the initial quest in the book (Eccl 1:3; 3:9).

The prophets often use *inclusio* as a means of reinforcing the declaration of judgment or the proclamation of salvation. Compare Hosea 1:10–2:1 to 2:21–23 and notice the bracketing language and content that embraces the subject matter between these prophetic statements. Also, *inclusio* is common in narrative as a means to surrounding the text with an opening or closing theme (often communicating the theological emphasis in the narrative).

Consider the reference to John the Baptist in John 10:40–42, for example. Why does the evangelist mention the Baptist here in his narrative? At first this seems rather puzzling, for John hasn't been heard of in the Gospel since chapter 5. Clearly, events have taken us far beyond John's ministry. In fact, the narrative is inching ever closer to Jesus's crucifixion in the midst of escalating conflict and controversy with the antagonistic Jewish authorities. The reason for mentioning John the Baptist here lies in the evangelist's desire to include an unmistakable structural marker that signals to his readers that the book dealing with John the Baptist is now approaching closure. What started in 1:19 with the public appearance of John the Baptist (anticipated in the prologue: 1:6–8, 15) has come to a close, as far as the narrative is concerned, in 10:40–42. With that, it's time to move on to the account of Jesus's crucifixion and resurrection. And what better way to do so than with the account of Lazarus's resurrection from the dead, in anticipation of the resurrection of none other than Jesus himself!

---

18. The metaphor of *hevel* (lit. "mist" or "vapor") describes various aspects, experiences, and judgments concerning the fallen world. See D. M. Clemens, "The Law of Sin and Death: Ecclesiastes and Genesis 1–3," *Themelios* 19 (1994): 5–8.

Table 7.2 — Three Basic Kinds of Boundary Features		
Boundary Feature	**Definition**	**Examples**
Initial Markers	The indicator that a new literary unit has begun.	2 Samuel 11:1; Jeremiah 11:1; Micah 4:4; Acts 10:1; 12:1; Romans 12:1; 1 Corinthians 7:1; 8:1; 12:1; 14:6, 20, 26, 39; 15:12, 35; Ephesians 4:1, 17; 6:10; Philippians 3:1; 4:8; Hebrews 12:1, 12; James 1:2; 2:1, 14; 3:1, 13; 4:1; 1 John 2:1, 12
Final Markers	The indicator that a literary unit has come to a conclusion.	2 Kings 17:7–23; 20:20–21; 21:7–18; 21:25–26; Ezekiel 36:38; Amos 5:17; Matthew 4:23–25; John 3:16–21, 31–36; 4:54; Ephesians 3:20–21; 6:23–24
Inclusio	A literary means to "wrap" a unit with parallel "bookends," often by employing parallel phraseology or subject matter.	Ecclesiastes 1:2; 12:8; Hosea 1:10–2:1; 2:21–23

Structural Formulas

While boundary features indicate the clearest demarcation between literary units, it's the structural form of the text that gives character to a particular literary unit. Observing the structure of the text isn't merely an academic exercise. Biblical authors communicate meaning through the arrangement and structure of the words they write, and thus an observation of literary form (how they say it) is a necessary first step in understanding the literary function of the text (even if merely aesthetic). Analyzing structural formulas can be a monumental task involving considerable literary expertise, and naturally not every Bible student will achieve expert status in this endeavor. However, there are common structural techniques employed through most literary genres that are rather straightforward. Learning to recognize standard structural patterns is a helpful aid in seeing literary units in the Bible, appreciating the aesthetics of the text, and ultimately understanding the function behind the framework of the text.

The following structural patterns are more often found in poetry than in prose, but a careful reading will find these patterns throughout most biblical genres. For the sake of conciseness, we are surveying the four most significant structural strategies in the Bible: repetition, parallelism, chiasm, and acrostic.

(1) Although *repetition* is a standard point of observation (covered in chapter 6), in broader structural terms repetition will often reveal the framework of literary units. Consider the literary structure of Genesis, built around the recurring phrase "these are the generations/history/record of . . ." (Gen 2:4; 5:1; 6:9; 10:1; 11:10; 11:27; 25:12; 25:19; 36:1; 37:2).[19] The repetition of this phrase throughout the book indicates an intentional, structural framework, a natural outline built according to the author's specifications.

A similar technique is used by John in his Gospel. A poignant example is the repetition of references to Jesus's "hour" in John 2:4; 7:6; 8:20; and 12:24. By including this phrase, and by repeating it from time to time, the evangelist gradually builds suspense, orienting his readers that there was an inexorable buildup to the crucifixion until, finally, in John 12:33 the veil is lifted (as far as the narrative is concerned) and the evangelist announces boldly that Jesus, by speaking of his own "lifting up," predicted "what kind of death he would die" (i.e., crucifixion).

Furthermore, songs and poetry in the Old Testament are often arranged around repeated refrains. The Song of Songs appears to be ordered by a repeated refrain (Song 2:7; 3:5; 8:4), while many Psalms are also similarly structured around refrains. In addition, the book of Ecclesiastes is in some form structured around the repetition of the "enjoy life" refrain (Eccl 2:24; 3:12, 22; 5:18–20; 8:15; 9:7–10; 11:9–10).

(2) *Parallelism*, common between lines of poetry, is also found in broader structural arrangements throughout the Bible. The book of

---

19. Known as the "*toledoth* formula," so named after the Hebrew phrase translated "these are the generations of."

Jonah has rich examples of parallelism in phrase and thought. For example, note the repetition and parallel phrases in the narrative describing Jonah's response to the repentance of Nineveh (4:1–4) and his response to the withered plant (4:5–9). The whole book of Jonah provides a great exercise in observation as one draws out the numerous parallels in word, phrase, and content throughout the narrative.[20]

(3) *Chiasm* is so named after the Greek letter *chi* which resembles the English X. Chiasm is a thematic "crisscrossing" between adjacent lines of poetry, sometimes occurring in extended passages of prose literature. Chiasm is most obvious when structured around parallel words and phrases, but careful observation will often reveal chiasm structured around concepts and themes (this is more common in narrative). Chiasm can exist between corresponding lines or broad literary units and may structure an entire book or just two adjacent lines.[21] Consider as an example Isaiah 6:10 (ESV); the first line corresponds with the sixth line, the second with the fifth, and the third with the fourth. The main body of thought then meets in the middle between lines three and four (thus the crisscross effect), with the seventh line (in this case) functioning as a capstone to the verse.

> A Make the heart of this people dull,
> > B And their ears heavy,
> > > C And blind their eyes;
> > > C' Lest they see with their eyes,
> > B' And hear with their ears,
> A' And understand with their hearts,
> > And turn and be healed.

---

20. Only later do we contemplate the function of these as an interpreter.
21. This sentence is actually chiastic in structure—can you see the pattern?

An example of chiastic structure framing the themes of a narrative can be observed in the book of Ruth. Consider the following proposal to outlining Ruth:[22]

A Introduction: Devastation of Naomi's family (1:1–5)

  B Naomi's two relatives deliberate whether to support her (1:6–22)

    C Ruth goes out to Boaz's field: Boaz's support and generosity (2:1–23)

    C' Ruth goes out to the threshing floor: Boaz's support and generosity (3:1–18)

  B' Naomi's two relatives deliberate whether to support her (4:1–12)

A' Conclusion: Restoration of Naomi's family (4:13–22)

Determining chiastic structure in a broad, thought-oriented framework is often subjective but nonetheless appears to be a valid literary observation, especially in the Old Testament. With eyes trained to see chiasm in Scripture, one comes to appreciate just how significant this is as a structuring device.[23] This highlights once again that literary genre is not a timeless, abstract phenomenon but has an important historical dimension. While some of the literary structuring devices found in the Bible (both Old and New Testament) are no longer used in modern English, Scripture mirrors ancient Near Eastern and Greco-Roman literary conventions that must be discerned by the careful interpreter of God's Word even where there are no contemporary literary parallels.

(4) As noted earlier, *acrostics* are highly structured arrangements where each line of poetry begins with a successive letter of the Hebrew alphabet (twenty-two consonantal letters). Perhaps the most famous of these is Psalm 119, where the entire Psalm is framed around the succession of acrostic subunits, each of which contains eight lines where the

---

22. David A. Dorsey, *The Literary Structure of the Old Testament: A Commentary on Genesis–Malachi* (Grand Rapids: Baker, 1999), 128. Although Dorsey makes many helpful observations in his structural commentary of the Old Testament, one could certainly accuse him of finding chiasm where none was ever intended by the biblical author. There is a danger in developing chiasm from the imagination.

23. See ibid. for a survey of chiasm in the Old Testament.

first letter of the first word of each line begins with the same letter of the Hebrew alphabet. Once eight lines are completed, the psalm proceeds to the next successive letter of the alphabet. Most English translations help the reader to see the acrostic by placing a Hebrew letter in the text to indicate which successive letter is next in line. Although many other psalms contain full or partial acrostics (9, 10, 25, 34, 37, 11, 112, 145), these are difficult to recognize as translation makes it impossible to retain the artistry of the pattern.

Table 7.3 — Four Kinds of Structural Formulas		
Structural Formula	**Definition**	**Examples**
Repetition	A recurring word or phrase within a unit.	Genesis 2:4; 5:1; 6:9; 10:1; 11:10; 11:27; 25:12; 25:19; 36:1; 37:2 John 2:4, 7:6, 8:20, and 12:24 Ecclesiastes 2:24; 3:12, 22; 5:18–20; 8:15; 9:7–10; 11:9–10
Parallelism	Corresponding phrases or thoughts.	Jonah 4:1–4 and 4:5–9
Chiasm	A thematic "crisscrossing" between adjacent lines of poetry.	Isaiah 6:10 Ruth 1–4
Acrostic	A poetic device where each line begins with a successive letter of the alphabet.	Psalm 119 Psalm 9, 10, 11, 25, 34, 37, 112, and 145 (all partial acrostics)

Cohesion

While boundary features provide some indication of where a literary unit begins and ends, the internal cohesion of the unit identifies a unit as such. Without cohesion, communication collapses and fails to provide coherent ideas. As George Guthrie aptly observes, "Cohesion is the quality of a text that gives it unity."[24] Observing cohesion in a textual unit is necessary to thinking according to contextual parts. Many of these observations are so "matter of fact" that it hardly seems necessary to address them here, but they are so foundational to interpretation that we would be negligent not to include them. There are a number of different qualities that hold a text together. Among the most basic of these are genre and subgenre, content, setting (in place and time), and language (vocabulary and grammar).

(1) *Genre and subgenre* provide one of the most obvious qualities that hold literary units together. Conversely, a change in genre or subgenre often (but not always) indicates a shift from one unit to another. This is perhaps clearest in the Old Testament prophets and the Gospels but can be seen throughout Scripture. Consider books such as Isaiah, Jeremiah, and Ezekiel. A survey of these books reveals numerous prophetic subgenres, including judgment speeches, salvation oracles, laments, visions, prophetic drama, biographical narrative, allegory, and even letters (see, e.g., Jeremiah 29).[25] Likewise, the Gospels contain diverse subgenres such as genealogy, songs, parables, allegory, woe speeches, narrative dialogue, sermons, and commentary. A quick glance at the first chapter of Matthew demonstrates a clear shift in genre between the genealogy in verses 1–17 and the narrative that begins in verse 18. A similar shift in genre separates the first eighteen verses of John's Gospel (the "prologue") from the opening narrative starting in verse 19. Recognizable shifts in genre can likewise be found chapter by chapter throughout the Gospels, and in virtually every book of the Bible.

(2) *Content* is perhaps the most obvious aspect of cohesion in the text. Cohesive subject matter lacks formal structure, but nonetheless constitutes a way in which textual units are identified. Actually, cohesion in content is at the core of what it means to have a contextually contained unit and thus has significant impact on interpretation. In the New Testament epistles, cohesion in content is often characterized by a progressive line of argument addressing a particular issue, while in the

---

24. Guthrie, "Discourse Analysis," 258.

25. For a fuller list and survey of prophetic subgenres, see Köstenberger and Patterson, *Invitation to Biblical Interpretation*, 321–40.

prophets it may revolve around the subject of an oracle. The content of narrative tends to cohere around characters and plot. Each book of the Bible will have its own matters of content typical of its genre and the purpose of the book itself, but within a book there are often numerous shifts in subject matter (again, the twists and turns of the narrative, nestled between recurring banquet scenes in the book of Esther, may serve as a convenient example). Analytical observation will discern cohesion in content and shifts between subject matter, considering these as foundational to contextual awareness.

(3) Cohesion in *setting*, including space and time, is foundational to distinguishing individual units (pericopes) in narrative literature (see, e.g., the initial setting indicated in Esther 1:1–4). As noted earlier, temporal and spatial markers indicate shifts in setting, but once established, the setting in narrative naturally remains intact until another marker indicates a change (the first of a series of banquets in the book of Esther commences in 1:5). Observing setting in narrative is typically clear. However, in prophetic literature setting is often more difficult to determine. While time and location is clearly marked in some oracles, in others we can only speculate on the setting.[26] Similarly, the setting of certain psalms is often open to conjecture. But even when initial markers don't provide clarity in determining setting, a cohesive setting, however inexact, nonetheless establishes the literary unit as such.

(4) *Common language* (grammar and vocabulary) provides an additional aspect of cohesion to the text. This is best observed in the original languages but is often apparent in translation as well. Any unified segment of the text ought to have grammatical cohesion (subject-verb agreement, relative pronouns, etc.). When these elements shift, this is normally an indication that a transition is taking place between units. For instance, in the Song of Songs the primary marker noting a shift in speaker (between the man and the woman) involves the gender of pronouns. In addition, in any discourse a cohesive line of argument is also dependent upon the

---

26. As anthologies, the prophetic books will often not provide a setting for spoken oracles, and even the events and situation of those oracles often lack chronological order in the prophetic books. However, some books provide clearly marked setting and chronological progression (Haggai is a notable example).

conjunctions and prepositions that tie the pieces together. When grammar indicates a shift in voice, or conjunctions indicate a change in direction, there may be movement from one unit to another.

Vocabulary also identifies unity in the text or disunity between texts. Common language is an obvious point of connectivity and cohesion within a text, whereas changes in vocabulary often mark a transition between literary units. Consider the complementary creation accounts in Genesis 1:1–2:3 and 2:4–4:26. The opening unit is noted for its use of *elohim* (translated into English as "God") while the later account applies the covenant name to God, *Yahweh* (often translated into English as "LORD"). An analytical reading of the first four chapters of Genesis should not ignore the distinction in vocabulary. At the very least, it's clear that two literary units exist in these opening chapters, even if an explanation is open to debate.[27]

The significance of structure and cohesion in analytical observation (and interpretation) is well illustrated with an example from the book of Amos. Chapters 1 and 2 of Amos contain a highly structured series of six sequential oracles against the nations surrounding Israel, each oracle corresponding to one another in genre, structure (including numeric formula), language, and content. After announcing a seventh oracle against Judah (Amos 2:1–3), the Israelite audience would expect closure, but instead Amos launches into the most stinging indictment against Israel, effectively trapping his audience by issuing an unexpected eighth oracle (also related to the previous seven in terms of form, language, and content). In whole, the first two chapters of Amos function together as a "rhetoric of entrapment,"[28] a self-contained unit within the book. The entire unit demands to be studied as a whole—to do otherwise would cloud the point and destroy the power of the message. However, in Amos 3:1 an entirely new oracle begins, distinct from the numeric oracles that comprise the first two chapters. It is appropriate, then, to study Amos

---

27. Although critical scholarship has traditionally attributed these accounts as originating from separate sources, literary explanation may in fact provide greater interpretive insight (separate units with distinct purposes in a unified, authored book).

28. Robert Alter, *The Art of Biblical Poetry* (New York: Basic, 1985), 144.

chapter 3 apart from chapters 1 and 2—a new unit has begun.[29] This illustrates the significance of observing structure and cohesion.

Table 7.4 — Four Kinds of Cohesion	
Type of Cohesion	**Definition**
Genre and subgenre	Classifications for types of literature which are based on similarities between form, style, and subject matter.
Content	Similarity in subject matter that unites a unit.
Setting	Common elements related to time and space.
Common language	Similarities in grammar and vocabulary that unite a unit.

Relationship

The observation of relationship within and between literary units is built upon the notion that communication requires a logical interplay between parts, and that how parts are conjoined reveals as much meaning as the individual parts. Analytical observation requires an awareness of basic relationships between the building blocks of written communication. Simply put, the parts of any given discourse, at whatever level, play roles in relationship with one another, and an analytical approach to observation will seek to identify those roles.[30] Those roles are identified by describing the function of words, phrases, and clauses in relationship to the broader text. Potential dynamics between phrases and clauses within a unit of discourse include cause and effect, sequential listing, contrast and comparison, reason, purpose and design, result or consequence, means, manner, inference, summation, elaboration, conclusion, analogy and illustration, command, and concession. However, our focus in this chapter is to review basic relationships between parts in the broad

---

29. Interestingly, Amos 3:2–8 is comprised of a series of interrelated rhetorical questions, each question functioning together to form a complete literary unit. With Amos 3:9, another unit begins.

30. Guthrie, "Discourse Analysis," 257.

arena of literary units rather than the details of sentence syntax. These relationships include interchange, inference (between broader literary units), prominence (within literary units), parenthetical commentary, pivot episodes, and hinge statements.[31] Detailed grammatical analysis lies beyond the scope of this book and is best relegated to the field of original language syntax.[32]

(1) *Interchange* involves the intentional contrast and comparison between narrative figures and events. With the use of interchange, the narrator is able to convey his message *through* points of contrast and comparison. Significant examples of interchange in biblical narrative include the narrative details contrasting or comparing Saul with David in 1 Samuel and Peter with Paul in the book of Acts. These examples transcend multiple pericopes within the books of Samuel and Acts, but often interchange is contained in tighter segments, such as the narratives contrasting Rahab with Achan in Joshua 2–7 (noted in an earlier illustration).

(2) As noted in chapter 6, conjunctions of *inference* suggest a logical relationship between conjoined literary units, especially in the New Testament epistles. In determining the relationship between literary units, one should not underestimate the significance of words such as "therefore" in directing the flow of major units of thought. Consider the example of Hebrews 12:1 in guiding the direction of discourse between major units of thought using a conjunction of inference ("therefore"). Based upon the writer's survey of the "faith hall of fame," he now moves on to exhort his audience to follow the Old Testament examples of faithfulness. Hebrews 11:39 brings the prior unit to conclusion, while Hebrews 12:1 begins a

---

31. For an alternative treatment of semantic, structural relationships, see David R. Bauer and Robert A. Traina, *Inductive Bible Study: A Comprehensive Guide to the Practice of Hermeneutics* (Grand Rapids: Baker Academic, 2011), 97–116. They survey the following list of semantic structures: contrast, comparison, climax, particularization, generalization, causation, substantiation, cruciality, summarization, interrogation, preparation/realization, and instrumentation.

32. For a thorough treatment of Hebrew syntax, see Bruce K. Waltke and Michael O'Connor, *An Introduction to Biblical Hebrew Syntax* (Winona Lake, IN: Eisenbrauns, 1990). The standard advanced Greek grammar is Daniel B. Wallace, *Greek Grammar beyond the Basics* (Grand Rapids: Zondervan, 1996); see also the abridgement *The Basics of New Testament Syntax* (Grand Rapids: Zondervan, 2000); and the intermediate grammar by Andreas J. Köstenberger, Benjamin L. Merkle, and Robert L. Plummer, *Going Deeper with New Testament Greek: An Intermediate Study of the Grammar and Syntax of the New Testament* (Nashville: B&H Academic, 2016).

new unit; yet this unit of exhortation is integrally related to the discourse survey in chapter 11. The point of inference—the "therefore" that introduces the new unit—does more to connect the two relationally than to divide them conceptually.

(3) An obvious feature of discourse is that all parts of the text don't function equally in terms of *prominence*. In other words, in order to communicate ideas writers will necessarily place emphasis on certain elements of the text, thereby minimizing others. Again, communication is more than simply the sum of lexical parts, and the ability of writers to place emphasis on certain points adds distinction between those parts. Without such emphasis, discourse would be flat, if not "virtually unintelligible."[33]

Discerning prominence in discourse is rather intuitive, yet there are observable strategies for conveying prominence (or emphasis) in writing. Punctuation (at least in English) does convey emphasis, but the flow of language itself can also communicate emphasis. This is often borne out in Paul's writing, where his style is anything but bland. Consider texts such as Philippians 3:2–10 or Romans 6–8. Even with the exclamation marks removed, an audible reading of these texts will reveal an ebb and flow that is intuitive and unmistakable.

However, in narrative, discourse prominence is often more subtle and relates to plot development and peaking. Thus Jesus's instruction to his followers to remain "in him" spiritually after his departure in John 15:1–10 may constitute the peak of the Farewell Discourse in John 13:31–16:33. More obvious is the climax of the account of the raising of Lazarus, which culminates in Jesus crying out with a loud voice, "Lazarus, come out [of the tomb]!" (John 11:43) and is resolved by Lazarus's immediate, albeit silent, compliance narrated in the following verse. Remarkably, once the narrative peak has been reached, the account immediately shifts gears with an abrupt change in setting, from the empty tomb of Lazarus to a meeting of the Sanhedrin plotting Jesus's demise (John 11:45ff).

---

33. Köstenberger and Patterson, *Invitation to Biblical Interpretation*, 598.

(4) Within narrative discourse, it's important to discern between the narrator's depiction of events, including dialogue, and his own *parenthetical commentary*. Many translations will include parentheses to mark what they believe are parenthetical comments, but their marks are not in the original text, and most translations won't include them either. As an exercise in discerning parenthetical commentary, read John 11:1–44 (the raising of Lazarus). Which verses appear to contain the comments of the evangelist, addressed to his "reading" audience? Are there any markers that distinguish these as parenthetical?[34]

(5) When reading prose literature, note major breaks in the storyline (for narrative) or the line of argument (for epistolary discourse). These shifts may be signaled by *pivot episodes* or *hinge statements* that indicate a change in the flow of thought or highlight the purpose of the discourse that precedes or follows the "hinge statement." In the David narratives, the David and Bathsheba pericope (2 Samuel 11) acts as a pivotal episode in David's life, with the tumult following the episode illustrating the consequences of the conditional aspect of the Davidic covenant (2 Sam 7:14).

Or consider Hebrews 8:1, a rather obvious hinge providing orientation within the complex line of argument of that book: "Now the main point of what is being said is this: We have this kind of high priest, who sat down at the right hand of the throne of the Majesty in the heavens. . . ." Just in case the reader needs clarification on what has been covered thus far, the writer of Hebrews provides a summary (the prior chapters 5–7 dealing with the high priestly role of Christ). But in Hebrews 8:2 the next tier in the author's line of argument is introduced, and the hinge is formed: "a minister of the sanctuary and the true tabernacle that was set up by the Lord and not man." What follows in Hebrews 8:3–10:18 is essentially an elaboration upon Hebrews 8:2, the "back end" of the hinge.

---

34. Discerning parenthetical comments is clear in translations such as the NET, which uses parentheses. The NET translators have placed John 11:2, 5, 13, 16b, 18–19, 30, 38b, 51–52, and 57 in parentheses.

Table 7.5 — Five Types of Discourse Relationships		
Type of Relationship	Definition	Examples
Interchange	Intentional contrast and comparison between narrative figures and events	Rahab and Achan (Joshua 1–7) Saul and David Peter and Paul
Inference	A logical relationship between conjoined literary units	Hebrews 12:1
Prominence	An emphasis on certain elements of the text	John 15:1–10 (within the overarching context of 13:31–16:33) Romans 6–8 Philippians 3:2–10
Parenthetical Commentary	Comments made by the narrator within a narrative text	John 11:1–44
Hinge Statements	Major breaks and pivots in the storyline or the line of argument in a discourse	2 Samuel 11 Hebrews 8:1–3; 8:3–10:18

Final Thoughts

For many, the observation of structure and form in inductive Bible study has been virtually synonymous with outlining (for preaching) and sentence diagraming (for exegesis). It's our contention that, while helpful, we must not place too high a priority on either of these as a means of organizing the text. It's highly unlikely that any of the biblical authors ever intended their messages to be outlined or diagrammed, and in some cases these procedures can actually impose a false structure on the text. However, as we observe the structure of the text intended by the original author, rather than outline the text merely to suit our own purposes in organizing the Scriptures for preaching and teaching, we believe that a more accurate approach to analytical reading is achieved.

As noted in the opening paragraph of this chapter, exegesis and inductive study have traditionally been preoccupied with the meaning of words and the function of grammar, often with little regard to genre or the literary structure of the larger discourse. What's more, traditional approaches to preaching have often taught that the biblical text (regardless of genre or inherent literary structure) should be compartmentalized into various "preachable" outlines compatible to congregational expectations (three points and a poem, etc.). However, by "tracing the concrete makeup and contours of the biblical text to teach and preach it accordingly," we believe that you can achieve a better, more accurate outcome.[35] We trust that this chapter has helped you make discernible progress toward that end.

---

35. Köstenberger and Patterson, *Invitation to Biblical Interpretation*, 594.

UNIT III

INTERPRETATION
Investigating the Text

Five Steps of Interpretation

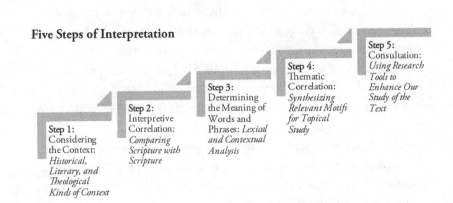

Step 1: Considering the Context: *Historical, Literary, and Theological Kinds of Context*

Step 2: Interpretive Correlation: *Comparing Scripture with Scripture*

Step 3: Determining the Meaning of Words and Phrases: *Lexical and Contextual Analysis*

Step 4: Thematic Correlation: *Synthesizing Relevant Motifs for Topical Study*

Step 5: Consultation: *Using Research Tools to Enhance Our Study of the Text*

8

Considering the Context
Historical, Literary, and Theological Kinds of Context

"Context, context, and context"—it should now be obvious that context is the number one factor in determining meaning. On the surface this seems rather simple. The meaning of words, phrases, and literary units of all sorts is always determined by context. However, as a matter of interpretation, considering the context is more complex than you might first think. There are various *kinds* of context that must be considered, all of which are vying for attention in accord with a careful reading of the biblical text. Interpreting Scripture begins by considering not just one but many aspects of context.[1]

Behind our philosophy of interpretation is the recognition that a valid, balanced approach to Bible study must incorporate an appreciation of the impact that history, literature, and theology has on the text. In simplest terms, the Bible is literature based in history that communicates a theological message. Put another way, God, who is immanent in history, inspired a text, and through this text has revealed himself. Thinking contextually must therefore incorporate an appreciation of the

---

1. This chapter focuses on aspects and facets of context that apply specifically to interpretation. In some sense, the context of the reader often influences interpretation through various forms of preunderstanding. However, in the spirit of attempted objectivity (as much as this is attainable), our emphasis in interpretation is on those aspects of context that flow from the author and the text, not the reader. This is not to deny that the reader has a context in which Scripture is appropriated. Indeed, application requires contextualization of the ancient text into one's own situation. However, in the interpretive stage of inductive Bible study, we aren't asking (yet) what the text *means* to me (or us) today but what it *meant* according to the intent of the original author. It's the context associated with the author and the text that we're exploring as interpreters of the sacred text of Scripture.

Bible as history, literature, and theology—to neglect any of these three components would be shortsighted, failing to understand what the Bible essentially is.

In this chapter we present a consideration of context that embraces each aspect of the hermeneutical triad.[2] Just as the historical, literary, and theological aspects of the Word of God don't stand or function alone, so the various kinds of context surveyed in this chapter don't function independently of each other. In most cases, considering the context will incorporate most if not all of the various kinds of context covered in this chapter. However, in order to grasp the unique characteristics and roles pertaining to each, we categorize the different kinds of context under the headings pertaining to each side of the triad (history, literature, and theology).

How do you consider the context as a step of interpretation? As with the steps of observation, it should be clear that interpretation is anything but formulaic. Yet even though context can't be grasped through a simple equation, there are points to consider along the way to thinking contextually. In our experience, there are three elements that are indispensable. The first is *awareness*. Simply put, we must be aware of the need to think contextually. Most interpretive breaches of context come as a result of ignorance rather than intentional neglect. For some, the idea of thinking contextually is new, a game changer of sorts. Many faithful Christians have simply never learned to think contextually, often because they have not had a contextually sensitive approach to the Bible modeled before them. What's more, many people lack an awareness of the various kinds of context that need to be properly distinguished and discerned in their study of the Bible. Even those who are aware of the general concept of thinking contextually may have never thought of thinking according to multiple aspects of context associated with history, literature, and theology. And so awareness is critical—first, an awareness of the need to think

---

2. For an in-depth presentation, see Andreas J. Köstenberger and Richard D. Patterson, *Invitation to Biblical Interpretation: The Hermeneutical Triad of History, Literature, and Theology* (Grand Rapids: Kregel, 2011); see also the abridged version by the same authors, *For the Love of God's Word: An Introduction to Biblical Interpretation* (Grand Rapids: Kregel, 2015).

contextually, and second, an awareness of the various kinds of context that need to be considered.

Figure 8.1: Three Keys to Thinking Contextually

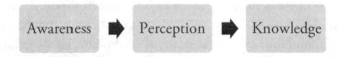

The second area that influences our ability to think contextually is *perception*. Interestingly, the Greek language has multiple words for seeing. On the one hand, there's the more basic word *blepō*, which simply refers to physical seeing. On the other is the more sophisticated *theaomai* (from which we get our English word "theater") that indicates actual perception beyond mere physical seeing. While this is admittedly simplifying matters, the following example bears out the importance of this distinction. When John writes that he and his fellow apostles "saw" Jesus's glory (John 1:14; the Greek word, you guessed it, is *theaomai*), his point is that they *perceived* in Jesus's words and actions that he truly was the One and Only Son of the Father, God incarnate (check out the context and ultimately the message of the entire Gospel). In other places, John makes mere reference to physical seeing.[3]

Thus the biblical record underscores that perception, moving beyond mere physical seeing, is of supreme importance in apprehending spiritual, theological truth. Thus Kevin Vanhoozer is correct when he observes that "Hermeneutics involves more than a wooden application of methodological principles; hermeneutics requires good judgment."[4] We would agree, and carry that sentiment to the specific realm of considering context. With experience, students learn to perceive when and how context is influencing the interpretation of the text. Interpreters must exercise restraint to avoid reading too much into a contextual inference and yet be open to embracing all that the text is actually saying in

---

3. E.g., John 1:18; 20:29.
4. Kevin J. Vanhoozer, *Is There a Meaning in This Text? The Bible, the Reader, and the Morality of Literary Knowledge* (Grand Rapids: Zondervan, 1998), 140.

context. Perception is the wisdom to discern the variables, to possess sensitivity to know to what degree context should (or shouldn't) influence interpretive conclusions.

Finally, the third area is *knowledge*. Although this is self-evident, we're here specifically targeting the knowledge of biblical background (pertaining to historical events, geography, and culture), literary genres, and theological motifs. All of these matters are explained under various kinds of context in the following pages. However, at this point it's worth noting that the more you know, the better equipped you become in applying that knowledge to the consideration of context, and ultimately to the interpretation of the text. This shouldn't discourage but rather encourage you. How could a new believer apply significant knowledge of first-century Jewish religious expectations to his reading of the Gospels? Or how could someone new to the Bible differentiate between prophetic subgenres? Obviously he'd be unable to do so without additional study, even if he were aware of the need to consider these things. The more you're able to apply your growing knowledge of background information—whether in history, literature, or theology—to the consideration of context, the more competently you'll interpret Scripture.

Considering the context is absolutely essential to accurate interpretation. Although there are challenges inherent in developing competence in this realm, these are far from insurmountable. In our experience, with time and applied effort, considering the context becomes almost habitual, a Bible study habit that we'd all do well to develop.

The following survey categorizes nine kinds of context under the three sides of the hermeneutical triad. As the foremost step of interpretation, it's only natural that these variations in context fit categorically within the structure of the hermeneutical triad. However, just as the sides of the triad function in relation to one another, so these kinds of context function interdependently. In virtually all examples where you might cite the relevance of context, there's more than one aspect of context impacting the proper interpretation of the text. A comprehensive approach to context will consider the impact of each kind of context every time one embarks on the interpretation of Scripture.

Figure 8.2: The Hermeneutical Triad

The Hermeneutical Triad

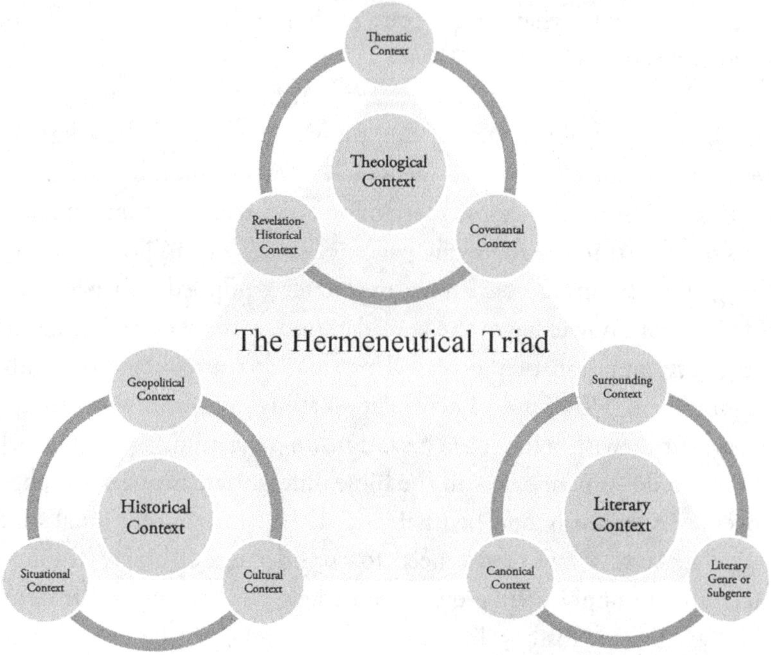

Context Pertaining to History

In the introductory chapters of this book we emphasized that the Bible can't be detached from its ancient, human context. Its pages reflect the events and experiences of real human history, and its origin is rooted in the causes and concerns of ancient peoples. As an interpreter, thinking contextually requires an awareness of three primary aspects of historical context: geopolitical, cultural, and situational.[5] However, it's not enough for you to consider the various aspects of historical context. You should

---

5. In chapter 2, under "The Contextual Principle," we labeled and reviewed three broad categories of context: historical-cultural, literary, and theological-canonical. Each of these quite naturally corresponds to the sides of the triad that we're now using to frame our comprehensive treatment of context. Historical-cultural context encompasses what we now distinguish as geopolitical, cultural, and situational context. Literary context encompasses surrounding, literary, and canonical context. Theological-canonical context encompasses thematic, covenantal, and revelation-historical context. Canonical context, as noted in this chapter, can refer to the relationship of the text to other texts within the framework of progressive revelation. Chapter 2 emphasized this aspect of canon; here we've chosen to emphasize the literary aspect of canonical context (the place of any given text within the broader literary corpus).

also note that historical context functions on two levels: (1) the context of the events reflected in Scripture; and (2) the context surrounding the development of the text itself.

Even a conservative approach to the history of the text recognizes that there are often centuries of distance between the events described in a biblical book and the written text.[6] For instance, historical books such as 1 and 2 Chronicles reflect a broad timeline of events spanning many centuries of Israelite history. Yet the book itself wasn't brought into its completed canonical form until the final events included in these books had taken place.[7] Thus historical context involves not only the historical events and cultures reflected by the events unfolding through the narratives within the books of Chronicles but also the historical setting of the chronicler himself.

The situational concerns of the author within his setting have immeasurable impact on the way in which a book is written, and thus we must also be concerned with that level of historical context.[8] In other genres, the distance between the event and the written text may vary. In the case of the prophetic books, the content often reflects a span at least a few decades of prophetic ministry that inevitably predates the written text.[9] In collections such as Psalms and Proverbs, there may be considerable distance between the origination of the psalm or proverb and its inclusion and arrangement within the canonical book. However, in the

---

6. In certain books, such as the New Testament letters, there may be no distance between the event and the development of the text. However, in other books there is considerable, albeit unknown, distance between event and text. Such is true with all historical books of the Bible, along with prophetic books and poetic collections (Psalms and Proverbs). On the diversity of means by which various books of the Bible underwent development, see John H. Walton and D. Brent Sandy, *The Lost World of Scripture: Ancient Literary Culture and Biblical Authority* (Downers Grove: InterVarsity, 2013).

7. Cf. 2 Chron 36:22–23.

8. This especially concerns the relationship between historical circumstances, authorial intention, and theological emphasis in the text of Scripture.

9. For instance, consider that Hosea's prophetic ministry spans the reigns of Uzziah, Jotham, Ahaz, and Hezekiah, kings of Judah, and Jeroboam II king of Israel. From the end of Jeroboam's reign until the start of Hezekiah's reign, at least thirty-five years transpire, including the cataclysmic events leading to the destruction of Samaria and fall of the Northern Kingdom of Israel to the Assyrians in 722 BC. Some of Hosea's prophecies occurred before the pivotal geopolitical events leading to Israel's demise, while others presumably occurred after these events. In either case, the authoring of Hosea's oracles and life drama into the book as we have it must have occurred after the fall of Samaria, which brings to bear some interesting questions regarding the intended audience of Hosea the book (as distinct from the audience that Hosea actually preached to prior to 722 BC).

New Testament epistles, there really is no distance between the text and its effective use and publication, and the notion of two levels of historical context virtually disappears.

In contrast to the Epistles, an awareness of these two levels of historical context is vitally important in the interpretation of the Gospels, where the events of Jesus's life are separated from the text by two or three decades. Again, the way in which the events are depicted, along with the theological emphases within the text, is influenced by the setting of the evangelist and his original audience. A great deal of geopolitical, cultural, and religious movement occurred in the decades following the life of Christ, and therefore we must be aware of those historical differences between the original set of events recorded in the Gospels and circumstances at the time of their composition.

The first two aspects of historical context, namely, geopolitical and cultural, primarily concern the first level of historical context (the context of the original events). Biblical narrative features an unfolding drama of events based in time, and while often personal in scope, historical events are typically measured and understood within the framework of geopolitical movement. This is certainly true in the Bible, where the focal point of God's activity among his people is so often touched by the rise and fall of rulers and kingdoms. Therefore the first aspect of historical context to concern the interpreter is the geopolitical context of the events described in any portion of Scripture.

The second aspect of historical context reflected by the ancient setting of Scripture is cultural context. The pages of Scripture reflect a wide range of ancient religious, social, and economic customs far removed from the experiences and expectations of modern readers. Understanding these cultural particulars is a vital component in reading the Bible according to its historical context. Cultural particulars are found in all literary genres and simply reflect the ancient setting of Scripture.

The third aspect of historical context surveyed in this chapter concerns both levels of history, and we call it "situational context." In reference to narrative literature, the events that unfold in biblical history were inevitably occasioned by the various events taking place in the ancient world. Understanding the circumstances *behind* an event will often provide necessary insight for understanding the event itself. In this sense, situational context affects the interpreter's understanding of Scripture on the first level of historical context (the context of the event itself). In addition, situational context also involves the second level of historical context. Biblical writers didn't find motivation for their work in a vacuum but rather were moved by circumstances taking place in the real world of their own experiences (and those to whom they wrote). This form of situational context involves the history and occasion surrounding the writing and development of the written text and often has significant impact on the underlying message of the book. While the situational contexts of some books are less definite, there are others (notably the New Testament epistles) that transparently reflect the occasion for their composition.

Figure 8.3: Context Pertaining to History

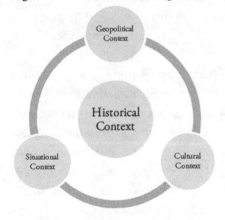

Geopolitical Context

Geopolitical context involves the historical, political, and geographical setting of the events reflected within a given portion of Scripture.[10] As with all forms of context, the relevance of geopolitical context for interpretation varies among books. For instance, the Old Testament prophets prophesied in the context of geopolitical events, and their prophecies were often fulfilled in the course of ancient geopolitical history (to realize the fulfillment of many biblical prophecies modern readers must know ancient Near Eastern history). However, geopolitical history has very little relevance to the interpretation of individual proverbs, and while some

---

10. It is certainly true that geopolitical events influenced how and when certain books were written, and thus involves both levels of historical context. However, the most pressing (and obvious) form of geopolitical context relates to the events described within the text.

psalms have an event-based background that impacts interpretation, many do not. In the New Testament, an informed interpreter of the Gospels must understand the political landscape of Jesus's day (Pharisees, Sadducees, etc.). An understanding of the Epistles, however, is less dependent upon geopolitical events and more contingent on the situational context prompting the writing of the letter itself.

In addition, how an interpreter accesses geopolitical context will inevitably vary depending on book and genre. For example, in the case of historical narrative, the geopolitical context is typically described at some point within the narrative (see, e.g., Esth 1:1–4). Once outside of narrative literature, geopolitical context is often speculative, and the details are rarely explicit and internal to the text. With the biblical authors regularly assuming that their audience had geopolitical awareness of their day, today's audience must engage in additional historical research to access and visualize the geopolitical context of the Scriptures. Thankfully, today's Bible reader has access to a plethora of helpful tools that provide assistance in understanding the varied geopolitical background of the Bible.[11]

As an example, consider one of the more profound (yet lesser known) prophecies from the book of Isaiah. While Isaiah contains numerous oracles of judgment against Egypt and Assyria (fulfilled in the seventh and eighth centuries BC), the promises of end-time blessing for these nations (Isa 19:23–25) are especially striking to the reader. Isaiah sees a day when there will be a "highway" between Egypt and Assyria (19:23) where these two nations will serve together. In this he is proclaiming something that would have been utterly shocking to his original audience. During Isaiah's day, Egypt and Assyria were mortal enemies, two superpowers vying for the upper hand in the ancient Near Eastern geopolitical arena. But what is even more shocking comes in verse 24, when Isaiah proclaims that "On that day Israel will form a triple alliance with Egypt and Assyria—a blessing within the land."

---

11. These tools include study Bibles, commentaries, Bible dictionaries, atlases, and a variety of specifically dedicated works describing the geopolitical context of the Bible. For a list of Bible study resources, see chapter 12, or alternatively, the appendix in Köstenberger and Patterson, *Invitation to Biblical Interpretation*, 809–32.

Israel was a small nation sandwiched between two larger enemies—an unenviable spot. Perhaps, as mentioned, an analogy exists in World War II-era Poland. While Hitler and Stalin were no friends to the Poles, their greatest enemies were in reality one another. This, of course, put Poland in a terrible spot, overrun twice during the course of the war (as bad as things were under Hitler, they were hardly better under Stalin)! If a 1940s prophet were to proclaim a future triple alliance between Germany, Poland, and Russia during the darkest days of World War II, this would have been roughly equivalent to the words of Isaiah pertaining to Egypt, Assyria, and Israel. But Isaiah takes it even further: "The LORD of Hosts will bless them, saying, 'Egypt My people, Assyria My handiwork, and Israel My inheritance are blessed'" (19:25).

Such a strong theological statement is only fully appreciated when considered within the geopolitical context of Isaiah's day. Again, turning back to our WWII analogy, imagine a Jewish prophet in 1944 proclaiming the day when God would bless "Germany My people, Russia My handiwork, and Israel My inheritance." Not an easy thing to imagine, and certainly not easy to accept (especially for a Jew living in 1944 Poland). When Isaiah spoke these words in the eighth century BC, he proclaimed what would have been widely considered absurd and potentially offensive. To understand the significance of this prophecy today, one must first appreciate the geopolitical context of Isaiah's day.

Cultural Context

Cultural distance is an inevitable result of modern readers engaging an ancient, historically based book. In the case of the sixty-six books of the Bible, multiple cultures are reflected in its pages. As interpreters, considering cultural context requires that we learn the customs and manners of biblical cultures, including their religious mores and expectations. There are literally thousands of examples where cultural understanding will provide clarity to the interpretation of the text, and in a sense one must always read Scripture with cultural context in mind. However, we'd like to register a note of caution at this juncture. In spite of the potential danger of misreading Scripture through Western eyes,[12] we must also avoid the temptation of reading too much into unlocking the text through "cultural keys." It's common to hear preaching that taps into cultural insights with little actual evidence to back up the claims.

In spite of that word of caution, we cannot neglect to consider cultural context in interpretation. In some cases interpretation is enhanced through an understanding of ancient practices (what *did* Peter mean when he said "Gird up the loins of you mind," 1 Pet 1:13 NKJV?). In other cases, a broader understanding of religious mores and expectations is required to fully grasp the argument of the text (what *does* Peter mean by "living stones" in 1 Pet 2:4–5?). Understanding cultural context often sheds light on the significance (and sensibility) of events we encounter in Scripture (consider the concept of a "kinsman redeemer" in reference to Ruth and Boaz). At other times, study of the cultural context allows us to grasp better what the author meant through instructions given in the context of ancient cultures. Certainly Paul's instructions to men and women in Corinth were framed within a certain set of cultural mores and expectations, even if based on universal principle.[13]

In biblical narrative, events are sometimes described that seem rather absurd to modern sensibilities. Consider the situation in Judges 21 where wives are provided for the men of Benjamin. As the daughters of Shiloh performed their dances, the men were instructed to hide in the vineyards, and as the women danced by each man was to jump out and "catch" a wife for himself (Judg 21:20–21). In this case there were admittedly unique geopolitical and situational events at work to create such an odd solution to the problem. For modern readers, just beginning to comprehend a culture where a solution (and event) of this kind is possible boggles the mind (because it is in the Bible, perhaps someone will one day develop a biblical methodology of dating and courtship based on Judges 21!).

---

12. This phrase is adopted from the title of the helpful book by E. Randolph Richards and Brandon J. O'Brien, *Misreading Scripture with Western Eyes: Removing Cultural Blinders to Better Understand the Bible* (Downers Grove: InterVarsity, 2012).

13. See 1 Cor 11:4–16.

The one consistent point in all of this is that the biblical authors *assume* cultural awareness that modern readers simply don't possess. Nevertheless, this is a challenge that can be overcome, even if we cannot do so perfectly by experiencing ancient cultures for ourselves. As with geopolitical context, modern readers will often depend on the work of experts in helping to understand the cultural particulars of the ancient world. But even when the details remain speculative, a cautious approach to cultural context provides the basis for research that invariably leads to interpretive insight.

Situational Context

Situational context pertains to both levels of historical context. In some sense, all of the events that take place in biblical narrative were occasioned by other events and circumstances in the world of the Bible. As noted earlier, the rather odd events you read about in Judges 21 came as a result of genocidal intertribal warfare in Israel (as described in Judges 20). Similarly, the practice of early believers "having all things in common" (Acts 2:44; 4:32) was occasioned by a specific situation in history.

Prior to evaluating the intention of Acts 2:44 and 4:32 for application, the interpreter must consider the situational context that created the environment and need for communal support. First-century Jerusalem attracted Jews from throughout the Roman Empire, with many who had traveled from afar for the Feast of Pentecost. Upon hearing the disciples speaking in their own diverse languages (Acts 2:8–12) and hearing Peter's explanation of these things, some 3,000 believed and were "added to them." These new believers didn't disband immediately but rather devoted themselves to the apostles' teaching and "to the fellowship" (Acts 2:42). While not all converts were pilgrims to Jerusalem, many were, requiring support as they remained in Jerusalem post-Pentecost to learn from the apostles before dispersing to their homelands. First-century travelers didn't carry credit cards or use ATM machines, and for those of limited means who had only intended on a short stay for Pentecost, the generosity of the community of believers

was needed for daily sustenance. Without undermining the importance of selfless generosity within the early church, the situational context must be considered if we are properly to understand the scope and
implications of what takes place in Acts 2 and 4.[14]

Genre comes into play here as well: remember that Acts is a historical
narrative, and so we should interpret the book primarily in terms of *what
happened* in the first days of the church (descriptive element), which may
or may not necessarily be required for believers of all ages (prescriptive
element). In addition, theological factors may also enter in, such as that
Luke may depict the early church in terms of inaugurated eschatology,
that is, as a foreshadowing of the community of redeemed in heaven.
This is supported by the fact that Luke casts the church along a salvation-
historical continuum, showing that subsequent to Jesus's ascension the
prophet Joel's vision of the end-time pouring out of the Spirit has been
fulfilled.[15]

Situational context also pertains to the context of the author, audience, and the events surrounding the writing or development of the biblical text. In at least a few obvious cases, specific books of the Bible can
be labeled as "occasional documents," meaning that their composition
was occasioned by historical events and situations.[16] For example, a personal letter such as the one written to Philemon is completely immersed
in the context of the situation involving Paul's encounter with the slave
Onesimus. Likewise, all of the New Testament epistles involve personal
concerns between the authors, their associates, and the churches or individuals to whom they wrote. Some were written to encourage, while
others take on a harsher tone, addressing some form of false teaching

---

14. Among other things, this means that Acts 2 and 4 cannot legitimately be used to make a case
for Christian socialism or communism, that is, for enforced or compulsory sharing of property in the
context of communal living.

15. Notice that we are also reading these Acts narratives in light of thematic context, which stems
from the Bible's expression of theological motif. In this sequence of events one might also see a biblical-theological motif in that the confusion of languages at the tower of Babel (Genesis 11) is shown to
be reversed when at Pentecost the Spirit miraculously enables people to hear the gospel in their own
languages (Acts 2).

16. Gordon D. Fee and Douglas Stuart, *How to Read the Bible for All Its Worth*, 4th ed. (Grand
Rapids: Zondervan, 2014), 60.

in the respective churches.[17] Knowing the situation between author and audience is a vital aspect of thinking contextually—to do otherwise would be akin to listening to a phone conversation on one end without any knowledge of the context of the conversation. Eavesdropping will provide some sense of what's going on, but the dangers of misunderstanding are obviously significant in such an encounter!

Other books have a less obvious connection to situational context, yet no biblical text was written in a vacuum. Understanding the biography of the author, his purpose and intent for writing, and the general circumstances of the recipients all play a role in the interpretation of Scripture. Consider, for example, how important introductory material is in the study of the book of Acts.[18] Discerning Luke's intention in writing Acts helps explain historical selectivity in the narrative, makes sense of theological emphasis in the book, and ultimately speaks to how modern readers appropriate a model of "doing church" in the first century (if Luke's intention was not to provide a normative model in "doing church," this also affects how we interpret and apply the book). For example, what do you make of the fact that Luke dedicated his work to his literary patron, Theophilus, who in all probability was a Roman government official?

In the same sense, while the book of Revelation speaks to future realities, it certainly had *some* function for its first recipients in their own situational context (the repetition of the call to "overcome," especially in the letters to the seven churches, highlights this function within

---

17. For a helpful study of the various heresies underlying New Testament letters, see Andreas J. Köstenberger and Michael J. Kruger, *The Heresy of Orthodoxy: How Contemporary Culture's Fascination with Diversity Has Reshaped Our Understanding of Early Christianity* (Wheaton: Crossway, 2010), chapter 3.

18. Matters pertaining to authorship, audience, text development, and situational context are typically covered in the area of "introduction." These matters are often quite complex, so students should not confuse "introduction" with "elementary." Also, in the field of biblical studies, "introduction" pertains to the background of the book (matters of authorship, audience, situation, etc.), in distinction from "survey," which provides a general review of the content of the book. Recommended introductions include Andreas J. Köstenberger, L. Scott Kellum, and Charles L. Quarles, *The Cradle, the Cross, and the Crown: An Introduction to the New Testament*, 2nd ed. (Nashville: B&H, 2016); and Eugene H. Merrill, Mark F. Rooker, and Michael A. Grisanti, *The World and the Word: An Introduction to the Old Testament* (Nashville: B&H, 2011).

the book).[19] For you as an interpreter, understanding this sense of how Revelation functioned in the first-century church depends in part on understanding the geopolitical and situational context of those who first received the Apocalypse: believers at the end of the first century AD living in the context of the Roman Empire with its emperor worship, pagan pantheon, and decadent society. An accurate interpretation of Revelation cannot ignore the situational context of the church in the late first century even if the vast majority of prophecy in the book awaits a future, end-time fulfillment.[20]

Figure 8.4: Context Pertaining to Literature

Context Pertaining to Literature

Interpreting the words of Scripture is far more involved than simply knowing Greek and Hebrew vocabulary, grammar, and syntax. Ultimately, the meaning of words and phrases in any language is determined by their intended usage, and this can be known only through a consideration of context. There are three primary facets of context pertaining to the written text of the Bible.

The first has been variously described as "surrounding context," "grammatical-syntactical context," and "co-text." Because this dimension of context deals with the meaning of words and phrases within the structural framework of surrounding sentences and paragraphs, we'll refer to this as *surrounding context*. Words and phrases have the capacity to convey multiple meanings (nuanced or otherwise), and ultimately it's the surrounding context that determines the meaning of those words

---

19. See Rev 2:11, 26; 3:5, 12, 21; cf. 6:2; 21:7.
20. See especially Köstenberger, Kellum, and Quarles, *Cradle, the Cross, and the Crown*, chapter 20.

and phrases. The thoughts that precede and follow any given portion of Scripture therefore constitute the surrounding context of that portion. In any coherent discourse, thoughts are expressed in association rather than isolation. Practically speaking, when you analyze the meaning of a word or phrase in the Bible, contextual meaning will always take precedence over lexical meaning. Although all forms of context influence the meaning of words in written communication, the surrounding context bears the most significant weight in determining word meaning.

The second facet of context pertaining to the Bible as literature involves the *literary genre* or *subgenre* of a textual unit. The Bible is a complex book reflecting a broad array of genres and subgenres. In order to interpret and apply Scripture accurately, the functional and structural traits inherent within the genre of the text must be considered as a facet of reading contextually. We've already seen in multiple illustrations that genre influences how we observe, interpret, and apply Scripture. As we consider the context of a portion of Scripture, we must think in terms of literary kind, not just in terms of what surrounds a portion of the text. We'll simply refer to the context of genre and subgenre as *literary context*.

There is a third facet of context that is unique to the Bible as a collection of sixty-six books. This is the *canonical context*, and it pertains to the context of individual passages within distinct books of the Bible as well as the placement of books within the one book we call "the Bible." As we begin to ponder canonical context, it's easy to see that all three sides of the hermeneutical triad warrant canonical consideration: regarding history, you should consider the *time* of the text within a chronology of events; regarding literature, you should consider the *place* of the text within the written corpus; and regarding theology, you should consider the *relationship* of the text to other texts within the progressive revelation of God to humanity. In this sense, you might find that canonical context ought to be considered through the lens of literature, history, and theology. However, we've already described geopolitical and situational context in reference to the place of biblical books in history. Also, we'll soon cover theological context, which considers the place of texts within the progressive framework of God's revelation to humanity. We therefore reserve the designation "canonical context" to describe the unique contributions and relationships between books arranged within the Bible.

Surrounding Context

Although thinking contextually goes far beyond the confines of surrounding context, this aspect of context deservedly receives the most attention for those who seek to interpret the Bible with accuracy and integrity. Alternatively, when preachers, teachers, and general readers take Scripture out of context, it's usually because they've ignored the surrounding context of a passage that they commit such interpretive malpractice.[21] In most situations, the Bible is taken out of context not because the reader lacks specialized training in history, literature, or theology, but rather because they have either (1) willfully ignored the surrounding context of a passage or (2) read the Bible without an awareness of how vital context is to the communication of ideas. You might say that the first is a crime of commission, while the second is a crime of omission. We see both committed frequently, though typically without malicious intent. Those who willfully ignore surrounding context usually do so as they teach right doctrine from the wrong texts, often for the sake of building up the body of Christ. Those who read the Bible with little awareness of surrounding context often do so because they have been trained (by example) to think through Scripture in terms of devotional nuggets, memorizing verses and reading for inspirational insight rather than interpretive understanding. Nevertheless, whether out of ignorance or misplaced motivation, to read and interpret Scripture without considering the surrounding context is careless and has led to a countless array of interpretive mistakes.

I (Al) was first struck with the importance of surrounding context as a teenager attending a missionary conference. The conference theme verse was Joel 3:14: "Multitudes, multitudes in the valley of decision! For the Day of the LORD is near in the valley of decision." Presumably,

---

21. For additional examples of Scripture taken out of context (often in popular Christian publications), see Richard L. Schultz, *Out of Context: How to Avoid Misinterpreting the Bible* (Grand Rapids: Baker, 2012).

the missionary conference "motto" committee was seeking to echo the idea of the "plentiful harvest" in Matthew 9:37 and "fields already white for harvest" in John 4:35. By associating the "valley of decision" with the "fields white for harvest," Joel 3:14 made a wonderful missions conference verse. The problem is that Joel 3:14 has nothing to do with evangelism, missionary labor, or willful souls waiting to make a decision for Jesus! Rather, the surrounding context makes it quite clear that the valley is the "Valley of Jehoshaphat," a name that literally means "Yahweh judges" (Joel 3:2). The nations are called to battle (3:9) and led supernaturally to the Valley of Jehoshaphat where Yahweh will bring them to judgment (3:12). The "decision" in 3:14 is Yahweh's decision to bring judgment against the nations; he will "decide" against them in that valley! Ironically, verse 13 does say that the "harvest is ripe," but in this context it is ripe for destruction! And so our missionary conference theme verse was actually an Old Testament prophecy calling the nations to the place of end-time judgment, popularly known as the Battle of Armageddon (Rev 19:17–21)!

The good folks who chose Joel 3:14 as their missionary conference theme verse harbored no malicious intent. However, a little attention to surrounding context might have kept the church from printing brochures and a rather sizable banner proclaiming Yahweh's judgment "in those days" (Joel 3:1)! To take into consideration the surrounding context of Joel 3:14 would have been a simple matter of reading beyond the confines of a single verse of Scripture. And while recognizing the boundaries of a contextual unit requires some level of analytical observation (in this case, Joel 3:1–16), the ability to follow the line of argument or subject matter in a passage typically requires no specialized training. Most breaches of surrounding context occur not because readers are unable to follow the subject matter or line of argument but rather because they simply aren't thinking of doing so.

Awareness, perception, and a sprinkling of common sense are the key factors for interpreting Scripture according to its surrounding context. However, it's not enough to simply suggest that readers be aware of the surrounding context of a passage. In addition, we've found that the following steps are helpful in assisting students to read Scripture in light of surrounding context.[22]

Table 8.1 — Tips for Understanding Scripture in Light of Surrounding Context	
1.	Determine the boundaries that comprise the unit of text being studied.
2.	Summarize the main idea of the unit.
3.	Explain how (or if) this segment relates to the units surrounding it.

First, *determine the boundaries* that comprise the surrounding context of the segment or passage under study. This coincides with the observation of literary units (as seen in chapter 7). Once a literary unit is determined, it is then possible to place limits on where the surrounding context of a passage begins and ends. As noted in chapter 7, a contextually contained unit of Scripture is marked by boundary features and cohesion. In most situations, the verses that immediately precede and follow a given portion of Scripture comprise its surrounding context. However, there are variations to this rule, and discerning surrounding context is often more complex than simply counting so many verses before and after the segment under investigation. If you're studying a segment of Scripture that concludes a literary unit, the surrounding context may in fact be a *preceding* context. In the same sense, if you're studying a portion of the text that begins a literary unit, the content that follows and concludes the unit may be the relevant *surrounding* context. Of course, following the standard steps of inductive study will ensure that literary units have been observed even prior to considering the impact of surrounding context on the interpretation of the text.

Second, *summarize the main idea* communicated through the contextually contained unit. Obviously this may help determine the boundaries of the unit (it's hard to summarize content without recognizing

---

22. These steps are adapted from J. Scott Duvall and J. Daniel Hays, *Grasping God's Word*, 3rd ed. (Grand Rapids: Zondervan, 2012), 159–61.

cohesion), but, more importantly, it'll help you to think through the subject matter that comprises the contextual content of a literary unit.

Third, once you've determined the boundaries defining the surrounding context and summarized the main argument or point of content in that segment, *explain how (or if) this segment relates* to that which precedes and/or follows. This third step is similar to the observation of relationship between literary units in chapter 7. However, at the point of interpretation, the goal is to determine the impact of surrounding context *beyond* the particular literary unit that comprises immediate surrounding context. As the concept of surrounding context broadens, the canonical and thematic contexts of entire books are considered regarding their impact on the interpretation of the text.

Finally, when thinking about how important surrounding context is to the interpretation of words, phrases, and verses in Scripture, consider always studying the biblical text according to contextually contained units. In some sense, this provides a safeguard against using Scripture in a manner that ignores surrounding context (it's hard to take a verse out of context when you're thinking in terms of literary units to begin with).

Literary Context (Genre and Subgenre)

When a refrigerator repairman accesses a schematics page, he has a certain framework of expectations for what he reads, and he "interprets" the page in accordance with the genre of "refrigeration schematics" (perhaps a subgenre within the "instruction manual" family!). Likewise, the lawyer reads a will or a trust with a certain set of expectations, understanding the "rules" of that literary specialty (as one should expect from a lawyer). In the evening, after work, both the lawyer and the repairman might pick up the same title of a popular suspense novel, and they each read it as a suspense novel, shifting their expectations and understanding to line up with the appropriate literary genre. Ignoring this shift would be a breach of literary context—it would be absurd for the repairman to read the novel as a repair manual or for the lawyer to read it as a legal document. For written communication to work, there must be a common understanding of rules and expectations that exist between author and reader in the realm of language (vocabulary, grammar, and syntax) and in the realm of literary genre.

There are literally hundreds of genres and subgenres within any literate culture, each with different formal and informal rules and expectations for communicating meaning. However, among all the literary works in the world, there is really no equivalent to the Bible, a collection of interrelated books where so many diverse literary genres are represented. Just as the lawyer and the repairman must shift their way of thinking when they finish work and turn to their suspense novel, so the reader of Scripture must be ready to shift the way they think between different literary genres in the Bible. Whether intentionally or intuitively (usually a combination of both), readers of the Bible understand that different rules apply when reading historical narrative versus law code versus prophetic oracle. Even without specialized training, there's an inherent understanding that one should not read the Song of Songs in the same manner as the judgment speeches of Jeremiah or the parables within the Gospels or the sayings within the book of Proverbs.

There are two points to consider when reading Scripture according to its literary context. The first pertains to observation and simply entails the ability to discern between different literary genres in Scripture. Considering literary context begins with recognizing the genre represented in a portion of Scripture and includes sensitivity to shifts between genres and subgenres within (and between) books of the Bible. Primary genres within the Old Testament include historical narrative, law code, psalms, wisdom literature, and prophetic literature. In the New Testament primary genres include historical narrative (Gospels and Acts), letters (epistles), and the apocalypse of Revelation. To further heighten the challenge of reading contextually, within each primary literary genre one finds typical subgenres. For instance, in any given prophetic book you might encounter apocalyptic visions, autobiographical narrative, historical narrative, prophetic drama, hymns, allegory, judgment speeches, woe speeches, salvation oracles, lamentation, and instructional discourse (and this list is not exhaustive!). In the New Testament Gospels, you're presented with narrative discourse, narrative commentary, genealogies, hymns, parables, sermons, and allegory (to name just a few). Virtually every book of the Bible has a diverse array of literary subgenres, and reading contextually requires an ability to discern the form and features distinguishing each while also appreciating the unique function that distinct literary subgenres carry.[23]

The second point applies more directly to interpretation and involves understanding the interpretive rules and expectations embedded within literary genres and subgenres. Just as language requires established rules of grammar and syntax for intelligible communication to exist, so there are also rules pertaining to genre that regulate the sense of communication between author and reader. The diversity of rules and expectations between literary genres in the Bible provide the basis for many discussions in biblical hermeneutics, and we would certainly agree that understanding the role of genre is an essential element of interpretation. Just as the repairman wouldn't read the refrigerator technician's manual with the same expectations and rules of engagement as the suspense novel, so the student of Scripture shouldn't read the book of Proverbs the same way he reads the book of Judges. The original language may be the same (Hebrew), but the genre is remarkably different. The same could be said of many New Testament books. Interpreting the Gospel of John and the book of Revelation requires a different set of interpretive rules and expectations, not because the language is different (both are written in Greek), or because they were written by different authors (both are attributed to John), but because the genres are distinct.

Knowing that different interpretive rules apply to the various genres in the Bible presents a significant challenge for interpretation, and to some extent all students of Scripture should strive to familiarize themselves with genre-specific hermeneutics. The lawyer in our earlier illustration will read a legal will or trust with an awareness of the nuances of literary context. Similarly, the experienced technician will read a set of refrigerator schematics with heightened knowledge based on his

---

23. For a detailed treatment of a vast array of Old and New Testament subgenres, see Köstenberger and Patterson, *Invitation to Biblical Interpretation*, chapters 5–11.

specialized training. We're not suggesting that the Bible requires specialized training in all of its diverse literary genres in order to be read. However, we're suggesting that you can gain a heightened understanding and appreciation of the text through an ability to navigate Scripture according to its literary context.[24]

Canonical Context

While the breadth of surrounding context is necessarily limited by literary units, there's a sense in which context extends beyond distinct units to include the literary setting of books (e.g., Amos), collections of books (e.g., the Minor Prophets or "The Twelve"), Testaments (Old or New), and ultimately the whole Bible (understood as a unified book). At the level of canonical context, you must first consider the role of a passage and its literary placement within the broader scope of a book. For instance, canonical context will consider why Isaiah's call to ministry is in chapter 6 of the book rather than at the beginning. And it'll ask what role (if any) this placement has in communicating the broader message of Isaiah.

To use another example, canonical context might consider the role that the messages to the seven churches in Revelation 2 and 3 have in relation to the rest of the book. What difference would it make if these were placed near the end of the book? Similarly, think about the poem on the virtuous wife that concludes the book of Proverbs (31:10–31). Does this poem relate to the rest of the book in any way? Is there a sense in which it correlates to "Lady Wisdom" from chapter 8 or that "Woman Folly" from chapter 9? Clearly, we're asking a thematic question as much as a literary one, but nonetheless these questions begin with a recognition that textual units tend to sustain a relationship within the context

---

24. One of the time-honored books on genre-specific hermeneutics is Gordon D. Fee and Douglas Stuart, *How to Read the Bible for All Its Worth*, 4th ed. (Grand Rapids: Zondervan, 2014). For Old Testament genres, we'd recommend D. Brent Sandy and Ronald L. Giese Jr., *Cracking Old Testament Codes: A Guide to Interpreting the Literary Genres of the Old Testament* (Nashville: B&H, 1995). See also Köstenberger and Patterson, *Invitation to Biblical Interpretation*, chapters 5–11; and the abridgement by the same authors, *Introduction to Biblical Interpretation* (Grand Rapids: Kregel, 2015).

of an entire given book. Essentially, we interpret literary parts in light of how they relate to the structure and content of the whole book.

Beyond the more obvious literary and thematic relationships within books of the Bible, canonical context also considers the relationship of content between books.[25] This is best illustrated among sections of the Bible but can easily expand to the context of a Testament or the whole canon. For instance, when reading the Pentateuch (the five books of Moses, i.e., Genesis, Exodus, Leviticus, Numbers, and Deuteronomy), there's a clear relationship between the five books of the law. Canonical context infers that the interpretation of any part of this corpus must be understood in light of the whole collection of five books. However, the context of these books extends beyond the Pentateuch to include the whole Old Testament.

The correlation between Deuteronomy 17 and 1 Kings 1–11 illustrates larger canonical context. The rise and fall of Solomon's kingdom can only be understood in light of the warnings and expectations of a king in Deuteronomy 17:16–17. This applies not only to the warnings about amassing silver and gold, multiplying horses from Egypt (military might), and multiplying wives (political alliances), but even to the more subtle elements of the Solomon narrative. For instance, to showcase Solomon's wisdom, 1 Kings 3:16–28 recounts Solomon's judgment in the dispute between two harlots over the death of a child. While a quick survey of 1 Kings would lead the reader to believe that this rendering of judgment was a positive thing for the new king, it should also be considered that Deuteronomy 17:8–13, just prior to stating principles on the governance of kings (17:14–20), provides principles (or laws) regulating matters of justice in Israel. Solomon didn't meet the guidelines for rendering legal judgment in Israel. Considering the narrative of 1 Kings 3 in light of the broader canonical context that includes Deuteronomy 17:8–13 *might* shed light on how the author of 1 Kings 3 actually intended his readers to receive the narrative.

---

25. It's difficult to divorce the literary placement of books within the canon from the thematic content of those books in considering canonical context. Interplay between the various kinds of context is simply an indication of the existence of interdependent relationships within the hermeneutical triad.

Beyond the Testaments, canonical context extends to include the whole Bible. Although perhaps more closely related to theology than literature, it's certainly true that continuity exists between books that cross between the Testaments. As an example, consider the fall of humanity in Genesis 3 and the redemption of creation in Romans 8. Canonical context suggests that there's a relationship between these chapters not simply based on thematic similarity but also on the grounds of canonical unity—although distant in terms of language, genre, and history, Genesis 3 and Romans 8 are nonetheless part of one story, one book. Therefore, when interpreting phrases such as "bondage of corruption" in Romans 8:19–22, Genesis 3:17–19 should be consulted. To neglect doing so would be to ignore the larger canonical context.

Figure 8.5: Context Pertaining to Theology

Context Pertaining to Theology

Areas of context that relate to the theological message of Scripture center on either the thematic content of the Bible or the process of God's revelation of himself through that content. There are three forms of context

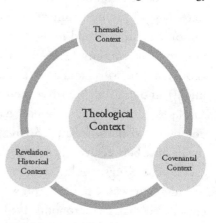

that relate to the theological message of the Bible: *thematic* context, *covenantal* context, and *revelation-historical* context. In each of these, reading the theological message of the Bible contextually is of primary concern. However, as suggested before, the message of the text can't be divorced from its history or its literature. When the following three forms of context are considered in conjunction with those treated under history and literature, we've formulated a comprehensive approach to context.

Thematic Context

Thematic context involves the consideration of theological motif as a form of context. The theological message of the Bible is communicated through repeated themes; when a theme repeats itself and carries prominence, it is labeled a "motif." Motifs can be seen in each book of the Bible, and certain motifs transcend individual books. Some motifs in Scripture can relate to practical matters, while others are of a theological nature. Situation and genre naturally influence the motifs within books, and ultimately motifs are nothing more than a reflection of the interests of a biblical writer.

Consider a few illustrations of thematic context from two of the wisdom books in the Bible: Ecclesiastes and Job. Observed via repetition and structural prominence, a reading of Ecclesiastes reveals certain themes that carry the message of the book. Most significant among these are: (1) the judgment that various elements in a fallen world are either "vain," "absurd," or "fleeting"; (2) the "under the sun" perspective that characterizes the reflections in the book; (3) the merits and limits of wisdom in a fallen world; (4) the sovereignty of God and the imposition of limitation on human existence; (5) the inevitability of death; (6) the good derived from the enjoyment of life; and (7) the fear of God in view of the final judgment.[26] Now consider the interpretation of Ecclesiastes 3:19: "For the fate of people and the fate of animals is the same. As one dies, so dies the other; they all have the same breath. People have no advantage over the animals since everything is futile." Jehovah's Witnesses have long used this verse as a proof-text for their theology of annihilationism, and many evangelicals might see this statement as the pondering of a lost soul without hope. The surrounding context provides little to clarify the statement, as the content of Ecclesiastes tends to skip between segments, highlighting recurring themes without necessarily following a linear form of argument. However, Ecclesiastes 3:19 is one among many statements in Ecclesiastes that ponders the inevitability of

---

26. This list is a slight adaptation of the motifs listed in Richard Alan Fuhr Jr., *An Analysis of the Inter-Dependency of the Prominent Motifs within the Book of Qohelet*, Studies in Biblical Literature 151 (New York: Peter Lang, 2013).

death, an obvious facet of living in a fallen world. The focus in Ecclesiastes is not on the resurrection as a solution to the fallen condition—the writer of Ecclesiastes doesn't yet know of Christ's atoning work on the cross, nor does he ever hint at it.[27] What he does emphasize is the *inevitability* of death—the fact that rich and poor, strong and weak, king and servant, wise and foolish all are going to the same place, the common destiny of all flesh: the grave. From an "under the sun" perspective, the writer is simply highlighting the fact that the wisest of wise people end up in the same place as stupid animals. Thematically, this complements his musings on the vanity of wisdom to stop the inevitable and the absurdity that all go to the same common place (i.e., the grave). Considering the thematic context, we find that the "Teacher" is not making a theological statement on the final destiny of the soul but rather simply stating the obvious fact that all mortal flesh dies. This is a true statement understood within the limitations of the author's intention.

Similar to Ecclesiastes, Job is built around recurring motifs. Throughout the dialogue between Job and his three "friends," Job repeatedly affirms his innocence, speaking with confidence that one day he'll be vindicated before God (13:15; 16:19; 23:10).[28] What vexes Job is that, try as he may, he can't access God in order to argue his case (a courtroom motif runs throughout the book of Job). At one point in the dialogue, Job states his confidence in a "living Redeemer" (19:25). On the surface, it's easy to see this as a messianic prophecy and foreshadowing of Christ in Old Testament wisdom literature. And certainly the New Testament affirms that Christ is our "living Redeemer," so it's tempting to read this

---

27. The "Teacher's" quest is to find out if wisdom provides any solution to the fallen condition. Ultimately, he finds that wisdom is good and gives an advantage in the fallen world but doesn't provide the solution to the dilemma of mortality. It's not until the New Testament that we find the solution to the grave in the resurrection of Christ (1 Corinthians 15), though hints of the resurrection are found in Scripture as early as in the book of Genesis: see Mitchell L. Chase, "The Genesis of Resurrection Hope: Exploring Its Early Presence and Deep Roots," *JETS* 57 (2014): 467–80.

28. Although Job suffered trials, there's little evidence to suggest that Job 23:10 is referring to the "refiner's fire," a place where Job proclaims confidence that his trials will bring him to a place of maturity and holiness (as with Jas 1:2–3 and 1 Pet 1:6–9). Rather, Job desires to plead his case before God (23:4), confident that God will consider the evidence for his innocence—yet he's frustrated that God can't be found (23:8–9). Nevertheless, consistent with parallel passages, Job affirms his confidence that one day when God does hear his case he'll be vindicated (23:10). Here the thematic context of Job (what Job is actually talking about) takes precedence over correlation derived from other texts.

back into the text of Job. However, in the context of Job the "living Redeemer" is the Judge who finally vindicates Job as innocent, even as Job is brought to the very point of death. In the New Testament, Christ is our "living Redeemer," but the sense of this role is completely different. Christ's death paid the price that our sin demanded, so that we as sinners could be liberated from the bondage of sin. Nowhere in the dialogues of Job is there any emphasis on soteriological doctrine, nor is there any clear expectation of resurrection or a coming Messiah. What is more, Job is about the business of proclaiming his innocence, not confessing his sin and need of a Savior. Although the statement in Job 19:25 is somewhat ambiguous, it's better to interpret it in accordance with the thematic context of Job than to make false interpretive associations, even when those associations are theologically true and desirable from a later, more fully developed Christian doctrinal vantage point.

These are rather stark (and somewhat controversial) examples, but there are literally thousands of situations in which thematic context will speak to the proper interpretation of a portion of Scripture. Whether confined to an individual book or reflecting a broader section of Scripture, the consideration of thematic context provides appropriate limitations on the extent to which Scripture can interpret Scripture. In a sense, thematic context provides a contextually sensitive approach to topical interpretation, understanding the parts in light of a limited whole. Not only does this invoke the tried-and-true hermeneutical principle of interpreting the parts in light of the whole, it also underscores the importance of keeping in mind the salvation-historical location of a given passage of Scripture (in particular whether the passage is found in the Old or the New Testament). We'll return to this important issue toward the end of this book when extolling the virtues of biblical theology.[29]

Covenantal Context

Covenantal context entails the consideration of the theological covenants that regulate God's relationship to his people throughout salvation

---

29. See chapter 15 on "doing theology."

history. These covenants provide the theological grounding that often explains God's relationship to his people in narrative texts. Moreover, the unfolding of events in biblical narrative is often the fulfillment of covenantal agreements, and therefore these covenants provide the theological basis that drives biblical history forward. The idea of covenant is also essential in understanding the promises and prophecies in the Old Testament prophetic books. The oracles and proclamations of the prophets were anchored to the covenants made between God and humankind. As the prophets spoke forth warnings of judgment and called the people to repentance, their words were based in the covenant made between God and his people Israel (mediated through Moses). As they prophesied with the expectation of future fulfillment, their oracles were anchored in the unilateral covenants of the Old Testament (Abrahamic, Davidic, and new covenant).

This anchoring in covenant can be illustrated through a few prophecies in the book of Micah. In Micah 1–3 the covenantal basis is the Mosaic covenant (Exodus 19–24), the stipulations are the law, the focal point is Israel, and the consequences of disobedience are death, destruction, and exile (Deut 28:15–68). The parallel oracles warning that Samaria (Mic 1:6) and Jerusalem (Mic 3:12) would be made a "heap of ruins" correlates with the expectations of consequences under the Mosaic covenant. But what is the basis of Micah's oracle of salvation in 4:1–8? Here the covenantal context has shifted—it is the new covenant, introduced in Deuteronomy 30:1–10.[30]

On a more practical note, an understanding of covenantal context will affect how interpreters appropriate for themselves the promises of the Bible. Although it preaches well to assure people that "every promise in the book is mine," in fact not all promises in the Bible belong to the church (and when it comes to promises of judgment, we should all be glad they don't!). Yet it's very common for preachers to take promises of blessing from the Bible and appropriate these in a universal sense for all New Testament believers without considering the covenant basis

---

30. Oracles of salvation in the prophets reflect promises based in the Abrahamic, Davidic, and new covenant. These covenants don't replace one another in the Old Testament but rather complement and refine the details of redemption.

for those promises. It's easy for the church to dismiss the thought of famine, plagues, and exile as a promise for disobedience (Deut 28:47–68), seeing that these are threatened for someone else (ancient Israel), yet how tempting it is to expect the blessings of prosperity regardless of their covenant basis (Deut 28:3–14)!

Revelation-Historical Context

The theological message of the Bible is intricately tied to the unfolding drama of God's interaction with his people. Moreover, the linear nature of God's historical self-revelation infers that the written Word should follow a similar linear pattern of revelation.[31] When reading Scripture, it's always important to determine at what point in revelation history a text is located. Considering the revelation-historical context of a passage in Scripture is based on the progressive principle (from chapter 2), Scripture wasn't revealed all at once, and the various authors of Scripture didn't all possess the same degree of knowledge of God. As a general principle, notwithstanding the omniscient authorship of God the Holy Spirit, a human author couldn't have intended that which he couldn't have possibly known (in other words, that which was revealed later in time; cf. 1 Pet 1:10–12). If authorial intent means anything to interpretation, then the words of the biblical text must align with the time in revelation history in which a biblical author lived.

Under "thematic context" we looked at an example from Ecclesiastes 3:19. In Ecclesiastes 3:20, the Teacher asks whether the "spirit of people rise upward," and later, in the poem allegorizing death, infers that the "spirit returns to God who gave it" (12:7). While there are numerous ways to approach these statements, many make the mistake of reading everything they know about death and the afterlife from the New Testament back into the mind of the Teacher. While the Teacher wrote "words of truth" (12:10), this doesn't mean that he was privy to all truth.

31. Interpreting Scripture according to this developmental pattern additionally infers that there's a trajectory of theological development in Scripture. A nuanced consideration of revelation-historical context will accommodate the fact that even when incomplete, there's a movement in Scripture that is (and was) orchestrated by an omniscient God. Thus, even while revelation is progressive, it was always on the track of leading to the full revelation of truth in the completed canon of Scripture.

In other words, even though he seemed to have some expectation that there was a coming time of post-mortem judgment (3:17; 12:14), the details were fuzzy at best, and he seemed to know little of what to expect after death (this was vexing to him as a wise man). Later in revelation history, God's people would learn about the resurrection of the just and the unjust, various appointments to judgment, and the vital distinction between heaven and hell. But these realities were revealed later in the New Testament, not in the Old. As interpreters, we must use restraint not to read more into the mind of the Old Testament author than revelation-historical context will allow.

Considering revelation-historical context implies that we understand the movement of covenants in Scripture, yet it goes beyond the recognition of covenant basis. Revelation-historical context considers the nature of linear progression in how God has revealed truth through the pages of the Bible. Not only does the history canvassed in Scripture span a period of thousands of years, but the actual development of all sixty-six books didn't happen all at once. In accordance with the activity of God in history and following the track of development from Genesis to Revelation, the interpretation of Scripture must be considered in context with the progressive history of revelation.

In keeping with the notion of salvation-historical progression, the apostle Paul saw himself as a steward of the mysteries of God, specifically of the new development that subsequent to the coming of Christ the church was constituted as a body consisting of both believing Jews and Gentiles.[32] Peter, likewise, conveys a clear sense of salvation-historical progression when he writes in his first epistle,

> Concerning this salvation, the prophets who prophesied about the grace that would come to you searched and carefully investigated. They inquired into what time or what circumstances

---

32. See, e.g., Rom 16:25–26; Eph 3:1–9; Col 1:25–27. For the biblical notion of "mystery," see G. K. Beale and Benjamin L. Gladd, *Hidden but Now Revealed: A Biblical Theology of Mystery* (Downers Grove: InterVarsity, 2014). See also D. A. Carson, "Mystery and Fulfillment: Toward a More Comprehensive Paradigm of Paul's Understanding of the Old and New," in *Justification and Variegated Nomism*, vol. 2: *The Paradoxes of Paul*, ed. D. A. Carson, Peter T. O'Brien, and Mark A. Seifrid, WUNT 181 (Grand Rapids: Baker, 2004), 393–436.

the Spirit of Christ within them was indicating when He testified in advance to the messianic sufferings and the glories that would follow. It was revealed to them that they were not serving themselves but you. These things have now been announced to you through those who preached the gospel to you by the Holy Spirit sent from heaven. Angels desire to look into these things. (1 Pet 1:10–12)

As Peter makes clear, try as they might, the Old Testament prophets were unable to pinpoint the exact time or circumstances at which the Messiah would be revealed. Now that the Messiah had actually appeared, Peter and his fellow apostles were able to proclaim the gospel of the Lord Jesus Christ as the fulfillment of Old Testament expectations. This is why Peter can later in the chapter claim that the reference to the word of the Lord in Isaiah 40:8 actually is "the word that was preached as the gospel to you" (1 Pet 1:25). In the telescope of history, hindsight is 20/20, but we shouldn't level the playing field unduly by overlooking the salvation-historical progression that needs to be taken into account when interpreting a given individual passage of Scripture.

Final Thoughts

Awareness, perception, and knowledge of context can come only with time, experience, and an intentional desire to interpret Scripture with accuracy and integrity. In this chapter, we've surveyed the essential aspects of context. For many, this survey was an eye-opening exposure to thinking contextually. What's more, now that you've read this chapter you should have an increased level of contextual awareness. Whether by ignorance or negligence, taking Scripture out of context is no longer a feasible option.

Considering the context is a skill that requires time to develop. This is true especially with regard to perception and knowledge—but we hope that through examples and instruction, we've contributed to your journey in this regard. Bible interpretation is not a hard science; neither is the process leading to it. Yet even so, there are guidelines to direct the process and ensure some level of objectivity in reaching conclusions. We trust that moving forward, your first step of interpretation will always be to consider the context.

9

Interpretive Correlation
Comparing Scripture with Scripture

Interpretive correlation is simply the practice of comparing Scripture with Scripture for the distinct purpose of informing the interpretation of a particular text based on other related texts. Texts may correspond through a variety of relationships, including parallel accounts, repeated phraseology, common subject matter, identifying markers, cause and effect, inference, and contrast. By observing corresponding relationships, interpreters will draw inferred meaning by making sense of these relationships. Put another way, interpretive correlation is the methodical pursuit of interpreting the parts in light of the whole. In Scripture, there are parallels and corresponding relationships between passages in the three areas of history, literature, and theology. Interpretive correlation involves researching parallels and making logical connections between related passages in each of these three areas.

We'll explore correlation as the means to "doing theology," the capstone to the inductive method, in chapter 15. But please take note: *interpretive* correlation shouldn't be confused with this latter kind of correlation. Both kinds of correlation involve comparing Scripture with Scripture, but they each have a different function and goal. As the culminating step of inductive Bible study, correlation, broadly conceived, involves the synthesis of related Scripture for the purpose of developing theology. It has an outward focus, synthesizing texts that have already been individually interpreted. *Interpretive* correlation, on the other hand, has an inward focus, serving to inform and safeguard the interpretation of Scripture. At its core, inductive Bible study demands that theology not develop on the basis of proof texting and selective use of evidence. Conversely, interpretation must also "be made on the basis of all the texts that speak to the issue."[1]

Scripture Interprets Scripture

Whether the goal is interpretation or theology, the valid practice of correlation is based on the harmony principle. Because there's one divine author who superintended the whole of Scripture, we can expect that Scripture will ultimately harmonize. Although the sixty-six books of the Bible reflect historical, literary, and even theological diversity (in terms of covenant, motif, and revelation-historical context), there's an unmistakable continuity born out of that diversity.[2] As a practical result, the student of Scripture can expect that the Bible will function as its own best commentary.

Although the continuity of Scripture suggests that interpretive correlation can bridge literary and canonical distance, interpretive correlation is nonetheless most useful when utilized within the same book or between books written by the same human author. As you draw connections between increasingly distant texts, the validity of those connections may become questionable.[3] For instance, if John repeats a particular word or phrase in his Gospel, you might expect that it carries the same meaning throughout the Gospel.[4] If he uses it in different books, the same may hold true, albeit with lesser certainty.

---

1. Grant R. Osborne, *The Hermeneutical Spiral: A Comprehensive Introduction to Biblical Interpretation*, rev. ed. (Downers Grove: InterVarsity, 2006), 29. Although Osborne is arguing for the "analogy of Scripture" in developing theology, the converse is certainly true as well.

2. For insight pertaining to the harmony and diversity of Scripture, see the excellent collection of essays in John Feinberg, ed., *Continuity and Discontinuity: Perspectives on the Relationship between the Old and New Testaments* (Westchester, IL: Crossway, 1998).

3. Interpretive correlation is most relevant within a book of the Bible rather than across different biblical books, but given the continuity of Scripture, many insights are valid even when comparing texts separated by canonical distance.

4. However, this is not a sure rule. Ultimately, you can't assume that a word or phrase means the same thing in two different contexts, even within the same book. Occasionally, writers may repeat words and phrases intending different meanings (e.g., as a form of wordplay).

However, that same word or phrase used in a given Old Testament book may have little bearing on John's use of the word (though John often does build his theology on Old Testament precedents). After all, in the original texts these are two different languages—in this hypothetical example they're not even the same word! Just because you find a parallel between two passages, this doesn't mean that the two passages are necessarily compatible.

Valid Correlation

For this reason using interpretive correlation is as much an art as it is a science. You must think through the validity of parallel relationships on a case-by-case basis, allowing the context of each reference and a good dose of sanctified common sense to determine the merits of the connection. Whether in reference to history, literature, or theology, interpretive correlation requires caution so as to avoid drawing false parallels or unwarranted conclusions.

The problem of invalid correlation is illustrated by the often assumed relationship between Job 23:10, "Yet He knows the way I have taken; when He has tested me, I will emerge as pure gold," and the New Testament texts of James 1:12 and 1 Peter 1:6–7. In the case of James 1:12, the text implies that "enduring trials" should be equated with passing a test and that this results in the reception of "the crown of life." In 1 Peter 1:7, the "genuineness of your faith," described as "more valuable than gold," is "refined by fire" through "various trials" (v. 6). It's very easy to assume a link between James 1:12, 1 Peter 1:6–7, and Job 23:10—especially knowing the suffering and trials of Job! After all, each reference is talking about fire, trials, refinement ("refined by fire"/"pure gold"), and testing. However, in spite of the fact that Job did experience suffering, the context of Job 23:10 is not affirming that God was using Job's trials to refine his faith. Rather, Job 23:10 is a statement affirming Job's confidence that when he does have the opportunity to stand before God in the courtroom of justice, he'll be proven blameless—vindicated of any wrongdoing. Although the language is similar between these three references, the contexts are quite distinct. Job 23:10 actually has nothing to do with the content of either James 1:12 or 1 Peter 1:6–7. Cross-references will not indicate whether this is a true or false parallel. The only way to evaluate the relevance of the connection is by reading each text in context, sprinkled with a dose of sanctified common sense. Correlation is indeed an artful step of interpretation.

Interpretive correlation contributes to the goal of accurate interpretation through two complementary roles. First, by comparing Scripture with Scripture, the Bible itself becomes a safeguard against errant interpretation. As a "safety net," the whole informs the parts in such a manner that the parts cannot contradict the whole.[5] This, however, doesn't deny the many examples of tension, contrast, and movement in Scripture that may at first glance appear contradictory.[6] What interpretive correlation does suggest is that the Bible, while reflecting historical, literary, and thematic diversity, won't contradict itself with regard to its essential theological message.

A classic example of interpretive correlation providing a theological and interpretive safety net is found when reading James 2:14–26, especially in the interpretation of verse 24, "You see that a man is justified by works and not by faith alone." Any interpretation of James 2:24 must be understood in relationship to Romans 4:5, "But to the one who does not work, but believes on Him who declares the ungodly to be righteous, his faith is credited for righteousness." Comparing James's argument with Paul's, each in its own unique context, results in a better understanding of what James may mean and what he cannot mean. The context of James indicates that true faith results in action—that works validate faith. However, a clear understanding of Romans 4 does provide helpful boundaries for the interpretation of James 2:14–26. Again, James *can* be interpreted accurately apart from Romans, but why would the interpreter not allow the words of Paul to inform the interpretation of

---

5. Howard G. Hendricks and William D. Hendricks, *Living by the Book* (Chicago: Moody, 1991), 230.

6. These issues are typically resolved through a proper understanding of context and the progressive nature of revelation. See Walter C. Kaiser Jr., Peter H. Davids, F. F. Bruce, and Manfred T. Brauch, *Hard Sayings of the Bible* (Downers Grove: InterVarsity, 1996), 15–34.

James's words? If all of Scripture is inspired by God, then the benefits of interpreting Scripture by Scripture are self-evident.

While the "safety net" function is inherently defensive, our second function is proactive—the pursuit of interpretation. Interpretive correlation isn't simply a safeguard but also a sophisticated interpretive tool, utilizing an understanding of broad relationships to answer and inform specific interpretive questions and issues. It is one thing to understand what a passage *cannot* mean based upon the principle that obscure texts won't contradict clear texts. It's another to realize that the meaning of an obscure text *can* be informed by an understanding of clearer, related texts. It's in the spirit of this proactive, "can do" role that interpretive correlation contributes most actively to the interpretation of Scripture.

Connecting the Dots

Although there are similarities between doing the work of interpretive correlation and thinking through certain forms of context, the distinctions are sufficient to consider this a separate step of interpretation. Most notable are the common features linking interpretive correlation to thematic, canonical, and revelation-historical context. Yes, interpretive correlation will seek to "connect the dots" between texts as themes are developed, will involve an understanding of how individual books relate within the whole canon of Scripture, and will be sensitive to the progressive nature of revelation. However, interpretive correlation as a process is wider than mere consideration of motif, canon, and the progressive nature of revelation. It is an active and methodical approach to informing interpretation through the analysis of a broad range of corresponding relationships.

Consider as an example the many connections required to understand the well-known verse from Jeremiah, "For I know the plans I have for you—this is the Lord's declaration—plans for your welfare, not for disaster, to give you a future and a hope" (Jer 29:11). Notwithstanding the significant points of context involved in the interpretation of Jeremiah 29:11,[7] there are texts in the book of Jeremiah that inform the meaning

---

7. Every aspect of context from chapter 8 should (and can) be considered in the interpretation of Jeremiah 29.

of Jeremiah 29, and in particular verse 11. Most significant of these is the direct link between the letter to the exiles in Jeremiah 29 and the vision of the good and bad figs in Jeremiah 24. Interpretive correlation actively engages the connection between these texts, even though they're separated by several chapters in the layout of the book.

In terms of history, the vision of the two baskets of figs is introduced "after Nebuchadnezzar king of Babylon had deported Jeconiah son of Jehoiakim king of Judah" (24:1), while the letter is written to those "deported from Jerusalem to Babylon . . . after King Jeconiah" (29:1–2). In other words, the introductions to each of these separate literary units link them historically—they are set within the same time period and refer to the same historical event. Although different in genre, the language of these texts speaks to their connection. In describing the good figs[8] the Lord testifies that he will "keep [His] eyes on them for their good and will return them to this land" (24:6). Moreover, he will "build them up," "plant them," "give them a heart to know Me," and "be their God" (24:7). In Jeremiah's letter to the exiles (those already in Babylon, taken in 597 BC), Jeremiah confirms the promise made through the vision of the figs—the language in 29:10–14 is the same language of restoration that describes the good figs in 24:5–7!

On the flip side, in describing the bad figs,[9] the language is that of destruction: "I will make them an object of horror," "a disgrace, an object of scorn, ridicule, and cursing," and "I will send the sword, famine, and plague against them" (24:9–10). In the same letter to the exiles noted above, Jeremiah describes the fate of those "who did not go with you into exile" (that is, those who remained in Jerusalem under King Zedekiah): "I am about to send against them sword, famine, and plague," "I will make them a horror," "an object of scorn and a disgrace" (29:17–18). As if the connection to the vision of the basket of figs needed any more support, Jeremiah states in the letter that these will be made "like rotten figs that are inedible because they are so bad" (29:17)! The language of the

---

8. The good figs refer to the exiles taken into captivity in 597 BC (eleven years before the destruction of Jerusalem).

9. The bad figs refer to those who remained in Jerusalem to experience the siege and destruction of the city in 586 BC, and by extension those who sought refuge in Egypt.

vision of chapter 24 and the letter of chapter 29 match in such a manner to confirm that Jeremiah is speaking of the same historical groups of people—those taken in 597 BC who would be spared destruction and would provide the remnant through which new covenant promises would be fulfilled and those who would experience God's wrath with the destruction of Jerusalem in 586 BC.

Theologically, the language of Jeremiah 24:5–7 and 29:10–14, in describing the good figs, clearly points to the new covenant. One can correlate this back to Deuteronomy 30:1–10 and forward to Jeremiah 31:31–34 and Ezekiel 36 and 37. The "I will" promises of geographical restoration, material prosperity, and spiritual renewal permeate these passages of Scripture. By the same token, the language describing the bad figs from Jeremiah 24:8–10 and 29:15–19 echoes the language of old covenant consequences in Deuteronomy 28:15–68. Even at a glance, one can quickly see how historical, literary, and theological correlation informs a proper understanding of the Jeremiah 29:11 promise. And our example really only touches the surface, connecting the major dots between these passages. One might also consider the thematic emphasis in Jeremiah warning the people of Jerusalem against going to Egypt for protection and refuge from the Babylonians (see Jer 24:8: does this remind us of a larger Old Testament theme warning God's people against "going back to Egypt"?). Notice the language of judgment proclaimed against "all you Judeans who live in the land of Egypt": "I am watching over them for disaster and not for good . . ." (Jer 44:26–27). Just as Jeremiah 29:11 uses the language of new covenant restoration to address the historical referents behind the vision of good figs, so Jeremiah 44:27 uses the old covenant language of judgment to address the historical referents within the vision of the bad figs. Connecting the dots is instrumental to relating the part to the whole—at the level of interpretation and even at the level of application. Has anyone ever considered Jeremiah 44:27 as a propositional, universal promise and then appropriated it to themselves?

As demonstrated in the above illustration, interpretive correlation is often multifaceted, and connecting the dots can quickly look more like a complex flow chart than simple movement from point A to point B. Corresponding relationships are of diverse kinds and varying levels of significance and often spread through a range of texts. However, even with that diversity, most connections fit nicely into the realms of history, literature, and theology. Utilizing this approach, we'll survey and illustrate the most relevant points of connectivity that contribute to the work of interpretive correlation.

Correlating Historical Content

In the realm of biblical history, most connections between related passages involve narrative sequencing (this happened after that), narrative causal inference (this happened because of that), or parallel passages (two texts describing the same approximate event). Sequencing and causal inference are typically communicated within close proximity. However, interpretive correlation seeks to draw connections between those passages that reflect a parallel history even when there's considerable distance between texts. The previous example from Jeremiah 24 and 29 illustrates this point. Although chapter 24 recounts a prophetic vision and chapter 29 a prophetic letter, and even though they are separated sequentially within the book of Jeremiah, they're both marked by matching historical introductions. These historical introductions establish that the referents of the good figs and the recipients of the letter are one and the same. At the same time, the bad figs relate directly to Zedekiah and those who remained with him in Jerusalem. As noted before, the matching language and theological content reinforce this conclusion, but the historical markers alone would be sufficient to make such a connection.

An example of parallel history between different books is found when comparing Malachi 3:13–16 to Ezra 9–10. Although Malachi doesn't mention Ezra nor the specific situation described in Ezra 9–10, there are inferred connections. In Malachi, Judean men are guilty of "acting treacherously" against the "wives of their youth." They were divorcing their Judean wives—in essence hating them—and with regard to this God states his clear displeasure (Mal 2:16).[10] No certain context is given for this event, but it's more than plausible to suggest a parallel to the contemporaneous narrative account in Ezra 9–10. In Ezra, Judean men were taking foreign wives and giving their daughters to foreign men. In reaction to this, Ezra actually commands that the Judean men divorce their foreign wives. It's likely that these are complementary historical references—that the Judean men were divorcing their Judean wives (Mal 2:13–16) to marry the same foreign women as seen in Ezra 9–10. The interpretation of each text is better informed through a correlation with the other. At the very least, one can see that between these texts there are two sides to divorce: Malachi indicts the men of Judah for acting treacherously against their wives by divorcing them (most likely to marry foreign women), while Ezra commands divorce as the solution to ridding the land of pagan influence. Correlation provides a framework for understanding these two texts in light of one another while in addition informing the manner in which we begin to develop a theology of divorce (and remarriage) from Scripture.

There are many examples of parallel history found between the Old Testament prophetic books and narrative books, and between the New Testament epistles and the book of Acts. But many of the most significant forms of historical correlation relate to "parallel passages" where narrative texts describe the same event in separate accounts. Parallel passages are found comparing the books of Samuel and Kings with Chronicles, Ezra with Nehemiah, and all four of the Gospels (in particular, the three Synoptic Gospels of Matthew, Mark, and Luke). As interpreters, our goal is to compare parallel narratives so far as it informs the interpretation of the text—not simply to recreate the

---

10. The translation of Mal 2:16 is notoriously difficult. Many translations have God as the subject of a propositional statement "I hate divorce," while others take the men of Judah as the subject, "He who hates and divorces . . . ," or as a conditional statement, "If he hates and divorces his wife . . ." (HCSB). For an overview of the exegetical issues involved in the translation of Mal 2:16, see Douglas Stuart, "Malachi," in *The Minor Prophets: An Exegetical & Expositional Commentary*, vol. 3, ed. Thomas Edward McComiskey (Grand Rapids: Baker, 1998), 1341–44.

historical event apart from the text. Consider the account of the feeding of the 5,000 in Mark's and John's Gospel:[11]

Table 9.1 — The Feeding of the 5,000	
Mark 6:35–44	**John 6:1–13**
[35]When it was already late, His disciples approached Him and said, "This place is a wilderness, and it is already late! [36]Send them away, so they can go into the surrounding countryside and villages to buy themselves something to eat." [37]"You give them something to eat," He responded. They said to Him, "Should we go and buy 200 denarii worth of bread and give them something to eat?" [38]And He asked them, "How many loaves do you have? Go look." When they found out they said, "Five, and two fish." [39]Then He instructed them to have all the people sit down in groups on the green grass. [40]So they sat down in ranks of hundreds and fifties. [41]Then He took the five loaves and the two fish, and looking up to heaven, He blessed and broke the loaves. He kept giving them to His disciples to set before the people. He also divided the two fish among them all. [42]Everyone ate and was filled. [43]Then they picked up 12 baskets full of pieces of bread and fish. [44]Now those who ate the loaves were 5,000 men.	[1]After this, Jesus crossed the Sea of Galilee (or Tiberias). [2]And a huge crowd was following Him because they saw the signs that He was performing by healing the sick. [3]So Jesus went up a mountain and sat down there with His disciples. [4]Now the **Passover**, a Jewish festival, was near. [5]Therefore, when Jesus looked up and noticed a huge crowd coming toward Him, He asked **Philip,** "Where will we buy bread so these people can eat? [6]He asked this to test him, for He Himself knew what He was going to do. [7]Philip answered, "Two hundred denarii worth of bread wouldn't be enough for each of them to have a little." [8]One of His disciples, **Andrew,** Simon Peter's brother, said to Him, [9]"There's **a boy** here who has five barley loaves and two fish—but what are they for so many?" [10]Then Jesus said, "Have the people sit down." There was plenty of grass in that place, so they sad down. The men numbered about 5,000. [11]Then Jesus took the loaves, and after giving thanks He distributed them to those who were seated—so also with the fish, as much as they wanted. [12]When they were full, He told His disciples, "Collect the leftovers so that nothing is wasted." [13]So they collected them and filled 12 baskets with the pieces from the five barley loaves that were left over by those who had eaten.

---

11. The feeding of the 5,000 is one of the few accounts that is found in all four Gospels, but because the accounts in Matthew, Mark, and Luke (the "Synoptic Gospels") are closely related, we will simply compare the accounts in Mark's and John's Gospel, which will be sufficient for our purposes.

When viewed in parallel columns, it becomes apparent that while the historical event underlying each of these accounts is one and the same, Mark and John each tell the story from their own particular vantage points. Strikingly, all the specific facts cohere very closely (indicated by underlining): the 200 denarii worth of bread, the five loaves and two fish, the twelve baskets, the 5,000 men who ate, even the people sitting down in the grass and Jesus praying and then distributing the food. At the same time, each evangelist supplies additional valuable detail, perhaps informed by eyewitness testimony:[12] Mark tells us that the grass was green and that Jesus had people sit down in groups of 150. John tells us the names of some of the disciples involved, Philip and Andrew, Peter's brother, as well as that it was near Passover (i.e., springtime, which nicely matches with Mark's information about the "green grass") and that the one who supplied the five loaves and two fish was actually a boy. Why don't you take a minute and look at these accounts more closely? We're sure you can register additional observations about similarities and minor differences in the way Mark and John tell the story. In doing so, the similarities and the differences ought to inform our understanding of the text, whether our primary focus is in Mark or in John.

In the realm of history, perhaps one of the most pragmatic forms of interpretive correlation happens when biographical parallels are drawn. Anytime you encounter a particular person in Scripture, it's always helpful to examine other portions of the Bible that might inform our understanding of this character. For instance, consider the characterization of Barnabas, "son of encouragement." Why was Joseph named "Barnabas" by the apostles (Acts 4:36)? This can likely be attributed to his sale of a field and the laying of the proceeds at the "feet of the apostles" (Acts 4:37). Presumably, this action by Joseph provided the example that encouraged the sale of other tracts of land and possessions among the believers (Acts 4:32–35). But tracing Barnabas throughout Acts, one finds that he's depicted as an encourager in each pericope in which he appears. When Saul came to Jerusalem to join the disciples

---

12. John, of course, was an eyewitness himself, as he was one of the Twelve. Mark most likely had access to Peter's eyewitness recollection (cf. 1 Pet 5:13), which explains why some of the information he includes sounds as if it came from someone who was actually present at a given event.

after his conversion experience, they were afraid of him, not believing that he was a disciple (Acts 9:26). However, he found support in Barnabas, who brought him before the apostles, acting as an intermediary, on one hand encouraging this new disciple and on the other hand encouraging the community of believers to accept him as one of their own (Acts 9:27–28). Later, Barnabas is again on the scene at a pivotal point, encouraging the Gentile converts in Antioch and, rather consequentially, recruiting Paul to join him (Acts 11:22–30; 13:1–2 reports that the church in Antioch sent these two men on Paul's first missionary journey). Barnabas's encouragement to the Gentiles at this juncture was historically critical, for this was the very inception of God's program for the worldwide expansion of the gospel. Finally, his aptitude for encouragement brought Mark under his wing, in the providence of God expanding the gospel ever further to Cyprus (Acts 15:36–41). What is more, through the encouragement of Barnabas, Mark remains an integral part of the expansion of the gospel, later writing a Gospel and being deemed by Paul as "useful" in the ministry (2 Tim 4:11). Connecting the dots between these narratives not only provides a clearer look at the role of encouragement in God's program of expanding the church (certainly a model for application), it also informs the reader as to why Joseph became known as the "son of encouragement" in the first place!

Correlating Literary Content

In the realm of language, correlation typically centers on the comparison of words and phrases. This begins with simple word parallels, where one compares how the same word is used in different texts. While this practice should focus on the Greek and Hebrew texts rather than words used in English translation, one can find value in comparing English words, albeit with caution. That said, a concordance allows English Bible students to quickly access original-language words behind translation, and thus there is little reason not to perform word studies in the original languages. Actually, doing word studies essentially is a matter of ascertaining what a word *can* mean through correlation (semantic range) and then discerning what a word *does* mean via context. Performing word studies involves correlation at its most basic level; we'll have more to say about this in the following chapter.

Word Use throughout Scripture

At this point, our primary concern isn't with semantic range and word definitions. We're rather interested in how the correlation of words through Scripture might inform the interpretation of words in particular texts. For example, Colossians 1:15 refers to Jesus as the "firstborn over all creation." Studying this portion of Colossians, we should ask, "What is meant by the word 'firstborn'?" Jehovah's Witnesses see the reference in verse 15 as depicting numerical order—Jesus was the first created being, and through him all other things were then made.[13] Similarly, Mormons view Jesus as the literal "firstborn"—the first child born to the "Heavenly Father" and one of his goddess wives. In reference to the person of Christ and his role in creation, how should Christians understand the word "firstborn"?

The Greek term *prōtotokos* can refer either to "first in order of time" or to preeminence in rank. Actually, in Colossians 1:18 Jesus is called the "firstborn from the dead," likely denoting the idea of "first in order" (he was the first to rise from the dead with a resurrection body). But is this the same sense in which Jesus is "firstborn over all creation" (v. 15)? The correlation of Scripture provides ample evidence to support the idea that preeminence in rank is the thought behind *prōtotokos* in verse 15.

In fact, the concept of the firstborn is found in many parts of the Old Testament to support the idea of preeminence.[14] In Exodus 4:22 Israel is described as "God's firstborn son," yet Jacob (Israel) was not the firstborn of Isaac's sons, nor was the nation of Israel the first nation

---

13. The New World Translation of the Jehovah's Witnesses actually inserts the word "other" five times in Col 1:15–20 to emphasize their theological interpretation of this text. According to the Jehovah's Witnesses, Jesus was the first created being, a "lesser mighty god," and through Jesus all "other" things were created.

14. The Greek translation of the Old Testament (Septuagint) lends some credibility to correlating *prōtotokos* from Old Testament texts, as this is the same Greek word used to translate the Hebrew in these texts.

to exist (Genesis 10).[15] Jeremiah refers to Ephraim as God's firstborn (Jer 31:9), yet Ephraim was not the firstborn of Joseph's children (Gen 48:14).[16] And Psalm 89:27 describes David as "My firstborn," yet David was the youngest among Jesse's sons (1 Sam 16:10–13). There's ample support in Scripture that the firstborn concept can refer to preeminence, even when birth order would suggest otherwise.[17] Here, interpretive correlation simply buttresses an interpretive conclusion that can be largely supported by context—just as Christ has "first place in everything" by nature of his position as "the head of the body" (Col 1:18), so he's preeminent over all things by nature of his being "the image of the invisible God" (Col 1:15).[18]

Grammatical and Literary Structures

As with word parallels, sometimes similar grammatical forms and literary structures between passages provide insight into meaning. When literary style is repeated, especially in close proximity, this *may* provide some exegetical clue to the interpretation of the text. Although repetition of phraseology, syntax, and grammatical structure may stem from stylistic choices, they're rarely accidental and may alert the reader to intended connections in meaning. For example, consider the rather ambiguous (if not cryptic) conclusion to the curse on women in Genesis 3:16: "Your desire will be for your husband, yet he will rule over you." There are generally two approaches to the interpretation of this part of the curse: (1) that desire has to do with sexual desire; or (2) that desire has to do with the ambition of authority. The first approach suggests that in spite of the fact that women will bear children in anguish, the command to "be

---

15. Interestingly, while Israel may have been Yahweh's firstborn in the sense of preeminence in rank (or election), the play on words contrasts this position with Pharaoh's literal firstborn child (first in order). See Exod 4:22–23.

16. Clearly Israel's blessing and choice of Ephraim over Manasseh illustrates the literary (and theological) emphasis on preeminence as the focal point of the firstborn concept found throughout Scripture.

17. Considering the irony embedded in this motif, this is as much a point of theological correlation as it is of literary correlation.

18. The semantic flexibility of *prōtotokos* is on full display in this passage, as Jesus's place in order as the first raised from the dead positions him uniquely to fulfill his role as the preeminent head of the body.

fruitful and multiply" stands intact—men and women are still attracted to each another, will still come together in marriage, and babies will still be born. The second approach suggests that after the fall what God created to be perfectly harmonious (the relationship between man and woman) will no longer be harmonious. With two sinners living together, there will be tension—a struggle that was never intended nor can ever be described as "good." At the very least, this approach suggests that subsequent to the fall there will be an ever-persistent struggle for authority in the marriage relationship.

While it's certainly possible that the cryptic nature of poetic language allows for multiple ideas in Genesis 3:16,[19] there's literary evidence to support that the second approach (tension in role relationship) is a component of this curse. Following the pronouncement of the curse, Genesis 4 transitions to illustrate the fallen condition of humanity in the narrative of creation's first murder. At the rejection of his offering, Cain became furious. In response to Cain, the Lord issues a cryptic warning: "sin is crouching at the door. Its desire is for you, but you must rule over it" (Gen 4:7). The similarity between the statements in Genesis 3:16 and 4:7 is quite fascinating, and almost certainly far from accidental. The language and syntax are almost identical between the two, and given the textual proximity, there is likely intentional symmetry between the statements. The point may be as follows: just as sin struggles for authority in the fallen heart of humankind, so the woman struggles with her husband for authority in marriage. The perfect relationship that God intended in the garden would be disastrously and irrevocably transformed by the fall—God's command that the man and the woman "be fruitful and multiply" continues to be in effect, but there will be great turmoil in the process of carrying out this command.

While the literary parallels between these statements suggest an interpretive link, context is ultimately the more significant player in determining the meaning of these statements. As is often the case, interpretive correlation supports a conclusion that is already drawn by way

---

19. Poetic script will often convey multiple ideas in terse style. This is obviously an exception to the one-meaning principle, but one that is supported by other poetic, programmatic texts (such as those reflecting covenant promises and announcements).

of the standard consideration of context and inherent word meaning. Nevertheless, interpretive correlation has its role in the process, and in this example can even be extended into the New Testament. For instance, would there be any value in reading the Pauline discourse of 1 Timothy 2:11–15 in view of Genesis 3:16 and 4:7? What do you think?

Correlating Theological Content

As an interpretive measure, correlating theological content in Scripture should not be viewed as a means to developing theology (as described in chapter 15). Nor is it simply to develop a better understanding of themes and motifs in Scripture (as described in chapter 11). As an aspect of interpretive correlation, we are simply recognizing that theological relationships often do inform the interpretation of individual texts. By drawing on the inferred relationships between or within theological themes and motifs, interpretive insight is achieved.

For instance, in studying Genesis 1:27, "So God created man in His own image; He created him in the image of God; He created them male and female," an obvious set of questions arise. In what manner is humankind (male and female) created in the "image of God"? What is the nature of that image? Does Genesis 1:27 imply that God has a body? There are many conceptions of image that have been suggested by theologians in response to those questions. Interpreting the concept of image in Genesis 1:27 is greatly enhanced through interpretive correlation, especially in deciding between a material and an immaterial construct of "image."[20]

The New Testament frequently alludes back to the book of Genesis. In the case of Colossians 3:10, there's an apparent allusion to Genesis 1:27: "You are being renewed in knowledge according to the image of your Creator." In the context of Colossians 3:1–11, spiritual transformation is in view, not physical transformation. This isn't to suggest

---

20. Although most Christians readily assume an immaterial sense of "image," there are some sects that view this image materially and physically. Mormons understand men and women to be created in the image of God in much the same way that sons and daughters bear the image of their father. After all, in Mormon theology we are the literal offspring of the one they call "Heavenly Father."

that physical transformation is outside of the scope of Christian expectation—in fact, the resurrection body is physical, not merely spiritual (1 Cor 15:35–50). But when 2 Corinthians 5:17 says, "If anyone is in Christ, he is a new creation," this doesn't mean that a believer receives a new physical body at the point of regeneration. No, this in fact comes at a later time—at the point of glorification.

What does all this imply? If Colossians 3:10 is alluding back to Genesis 1:27, and if Paul is arguing that spiritual transformation is in some sense a matter of being renewed back into the image of God (cf. Gen 1:27), then logic would have it that this image is an immaterial image and not a material, physical image. While Colossians 3:10 isn't directly addressing the "image of God" question, it does imply the answer. Often interpretive correlation leans on inferred connections to draw implied solutions.

Continuing to address the "image of God" issue, correlation also helps answer the associated question: Does Genesis 1:27 imply that God has a body? Here one might consider John 4:24, which states that "God is spirit" and Luke 24:39, where Jesus distinguishes his resurrection body by asking the disciples to "Handle Me and see, for a spirit does not have flesh and bones as you see I have" (NKJV). While we should exercise caution not to overemphasize the point (Jesus is clearly not dealing with the same issue between these texts), there's inferred support from these texts suggesting that the Genesis 1:27 "image" has nothing to do with the physical body.

Final Thoughts

Although we're presenting interpretive correlation as a step of interpretation, it should be rather obvious that this is as much a way of thinking through Scripture as it is a mechanical step of inductive study. With time, connecting the dots throughout Scripture becomes a matter of habit, an interpretive skill that reads Scripture in light of Scripture. Through practice, this skill is quickly implemented in all Bible-reading forums, from early-morning devotional reading to late-night formal study. But as this interpretive skill develops, how do you find the material to engage in interpretive correlation as a part of inductive study? How do you connect the dots when you don't even know where the dots are found—or if they even exist at all?

The answer to this is relatively simple, but it may not be the answer that most would expect. The truth is, while there are helpful resources that assist in the work of interpretive correlation, there's no substitute for biblical literacy and a familiarity with the basic contents of Scripture. As biblical literacy increases, the speed and thoroughness by which connections are observed and drawn through Scripture will increase. It's only natural that new believers opening the Bible for the first time won't make connections or realize historical, literary, or theological relationships as they read. However, with time a broader picture of Bible knowledge develops. What was once obscure becomes clear, and they begin to see connections that they never saw before. Reading Scripture with an expectation of harmony, one soon finds relevant connections throughout the Bible—even without the use of study tools.

If the best tool for interpretive correlation is biblical literacy, then what should one do in the transition as this develops? After all, even the seasoned Bible student won't always know where all relevant passages are located that correlate to a given text. One of the most basic tools for cross-referencing Scripture is a good study Bible. All study Bibles are different, but most will integrate the references to relevant passages within the commentary study notes or will cite cross-references (without commentary) in the center margin. Also, various tools such as topical Bibles and topical analytical encyclopedias will supply associated references under topical headings. Computer software continues to refine the process of topical cross-referencing, and with practice may prove to be the most useful tool for correlation. And with the study of words, the basic concordance is the most useful tool for finding cross-references in doing interpretive correlation.

However, you should exercise caution when using study Bibles and related tools to find lists of cross-references and parallel passages. In the end, context is always key to determining if related texts are really relevant to interpretation. Just because the same word or phrase is found in two different texts doesn't mean they're speaking to the same issue, and even when the same issue is dealt with in two or more texts, there may be varying degrees of relevance to interpretation. Therefore interpretive correlation requires that readers understand terms and topics within *each* relational context. Parallel language alone doesn't indicate a relevant connection. At some point, you must assess each connection between cross-referenced texts on its own merit. Some parallels are true and relevant, while others are suspect. Only by reading each text in context will you be able to discern whether a point of correlation is valid or not.

10

Discovering the Meaning of Words and Phrases

Lexical and Contextual Analysis

Who determines the meaning of words? Are dictionaries the final authority, a sort of Supreme Court of language? Did that Greek or Hebrew lexicon which many of us quote so confidently fall out of heaven, so to speak, as inspired and infallible? Or is there some other standard-bearer or authority who can say with confidence, "The Greek (or Hebrew) means such-and-such"? Pastors and students alike are fascinated with the meaning of original-language words, and rightly so. Words are the building blocks of language—without them, there's no such thing as a written "word" from God. Yet what impact does word meaning have on Bible interpretation, and how does one inductively discover the meaning of words in Scripture?

For the interpreter, an understanding of the meaning of words is essential to the interpretation of Scripture as a whole. But while tremendous importance is attached to the accurate understanding of words, words mean nothing apart from their collective use in sentences, paragraphs, and larger discourse units. Therefore, while the concern of this chapter is the meaning of individual words and phrases, it's vital to understand that meaning is ultimately conveyed through the relationship *between* words in broader segments of biblical discourse.[1] Nevertheless, word study is very important, because, conversely, without a clear

---

1. Andreas J. Köstenberger and Richard D. Patterson, *Invitation to Biblical Interpretation: Exploring the Hermeneutical Triad of History, Literature, and Theology* (Grand Rapids: Kregel, 2011), 576, 624–26.

understanding of word meaning, a broader understanding of discourse meaning is impossible to attain.

Word study is not an end in itself. As mentioned, a word means virtually nothing apart from its context, and so word study is merely one (albeit vital) component part in the overall process of interpretation. Inductive Bible study isn't concerned with developing word-by-word lists of lexical definitions. That's not interpretation. Inductive Bible study is, however, concerned with the potential meaning of words in the biblical languages and, ultimately, with the actual meaning of words in their biblical contexts.

Context always takes precedence over lexical definitions. In biblical discourse, words mean what their authors *intended* them to mean, not what word studies, lexical entries, or exegetical dictionaries determine they *could* mean. Yet there's some give-and-take—the meaning of a word in any context is constrained and informed by its semantic range. It does matter what a word can mean in a given language. We'd therefore be shortsighted to minimize the importance of word study as a part of the interpretation of Scripture.

Robert Plummer observes that "Never before in the history of Christianity has there been less need for word studies."[2] In a sense, he's correct. The myriad of tools available in print and electronic format essentially provides the results of word study at the fingertips of interested students. Bible students are no longer forced to perform the labor of word study from scratch, finding and analyzing each occurrence of a word throughout Scripture, distinguishing semantic categories and determining the semantic range for the word. Yet in the information age we find that students often misunderstand the function and utility of word study in Scripture, frequently reading too much into the lexical definitions of words or alternatively neglecting word study altogether.

This is why a balanced approach to word study in the inductive method is both beneficial and necessary. With the availability of modern tools, students can easily access the raw data pertaining to Bible

---

2. Robert L. Plummer, *40 Questions About Interpreting the Bible* (Grand Rapids: Kregel, 2010), 119.

vocabulary. At the same time, students must also gain a sense of how to *interpret* that data—to know what matters and what doesn't, to understand the impact lexical information might have on the interpretation of broader discourse in Scripture. Our goal in this chapter is to provide a theoretical basis and methodological process for word study, one that is easily adapted to ever-changing tools. Within the inductive method, the study of words and phrases combines aspects of considering context and interpretive correlation, applying these specifically to the study of words and phrases within Scripture.

Identifying Significant Words for Study

As a step for observation, we emphasized the importance of choosing the right words and phrases for focused word study. In determining nonroutine terms, we weren't simply discerning between routine and nonroutine terms as an end in itself. The purpose behind discriminate observation was always to narrow the field of concern for interpretive study. Nonroutine terms constitute the words and phrases within a text that warrant further attention. It's simply impractical to study every word of the text with equal focus and vigor. Most words are straightforward and easily defined within their context. What's more, a more precise understanding of a particular word doesn't always translate into a clearer understanding of the author's point in a broader discourse.

We must be careful to choose the right words for word study—those terms that are especially crucial in communicating the meaning of the broader message or those terms that are especially difficult to understand. Earlier, we categorized nonroutine terms into six different kinds: (1) contextually crucial terms; (2) theologically profound terms; (3) historically particular terms; (4) exegetically or textually uncertain terms; (5) figurative terms; and (6) symbolic terms. We'd suggest selecting pertinent words from among the nonroutine terms for word study. Even then, depending upon the nature of the text, there may be some words that are especially suited for word study. These are typically those few words that are crucial *and* either theologically profound, historically particular, or exegetically uncertain. If a particular word represents the primary locus of meaning in a passage, or if translators are in disagreement over how to translate a given word, then we're well advised to investigate the word for ourselves.

Remember also that selectivity in word study may be partially determined by genre. Word study tends to provide the greatest benefit in the logical discourse of the New Testament epistles, whereas the storyline in Old Testament narrative is less impacted by the meaning of individual words. Moreover, as we've seen, Old Testament poetry is characterized by parallelism, where repetition of synonymous words tends *not* to emphasize nuanced distinctions in word meaning. For example, to emphasize word definitions between the parallel lines of Psalm 19:1—"The heavens declare the glory of God, and the sky proclaims the work of His hands"—would likely draw the reader *away* from the point being communicated through the corresponding lines of poetry, and at the very least would produce little exegetical insight. In poetry, repetition, assonance, and word variation intensify the sense of movement between lines of poetry, but you should be careful not to read too much into an author's varying choice of words.

Traditional Word Study

Traditional word study is a matter of first determining what a word *could* mean within the realm of a given language and, second, determining what a word *does* mean in a given context. The question regarding what a word *could* mean is a matter of discovering its semantic range. The question regarding what a word *does* mean is a matter of discerning authorial intention in a particular context. However, before performing these primary steps, the English Bible student must first discover the underlying original language word (or words) behind the English text.

Basic Resources for Word Study

There are various tools available to English Bible students for locating the original Greek or Hebrew words behind an English translation.[3]

---

3. More technical resources for doing word studies are listed later in the chapter.

The most common tool used for this procedure is the exhaustive concordance. An exhaustive concordance will have a Greek and Hebrew dictionary of words that corresponds with the English main text concordance (most English words found in a given translation have a basis in a corresponding Greek or Hebrew word, although direct one-for-one correspondence doesn't always exist). Concordances use a numbering system that allows students with limited knowledge of the original languages to discover the underlying Greek and Hebrew words that correspond to English words within a translation. To find Greek and Hebrew words in an exhaustive concordance, you simply need to look up the English word in the main concordance, find the verse from which the word under study is drawn, and locate the attendant number.[4] With that number, you can find the underlying Greek or Hebrew word in the corresponding original language dictionary (usually located in the back of the concordance). With the numbering system in place, you don't need to know original language alphabets or vocabulary in order to find words in their concordance dictionaries.

Examples of exhaustive concordances include the *Strong's Exhaustive Concordance of the Bible* for the KJV, the *Strong's NASB Exhaustive Concordance* for the NASB, and the *Strong's NIV Exhaustive Concordance* for the NIV.[5] Please note, however, that not every English translation has an accompanying exhaustive concordance with corresponding dictionaries and numbering systems.[6] A unique tool is *The Book Study Concordance*, which enables study of New Testament vocabulary book by book.[7] While not a substitute for traditional concordances, *The Book Study Concordance* breaks down the vocabulary one book at a time, from Matthew to Revelation, and includes helpful vocabulary statistics as well.

---

4. It is critical that the translation and concordance match.

5. Edward W. Goodrick and John R. Kohlenberger III, *Strong's NIV Exhaustive Concordance* (Grand Rapids: Zondervan, 1999). The *Strong's NASB Exhaustive Concordance* is published by Zondervan (2000) through special arrangement with the Lockman Foundation.

6. An example of a comprehensive but not exhaustive concordance is William D. Mounce, *ESV Comprehensive Concordance of the Bible* (Wheaton, Illinois: Crossway, 2012).

7. Andreas J. Köstenberger and Raymond P. Bouchoc, *The Book Study Concordance of the Greek New Testament* (Nashville: B&H, 2003).

In the absence of the traditional exhaustive concordance, students often utilize concordances generated within computer software platforms such as WORDSearch, Logos, and Accordance. These programs feature concordances matching a broader variety of English translations and usually have enhanced search features that extend beyond the capacity of hardcopy concordances. With concordance software, students can simply hover over or click on an English word in a given text and all its occurrences in a given translation appear on the screen. Moreover, most programs supply additional word study features, including easy access to the underlying original language words and their semantic ranges (see the next step below).

Getting Started: Range of Meaning

Once the Greek or Hebrew word behind a translation is discovered, actual word study can begin. Our first step in original language word study is to discover what the word *could* mean. This involves delineating the *semantic range* of that original language word. There are two paths to discovering a word's semantic range. The quick path is through a Greek or Hebrew lexicon, exegetical dictionary, or word study software. Through these tools the semantic range of a word is listed and explained—someone has essentially done the step of word study for you. The availability of such tools should come as no surprise. Standard English dictionaries provide the semantic range of English words in a concise format. Why shouldn't we expect the same for the biblical languages?

While lexicons and related tools are helpful and pragmatic, it's a worthy exercise now and then to conduct this first stage of word study on your own, correlating and synthesizing all the biblical references to a nonroutine term. This, of course, requires a certain amount of effort and is most feasible when applied to a word found less than twenty-five times in Scripture. To see the semantic flexibility of a word within Scripture is an eye-opening exercise and will greatly benefit your ability to grasp the semantic range of a word and its application of meaning to specific contexts.

What makes do-it-yourself word study feasible is the closed system of references found in the canonical books of the Bible. While the use of words outside of Scripture may be influential, for the Bible student word study is primarily conducted within the confines of the Bible. It's the use of words in Scripture that most acutely informs our understanding of how they function within Scripture. What is more, through the use of a concordance students can study the use of words within particular books, among particular authors, or within particular segments of Scripture (i.e., the Gospels).[8] You can study the way in which particular words are distributed within books and how they are distributed among books. These observations will often raise interesting questions and will also inform you of particular concerns and interests by the various biblical authors.

Performing original-language word study also helps inform the English Bible student about words for which there's no precise equivalent in English.[9] Consider, for example, the Hebrew word *sheol*. This word is found sixty-six times in the Old Testament. It's translated variously as "grave," "death," and "depths." The KJV renders the word as "hell" in roughly half of those sixty-six cases, while many modern translations choose to simply transliterate the word in contexts where an English equivalent is lacking (as demonstrated by the HCSB). You could simply turn to *sheol* in a Hebrew lexicon or exegetical dictionary to discover more about this word, but wouldn't it be a fascinating study to look up each of the sixty-six places where the word *sheol* is found in the Old Testament and in the process determine by way of context exactly how the word is used in each of those individual contexts? Once each of those sixty-six usages of the word *sheol* is grouped, synthesized, and compiled, you can accurately delineate the semantic range of the word in the Old Testament.[10]

---

8. A particularly helpful tool in this regard is the *Book Study Concordance*, on which see the brief description above. See also the review by John Kight, "One Useful Tool for the Study of the Greek New Testament," *B&H Academic Blog*, September 2, 2015, http://www.bhacademicblog.com/one-useful-tool-for-the-study-of-the-greek-new-testament.

9. Many words in the original languages don't have exact corresponding terms in English. More commonly, segments of the semantic range of a Greek or Hebrew word overlap a segment of the semantic range of an English word. This overlapping correspondence makes translation possible. Through word study, students can see for themselves where overlap occurs and where it does not.

10. For a comprehensive study of the word *sheol*, see Philip S. Johnston, *Shades of Sheol: Death and Afterlife in the Old Testament* (Downers Grove: InterVarsity, 2002).

Ever wonder how dictionaries are written?[11] How exactly are words defined and a semantic range developed? For living languages, this happens through research into popular word usage. In the development of biblical Hebrew and Greek lexicons, the same process is followed, except instead of a survey of popular usage, it is a survey of biblical texts that constitutes the range of research. In a sense, by doing your own word study, looking up and discerning how a particular word is used in the Bible, you're able to determine for yourself what a biblical word could mean—you're writing your own lexical entry on a biblical word.

Contextual Meaning

After determining what a word *could* mean through the discovery and delineation of its semantic range, the second stage in traditional word study is to discern what it *does* mean in a particular context. Words typically don't convey all (or even multiple) aspects of potential meaning in a single context—usually only one meaning from among semantic options is intended.[12] The challenge of word study (and interpretation) is to understand what sense of meaning a word carries in a particular context—a sense drawn from among multiple possible definitions housed in a word's semantic range. Consider the example of the Hebrew word *shamem* in Ecclesiastes 7:16: "Don't be excessively righteous, and don't be overly wise. Why destroy [*shamem*] yourself?" (HCSB). A study of what the word could mean in the Old Testament reveals a semantic range divided into three groups of related senses: (1) the word can refer to the state or process of destruction ("to be destroyed"); (2) the word can refer to fear and consternation ("to be appalled"); or (3) the word can refer to dismay and bewilderment ("to be astonished"). Various English words may best nuance the intended sense of *shamem*, with context ultimately

---

11. For some fascinating reading on the making of the premier English-language dictionary, see Simon Winchester, *The Meaning of Everything: The Story of the Oxford English Dictionary* (New York: Oxford University Press, 2004); idem, *The Professor and the Madman: A Tale of Murder, Insanity, and the Making of the Oxford English Dictionary* (New York: Harper Perennial, 2005); and John A. L. Lee, *A History of New Testament Lexicography*, Studies in Biblical Greek (New York: Peter Lang, 2003).

12. There are exceptions to this general rule. Metaphors often carry the capacity to communicate multiple sets of ideas depicted through corresponding referent and image, and rhetorical wordplay often capitalizes on multiple senses with a word's semantic range.

determining the intended meaning. In the case of Ecclesiastes 7:16, translations take a rather uniform approach in translating the word as "destroy." Based off of this translation, most English readers will assume that the broader context of Ecclesiastes 7:15–18 is teaching the "golden mean," a form of moral moderation unique to the teachings of Ecclesiastes. However, the word *shamem* could convey the idea of "dismay" and "bewilderment" rather than "destruction." The NET Bible reflects this approach to Ecclesiastes 7:16: "So do not be excessively righteous or excessively wise; otherwise you might be disappointed." This raises the question, "Disappointed *in what?*"

The context of Ecclesiastes 7:15–18 would suggest disappointment (or even astonishment) at the exception to expected outcomes—having seen the righteous person perishing in spite of their righteousness (v. 15), the Teacher advises the wise not to depend on their righteousness as a security against premature death (v. 16). Those who trust in their righteousness as a security might be "shocked" nonetheless to experience trouble in their life. On the flip side, the Teacher also advises against flirting with disaster even though he has seen the wicked live long in spite of his evil (v. 15)—why die by retribution for your sins? (v. 17). The main point is to live soberly in view of the possibility of divine retribution but not to live so confidently to think that there may be no exceptions in a fallen world (v. 18). After all, good times and bad times are in the hand of God (v. 14), yet both are experienced equally and unexpectedly in the common experience of man (Eccl 9:11–12).[13]

The above illustration relies upon the knowledge that *shamem* could mean "destroy" or "disappoint." A comprehensive survey of *shamem* as used throughout the Old Testament would demonstrate the flexibility within the word's semantic range—this is the first stage of word study. But ultimately our word study leads us to the place where we must discern what the word *does* mean in the context of Ecclesiastes 7:16. Either option, "destroy" or "disappoint," is possible. The question for the reader is to discern what sense is most probable (or plausible) *in this context*. Translations

---

13. For a detailed treatment of Eccl 7:15–18, see Wayne A. Brindle, "Righteousness and Wickedness in Ecclesiastes 7:15–18," *AUSS* 23 (1985): 243–57.

have to choose one or the other. But if you've done your own word study, you're not constrained by translations. Now you can decide for yourself what sense of the word makes best sense (literally!) in context.

Table 10.1 — How to Do a Word Study	
1.	Discover the Greek/Hebrew word behind a translation. Use a concordance if needed.
2.	Discover the Greek/Hebrew word's semantic range in the original language. This determines what a word *could* mean.
3.	Discern what a word *does* mean according to its use in context.

Semantic Field Study

Traditional word study focuses on the semantic range of a word and the attendant sense of that word in a particular context. This kind of word study is especially helpful in the interpretation of individual nonroutine terms and the texts associated with them. However, meaning is conveyed in Scripture not only by individually interpreted texts but also through recognized subject matter—the theological threads, themes, and motifs found within and among books of the Bible. Theology is simply the correlation and synthesis of individually interpreted, yet *related*, texts. The structure of theology is formed by the themes, threads, and motifs that run through these related texts. While theology is inherently topical, it is supported by an underlying linguistic foundation—related words that comprise a semantic field. Thus there is an alternate word study track that best facilitates an understanding of theological motif—semantic field study.[14]

---

14. In the framework of the inductive method, the development of theology constitutes the fourth and final step of induction. However, interpretation and the development of theology are inherently linked, as is the influence of word meaning on each. While our focus here is on word study, there is much more to be said on doing theology in chapter 15. For a helpful resource for semantic field study, see Johannes P. Louw and Eugene A. Nida, *Greek-English Lexicon of the New Testament Based on Semantic Domains*, 2 vols. (New York: United Bible Societies, 1988, 1989). For a helpful introduction to linguistic issues affecting biblical interpretation, see Peter Cotterell and Max Turner, *Linguistics & Biblical Interpretation* (Downers Grove: InterVarsity, 1989).

Although the terms are easily confused, there's a distinction between semantic *range* and semantic *field*. *Semantic range* is the range of potential meanings that a given word might convey. The actual sense of that word depends upon its role in a specific context, but that sense is always drawn from that word's semantic range. As demonstrated earlier, knowing a word's semantic range is an essential first step in discerning actual word meaning. *Semantic field* is distinct in that it refers to a collection of related words (including synonyms and antonyms) within a given language. While "semantic range" refers to meanings housed within a *particular word*, "semantic field" refers to *associated words* housed within a particular language.

To illustrate this distinction, consider the English word "car." Its semantic range includes the following: (1) an automobile; (2) an individual unit of a vehicle running on tracks (i.e., a freight car); (3) the part of an elevator that carries passengers or freight. The semantic field, however, includes associated vocabulary and concepts related to the English word "car"—words such as vehicle, truck, convertible, bus, and limousine. Some of these words specify particular kind of automobiles, some relate to associated means of transportation, and others can function as synonyms (such as "vehicle"). However, note that the term "vehicle" could refer to "the means to accomplish a purpose or goal," an aspect of its semantic range that has nothing to do with automobiles. Terms within a semantic field may include ranges that divert significantly from any unifying idea. It's especially important to keep this in mind when doing original-language word study.

When applied to original-language vocabulary, semantic field study equips you to better understand the concepts communicated by the biblical writers through the words that they use. Because theology is developed through the foundation of related terms, it's critical to understand the relationship between words as they inform a particular topic or motif in Scripture. Semantic field study therefore complements traditional word study at the level of interpretation and correlation. You should be interested not only in the words a biblical writer *did* in fact use but also those related words that he *could* have used but did *not* (you may need to read this sentence more than once, but grasping this point is crucial as you read on).

Examples of Semantic Field Study

So what exactly does semantic field study look like, and what are its benefits in the study of Scripture? Let's consider the word "fool" in Psalm 14:1, "The *fool* says in his heart, 'God does not exist.'" In English, the word "fool" can be a noun or a verb, and its semantic range includes definitions such as (1) a silly or stupid person; (2) a person who lacks judgment; (3) a person who has been tricked or deceived; (4) a professional jester; (5) to trick or deceive; and (6) to jest. In certain phrases, the word can be nuanced to infer wasting time (to "fool around") or wasteful activity (to "fool with"). However, in reference to Psalm 14:1, we're not dealing with an English term but rather a Hebrew word. The Hebrew word translated "fool" in Psalm 14:1 is *nabal*, and a study of its semantic range will reveal that the word connotes the idea of unbelief or irreverence toward God (see also Prov 17:7, 21; Isa 32:5–6). In this case, a traditional word study is quite informative regarding the interpretation of Psalm 14:1, especially due to the fact that the English word "fool" doesn't directly infer anything about unbelief or irreverence toward God.

Perhaps equally informative is a semantic field study that involves related Hebrew terms such as *ehviyl* and *kesiyl*. Both are translated "fool," but *ehviyl* conveys the idea of moral disdain and lack of judgment (see Prov 14:9; 15:5; 20:3; Isa 35:8), while *kesiyl* signifies "hardheadedness" and senseless behavior (see Prov 12:23; 14:7; 17:10). These three terms, along with other Hebrew terms within the semantic field, each demonstrate something about the concept of foolishness within the Old Testament, and in particular Hebrew wisdom literature. For the interpretation of Psalm 14:1, semantic field study reveals that the psalmist specifically chose the word *nabal* because it connotes unbelief and irreverence towards God *more so* than other related terms.

What is more, in the development of a biblical theology of wisdom, a study of Hebrew synonyms reveals that the semantic field of terms related to "foolishness" emphasizes the idea of negative moral disposition (as seen by a study of *ehviyl* and *kesiyl*) over low IQ. A semantic field study also includes antonyms related to *nabal*, seen by English words such as "wise" (*hakam*; Prov 14:1; 20:26; 24:23), "wisdom" (*hokmah*; Prov 8:11; 13:10; 14:6), and "understanding" (translated from *tevunah*; Prov 2:3, 6; 3:13; 18:2; and *binah*; Prov 4:1, 5, 7; 9:10). A study of the full semantic field of *nabal*, including antonyms, enhances the idea that moral disposition is an essential component of biblical wisdom and that orientation toward God determines whether one is labeled as "wise" or "a fool." The merits of semantic field study are far reaching, benefiting the student in the interpretation of individual texts and the development of a broad-based understanding of biblical motifs.

To close with a New Testament example, suppose you're interested in studying the concept of teaching in the letters to Timothy and Titus, a major theme in these writings. If you were to take as your starting point a given passage where the Greek word for "teaching," *didaskalia*, is used (e.g., 1 Tim 1:10), traditional word study would entail looking up all the other instances of the same word in a Greek or Greek-based concordance.[15] This would enable you to study all the passages where Paul uses this particular Greek term, so you could see the range of meaning of this expression in different contexts and develop a comprehensive understanding of the use of *didaskalia* in these writings.

But what if you were to include related words in your study, such as "to teach" (*didaskō*; 1 Tim 2:12; 4:11; 6:2; 2 Tim 2:2; Titus 1:11), "to teach false doctrine" (*heterodidaskaleō*; 1 Tim 1:3; 6:3), and "teacher" (*didaskalos*; 1 Tim 2:7; 2 Tim 1:11; 4:3)? And what about other conceptually relevant terms such as "deposit" (*parathēkē*; 1 Tim 6:20; 2 Tim 1:12, 14), "faith" (*pistis*; over 30 times: e.g., 1 Tim 1:2, 4, 5) or "entrust" (*paratithēmi*, 1 Tim 1:18; 2 Tim 2:2)? What would expanding your word study into a full-orbed semantic field study add to your understanding? And what significance would you attach to the fact that an important Pauline word such as "tradition" (*paradosis*) doesn't occur in the letters to Timothy and Titus at all?[16]

---

15. In the present case, this would lead you to the following passages: 1 Tim 4:1, 6, 13, 16; 5:17; 6:1, 3; 2 Tim 3:10, 16; 4:3; Titus 1:9; 2:1, 7, 10.

16. For Pauline references in his other letters, see 1 Cor 11:2; Gal 1:14; Col 2:8; 2 Thess 2:15; 3:6.

Again, the benefit of studying not merely one given word that is used but also related terminology seems worth the extra effort if your goal is understanding word usage in a particular body of writings, especially with regard to nonroutine terms that possess biblical-theological significance. Depending on your word study and original language skills, and depending on the time you have available, you could narrow or broaden the scope of your study as desired. Just make sure you don't claim too much and realize the limitations of your findings depending on the degree of thoroughness with which you went about studying a given word or concept in Scripture.

Table 10.2 — Understanding the Distinction between Semantic Range and Semantic Field	
Semantic Range	Semantic Field
The range of potential meanings that a given word might convey	A collection of related words (including synonyms and antonyms) within a given language

Common Dangers

A chapter dedicated to proper word study technique is incomplete without an adequate warning against committing word study fallacies. Too often, students and preachers step into the quagmire of misguided thinking when studying the words of Scripture, especially when dealing with the original languages. This isn't to suggest a form of Christian elitism that requires linguistic expertise in order to dissect the fine parts of Scripture. It does, however, suggest that the words of an inerrant, infallible text are important and must be treated with care.

What's more, with a little caution and humility, English Bible students can interact with the issues pertaining to original language word study. It's helpful to know the basics of Greek and Hebrew vocabulary and grammar, but even those well versed in the languages often use them inappropriately. Our point is this: Don't trust everyone blindly who says in their sermon or Bible lesson: "The Greek (or Hebrew) says such-and-such"! An understanding of what can and cannot be understood through the study of Greek and Hebrew words provides a great advantage even to those with only minimal original language background.

In certain disciplines it's highly beneficial to understand what not to do even before fully knowing how to perform the task at hand. This is perhaps nowhere better seen than in the realm of Bible word study. The following list includes four of the most common word study fallacies that we've seen students and pastors commit.[17] Learn to recognize and avoid these pitfalls and you'll be better equipped to study the words of Scripture with the respect they deserve.

Full Semantic Range Fallacy

Word meaning is generally not confined to singular usage—as mentioned, most words have a semantic range of varying breadth and capacity. In popular usage, we typically assume that only one potential meaning is conveyed through any given use of a word in context. For instance, the English word "run" can mean a wide variety of things depending upon its intended use in context—the *Random House College Dictionary* lists 135 lexical options![18] It would be foolish to think that every time the word "run" is used all 135 potential meanings are in play or even that a handful of those options are intended. Typically, in any single context only one definition of the word is intended by the author—determining that intended meaning is largely a matter of inferring its role in context. There may be exceptions with certain words in certain contexts (often associated with wordplay and the use of metaphor), but the standard expectation is for singular word meaning in any given context.

What's common sense in conventional language is too often dismissed in Bible word study. Students often assume that a word used in

---

17. For a more comprehensive treatment of exegetical word study fallacies, see D. A. Carson, *Exegetical Fallacies*, 2nd ed. (Grand Rapids: Baker, 1996), 27–64. Some of the examples we use are adapted from Carson's book. See also Köstenberger and Patterson, *Invitation to Biblical Interpretation*, 630–50.

18. See the respective entry in *The Random House College Dictionary*, rev. ed. (New York: Random House, 1988).

a particular biblical context is in some manner communicating aspects of its entire semantic range, a fallacy also known by its technical name, "illegitimate totality transfer." Or even worse, students select a portion of that semantic range to make a point, without necessarily finding a basis for such selectivity in the actual context. To transfer a significant portion or even the totality of a word's semantic range into a single context is a word study fallacy. No word, whether Greek or Hebrew, will convey every sense of its semantic range any time it is used in Scripture.

Caution should also be exercised when studying descriptive characteristics of words used as metaphors. Words used as metaphors can often refer to one definition of a word in multiple contexts but vary in relation to the point of emphasis highlighted by each context. As an example, consider the use of sheep imagery in the Bible. In Isaiah 53:6, for instance, we read that "We all went astray like sheep; we all have turned to our own way." In this case, the characteristic of sheep that is referenced in the prophet's illustration is their well-known waywardness, stubbornness, and intransigence. Sheep, like many of us, have a mind of their own! But then, look at the way Jesus uses the same metaphor—that of sheep—in his well-known discourse in John 10. Speaking of the "good shepherd," Jesus asserts that "the sheep hear his voice. He calls his own sheep by name and leads them out. When he has brought all his own outside, he goes ahead of them. The sheep follow him because they recognize his voice" (vv. 3–4). What is the characteristic of sheep emphasized in this passage? It is the intimate relationship with their shepherd who knows them and cares for them (today, we might extend this illustration to our dog, "a man's best friend"). To go no further (and examples could be multiplied), it appears that Isaiah and Jesus used sheep metaphors in entirely legitimate yet clearly different ways. In fact, in their respective utterances, they highlight diametrically opposite qualities of sheep: Isaiah, their waywardness; Jesus, their intimate relationship with their shepherd. How do we know which meaning is intended? Context must decide.

Common Priority Fallacy

Although a word may mean one thing most of the time, it may not mean that one thing all of the time. While we rarely think of this as an issue in popular communication, it is a common fallacy in Bible word studies to assume that the most common usage of a word has priority over less common usage. The most common meaning of a word in Scripture may have no bearing on a word when used in a particular context. What is more, even when a biblical author *frequently* uses a word in a certain manner, this doesn't mean that he *always* uses the word in that same manner. *Frequency* does not determine *priority* in word meaning— ultimately each word must be tested according to its use in each context in which it is found.

A possible example is Paul's use of the common Greek word for "to save" (*sōzō*) when speaking of women's "salvation through childbearing" in 1 Timothy 2:15 (by any token a difficult passage to interpret!). The apparent difficulty of Paul teaching salvation *by works* (childbearing?), which runs flatly counter to his teaching elsewhere (e.g., Eph 2:8–9), is alleviated when we realize that Paul here may use the common word for "to save" in a less common (or even rare) sense, namely to convey the notion of preservation from falling into error. Paul's point, in context, thus may be that women in his (and, by extension, our) day, rather than Eve at the original temptation, can resist the devil's efforts to lure them into usurping the man's leadership role—if, that is, they adhere to their God-given primary role epitomized by childbearing (which, in turn, is part of their larger role of supporting their husband, nurturing their family, and managing their household).[19]

---

19. See Andreas J. Köstenberger, "Ascertaining Women's God-Ordained Roles: An Interpretation of 1 Timothy 2:15," *Bulletin of Biblical Research* 7 (1997): 107–44; and the popular summary "Saved through Childbearing? A Fresh Look at 1 Timothy 2:15 Points to Protection from Satan's Deception," *CBMW News* 2/4 (1997): 1–6.

Table 10.3 — Word Study Fallacies	
Fallacy	**Definition**
Full Semantic Range Fallacy	Also known as the "illegitimate totality transfer," this occurs when a person imposes a significant portion or the totality of a word's semantic range into a single context.
Common Priority Fallacy	This fallacy occurs when a person gives the most common usage of a word priority over its less common usage(s).
Root Fallacy	Also known as "etymological fallacy," this is the assertion that the meaning of a word is a conglomeration of its morphological parts or constrained by its etymological root.
Exegetical Distinction Fallacy	The presupposition that the biblical writer is always intending heightened theological distinctions between different words.

Root Fallacy

Words have a history, and the study of a word's development is an important aspect of ancient language study. However, words rarely retain all of the meanings associated with their developmental component parts. When we assume that the meaning of a word is a conglomeration of its morphological parts (e.g., "pineapple" means "pine" + "apple"), or constrained by its etymological root ("nice," being derived from Latin *nescius* [literally, "not knowing"], means "ignorant"), then we're in danger of committing the etymological fallacy. The folly of such thinking is easily illustrated through common English compound words (in addition to "pineapple," consider the word "butterfly," hardly a composite of "butter" + "fly").

Unfortunately, when students are exposed to the concept of root words in Hebrew and Greek, they often assume that current word meanings are necessarily informed or constrained by root origins. There may be associations involved, but these are typically quite distant. In any case, you must never *assume* that a word *means* at the time of writing what it *meant* when it was first coined! Word meanings (or at least their nuances) tend to change over time, and we must not collapse the history of the meaning of a particular word. Don't allow etymology to take precedence over context. A word's meaning is ultimately determined by *present* intention, not etymological *past*.

Exegetical Distinction Fallacy

In performing word studies, students should rightly ask why a certain word is used as opposed to other related terms, and with that, what distinctions lie between near synonyms (these *might* convey intended nuanced distinction). However, it's important that readers not assume at the outset that writers are *always* intending heightened theological distinctions between different words. Just because a biblical writer uses one word rather than another doesn't invariably indicate this is significant to the interpretation of the text. This is similar to the way we use rough synonyms in English to avoid repetition without intended distinction in meaning.

As demonstrated earlier, this is especially important in the study of Old Testament poetry, where parallelism gives stylistic priority to the use of synonyms (e.g., "The heavens declare the glory of God, and the sky above proclaims his handiwork"; Ps 19:1). Even in prose literature, a biblical writer may use synonyms interchangeably for nothing more that stylistic variation. Readers must determine the degree to which a writer uses words for theological distinction. There may be significance in word distinction—or there may not be. When performing Bible word studies, it's important not to blow lexical distinctions out of legitimate proportion.

Tools for Word Study

In the ever-expanding world of Bible study software, tools for word study are becoming increasingly streamlined and integrated. That said, students should be aware of primary word study tools and their basic functions for inductive Bible study.

Exhaustive Greek and Hebrew Concordances

Concordances, that is, complete listings of the use of words in Scripture (or separately of the Old and New Testament) are foundational to doing traditional word study. They allow you to find words in references throughout the Bible, provide broad perspective on word distribution, and align English words in translation with their underlying original-language terms. If you're capable of working in the original languages, consider bypassing concordances based on a given English translation and use Greek and Hebrew concordances such as the *Hebrew-English Concordance to the Old Testament*, the *Greek-English Concordance to the New Testament*, or the *Greek Exhaustive Concordance*.[20] With regard to English concordances, however, keep in mind that these are translation-specific (i.e., there are separate concordances for different translations such as the NIV, the ESV, or the NASB).

Lexicons

Lexicons are simply dictionaries that include word definitions for original-language Bible vocabulary. They provide detailed definitions that assist in knowing a word's semantic range. It's important, however, that you not depend solely on lexical definitions—after all, doing so negates the discovery of word meaning through personal word study. Lexicons are, after all, the product of someone else's word study. They're dependable but not inspired. They provide definitions pertaining to what a word *can* mean, but they don't necessarily indicate what a word *does* mean (you may want to read this sentence again and take special note of it). Ultimately, context will always take precedence over lexical definitions. The standard lexicon for the New Testament is *A Greek-English Lexicon of the New Testament and Other Early Christian Literature* (3rd

---

20. John R. Kohlenberger III and James A. Swanson, *The Hebrew-English Concordance to the Old Testament* (Grand Rapids: Zondervan, 1998); John R. Kohlenberger III, Edward W. Goodrick, and James A. Swanson, *The Greek-English Concordance to the New Testament* (Grand Rapids: Zondervan, 1997); John R. Kohlenberger III, Edward W. Goodrick, and James A. Swanson, *The Exhaustive Concordance to the Greek New Testament* (Grand Rapids: Zondervan, 1995).

edition); for the Old Testament it is *The Brown, Driver, Briggs Hebrew and English Lexicon.*[21]

Exegetical Dictionaries

Exegetical dictionaries are abridged dictionaries that provide more detailed entries than standard unabridged lexicons. By selecting limited but important vocabulary, they're able to describe in paragraph entries how a word functions throughout Scripture. They essentially are tools that do the word study for you and can provide the benefits of word study analysis without the hard effort of actually doing a traditional word study. While the entries in these dictionaries are written by reputable scholars, again, they are not infallible or inspired. Scholars have at times been known to be wrong! At other times, multiple scholars disagree, which raises the question: Which scholar do you believe?

For this reason there's no substitute for your engagement with inductive Bible study, including in the area of determining word meanings through, at the very least, intelligently and discerningly assessing the results arrived at by others. Exegetical dictionaries function much like commentaries—in this case, commentaries on words. They are subject to interpretive opinion and should be used as a tool for consultation used alongside personal word study. Widely used exegetical dictionaries include the five-volume *New International Dictionary of Old Testament Theology and Exegesis* and the five-volume *New International Dictionary of New Testament Theology and Exegesis.*[22]

---

21. William Arndt, Frederick W. Danker, and Walter Bauer, *A Greek-English Lexicon of the New Testament and Other Early Christian Literature* (Chicago: University of Chicago Press, 2000) and Francis Brown, Samuel Rolles Driver, and Charles Augustus Briggs, *Enhanced Brown-Driver-Briggs Hebrew and English Lexicon* (Oxford: Clarendon, 1977).

22. Willem A. VanGemeren, ed., *New International Dictionary of Old Testament Theology and Exegesis* (Grand Rapids: Zondervan, 1997); Moisés Silva, ed., *New International Dictionary of New Testament Theology and Exegesis* (Grand Rapids: Zondervan, 2014).

Final Thoughts

By correlating and analyzing the use of words in Scripture, students can carefully ascertain what a biblical word *could* mean. By considering how a word is used in context, students can also determine what it *does* mean. Word study is in large part a matter of applying the two primary aspects of interpretation—interpretive correlation and the consideration of context—to the study of individual words and phrases. There's nothing special or mysterious about the lexical definitions of original language words that Bible students cannot understand. After all, lexicons and exegetical dictionaries employ the same inductive process of interpretive correlation and the consideration of context to the study of words that we've demonstrated in this chapter. Certainly, it helps to understand how words function in a language, and subsequently, how they function in literary discourse. But word study is not the holy grail of inductive Bible study. All students of Scripture, even those relying on a translation, can apply proper and competent word study methodology to the interpretation of the Bible.

As a final word of caution, we advise you to be careful with the selective use of evidence in transferring observations from word study into the interpretation and especially the teaching of Scripture. It's a great temptation to stress a potential aspect of what a word could mean if it suits the context of a message—even when it is not supported by the context of the passage or is not the most plausible meaning. To commit such a breach out of ignorance is common, but to do so knowingly is inexcusable. Again, a measured approach to word study may not provide the pearls and nuggets that wow an audience every Sunday or that provide points of dramatic insight never before seen in a standard resource, but it is better to approach the words of Scripture with caution and yet retain one's integrity.[23]

---

23. For a survey of examples of the selective use of evidence in popular Christian writing, see Richard L. Schultz, *Out of Context: How to Avoid Misinterpreting the Bible* (Grand Rapids: Baker, 2012), 57–72.

11

Thematic Correlation
Synthesizing Motifs for Topical Study

Inductive Bible study has traditionally been associated with an expositional, verse-by-verse approach to the study of Scripture. To some degree, we've implied this approach throughout the book, referring to passages, verses, and literary units as the focus of Bible study. In a general sense, an expositional reading of Scripture is the default pattern for inductive Bible study, embracing contextual boundaries and following the logical progression of thought within literary discourse. Inductive study, however, is broad enough to recognize that a contextual reading is not limited to verse-by-verse exposition. The message of Scripture is communicated not only through literary discourse but also through thematic and topical relationships. Although we dealt with the consideration of thematic context in chapter 8, in this chapter we'll further develop the case for topical study within the paradigm of inductive Bible study.

While inductive study remains tied to the interpretation of individual texts, this doesn't demand an exclusive embrace of exposition as the only approach to the study of God's Word. Within the sphere of inductive interpretation, there's a place for topical study. Inductive sensitivity might even suggest that some texts are better studied topically rather than expositionally. Therefore we turn now to thematic correlation as an additional, important component to the inductive interpretation of Scripture.

Correlation is an essential component of interpretation. By comparing Scripture with Scripture, the Bible itself functions as its own best commentary, informing the parts through awareness of the whole. The purpose of interpretive correlation, which was introduced in chapter 9, is primarily expositional, focused on developing insights to a particular passage by drawing upon related passages. In this sense, interpretive correlation is an exegetical exercise, drawing the meaning of the text from related texts. Although interpretive correlation may draw on a diverse array of historical, literary, and theological relationships, the focus remains on answering interpretive questions aimed at a single passage of Scripture.

The difference between *interpretative* and *thematic* correlation is simple and relates primarily to its purpose. Both involve the comparison of related portions of Scripture. Yet with thematic correlation, the focus shifts from a purely exegetical goal to a broader synthetic understanding of Scripture. In other words, thematic correlation involves an analysis of topical meaning. Its interests are not in the mere interpretation of an individual passage of Scripture but the interpretation of broader thematic elements within Scripture. It is the interpretation of practical and theological motifs.[1]

Thematic correlation involves an analysis of relevant themes and motifs *within* a passage, and *that* passage's contributions to the broader biblical message pertaining to those motifs. In the process of interpreting any passage of Scripture, you should always consider ways in which the passage you're studying relates to other passages thematically. This involves the regular exploration of thematic correlation.[2]

Table 11.1 — Thematic Correlation's Two Inductive Stages of Implementation	
1.	Find relevant themes and motifs in a biblical passage.
2.	Synthesize meaning among passages that correspond regarding a particular theme or motif.

---

1. A motif is simply a repeated theme that reflects the interests of the biblical writer(s).

2. Thematic correlation is not quite the same as doing theology, the final application of inductive correlation. The development of theology is a cumulative exercise that reflects a lifetime of inductive study. Thematic correlation is an interpretive step that involves a discovery and understanding of themes and motifs reflected in those Scriptures being presently studied.

As a step of interpretation, thematic correlation requires two inductive stages of implementation. First, you must learn to find relevant themes and motifs in a biblical passage. This involves the kind of sight and perception that reflects an observational posture—the ability to see the text in topical categories. Second, you must learn to synthesize meaning among passages that correspond regarding a particular theme or motif. This is the heart of thematic correlation—a synthetic understanding of the interpretive meaning of a particular topic in Scripture.[3]

Table 11.2 — Four Stages of Inquiry for Discovering Relevant Themes	
1.	Consciously pursue relevant topical content.
2.	Broaden the scope of the investigation by looking beyond a single literary unit to the surrounding literary units in a given book.
3.	Think categorically in terms of biblical-theological motif.
4.	Look for repetition and contrastive relationships.

Discovering Themes within Biblical Texts

One of the foremost challenges to thematic correlation is simply recognizing relevant themes and motifs within a passage of Scripture. This is especially true for beginning students unfamiliar with theological and practical topics within the Bible. For those unacquainted with the vast array of motifs in Scripture, how do you discover legitimate themes for topical study? Are there clues that distinguish thematic elements and motifs in a passage of Scripture?

To start with, themes and motifs tend to reflect the interests of biblical writers. Within a book, collection of books, or the whole canon of Scripture, prominent themes are supported, developed, and defended. Although themes aren't always stated through explicit means (such as

---

3. Most inductive Bible study textbooks don't discuss thematic correlation. Hans Finzel includes a segment on topical study in his text, breaking topical study down according to the inductive steps of observation, interpretation, and application. See Hans Finzel, *Unlocking the Scriptures: Three Steps to Personal Bible Study* (Colorado Springs: David C. Cook, 2003), 163–78.

repeated vocabulary), there's a sense of repeated subject matter in the development of a motif. It may be conceptual and implied, or concrete and explicit, but thematic subject matter will always reflect those ideas that the author really sought to communicate in a discourse.

Pursue Relevant Content

For the reader seeking to discover relevant themes, four stages of inquiry should be pursued in the study of a biblical passage. First, you must cultivate an eye for discovery—the *conscientious pursuit* of relevant topical content. This may seem rather obvious, but you should frame your interpretive questions to enhance your search for topical material. When looking for thematic motifs in Scripture, an inductive approach must seek out thematic content that reflects the text and avoid imposing contemporary topical interests onto the text. You must observe the text inductively, asking what it reveals about the interests of the biblical author rather than your own interests and concerns. You should be careful not to impose topical content onto the text but rather draw it from the text.

Broaden Your Scope

Second, to discover relevant themes and motifs within a passage, you must *broaden your scope* of discovery, looking *beyond* a single literary unit to the surrounding literary units in a given book. Thematic content is rarely obvious in the limited view of a single passage. The discovery of a biblical motif demands a wide-angle lens on the text, even if the primary interpretive interests lie within a single literary unit. To discover thematic content in a passage, you must look beyond that passage to gain perspective. Thematic correlation doesn't take place in confined literary quarters.

Think Categorically

Third, you must come to a place where you *think categorically* in terms of a biblical-theological motif. When you have no idea what biblical motifs *might* exist in a passage, you're unlikely to see those motifs when they *do* exist in a passage. Developing biblical-theological awareness takes time and usually corresponds to an ever-growing grasp of biblical content. It requires a general familiarity with those things that interest the biblical writers, both practical and theological. What is more, you should think conceptually, as topical categories may not be represented by explicit language. For example, you can trace a theology of remembrance throughout both Testaments, even though this is more conceptual than concrete. On the other hand, some motifs are framed in categorically representative language. A clear example of this is the "Day of the Lord" motif emphasized in certain books (e.g., Joel and Zephaniah) and found in both Testaments. "Day of the Lord" can refer to a diverse array of contextual realities describing God's activity on earth, yet this variance within the motif follows uniform descriptive language.

Look for Repetition and Contrast

Fourth, you ought to look for *repetition* and *contrastive relationships* when drawing out thematic content from Scripture. Motifs are often framed in terms of relationship. For example, in the book of Proverbs, rather than study wisdom or folly independent of one another, it's better to think in terms of their relationship to one another. The same might be said of the relational contrast between law and grace in Paul's letters or love and hate in John's writings. Although these stages provide some assistance in drawing themes from Scripture, there's no substitute for experience in discerning thematic content from the rest of the biblical text. A growing sense of biblical and theological literacy is critical to seeing the thematic content in Scripture. A new believer will simply not see the text categorically the way a seasoned reader will. However, proper topical study is possible for any student of Scripture, beginning with careful and conscientious reading. Building thematic categories will follow, and knowing what to look for comes quite naturally with time.

Discovering Motifs: An Example from Galatians

Before moving on, it'll be helpful to examine at least one passage of Scripture to see if we can discover motifs for thematic correlation within that passage. Remember, at this point we're simply distinguishing themes or motifs from the text that warrant topical study. Galatians 5:22–26 is a concise passage that illustrates our point well:

> But the fruit of the Spirit is love, joy, peace, patience, kindness, goodness, faith, gentleness, self-control. Against such things there is no law. Now those who belong to Christ Jesus have crucified the flesh with its passions and desires. Since we live by the Spirit, we must also follow the Spirit. We must not become conceited, provoking one another, envying one another.

There are different themes that stand out in this passage, but categorizing those themes may require careful thought. For example, one rather obvious theme that this passage addresses is the "fruit of the Spirit." However, you'd need to decide if the "fruit of the Spirit" should be studied as a whole or if it would be better to examine each of these independently. Given the broad, somewhat generic nature of the independent "fruits" (e.g., love), it's perhaps better to focus on the fruit of the Spirit as a full-bodied motif. In association with the fruit-of-the-Spirit motif, you might also see in this text some contribution to the New Testament's description of the role of the law (especially in relationship to grace). However, in the spirit of selectivity, there's really not enough significance given to the role of the law in *this* text to examine it as a motif for thematic correlation (as based on Gal 5:22–26).

Another motif that stands out prominently in this text is the "crucifixion of the flesh." This is very much a New Testament theological motif that uses the imagery of crucifixion to identify the believer with spiritual realities involving his or her relationship with Christ. What is more, if one is looking for a comprehensive list, "life in the Spirit" could be seen as a motif reflected in Galatians 5:22–26. Finally, on a practical note, one could easily see in this text a contribution to the New Testament's teachings on "relationship dynamics" within the church, possibly studying the final three imperatives in the passage under this thematic umbrella.

We purposefully chose a concise passage for this illustration, although we could easily broaden the text to reinforce the relevance of these themes. A study of the fruit of the Spirit is enhanced when examined in contrast to the "works of the flesh" (Gal 5:19). You might also study the role (and power) of the law when set in relation to the role (and power) of the Spirit (Gal 5:16–18). Language that identifies believers with the crucifixion of Christ is found elsewhere in Galatians (Gal 2:20), and the subject of relationship dynamics is established in the preceding passage (Gal 5:15). Thematic correlation will involve interpreting these themes in light of corresponding texts throughout the Bible. But even this begins by examining the context of Galatians on the premise that these motifs reflect the legitimate interests of the author Paul to the church of Galatia.

Interpreting Themes between Biblical Texts

Once you've discovered relevant topics that merit thematic study in a passage, the next stage is to implement a synthetic approach to interpretation—the actual practice of thematic correlation. But this requires that we examine what a synthetic approach to interpretation involves, or put more simply, how we interpret topics in Scripture.

As an interpretive endeavor, thematic correlation involves two primary elements. First, you must accurately interpret the individual references that speak to the topic being studied. Second, assuming that you've accurately interpreted the individual texts, you must also understand the relationship between those passages.

So now we arrive at the interpretive crux of thematic correlation. Not only must you interpret topical content within individual texts accurately, you must also correctly interpret the synthetic relationships between those passages.

In this sense, thematic correlation involves a two-horizon interpretive venture—the correct interpretation of texts *and* an accurate understanding of the relationships between those texts.[4] We've been dealing with the accurate interpretation of texts throughout this book, so let's now focus on the crux of thematic correlation—the interpretation of relationships between thematically aligned texts.

Finding Corresponding Passages

Before you can interpret the relationship between texts, you must first know what references are in play. It's not enough to discover relevant themes in a passage. You must also discover corresponding passages that speak to that common theme being studied. The process of finding corresponding passages for thematic correlation is the same as that of interpretive correlation. If a topic is built around specific vocabulary, then a concordance is a good starting point. However, finding correspondence only through vocabulary is limiting and makes no qualitative judgments regarding the relevance of corresponding texts. Other cross-referencing tools such as topical Bibles and study Bibles are also useful as a starting point, but these too rarely make qualitative judgments linking passages together.

Most students will find alternate resources more helpful in finding relevant cross-references. Included among these are the numerous varieties of biblical-theological dictionaries available on the market today.[5] Theological dictionaries will usually list topics alphabetically, so if a dictionary has an entry on a topic, it's easy to find. However, publishers will often market specific interests in theological dictionaries, and therefore not all dictionaries cover the same array of topics—so you may need to look at multiple sources to find a treatment on your topic. However, if an entry is available on a specific topic within one of these resources, then all the relevant texts that speak to that topic will usually be listed, making these quite valuable for thematic correlation.

Moreover, in the electronic age more and more search engines carry the capacity to bring together corresponding biblical passages.

---

4. David R. Bauer and Robert A. Traina, *Inductive Bible Study: A Comprehensive Guide to the Practice of Hermeneutics* (Grand Rapids: Baker, 2011), 340–41.
5. For a list of examples, see the description of Bible dictionaries in chapter 12.

These include dedicated Bible software programs as well as online general use search engines. The short side of electronic search platforms is that cross-references are often listed without evaluation regarding their relevance, but this is beginning to change as software becomes more "intelligent." While resources are helpful and even necessary for comprehensive thematic correlation, there's no substitute for biblical literacy and common sense in drawing legitimate connections between passages that correlate around biblical motifs.

Exercise in Cross-Referencing: Galatians 5

In the earlier illustration we discerned that the "crucifixion of the flesh" was a relevant theme in Galatians 5:22–26. To reap the insights of thematic correlation, we must not only recognize a theme as such; we must also find corresponding passages that speak to the topic, "crucifixion of the flesh." So what texts correspond to the theme "crucifixion of the flesh"? Through a simple word search we find similar terminology in Galatians 2:19–20, "I have been crucified with Christ and I no longer live, but Christ lives in me," and Romans 6:6, "For we know that our old self was crucified with Him. . . ." We also find similar language in Galatians 6:14, "The world has been crucified to me through the cross, and I to the world," and thematic correspondence in Colossians 2:14, "He erased the certificate of death, with its obligations, that was against us and opposed to us, and has taken it out of the way by nailing it to the cross."[6]

Our research is not limited to these four references, however. By looking up the words "crucified," "crucifixion," or "cross" in a concordance, you'll find many more examples of crucifixion language than those cited above. Yet we've already made some judgments regarding the relevance of the many texts that speak of crucifixion—that's why we didn't list them all. Most are referring to Christ's actual historical

---

6. Gal 6:14 and Col 2:14 don't tie directly in with the "crucifixion of the flesh" and therefore may be less relevant than Gal 2:19–20 and Rom 6:6. However, the similarity in experiential relationship to the crucifixion of Christ makes these references worth examining in a study of Gal 5:22–26.

crucifixion, and only a few speak to the issue of the believer's experiential self-identification with the crucifixion of Christ. We must discern the relevance of thematic correspondence at the level of contextual meaning rather than simple word repetition.

In studying the "crucifixion of the flesh" motif, why focus on the word "crucified" rather than "flesh"? The answer is twofold. First, there are many more references to "flesh" in the New Testament, and there's greater variety of senses affixed to the term. Sifting through these would be laborious and fail to ultimately deliver much insight on the motif "crucifixion of the flesh." Second, the primary point of focus in the motif is identification with the act of crucifixion, not the object of the "flesh." This is not to suggest, however, that the New Testament motif of "the flesh" is irrelevant here. Actually, what is really under consideration in our example are those references where "crucifixion" and "flesh" are brought together in relation to the believer's sanctification and identification with Christ.

The concept of the "flesh" and the believer's battle with it is itself a significant New Testament motif. It is associated with a variety of complementary motifs that may infer identification with the crucified self, including the passing of the "old man" and the putting on of the "new man" (Col 3:9). There is thematic language used in the New Testament that mirrors the "crucifixion of the flesh," especially in regard to terms such as "death," "baptism," and "resurrection" (cf. Rom 6:1–23; Col 2:20–3:11). Interestingly, another motif associated with the "crucifixion of the flesh" incorporates circumcision imagery (cf. Rom 2:25–29; Gal 5:1–6; 6:11–15; Col 2:11–15). At some level, you will find that thematic correlation often leads to the analysis of interrelated and interdependent motifs throughout Scripture.

The illustration above demonstrates that the process of finding relevant cross references involves interpretive judgments being placed on corresponding texts. Thematic correlation may begin by simply linking corresponding texts discovered through concordances, topical dictionaries, and collective memory, but it quickly transitions into an interpretive venture where texts are judged according to how they relate to one another. More than anything else, interpreting motifs in Scripture requires an appreciation of the "dynamic conversation" between related passages.[7] The danger of thematic correlation is that false connections can be made from wooden observations or that superficial connections are built through the mere observation of common language. Thematic correlation requires careful discernment as to the actual relationship between texts. Ultimately, it involves the interpretation of meaning between texts.

Developing Thematic Summary Statements

Connecting the thematic dots in Scripture enables the identification and exploration of a given biblical motif. The outcome of interpreting texts in a balanced manner is the representative teaching of Scripture regarding a particular topic, theme, or motif. Often there are different angles on a topic presented in Scripture. The challenge of thematic correlation is to accurately summarize biblical teaching through a balanced synthesis of what all texts are teaching on a particular subject, with each text understood within its own context. For the interpreter, the most helpful aid to ensure clarity and accuracy in synthetic interpretation is the "thematic summary statement." This involves doing the work of synthetic interpretation and then summarizing the conclusions through a theological snapshot of the topic. It's a matter of considering a topic in all its literary manifestations but then condensing it down to describe in writing what Scripture is teaching in a concise yet thorough summary. It's a practical step—certainly not required for interpretation to take place, but helpful in bringing clarity to the interpretation of related parts.

Example: Thematic Summary in Proverbs

To illustrate the process leading to a thematic summary statement, let's consider a book that lends itself to thematic correlation—the book of Proverbs. The book of Proverbs explores numerous wisdom-based,

---

7. Bauer and Traina, *Inductive Bible Study*, 346.

practical motifs. One such motif involves the relationship between wealth and poverty. Wisdom's teachings on wealth and poverty aren't treated through linear discourse. To benefit from a study of "money matters" in the book of Proverbs, you must use thematic correlation to arrive at a sensible understanding of wisdom's teaching on the subject. This is simply due to the fact that proverbs on wealth and poverty are scattered throughout the collection, each tackling the subject from different angles and perspectives. Interpreting the relationship between individual proverbs, you'll eventually come to the place where you can summarize wisdom's teachings on wealth and poverty through the development of a thematic summary statement.

How is this done? It all begins with an understanding of each proverb that falls within the boundaries of the "wealth and poverty" motif. Individually understood, each proverb contributes to the broader motif from a different angle, although often more than one proverb will speak in similar fashion to the subject. Consider the following summations as a starting point:

- Lazy behavior results in poverty, while diligence results in wealth (Prov 10:4; 20:13). However, poverty may also result from corruption and injustice (Prov 13:23).
- A degree of practical security comes with wealth, while poverty results in numerous pitfalls (Prov 10:15). However, there's a limit to the security that wealth provides (Prov 11:4, 28). Moreover, wealth may even become a liability (Prov 13:8).
- Mere talk leads to poverty, while diligent action brings prosperity (Prov 14:23). Furthermore, those who seek the benefits of wealth without working for it will find themselves in poverty (Prov 21:17; 28:19).
- In a world where injustice is common, favoritism often benefits the rich (Prov 14:20; 19:4). However, wealth without the peace of God has little benefit (Prov 15:16; 28:6).
- Profit comes not only as a result of hard work but also wise planning. Meanwhile, haste leads to poverty (Prov 21:5).

- Wealth brings power in society, while poverty results in servitude (Prov 22:7).
- Wealth gained through corruption will eventually be judged (Prov 22:16, 22–23; 28:8, 20).
- Riches are a fleeting entity; the wise will not be consumed by the pursuit of wealth (Prov 23:4–5).
- Those who lack generosity will find themselves in poverty (Prov 28:22, 27).
- While corruption is the bane of the rich, it is not exclusive to them (Prov 28:21).

While a summary of each facet of this motif is a helpful starting point, thematic correlation is especially interested in understanding how these proverbs relate to one another. A thematic summary statement will therefore seek to bring these teachings into synthetic harmony, even if there's tension and contrast between them. What, then, might a thematic summary statement of wisdom's teachings on wealth and poverty look like? We'd suggest the following:

> There'll always be some who are poor and some who are rich. Yet the reasons why some are rich and some are poor are multifaceted and not always in the control of the individual. Some are poor due to misfortune, while others are poor due to their own laziness. Some are rich because of greed and corruption, while others achieve wealth through diligent behavior and wise planning. Wealth brings benefit and security, yet can also be a liability. Wealth is good at the moment, yet fleeting; only the fool wastes his efforts in the pursuit of wealth. All things considered, a person may have an advantage in gaining wealth through hard work and discipline, yet ultimately wealth comes through the hand of God. Money is a blessing and to some extent, a necessity. But the wise will learn to control it, while the fool is controlled by the pursuit of wealth.

Developing a thematic summary statement requires reflection and precision. As an interpretive exercise, it forces us to slow down and articulate the collective interpretation of texts that speak to topics in Scripture. What's more, it helps to contribute to an understanding of thematic teaching points that provide the basis for the appropriation of topical content in the life of the believer.[8]

Final Thoughts

Scripture communicates thematically; to avoid topical study is not to approach Scripture on its own terms. A careful reading of the Bible will reveal that the writers cared about topics and addressed these subjects through the written word. To avoid topical study is to ignore the very substance of Scripture. However, in the pursuit of topical study, you should be cautious not to impose artificial topical interests onto the biblical text. Unfortunately, we see this happen all too often in topical preaching. Yet there's a better way—a more careful approach that implements thematic correlation in the inductive process. Therefore, as you prepare to study and teach the Word of God faithfully in line with its own thematic content, we'll leave you with a few additional thoughts to ponder.

First, remember that different passages will provide different angles on content. Look for correlation to reveal how separate passages complement one another in the development of content, but don't expect complete uniformity. If there were no thematic diversity in Scripture, thematic correlation would be unnecessary. Come to expect that there'll be tensions in the text as related passages are examined. Don't, however, fall into the trap of attempting to forcibly harmonize texts. There are places where tension within a motif is an essential component of Scripture's teaching on the subject. Learn to embrace tension when it's real, and don't improperly resolve complementary truths that stand in tension in Scripture (e.g., divine sovereignty and human responsibility or faith and works).

Second, understand that themes and motifs may extend between books of the Bible, but language will often shift from one author to the

---

8. See chapter 13 on the development of "teaching points" as an inductive step of application.

next. For instance, John frequently uses the imagery of light and darkness, and in his first epistle he contrasts those who "walk in the light" with those who "walk in darkness." Meanwhile, Paul uses very different language, often referring to those who "walk in the flesh" and those who "walk in the Spirit." While these two biblical authors may be speaking to very different realities, it's worth exploring whether or not there's any overlap between them. Thematic correlation will explore that question, understanding that different authors of Scripture can speak to the same topic through their own unique language and imagery.

Finally, as a word of encouragement to pastors and teachers, consider the merits of preaching and teaching in a biblical-theological manner rather than the more traditional (and typical) topical manner. Topical study can easily go astray and can lead to proof texting—much of this because pastors and teachers are addressing topics related to their own interest or those of their congregation. But what if pastors were to preach topically *according to the interests of the biblical authors?* In this they may by necessity move from one text to another as they unpack the motif for their audience, but they'd be doing so because the biblical text naturally leads them from one text to the next.

As an example, I (Al) was once asked to provide pulpit supply for a pastor who was preaching through the book of Joshua. The text I was given was Joshua 5:1–12—the account of the men being circumcised before entering the land of Canaan. Since this is not an easy passage to preach expositionally, I chose a topical approach, tracing the significance of the rite of circumcision in Israel's covenant relationship with God and then transitioning to the significance of the imagery as it relates to the new covenant.[9] This was not a standard topic to address, but it provided an excellent opportunity to unfold a biblical-theological motif that is found in Scripture and provided a practical opportunity for gospel exhortation.

Biblical-theological preaching communicates truth topically, even if not following a strict verse-by-verse approach. Following this methodology, you'll be able to teach or preach the text inductively, even if not

---

9. Cf. Deut 30:6; Jer 4:4, 9:26, 31:33; Rom 2:29.

expositionally. Those of us who preach regularly, especially those serving in pastoral ministry, have a unique opportunity not only to teach people in our congregation how to think biblically and how to study the Bible, but also how to draw connections between various passages and books in the Bible. There's a dire need for theological—read: biblical-theological—preaching in our churches today. In this chapter, we've sought to sensitize you to the importance of discerning thematic correlation and to help you develop skills in synthesizing themes and motifs for topical study. Our hope is that this will be beneficial not only for your personal study but also for your ministry of preaching and teaching so that it might bless people in churches everywhere for God's greater glory.

12

Consultation

Using Research Tools to Enhance Our Study of the Text

Advocates for inductive Bible study have traditionally taught that by learning the inductive method, students of Scripture can be unchained from their dependence upon commentaries, set free to interpret the Bible for themselves. Some take a strict stance against the use of all commentaries, while others suggest consulting commentaries only after completing the process of unaided study. However, we suggest an integrative approach to commentaries, viewing commentaries and other biblical studies resources as opportunities to dialogue with others in a "virtual community . . . about the text."[1]

Balance is obviously required. Too often we've seen students engage with commentaries as a crutch, taking the conclusions of their favorite (or most convenient) resource without reflective evaluation. Consultation within the process of inductive study provides an opportunity to enhance one's own thinking and to engage critically with scholarship over the meaning of the text. It's not meant to be a crutch, a replacement for doing the hard work of inductive thinking, but a complement to one's own study, an opportunity to gain insight and knowledge from the cumulative expertise represented within Christian scholarship.

We know that very few will develop expertise in all aspects of biblical studies, whether historical, literary, or theological. Therefore, we find that gaps can be filled by consulting with others through available

---

1. Robert L. Plummer, *40 Questions about Interpreting the Bible* (Grand Rapids: Kregel, 2010), 121.

resources and reference works. This isn't a crutch or an excuse for lazy Bible study habits. The collective influence of biblical scholarship is an integral component to the edification of the church. Even those who teach in professional ministry ought to value the insights and contributions of others. We'd rightly view a pastor claiming no need of counsel and instruction as arrogant. Why should we think that there's no value in consulting the work of others in our study of Scripture?

Commentary consultation is part of the unit on interpretation, making this step the third amongst the "3 Cs" of interpretation (context, correlation, and consultation). However, with consultation, order and process need not be rigid. Structurally, the most natural place to incorporate consultation is at the end of interpretation. Logically, the most beneficial point for a concentrated dose of consultation is *after* observation and interpretation. This provides a safeguard against using commentaries as a crutch while bypassing personal inductive study. However, in both practice and theory, we suggest consultation *throughout* the inductive process, drawing from sources to enhance and invigorate each step of the inductive method from observation through application.

Consultation involves a plethora of potential resources. Never in history has the church, especially the English-speaking church in North America, had access to so many quality research materials for Bible study. The amount of literature is quite staggering. But unfortunately, not all resources are of equal value, and some are outright dubious. For this reason, we find that direction is needed in choosing and using resources for inductive consultation. We trust that this chapter will provide that needed direction, arguing the case for consultation's utility while incorporating helpful suggestions for both choosing and using commentaries within the compass of an inductive method.

Consulting the Historical, Literary, and Theological Depths of Scripture

Why should we use commentaries or other reference works? Certainly the purpose isn't so they'll do all the work for us or to deny the serious Bible student the pleasure of discovering the meaning of the text on his or her own. However, as we've stressed throughout this book, the Bible is an ancient, literarily diverse book communicating divinely inspired truth. Breaking this down according to the hermeneutical triad—history, literature, and theology—we find that digging into the depths of Scripture often requires access to information not readily available or naturally known. This information may pertain to any number of specialized interests, including historical backgrounds, original-language grammar and syntax, ancient literary form, and theological motifs. By consulting commentaries and related resources, students have access to technical information they might not otherwise know. The primary reason we use commentaries is not to have others tell us what the Bible means. Rather, it's to provide information and insight that better equips us to make our own decisions about what the Bible says.

Table 12.1 — Purposes for Commentaries	
1.	Uncovering the Historical
2.	Unlocking the Literary
3.	Unveiling the Theological

Uncovering the Historical

Acquiring thorough familiarity with the history and culture of the Bible requires years of study. In time, committed, regular study of Scripture provides us with a good general working knowledge of Bible background information. However, when specific geopolitical, situational, geographical, and cultural elements inform particular texts, a commentary is often the primary means to engage with relevant historical information. Recent years have seen the development of many specialized commentaries, including Bible backgrounds commentaries, which often constitute a goldmine of information in areas of cultural and archeological interest.[2] In addition, you may want to consult Bible dictionaries (great for historical people, places, and things) and Bible atlases

---

2. See in particular the multi-volume *Zondervan Illustrated Bible Backgrounds Commentary* and the forthcoming one-volume *Baker Illustrated Bible Backgrounds Commentary*.

(providing geopolitical overview and geographical locations). What is more, Bible introductions provide a great resource for unpacking the situational context of books.[3] Add to these standard commentaries and most of us will have little trouble discovering the ancient world of the text we're studying.

Unlocking the Literary

As we get deeper into the intricacies of Bible study, we can't help but engage the text through the original languages: Greek, Hebrew, and to a much lesser extent, Aramaic. One of the more significant benefits of a good commentary is the insight it provides into original-language vocabulary, grammar, and syntax. While we encourage students to learn Greek and Hebrew whenever possible, we understand that most Bible students will have limited exposure to these languages. For those with limited knowledge of Greek and Hebrew, commentaries can provide helpful insight. However, caution is advised. Know the word study fallacies—sometimes commentators will commit them.[4] Also, know your own limitations with the original languages. As the saying goes, "A little knowledge is dangerous." One of the benefits of learning even a minimal amount of Greek and Hebrew is that the exegetical discussions in the advanced commentaries become accessible. If you are unfamiliar with the original languages, it's better to tread cautiously over these discussions.

Thankfully there are a variety of commentaries on the market, and many are written for audiences with little or no background in the biblical languages. Some commentaries use informal transliteration in the main text and original language characters in the footnotes. This allows the English-only reader to engage with the primary points involving original-language vocabulary while not eliminating technical language discussions. What is more, when the original languages inform the

---

3. See individual descriptions and recommendations for each of these resources in the later portion of this chapter.

4. For an abbreviated list, see chapter 10. In addition, see D. A. Carson, *Exegetical Fallacies*, 2nd ed. (Grand Rapids: Baker, 1996); Andreas J. Köstenberger and Richard D. Patterson, *Invitation to Biblical Interpretation: Exploring the Hermeneutical Triad of History, Literature, and Theology* (Grand Rapids: Kregel, 2012), 630–50.

meaning of the text, the better commentaries will do more than assume technical competency. As appropriate, they'll explain grammatical function in the text and define Greek and Hebrew terms as determined by context. Non-technical exegetical commentaries will provide balance, incorporating learned insight from the original languages without requiring first-tier competency in those languages.

Commentaries can also assist in alerting the reader to text-critical issues. Although comparing translations may alert the reader to text-based issues, comparing translations will do little to explain the background involving such discussions. For English Bible students, further consultation is almost always needed in the analysis of text-critical issues. Academic commentaries will provide an explanation and analysis of textual variants, allowing you to understand the reason behind differences in translations and to decide for yourself the preferable reading.

Commentaries often assist the reader in recognizing literary structure and rhetorical function. While meaning is typically conveyed beyond the level of words and sentences, this aspect of literary influence on the interpretation of the text is essential. Commentaries are regularly structured around the literary units in the biblical text, and insight is often drawn from the literary and figurative devices employed by the biblical authors. Some commentary series are even quite intentional in highlighting the analysis of structure and the rhetorical function of the text.[5]

Perhaps most significant in the realm of word and phrases is the assistance commentaries provide in the work of interpretive correlation. While cross-referencing tools are helpful in providing correspondence between matching words and phrases, they fail to assist the reader in making relevant connections between passages. Commentaries not only provide the ammunition for interpretive correlation—cross-referenced words and phrases—the better ones specify when a connection is relevant and when it is not, even analyzing the relevance of corresponding texts for interpretation.

---

5. See the series introduction to any volume of the Hearing the Message of Scripture Commentary Series published by Zondervan. See also the relevant portions in the ZECNT (Zondervan), EGGNT (B&H), and BECNT series (Baker).

Unveiling the Theological

Commentaries tend to specialize in the language of Scripture—the study of words, phrases, and literary units. Motifs and broad-based themes are difficult to address in a verse-by-verse format, and therefore theology is often overlooked in exegetical commentaries. However, commentaries are now beginning to demonstrate the importance of thematic context in the interpretation of the text. Prominent motifs often factor into the interpretation of biblical texts, and when bypassed in exposition, they're often treated through excurses or appendices. With the resurgence of biblical theology, many commentaries are now devoted to the analysis of relevant themes, no longer relegating these to treatments outside of the scope of verse-by-verse exposition. When commentaries give adequate attention to theological motifs within the text, this analysis helps readers see the theological threads that impact interpretation—threads not readily seen apart from the assistance provided by outside scholarship.[6]

Table 12.2 — Tips for Choosing Commentaries	
1.	Skim through the commentary and test it with a known problem passage.
2.	Know what you're getting. What is the background of the author? When was the commentary written?
3.	Choose utility over style. Pick what you know you will use, and use it.

Tips for Choosing Commentaries

Students frequently ask us to recommend commentaries. While we certainly have our favorites, we prefer that students learn to discern for themselves the most valuable among the many resources on the market today. This doesn't preclude us from offering suggestions on how to make those choices—we simply want students to test the field and learn to discern what's out there. Even then, we realize that recommendations have their place, and so we offer a few recommended commentary

---

6. Relevant series include the BTNT (Zondervan) and BTCP series (B&H Academic), both of which focus on biblical theology.

sources that we find beneficial in complementing the inductive study of the Bible. But first, let's think through a few suggestions that might aid in making wise decisions when purchasing or selecting commentaries.

Tip #1: Take It for a Test Drive

One of the best ways to know if a commentary is really helpful is to test it with a known problem passage.[7] If a commentary bypasses the difficult questions in one problem passage, then it is likely to do that with most or all of the others. If that's the case, then its value for consultation is limited. In addition to tackling the hard questions, look to see if the commentary surveys the various options for interpreting those difficult passages. The best commentaries will not only present the author's interpretation of a passage but will also provide analysis into the pros and cons of various approaches, along with the rationale behind the author's preferred conclusion.[8]

Tip #2: Look Under the Hood

Before putting much stock in a commentary, and especially before purchasing it, make sure that you know what you're getting. First, ask whether the commentary is geared to a popular or academic audience. Popular-level commentaries are not necessarily bad, but they're more likely to bypass the harder interpretive issues in the text. Also, they rarely include detailed citation. Not only does this make it difficult to verify any information they provide, it also limits their utility as a springboard for further research.[9]

Second, check to see if the commentary represents an evangelical, faith-based stance toward Scripture or embraces a critical approach. This distinction is often laid out in the commentary preface and is usually

---

7. Gordon D. Fee and Douglas Stuart, *How to Read the Bible for All its Worth*, 4th ed. (Grand Rapids: Zondervan, 2014), 277.

8. Ibid.

9. Although the designation of popular versus academic denotes a distinction in depth and style, one of the best ways to differentiate between them is by citation. An academic commentary will include extensive footnotes or endnotes, while a popular-level commentary may have no documentation whatsoever.

a function of the stated aims of a given series. We can't stress enough how important it is to become familiar with the overall orientation of a commentary. Over time, you'll learn the flavor of most commentary series and their publishers. In addition, it'll be helpful to research the theological persuasion of the individual author.[10]

Third, check the publication date on commentaries. Newer does not always mean better, but newer commentaries will naturally reflect more recent scholarship. This results in exegetical treatments that reflect current conversations and trends in biblical scholarship. The bibliographies in newer commentaries also reflect a broader and more current pool of resources, therefore providing an advantage for further research. Finally, newer commentaries are typically set in a more user-friendly style and format than older ones. This is simply a byproduct of the marketplace, where more appealing presentation produces better sales for the publishers.

Tip #3: Choose Utility over Style

Choosing between commentaries is a matter of preference. Some like a certain style of writing; others prefer a particular format. Today one of the major factors to consider is whether to go with electronic resources or books in hard copy. The actual text may read the same, but the way in which the resource is used may differ considerably. Most commentaries are now available in powerful Bible software programs, including WORDsearch, Logos, and Accordance. Keep in mind that Bible study software simply provides the platform for an electronic library. These programs are not themselves libraries, nor do they often come with the best in published commentary resources. Current commentary series are usually not preloaded into basic software packages. While older commentaries are often preloaded, many of these are in public domain or they have little value in the marketplace. You will pay for recently published commentaries, usually at a price similar to the hard-copy volumes. Yet

---

10. In any given series, authors will often represent a variety of individual theological persuasions and commitments. In researching the background of an author, the internet will often be a useful resource. As with any internet research, of course, please use discretion and double-check to make sure the information is accurate.

once a collection is built into a software program, the search capabilities within an electronic library are substantial. In the end, choosing between electronic and hard-copy versions is a matter of personal preference. If you are inclined to use electronic resources and are comfortable reading books on a screen, then building a library integrated within Bible study software may be a wise choice. The main rule is to be comfortable using the system that you choose. Pick what you know you will use, and use it.

Tip #4: When in Doubt, Consider These

There are numerous varieties of commentary resources, including one- and two-volume commentaries on the whole Bible, single-book commentaries, and commentaries on segments of Scripture (i.e., the Minor Prophets). Between these are popular-level and academic-level commentaries. Beyond that, you might distinguish between broadly evangelical and critical works. Below we have listed suggested commentary series in alphabetical order that cover either whole Testaments or the entire Bible.[11] Our suggestions are divided between evangelical and critical works, with the first list recommended for normal consultation. The second list is cautiously recommended in adjudicating difficult interpretive issues, as in many cases these works may provide the most detailed assistance available.

Broadly Evangelical Commentary Series:

(1) Baker Exegetical Commentary on the New Testament (BECNT)
(2) Biblical Theology for Christian Proclamation (BTCP)
(3) Exegetical Guide to the Greek New Testament (EGGNT)
(4) IVP New Testament Commentary (IVPNTC)
(5) Kregel Exegetical Library (KEL)
(6) New American Commentary (NAC)
(7) New International Commentary on the Old/New Testament (NICOT/NICNT)
(8) New International Greek Testament Commentary (NIGTC)

---

11. Publishers often produce individual volumes with the intention of eventually completing the entire series. However, this often takes many years, and thus some of our recommended series are only partially available.

(9) NIV Application Commentary (NIVAC)

(10) Zondervan Exegetical Commentary on the New Testament (ZECNT)

Critical Commentary Series:

(1) Anchor Bible (AB)

(2) Eerdmans Critical Commentary (ECC)

(3) Hermeneia

(4) International Critical Commentary (ICC)

(5) Interpretation

(6) Word Biblical Commentary (WBC)

Table 12.3 — Recommended Commentaries	
Evangelical Commentary Series	**Critical Commentary Series**
Baker Exegetical Commentary on the New Testament (BECNT)	Anchor Bible (AB)
Biblical Theology for Christian Proclamation (BTCP)	Eerdmans Critical Commentary (ECC)
Exegetical Guide to the Greek New Testament (EGGNT)	Hermeneia
IVP New Testament Commentary (IVPNTC)	International Critical Commentary (ICC)
Kregel Exegetical Library (KEL)	Interpretation
New American Commentary (NAC)	World Biblical Commentary (WBC)
New International Commentary on the Old/New Testament (NICOT)	
New International Greek Testament Commentary (NIGTC)	
NIV Application Commentary (NIVAC)	
Zondervan Exegetical Commentary on the New Testament (ZECNT)	

Tips for Using Commentaries

We obviously want to do more than just choose the right commentaries—we want to know how to use them! Choosing commentaries and using them well comes with experience, yet a few helpful suggestions will go a long way in establishing good habits for commentary consultation. Consider the following as a collection of related thoughts rather than a series of steps to follow. Put them into practice, and commentary consultation will complement and enhance your own study of Scripture.

Table 12.4 — Tips for Using Commentaries	
1.	Use commentaries with varying biases and backgrounds. Three to five sources with varying backgrounds is a great start.
2.	Keep track of each commentary's interpretive conclusions.
3.	Continue asking questions as you go.
4.	Use the information included in a commentary's footnotes and make use of its bibliography.
5.	Use a commentary or reference book's Scripture index to find more information on the verse or passage you are researching.

Tip #1: Diversify between Opinions

Commentators are not inspired, and their opinions are not infallible. One only needs to survey the commentaries from our lists above to realize that on problem passages, commentators rarely express uniform conclusions. They may be working from the same text and even have a similar hermeneutical approach, but their conclusions are often quite diverse. Therefore we recommend addressing the diversity of opinions by diversifying amongst the sources used in consultation similar to the way in which one may diversify one's investments by including various kinds of stocks and bonds in one's portfolio.

When consulting commentaries, we suggest using at least three to five sources in any serious study of Scripture. This is especially important when studying difficult or controversial passages. There are two primary advantages to diversifying amongst sources in consultation: (1) diversification provides greater opportunity to find keen insight in addressing the hard questions of the text; (2) diversification acts as a safeguard and balances out one's grasp of the relevant exegetical issues involved. In this the wisdom conveyed in Proverbs 18:17 is true: "The first to state his case seems right until another comes and cross-examines him."

Tip #2: Engage in the Discussion between Opinions

When consulting commentaries, it's helpful to keep track of the interpretive conclusions reached by various commentators. Begin by writing down the interpretive question that you are asking, followed by a list of commentaries consulted.[12] With each commentator, state in summary how they answered the interpretive question. This will generate a list of possible interpretations (or positions) for a particular verse, passage, or interpretive issue. Beyond stating the conclusion, also summarize the interpretive rationale behind the author's conclusion. The better commentaries will always provide sufficient support for any stated conclusion. If commentators routinely bypass supporting their conclusions to hard questions, then the commentary may be a poor choice. In addition, a commentary that altogether bypasses the hard questions may not be the best choice for consultation.

A written list of interpretive conclusions and supporting rationales provides a one-stop shop to engage with scholars over the questions of the text. But engagement requires more than simply reporting what commentators are saying. Once a list of conclusions and supporting rationales is developed, expand upon this by stating why you agree or disagree with an author. Always feel free to disagree with a commentator on a particular issue, but in doing so be sure to state why you disagree. When you agree, be sure to state why you do so, making reference to any supporting exegetical rationale that has persuaded you. You may find it helpful to rate the conclusions of commentators on a scale of plausibility.

---

12. Include the author, title, and commentary series.

Most interpretive conclusions lie somewhere between slightly possible to highly probable. Herein lies the rub—quite regularly commentators will assert a given interpretation that is barely *possible*, but what they would need to show is not only that their interpretation is *possible* but that it is *plausible* and in fact the most *probable* way to read the text. Therefore, don't confuse possibility with plausibility or even probability. Not everything that is possible is also probable. In all of this, the primary goal is simply to engage commentators in their treatment of the biblical text. This will spur you on in your own engagement with the text and provide a safeguard against simply buying into the conclusions of the first author you read without critical evaluation.

Tip #3: Continue to Be Inquisitive as You Research

One of the advantages to consultation, especially when using multiple sources, is that through research you're exposed to issues and problems not caught in observation. Therefore approach commentaries with an eye to learning the issues as much as to answering the questions. When commentaries are used in the later stages of interpretation, interpretive questions will often be revised as new issues come to light. This is fine—as noted, inductive methodology is not perfectly linear. We stress the importance of doing our own study prior to consultation, yet we also recognize that research provides a new set of eyes on the text, and from this, a new set of questions. Commentators will often bring to light issues in the text that we missed in observation. Stay inquisitive even when consulting commentaries, and always retain the freedom to augment or add to the interpretive questions that drive you to a better understanding of the text.

Tip #4: Use Consultation as a Springboard for Further Study

Consultation is not the end of study—it often constitutes the beginning. One good, recent commentary resource will often direct you to other quality sources through the footnotes and bibliography. But this will only happen when you pay careful attention to footnotes and bibliographies. Don't skip footnotes in commentaries, as they may contain information even more helpful than what you find in the main text. And consider bibliographies as an aid pointing the way to further research. If you're struggling to find quality sources that address a particular issue or interpretive question in the biblical text, but you have one recent, academic resource in hand, then use its bibliography as a springboard to find the other sources that speak to the topic you're addressing.

Tip #5: Use Scripture Indices

When studying a passage of Scripture, don't limit yourself to sources arranged in standard, verse-by-verse commentary format. A wide variety of books can function similarly to commentaries even if they don't fit the traditional format. Most books outside of commentary series are formatted topically rather than textually, making them more difficult to use for inductive study. Yet books based in biblical studies topics often answer interpretive questions with as much depth and precision as commentaries. So how do you find content with specific exegetical value in topically arranged books? Try the Scripture index.

Most academic resources in the field of biblical studies will include a Scripture index along with other indices. These indices are highly useful in accessing specific content within a given book addressing specific biblical texts. Don't be disappointed, however, if a book doesn't address the questions you're asking, even when it does cite the verses you're studying. Sometimes a reference is found in an index but little is stated about it in the main text. Conversely, it's not uncommon to find a goldmine of text-specific information in the most topical of sources.

Consulting Other Resources

For the bulk of this chapter, we've focused on commentaries. Now that we've explored commentaries in some detail, let's consider other resources that contribute to the inductive process of Bible study. The following resources provide an alternative to commentaries, meeting the same need for consultation but offering specialized content and presentation.

Table 12.5 — Other Resources for Consultation	
1.	Translations and concordances
2.	Study Bibles *(ESV Study Bible, HCSB Study Bible, The MacArthur Study Bible, NET Bible, NLT Study Bible,* and the *Zondervan NIV Study Bible)*
3.	Bible atlases
4.	Bible introductions
5.	Monographs (volumes on single topics) and journal articles

Translations and Concordances

As part of the interpretive process, serious students of Scripture should typically consult multiple translations. We've devoted an entire chapter to translations (chapter 3). Concordances, for their part, are an important part of studying significant terms in Scripture, which we've already discussed as well (chapter 10).

Study Bibles

In today's market, there are study Bibles to suit just about every theological and social demographic within the church. These include women's study Bibles, teen study Bibles, military study Bibles . . . even inductive study Bibles! Several are excellent, many are helpful, some are gimmicky, and a few may even be dubious. We encourage the use of study Bibles for three reasons: (1) to help in correlation; (2) to provide textual insight; and (3) to provide historical background.

For correlation, the quick access to cross references, especially the relevant references found in study notes, is tremendously helpful in connecting the dots for interpretive correlation. Regarding text-based questions, academically oriented study Bibles will often alert you to textual variants and include some commentary on the issue. With regard to historical background, most study Bibles provide dates, geopolitical setting, maps, and cultural particulars that can enhance your appreciation for the history behind the text.

Beyond these, you may find interpretive notes helpful in the same way in which you may appreciate abridged commentaries. Be cautious, though—the easy access provided by study Bibles makes it tempting to use interpretive notes as a crutch. Devotional reflections found in some study Bibles can also be beneficial, but we'd prefer that you think things through on your own in studying Scripture. For correlation, textual insights, and historical background, nothing combines utility and convenience quite as well as a good study Bible. Recommended study Bibles include the *ESV Study Bible*, the *HCSB Study Bible*, the *MacArthur Study Bible*, the *NET Bible* (with notes), the *NLT Study Bible*, and the *Zondervan NIV Study Bible*.

Bible Dictionaries

Bible dictionaries come in many varieties, with traditional dictionaries covering general Bible topics and a new generation of dictionaries tackling a plethora of dedicated fronts. Traditional Bible dictionaries are alphabetically arranged just like any dictionary. The entries, however, tend to relay substantial explanations rather than mere definitions. Bible dictionaries include entries on biblical places, people, and things, focusing mostly on historical names and biblical themes. Traditional dictionaries are rather comprehensive and are the best place to go for concise explanations of obscure terms in the Bible. One of the better examples of a traditional Bible dictionary is the *Holman Illustrated Bible Dictionary*.[13]

A new phenomenon in Christian publishing is the dedicated Bible dictionary. The variety of these dictionaries in today's marketplace is quite overwhelming. For exegetical study, there is the IVP family of "black dictionaries," such as *The Dictionary of Jesus and the Gospels* or *The Dictionary of Paul and His Letters*.[14] For figures of speech and rhetorical

---

13. Chad Brand, Charles Draper, and Archie England, eds., *Holman Illustrated Bible Dictionary* (Nashville: Holman, 2003).

14. Joel B. Green, Jeannine K. Brown, and Nicholas Perrin, eds., *Dictionary of Jesus and the Gospels*, 2nd ed. (Downers Grove: InterVarsity, 2013); Gerald F. Hawthorne, Ralph P. Martin, and Daniel G. Reid, eds., *Dictionary of Paul and His Letters* (Downers Grove: InterVarsity, 1993).

devices there is the *Dictionary of Biblical Imagery*.[15] For all things pertaining to theological themes and motifs, there is the *New Dictionary of Biblical Theology*.[16] For the biblical ethicist (or those simply interested in practical theology), there is the *Dictionary of Scripture and Ethics*.[17] And for all things hermeneutical (and beyond), there is the *Dictionary for the Theological Interpretation of Scripture*.[18] These dictionaries—and the many others that are now being published—are arranged much like traditional Bible dictionaries but treat a narrower range of dedicated subject matter. This allows for detailed treatments and substantive content within fewer entries. If you are studying a passage that touches upon a specific range of interest, then a dedicated Bible dictionary may be one of the more useful resources available.

Bible Atlases

Bible atlases are books of maps, in this case, maps of the biblical lands. However, modern Bible atlases often provide more than only maps. Beyond geographical orientation, they also provide historical background of various kinds. They're usually complemented by a range of pictures, and many provide helpful archeological sidebars and insets. They provide geopolitical background and illustrate major movements in Scripture, tracing the rise and fall of kingdoms in the biblical era. They also coordinate chronological and canonical sequencing throughout the Bible, providing valuable assistance in historical and geographical orientation to the Bible. Recommended Bible atlases include the *Crossway ESV Bible Atlas*, the *Holman Bible Atlas*, the *Zondervan Atlas of the Bible*, and the *IVP Atlas of Bible History*.[19]

---

15. Leland Ryken, James C. Wilhoit, and Tremper Longman III, eds., *Dictionary of Biblical Imagery* (Downers Grove: InterVarsity, 1998).

16. T. Desmond Alexander, Brian S. Rosner, D. A. Carson, and Graeme Goldsworthy, eds., *New Dictionary of Biblical Theology* (Downers Grove: InterVarsity, 2000).

17. Joel B. Green, ed., *Dictionary of Scripture and Ethics* (Grand Rapids: Baker, 2011).

18. Kevin J. Vanhoozer, ed., *Dictionary for the Theological Interpretation of Scripture* (Grand Rapids: Baker, 2005).

19. John D. Currid, *The Crossway ESV Bible Atlas* (Wheaton: Crossway, 2010); Thomas V. Brisco, *Holman Bible Atlas* (Nashville: B&H, 1998), Carl G. Rasmussen, *Zondervan Atlas of the Bible*, rev. ed. (Grand Rapids: Zondervan, 2010), and Paul Lawrence, *The IVP Atlas of Bible History* (Downers Grove: InterVarsity, 2006).

Bible Introductions

In the realm of biblical studies, introduction shouldn't be confused with survey. Survey deals with an overview of content; introduction deals with issues behind that content. Nor should one think of introductory issues as elementary. Surveys overview the basic contents; introductions address rather complex issues germane to a book's background. Biblical introductions deal with historical, literary, and theological background. Therefore, a good Bible introduction will address matters of history, including date, author, audience, purpose, and occasion. It'll also deal with textual issues and linguistic particularities, along with an overview of genre, literary structure, and rhetorical strategies in a given book. Introductions deal with the theological motifs and general emphases of every book of the Bible. Recommended Bible introductions include *The Cradle, the Cross, and the Crown: An Introduction to the New Testament* and *The Word and the World: An Introduction to the Old Testament.*[20]

Monographs and Journal Articles

Monographs are books that address focused subjects. In biblical studies, relevant topics are varied and could apply to any matter of historical, literary, or theological concern. With the use of Scripture indices, monographs can be used like a commentary; if the verse or passage you're studying is listed in the Scripture index, there may be a treatment that specifically answers the questions you're asking. Monographs tend to provide more detail on specific issues than commentaries and dictionaries and should therefore not be missed when doing biblical studies research and consultation.

More focused and concise than monographs, journal articles are often the best resource for specific issues in Bible interpretation. Journal articles are by their very nature academic. Therefore you should expect more controversial topics to be taken up by journals. You should also

---

20. Andreas J. Köstenberger, L. Scott Kellum, and Charles L. Quarles, *The Cradle, the Cross, and the Crown: An Introduction to the New Testament*, 2nd ed. (Nashville: B&H Academic, 2016); and Eugene H. Merrill, Mark F. Rooker and Michael A. Grisanti, *The Word and the World: An Introduction to the Old Testament* (Nashville: B&H Academic, 2011).

understand that the conclusions reached in journal articles may not be standard or reflect consensus opinion. Journals are in the business of publishing new and innovative approaches to old issues—you should be cautious in assuming that perspectives in journal articles are the end of the conversation. But for detailed treatments on difficult interpretive questions, journal articles often provide the most in-depth treatment available on a given subject.[21]

Final Thoughts

Commentary consultation is not a crutch or a replacement for in-depth, personal Bible study. Neither is it contrary to inductive methodology. Incorporated within the inductive method, commentary consultation—or to broaden the scope, biblical studies research—complements and enhances personal study at every level. In all of this, it's important to remember that consultation is conversation, not capitulation. This means that you must enter into the conversation with wisdom and discretion, knowing when to chew the meat and when to spit out the fat. We trust that the guidelines and suggestions put forth in this chapter will aid you in doing so.

Speaking of discretion, we'd be remiss not to conclude with a final word of caution. For many, the internet has become the first place to turn with questions about all of any number of things. And while the internet has its place, it is generally not recommended for biblical studies consultation. This is not to say that all information on the internet is dubious. In many fields, especially the sciences, up-to-date, peer-reviewed research is readily available. However, this is often not the case with online, open-forum content in biblical and theological studies. Be very careful; nowadays anyone with an opinion can generate a website and publish their thoughts.

---

21. Helpful journals include the *Journal of the Evangelical Theological Society* and the *Bulletin of Biblical Research*, along with a plethora of other specialized journals.

UNIT IV

APPLICATION
Acting on the Text

Steps of Application

Step 1: Establishing Relevance and Legitimacy: *Assessing the Text's Applicability to Us Today*

Step 2: Appropriating the Meaning: *Living Out the Text's Teaching in Our World*

Step 3: Doing Theology: *The Outflow of an Inductive Approach to Scripture*

13

Establishing Relevance
and Legitimacy
Assessing the Text's Applicability to Us Today

Application is vital yet tricky business.[1] While the interpretation of the text is reasonably objective and concrete, being tied to authorial intent, application moves into a much more subjective realm, the realm of the reader. Interpretation depends largely on an accurate understanding of words, phrases, and clauses functioning together in biblical discourse, written communication designed to convey the author's message to his readers. Interpretation can be discovered through a study of the historical, literary, and theological contexts of the original setting in which Scripture was written and received. However, application requires movement from the original context to our contemporary context, a journey laden with questions of relevance and legitimacy. Ultimately, it's a journey that requires great wisdom—or at the very least, a healthy dose of sanctified common sense. Kevin Vanhoozer presents this distinction well when he states that "intended meaning . . . is a matter of historical and literary knowledge; discerning significance, on the other hand, is a matter of wisdom, for it concerns not the achieving of knowledge but the appreciation of knowledge and its right use."[2]

Although application is inherently subjective, this is not to suggest that there are no objective constraints on application. While the reader

---

1. For a thorough discussion, see chapter 16 in Andreas J. Köstenberger and Richard D. Patterson, *Invitation to Biblical Interpretation: Exploring the Hermeneutical Triad of History, Literature, and Theology* (Grand Rapids: Kregel, 2011), esp. 784–97.

2. Kevin J. Vanhoozer, *Is There a Meaning in This Text? The Bible, the Reader, and the Morality of Literary Knowledge* (Grand Rapids: Zondervan, 1998), 423.

must evaluate the relevance of the text for his own day, and ultimately for his own situation, this doesn't mean that the reader has full control over what is potentially meaningful for today. Application may be broad, reaching out to a multitude of modern contexts and situations, but it is not unlimited. It's possible to draw illegitimate applications from the text of Scripture. The one constraint on application that sets the boundaries and limits the perimeters of what is possible is interpretation. Therefore, the guiding principle to application can be summed up as follows: *that which is meaningful for our day must have its foundation in correct interpretation, the meaning of the text in its original context.* Put another way, a text cannot be meaningful today in a way that is inconsistent with the original author's intended meaning.[3]

The inductive method of Bible study provides the necessary safeguards for the application of Scripture. While we recognize that most readers of the Bible will move through the steps of inductive study in abbreviated form, even a devotionally oriented reading of Scripture requires interpretation as a necessary prerequisite to application. It's always tempting to bypass the hard work of interpretation and move too quickly to the application of the text. However, thorough interpretation provides needed direction for the proper application of the text, establishing boundaries that limit the possibilities and provide sensible perimeters for applied meaning in our day.

Assuming that a given portion of Scripture has been properly interpreted, how do you transition from interpretation to application? What are the steps involved in appropriating the Word of God—in doing the head-work that eventually culminates in leg-work (that is, being "doers of the Word and not hearers only")?[4] Essentially, this process begins with

---

3. Fee and Stuart state, "A text cannot mean what it could never have meant for its original readers/ hearers." See Gordon Fee and Douglas Stuart, *How to Read the Bible for All Its Worth*, 4th ed. (Grand Rapids: Zondervan, 2014), 34. We agree with the essence of this statement. However, while current relevance must be informed and restrained by past, exegetical meaning, the shift between the original context and our contemporary context must allow for some degree of departure. Nuancing the degree of departure is often the crux of application.

4. In some sense, the greater problem is that we're simply unwilling to put into practice the clear teachings of the Word of God. However, application often does require deep thought and intellectual processing. We trust that a greater understanding of this process will aid in bringing the mind and the heart together, with the result of becoming "doers of the word and not hearers only" (Jas 1:22).

asking two primary questions for application. The first question is this: "How *might* this text (whether commandment, exhortation, precept, instruction, example, situation, principle, etc.) relate to *us* today as the people of God?" The second question logically follows: "What *does* this text mean for *me* today as a follower of Christ?" The task of answering the first question is the subject of this chapter. The subsequent task of answering the second question is the subject of the next chapter. Both are related; you can't fully appropriate what's meaningful in *your* life without first considering how the text might be meaningful in *our* life—that is, the broader corporate context of the twenty-first-century church.

In answering the first question, you should process the interpreted text through three sequential stages. The first is to evaluate the *relevance* of the text for application in our world today. Such evaluation is necessary due to factors that distance the contemporary reader from the original audience of Scripture. The second stage is to determine *legitimacy* by drawing parallels between the interpretation of the text and potential applications. Finally, the third stage answers the primary question through the discernment and articulation of *teaching points*—clear, concise statements that summarize what God's Word is teaching at any particular point in Scripture. Our goal is to articulate sensible, if possible even memorable, statements that accurately reflect the interpretation of the text along with its eternal relevance as the Word of God. In the discernment and development of these teaching points, you'll gain clear perspective regarding that which is meaningful for today.

Table 13.1 — Three Sequential Stages for Assessing Application	
1.	Evaluate the relevance of the text for today.
2.	Determine legitimacy by drawing parallels between the interpretation of the text and potential applications.
3.	Use teaching points and discernment to answer the primary questions of application.

Establishing Relevance in Application

Thinking back to the hermeneutical triad, we understand that the Bible is an ancient document rooted in real human *history*, reflecting historically particular situations and cultures far removed from our own. What's more, we are dealing with a *literary* text, written in real languages, governed by the conventions of grammar and syntax, and displaying all the traits and texture of a literary masterpiece. Finally, the Bible conveys a *theological* Word from God, God's revelation of himself and his program to mankind. This is what the Bible consists of; this is what it is.

In short, therefore, as interpreters we're faced with three inescapable realities as we seek to study Scripture: the reality of history, the reality of a text requiring interpretation, and the reality of God (theology). Not only do these traits result in challenges to understanding the Bible (various gaps needing to be overcome; chapter 1), they also inform how you should interpret the Bible (chapter 8). Yet the impact of the hermeneutical triad doesn't stop at interpretation. Just as the hermeneutical triad influences the way in which we read and interpret the Bible, it also impacts the way we go about establishing the application of Scripture.

Applying a historically particular, literarily diverse, and theologically laden message from God requires great care. Because the Bible was inspired within the context of real historical events, it is marked by cultural and situational particularities. Because the Bible reflects an astounding diversity of literary genres, not all texts speak directly to application. Because Scripture reflects a progressively revealed theological message, we must be careful in determining whether expectations and imperatives are for the original readers only, for us today, or for both. We know that the Bible has eternal relevance, transcending historical, literary, and theological distance. But the bridges that transcend these gaps aren't always obvious, and sometimes even non-existent.

While underlying principles saturate the biblical text, and while many principles speak to God's self-disclosure rather than provide directive commands and expectations, there are nonetheless cases where the relevance of the biblical text must be brought into question. For instance, what is one to do with Numbers 5:11–31? How might this text be practiced today? Should the jealous husband still have authority to bring his wife suspected of adultery, an act for which no witness exists, to the authorities? Is there a modern equivalent to the "bitter water that brings a curse" (whatever that means) that might be applied in our day? Here the issue is not interpretation but rather evaluating the relevance of the text for application. Finding legitimate parallels for application is beside the point if the text has no lasting relevance for our day.

Establishing relevance relates to the matter of processing *whether* Scripture should have any directly applicable function for today or, in some cases, deciding to *what degree* a text is still relevant.[5] The issue of relevance stems from the fact that the Bible is historically particular, literarily diverse, and theologically progressive. For instance, in relation to historical particularity, one must wonder if every commandment, exhortation, or example laid out in Scripture is meant to be normative in terms of application. Are there some things in the Bible that are so situationally particular, or culturally contingent, that perhaps there's no eternal relevance at all (aside from contributing to our understanding and appreciation of God's historical program of redemption)?

Or in the case of the literary topography of Scripture, we quickly realize that the Bible isn't built around a uniform set of commandments, instructions, or promises. The diversity of literature in the biblical text requires the evaluation of literary relevance. By its very nature, a proverb is meant to be applied, but can the same be said for a genealogy? It's easy to see the direct link between New Testament exhortation and application, but does historical narrative provide the same easy correspondence between text and relevant application?

Also, in reference to the theological nature of Scripture, the progressive nature of covenantal relationships requires the evaluation of ongoing relevance. Although the Old Testament law functioned as legal code for ancient Israel, does that automatically make it law for people today? Moreover, issues in application often extend beyond covenant, reflecting

---

5. On the other hand, determining legitimacy involves one in the process of thinking through *how* Scripture might function as God's Word for today. The evaluation of relevance and the determination of legitimacy are clearly companions in application, but there is a different goal in view.

instead broader ethical movement in revelation history. For instance, what does one do with the many Old Testament texts that assume the practice of polygamy? What about the texts that support the regulation of slavery in both Testaments? Clearly there must be some rationale behind why we might apply some texts in Scripture but not all of them—or at least not all of them in the same manner or to the same degree.

As implied through the questions above, evaluating the relevance of Scripture relates to factors born out of each side of the hermeneutical triad. As we evaluate the text in relation to history, the relevance of its message is filtered through questions of cultural and situational relativity. As we evaluate the text in relation to literature, the relevance of the text is filtered through questions pertaining to literary dimension. Finally, as an inherently theological revelation from God, we must assess Scripture for theological movement and potential discontinuity between covenants.

Regarding History

Cultural Relativity

Due to the cultural particulars found in Scripture, modern readers are often faced with questions of cultural relativity. While interpretation requires an awareness of biblical cultures to inform our understanding of the meaning of many biblical texts, application requires that the reader evaluate the relevance of texts saturated by cultural particularities. Many commandments, instructions, and examples in the Bible reflect a culture rather foreign to our own. In these passages, the direct application of a biblical example or directive would result in a cultural absurdity, something very different in our culture than what was ever meant in the original culture.

Example: Holy Kiss. Consider the imperative found four times in Paul's letters and once in Peter, "Greet one another with a holy kiss."[6] The goal of interpretation would be to understand everything possible regarding this ancient practice. This might include an understanding of

---

6. Rom 16:16; 1 Cor 16:20; 2 Cor 13:12; 1 Thess 5:26; 1 Pet 5:14.

the form of the practice (a kiss on the forehead, cheek, or lips?) along with its function in society. One might also research a number of related questions: Was the holy kiss an adaptation of an ancient secular practice implemented in a special way in the church? Was it adopted from Jewish or Greco-Roman culture? Did it have a nuanced function in the church that differed from society in general? What exactly did such a kiss convey culturally and socially? How does each example of the imperative function in each individual letter?

However, while interpretation would require research and immersion into the cultural backgrounds of the New Testament, the real crux of the issue here is application, and more precisely, cultural relevance. Whatever the holy kiss would have entailed in Paul's day, whether in form or function, we're quite sure that practicing the holy kiss today would not convey the same intended meaning![7] The issue isn't one of interpretation; knowledge of New Testament cultural backgrounds should provide an understanding of what the New Testament writers meant and how the recipients of their original communication would have understood those instructions. The issue is one of cultural relevance—to practice the holy kiss today would be culturally inappropriate, at least in most Western cultural contexts, and would almost certainly not reflect the underlying principle in the text. We know that God can't be telling us to do *that*, right?

Notice that with the holy kiss, the issue is not related to *historical*, situational particularity. In other words, the fact that this exhortation is repeated five times in the New Testament suggests that it was not a particular command related to the situational context in one church or community. If anything, the repetition of this command five times by two different authors in five books makes it one of the most normative commands in all the New Testament! Neither is the issue related to its *literary* dimension. These are all instructive exhortations found in epistolary literature. In terms of literary genre, they are as inherently applicable as anything in Scripture. Nor is the issue bound up with *theological*

---

7. We understand that in other parts of the world, a form of the "holy kiss" is still practiced today. We are, however, writing primarily to a North American audience, highlighting the fact that perspectives on cultural relevance must be adjusted even between twenty-first-century audiences.

discontinuity. These are New Testament texts written to churches—our covenant, our people, our apostles. The only barrier to direct application appears to be cultural. Thus the relevance of these texts must be assessed through the filter of cultural relativity.

How does one apply texts that appear culturally relative? How does one even evaluate whether a text is culturally relative? Similar to almost all issues in hermeneutics, there's no precise scientific formula or rule that applies to the evaluation of cultural relativity. However, in general, if the direct application of a biblical commandment, instruction, or example would result in a cultural absurdity, or would fail to convey the originally intended purpose to a modern audience because it is out of step with current cultural practices, then one might suspect cultural relativity. If the barriers to application appear most directly related to cultural distinctives, then one might evaluate whether or to what degree the text is relevant for today.

In the evaluation of culturally relative texts, rarely must you decide between direct application and no application whatsoever. Rather, whenever possible, you ought to look for application through a cultural equivalent, a tangible practice that translates intended meaning from their culture to our own. In the case of the holy kiss, this could involve a "holy hug," "holy handshake," or any number of physical acts that convey what Paul and Peter intended to convey through the holy kiss. However, cultural equivalents aren't always apparent. In some cases, it's more sensible to apply the underlying principle within the culturally relative text. Here evaluating relevance leads directly to the practice of determining legitimacy (as seen in the following pages). In the case of the holy kiss, you might determine that application is best practiced by simply applying the underlying principle (perhaps understood as the need to reinforce brotherly love through an outward display of non-sensual love and affection within the community of believers). The underlying principle, distilled and summarized in a coherent teaching point, could then be practiced through numerous legitimate scenarios.

In addition, you might ask whether there are some commandments, exhortations, and narrative examples so far removed from us culturally that they've become completely irrelevant for the Christian today. In most cases, these involve situations related to normativity and theological discontinuity. For instance, with the example cited earlier from Numbers 5, the issue isn't just cultural but rather situational, particularly in terms of the covenant and law established for ancient Israel. We'd argue that the instructions laid out in Numbers 5 concerning "unfaithful wives" shouldn't be applied in any prescriptive sense for today. However, this is determined primarily on the basis of theological discontinuity and situational relevance, reflecting a unique ritual apparatus within ancient Israel. It's only a secondary matter that the whole scenario is also culturally distant.

Situational Relativity (Normativity)

The situational particularity of Scripture leads to the frequent need to evaluate situational relativity (or normativity) in relation to biblical commands, exhortations, examples, and expectations. Just because a biblical writer lays out a commandment or uses the imperative, does this necessarily imply a normative expectation for all readers? Just because an event is described in Scripture, does this imply that we ought to receive it as a normative example? Just because an action is prescribed in Scripture, does this mean that such an action was ever intended for anyone other than the original audience? Just because something happens to someone in Scripture, whether positive or negative, does this then imply a normative expectation for all? Evaluating Scripture through the lens of situational particularity, one must ask whether a text is meant to be normative or not—or perhaps more precisely, to what degree is a text meant to be normative for later generations?

Evaluating situational relativity concerns the reader with the movement from situationally particular settings to universally broad relevance. Such an assessment crosses literary boundaries, relating to propositional directive and narrative example. It also crosses theological boundaries, involving texts based in both Testaments and involving all biblical covenants. As with cultural relativity, the need to evaluate normativity is contextually driven, but instead of cultural context it is situational context that generates these questions of relevance.

Evaluating situational relativity isn't simply a matter of determining whether a text is descriptive or prescriptive. In some sense, this distinction doesn't accurately reflect the issue stemming from historical, situational particularity. Rather, the evaluation of situational relativity is a matter of determining the degree to which situational particularity limits the relevance of a text for application today. Scripture often reflects individual focus and specific circumstances that don't apply outside of the situational context.[8]

How do you evaluate situational relativity? To a large extent, this is a matter of discernment and wisdom. However, evaluating normativity begins with the objective task of interpretation. As a text is understood through interpretation, you engage situational context along with the intention of the author and the nature of his audience—the very elements that speak to inherent normativity and situational uniqueness. This may entail oversimplification, but if the circumstances of a text are repeated in a variety of settings, or if a text appears to be addressed to a universal audience, then it is likely normative. Conversely, if a text is bound by unique circumstances in an uncommon setting, its relevance may be limited to its original audience within the context of its original setting. Even then, rarely is situational relevance determined by black-and-white distinctions. Determining the degree to which a text is meant to be normative is in large part a matter of discernment.

Examples from 1 and 2 Timothy. At this point it may help to illustrate the issue of situational relativity. Consider first a simple example, and then let's examine a few that are more challenging. In 2 Timothy 4, Paul instructs Timothy to "make every effort to come to me soon" (v. 9), and when he comes to "bring the cloak I left in Troas with Carpus, as well as the scrolls, especially the parchments" (v. 13). A little bit of sanctified common sense will suggest that this imperative, while prescriptive for Timothy, was never meant to be normative for a broader audience in universal contexts. The command itself is inherently tied to its situational context. This doesn't mean that this kind of passage is completely

---

8. A context in which there may be prescribed instruction or a described procedure and outcome. The issue is not prescription versus description, but rather a question of normativity.

devoid of contemporary relevance. For example, you might suggest that there's an underlying principle regarding relational expectations between Timothy and Paul that could serve as a model (such as honoring one's teacher by performing some helpful service).[9] Of course, there's no harm done if this text doesn't carry a direct and tangible point of application.[10]

Moving on to more challenging examples, the entire section from 1 Timothy 4:11 to 6:19 contains numerous points for potential application. However, you must first assess the relevance of these before moving ahead to the development of teaching points. For instance, the segment providing instructions for the support of women who are "genuinely widows" (1 Tim 5:3–16) requires some level of cultural and situational evaluation.[11] Widows are not as helpless in twenty-first-century Western society as they were in the first century, and we certainly should pause before requiring that the "test of good works" be determined by widows "washing the feet" of the saints (1 Tim 5:10). While many of these issues are more properly evaluated through the filter of cultural relativity than normativity, some particulars in this passage are quite situational. For instance, should all churches be required to place "genuine widows" on an official support list (v. 9)? Should such widows be at least sixty years old (v. 9)? Should churches today mandate that widows who are put on such a roll also make a "pledge" (v. 12)? Doesn't the fact that Paul instructs Timothy within a context of some having "already turned away to follow Satan" (v. 15) imply a degree of situational relativity?

Moving beyond the care of widows, there's an even more obvious example of situational relativity in 1 Timothy 5:23, "Don't continue drinking only water, but use a little wine because of your stomach and your frequent illnesses." Paul is clearly not inferring drunkenness; the preceding command in verse 22 is to "keep yourself pure." But Paul's

---

9. See in this regard Andreas J. Köstenberger, "Jesus as Rabbi in the Fourth Gospel," *Bulletin of Biblical Research* 8 (1998): 97–128.

10. The value of this text may actually be more significant for its apologetic relevance (recognizing that "scrolls and parchments" were being circulated between cities in the first decades of the church). In any case, we'd suggest that these imperatives are so situationally particular that they were never intended as normative, universal instructions.

11. Often cultural and situational relativity will overlap in the same passage of Scripture. This is certainly the case in 1 Tim 5:3–16.

instruction for Timothy to "drink a little wine" is quite clear. Evidently Timothy was abstaining from all consumption of wine, thus subjecting himself more frequently to the unpurified water that was the norm in the ancient world. The work of interpretation would investigate such variables as the medicinal assumptions related to wine in Paul's day along with the alcoholic strength of wine in the first century (it may have been diluted with water more than it is today).[12] However, assuming that the wine Paul refers to was sufficiently alcoholic (comparable to wine today), and assuming that Paul intended Timothy to seek some relief from digestive troubles through the consumption of wine (perhaps caused by the presence of sinning elders that he needed to censor and remove; look at the surrounding context: vv. 22 and 24!), we must still evaluate the significance of this passage for today. Are these instructions so particular to Timothy's circumstances that they are completely devoid of contemporary relevance, especially in light of the availability of pure non-alcoholic drink in our day? Are there circumstances in which one might find a parallel, perhaps in locations where contaminated drinking water still is an issue (and where wine is an available alternative)? Or should we simply take this as an endorsement of wine as a sensible beverage for the sake of maintenance of good health? These are questions of situational relevance.[13]

Regarding Literature

Literary Dimension

Just as genre informs interpretation, so it also impacts the application of Scripture. As one navigates the literary diversity of Scripture, it's obvious that some texts by their very nature are inherently more applicable than others. Commandments, precepts, and admonitions are clearly oriented toward application, narratives and parables less so, and

---

12. See Andreas J. Köstenberger, "Wine," in *Dictionary of Jesus and the Gospels*, 2nd ed., ed. Joel B. Green, Jeannine K. Brown, and Nicholas Perrin (Downers Grove: InterVarsity, 2013), 993–95.

13. Whatever conclusion one reaches in the evaluation of this instruction, this verse does play an interesting role (even if minor) in the development of a biblical and practical theology of alcohol.

genealogical listings have little intrinsic bent toward application. Among the hundreds of subgenres in Scripture, each will be applied through a literary filter, an inherent sense of orientation that we call "literary dimension." While context and content have greater control in communicating the relevance of the text for application, one should not neglect the impact of literary factors in influencing how a text is received for today.

Some texts are naturally oriented toward application—commandments, exhortations, precepts, and imperatives are inherently meant to be applied. However, most literary forms in Scripture take a less direct path to application. In the pages of Scripture lie many texts that are difficult to apply not because of historical or theological barriers but due to *literary* barriers. Consider the many pages of narrative in Scripture. While there's certainly application to be drawn from these texts, historical narrative is inherently informational. Also, application is rendered more complex by subtle differences between the original historical and theological contexts of most biblical narratives and our contemporary situation.

For example, people often suppose that Peter, or other disciples mentioned in the Gospels, serve as examples for us today, such as in Peter's occasional doubts or misunderstandings. Similar to Peter, it's therefore often argued, we may be plagued by doubt or failure. Yet this straightforward application overlooks the fact that unlike Peter in the Gospels, believers today have the indwelling Holy Spirit from the moment they believe. Peter, on the other hand, while benefiting from the earthly presence of Jesus with him, had to await the pouring out of the Spirit at Pentecost, which didn't occur until Acts 2 (and thus *after* the Gospels!). Any attempt to apply the lessons gleaned from Peter's experience as narrated in the Gospels must therefore of necessity be more indirect and allow for differences in his and our situation.[14]

Granted, knowledge of historical information can influence the tangible world of behavior. Similarly, as one's theological perspectives are informed through instructive discourse, behavioral changes come as a

---

14. For a treatment that wrestles with questions such as these see Andreas J. Köstenberger, *The Missions of Jesus and the Disciples according to the Fourth Gospel* (Grand Rapids: Eerdmans, 1998), chapter 4.

result—but the nature of the literature isn't inherently directed toward application. What's more, a text's literary dimension implies that diverse and often nuanced approaches must be considered in *how* different forms of biblical literature are applied. The approach one takes to applying narrative will inevitably be different than that taken to Old Testament law. Certain rules guide the appropriation of proverbial wisdom—rules and guidelines determined by the literature itself. In the same manner, there are guidelines that affect the application of psalms, parables, and virtually every distinct genre and subgenre in Scripture.

While we recognize that literary genre influences the application of the text just as much as the interpretation of the text, our focus is evaluating the relevance of the text in terms of literary genre. A comprehensive survey of literary dimension is impossible here, but the issue can easily be illustrated through a sampling of genres. Obviously, a more exhaustive survey of literary dimension in application would be beneficial, along with examples and nuanced case studies. However, the following provides a representative survey of genres that illustrate how the literature of text factors into the evaluation of relevance.

Narrative Examples. Is the primary function of biblical narrative to provide examples for behavior? Should narratives be probed and sifted to find points of application within each supporting element, within each twist and turn of the plot? Does the literary genre itself support the common approach taken in popular preaching and devotional reading, where narratives are primarily understood as direct examples for application today?

As we consider the literary aspect (or dimension) of narrative, we find that narratives are not given to directive application. This, of course, doesn't mean that narratives have no relevance for application. However, the natural literary aspect of narrative suggests that individual segments are often not directly relevant for application. In typical narrative fashion, relevance is communicated through entire pericopes (narrative literary units) and the interface between them. Narratives tend to communicate significance to the modern reader in broad, informative segments rather than concise, imperative instruction. Application derived from individual components within narrative must be approached cautiously. When you look for a nugget of applicable truth in every element of a narrative, the tendency is to find more application than what the literature naturally communicates.

What's more, narratives tend to illustrate theological commitments as they unfold in the course of history. They don't necessarily model proper behavior. Consider the patriarchal narratives in Genesis. While these illustrate God's faithfulness to the covenant made with Abraham, they do so in broad segments and often in spite of the somewhat suspect morals of the patriarchs themselves. Again, you should exercise caution in the way in which you discern relevance for application from biblical narrative. If you fail to assess the relevance of the text in terms of its functional literary dimension, you may apply the text incorrectly. Consider the example of Jacob's deception in Genesis 27. To follow the narrative describing Jacob's deception as a model for behavior is not a failure of interpretation but rather of application.

It constitutes a failure to evaluate the text in terms of its literary function—narratives are not necessarily meant to be followed as models for behavior. Just think of the example of Peter in the Gospels cited earlier. Or think of the many narrative examples in the book of Acts. First and foremost, Luke wrote his account of the history of the early church because certain events truly inspired, and he judged them significant for inclusion (or course writing under inspiration). Whether or not the actions of a given character in the narrative are to be emulated by believers today is another matter. This must be established by more indirect means and cannot simply be assumed at the outset.

Even an overwhelmingly positive character such as Paul may at times engage in conduct that is not condoned by Luke. Thus Paul loses his temper and lashes out against the high priest in Acts 23:3 (though he promptly backtracks in verse 5). At another time Paul brushes aside the warning by the prophet Agabus not to go to Jerusalem and subsequently gets arrested, though this was still in keeping with the sovereign will of God (Acts 21:10–14). Peter, along with the other disciples, is told by Jesus to wait for the pouring out of the Holy Spirit (Luke 24:49), but characteristically he got tired of waiting and initiated the replacement of

Judas with another disciple, casting lots (Acts 1:15–26; cf. John 21:3). Perhaps this was what God intended, but the replacement disciple, Matthias, is never heard of again in Acts, while Jesus later handpicks Paul as the apostle who is to take the gospel to the ends of the earth (Acts 9). Whether or not one agrees with all of these examples on an interpretive level, our point here is simply that the reader of historical narrative should not uncritically assume that merely because a given action is recorded, this necessarily means it is commanded or held up as normative.

We could go on, but the point should be clear: Don't assume that a given character or behavior in biblical narrative is meant to be emulated merely because it is recorded. Take a more indirect approach and recognize any differences in circumstances between your own situation and that of the biblical character. Then, see if you can discern a universal principle that allows you to bridge the application gap.

Legal Commands. A command is a command, about as inherently applicable as any text can be. However, legal commands in Scripture are formally stipulations that bound covenant participants to a particular agreement, and therefore what was legally binding for the ancient Israelite may not be legally binding for the twenty-first-century Christian. For the Christian reader, the barriers in drawing relevant application from Old Testament legal code have more to do with theological discontinuity than a text's literary dimension. The question faced by modern readers is whether the law is legally binding outside of the covenant relationship God had with ancient Israel.

Again, the issue is a matter of discerning to whom the law applies. One might imagine that for the ancient Israelite there was no question whether or not individual laws were relevant—they were all meant to be obeyed. The literary essence of law suggests a direct link to application; after all, laws are by their very nature meant to be applied. Yet today, legal code must be evaluated from the perspective of the new covenant— the church is no longer under the law.

Wisdom Precepts. Although Old Testament wisdom wrestles with the hard theological questions of perceived injustice and the providence of God, most wisdom is inherently practical, the implementation of precepts for living day by day. In this sense, the bulk of wisdom, especially proverbial wisdom, is naturally applicable. To question the relevance of a proverb is itself folly—the literature itself drives the reader to ponder how it is meant to be applied, to process its relevance for today.

Not only is the literature of proverbial wisdom naturally oriented to application, it's also free from the constraints of situational and covenantal context. Proverbial wisdom tends to communicate truth in an ahistorical, timeless fashion. Proverbs are intrinsically normative— although general truths with merely probable outcomes, they're not relationally bound as are covenantal stipulations and promises. Moreover, proverbial wisdom takes a very direct route from ancient origin to modern relevance (though they're often similar to riddles, needing to be unpacked as to their intrinsic culturally constrained meaning and message). The underlying principles embedded in most proverbs aren't limited by situational relevance. The literature of wisdom lends itself to application in a more direct manner than perhaps any other form of text in Scripture. This reality is even further enhanced because wisdom reflects an approach to life in keeping with the built-in principles of God's creation—principles that transcend culture and history.

Prophetic Oracles. If the Word of God can be compared to a double-edged sword (Heb 4:12), then prophetic oracle may comprise the sharpest point of the blade. The prophets spoke to get the attention of the people, and their rhetoric reflects a verbal commitment to bring the people to a place of repentance. While the Old Testament prophets must be understood within the framework of a given geopolitical and situational context, their message tends to transcend the confines of their own historical setting. Just as a pastor preaches with the intention to affect change in attitude and behavior, so the prophets did as well. Therefore, it should come as no surprise that the content of most prophetic oracles, whether announcements of judgment or oracles of salvation, is intrinsically oriented toward application. To be sure, one may need to sift through matters of historical distance and covenant relationship in the evaluation of a given prophetic oracle, but the literary genre of prophetic oracle offers a straightforward path to application.

Epistolary Exhortations. The New Testament epistles are clearly a word for the church—after all, these letters were originally addressed to real historical churches in space and time. However, as noted earlier, this very fact necessitates the evaluation of the text in terms of cultural and situational relativity. And in many cases the modern reader may determine that particular portions of these letters require a detour around cultural and situational relevance. But what shall we say about the literary dimension of epistolary literature? Are the New Testament letters inherently oriented toward application?

The answer to this question requires that we distinguish between literary subgenre in the Epistles. There are some structural elements (greetings, benedictions, etc.) in epistolary literature that aren't quite as tuned toward direct application. But for the most part, the main body of epistolary literature is geared toward practical application. This is the case particularly because the same covenant—the new covenant—is in effect for the recipients of the New Testament letters and for Christians today.

Thus when Paul writes to the Corinthians, for example, they're essentially in the same situation as believers today, at least in terms of covenant.[15] Even instructive theological discourses in the Epistles tend to carry a practical function, often providing the necessary foundation for addressing the practical, behavioral concerns of the day. Whether through instruction, exhortation, or apostolic command, we know from the literary features of these words that they were meant to be applied. Any barrier to application will come by way of historical distance, not literary or theological disconnect.

---

15. See further the discussion of theological continuity and discontinuity that follows.

Regarding Theology

Theological Continuity and Discontinuity

One of the more striking issues in evaluation pertains to theological continuity and discontinuity.[16] Simply stated, there are many commandments, instructions, and narrative examples in Scripture that reflect covenantal relationships not possessed by modern readers. When assessing the relevance of the text for application, you must always consider covenant distance and its impact on application. Most recognize general theological continuity between the New Testament and the twenty-first-century church, so it's quite natural to assume a direct theological link between the letters of the New Testament and the contemporary reader. However, this is clearly not the case in the Old Testament, where the prevailing covenant is different from the new covenant.

The issue of covenant distance is tremendously important in evaluating the Old Testament. How should the Old Testament law be appropriated for application? Do laws pertaining to an ancient system of worship, including priests, sacrifices, and ritual cleanliness, have any relevance for today? How much of this is based in culture, and how much in covenant? Should believers today expect the same blessings and curses for covenant obedience or disobedience as the ancient Israelite expected (Leviticus 26; Deuteronomy 28)? Should we not see that the unfolding of Old Testament narrative reflects the consequences of covenant fidelity or infidelity? Knowing that the prophets spoke in the context of covenant warning, should one expect the same announcements of impending judgment for disobedience today (loss of land, destruction of resources—even exile!)?

The fact that covenant affects the relevance of certain biblical texts doesn't negate legitimate appropriation of these texts. Whether by

---

16. Although these terms involve broader issues in biblical theology, for the purpose of evaluation we're focusing on the question of covenant relationship and its impact on relevance for application. For a sampling of issues in biblical theology, see John S. Feinberg, ed., *Continuity and Discontinuity: Perspectives on the Relationship between the Old and New Testaments* (Westchester, IL: Crossway, 1988). More recently, see James Mead, *Biblical Theology: Issues, Methods, and Themes* (Minneapolis: Westminster John Knox, 2007). There's also some helpful reflection in James Barr, *The Concept of Biblical Theology: An Old Testament Perspective* (Minneapolis: Augsburg Fortress, 1999).

appropriating the underlying principles with some texts or by simply understanding God's program through redemptive history, all of Scripture has a critical function as the revealed Word of God. However, the degree and manner of relevance will be affected by covenant distance. The reason we tend not to consider the food laws of Leviticus 11 as binding for today has little to do with cultural or situational relativity, and if just a matter of literary factors, we'd find a rather direct path to applying these laws. Rather, the issue is one of theological discontinuity. These laws, along with the many others in the Levitical code, pertain to a covenant that is not our covenant today. Their relevance must therefore be evaluated accordingly.

Salvation-Historical Progression

There's an undeniable salvation-historical progression throughout Scripture that needs to be taken into account when interpreting and applying individual texts.[17] For example, consider the basis for not applying Old Testament texts concerning slavery. One can find instructions regulating slavery in the Old Testament, while the New Testament contains instructions to slaves. But it's interesting that neither Testament forbids or abolishes slavery. While slavery texts are obviously set within an ancient context, they shouldn't be dismissed simply in terms of cultural and situational relevance.[18] However, if a historical and theological trajectory can be discerned through the pages of Scripture that reveals a divine ideal abolishing slavery, then the modern reader is better justified in evaluating slavery texts as non-relevant or less relevant for application today. The same might be said for texts referring to the practice of polygamy. While we may see the pitfalls of polygamy in certain Old Testament narratives, one doesn't find explicit commandments or instructions

---

17. Although the term "redemptive movement" has been embraced by some as a hermeneutic based in "the recognition of progressive patterns that reach their climax beyond the actual words of Scripture," we're not advocating such an approach. For a monograph-length treatment and critique, see Benjamin Reaoch, *Women, Slaves, and the Gender Debate: A Complementarian Response to the Redemptive-Movement Hermeneutic* (Phillipsburg: P&R, 2012). Cf. Robert L. Plummer, *40 Questions about Interpreting the Bible* (Grand Rapids: Kregel, 2010), 324.

18. Notice that the instructions Paul gives to slaves and masters in Eph 6:5–9 are in the same situational and cultural context as instructions given to husbands, wives, and children.

forbidding the practice. This may reflect a cultural norm (at least in the Old Testament), but does cultural relativity alone explain why polygamy should be discarded? Evaluating the text through the lens of progressive movement in revelation history may provide the needed rationale in explaining why the appropriation of some texts is relevant for today while that of others is not.[19]

Relevance Continuum

As implied above, assessing the relevance of the text for application is rarely a black-and-white, either-or proposition. More often, due to historical, literary, and theological factors, some Scripture passages are inherently *more* and other texts *less* relevant for application today. Bauer and Traina refer to this phenomenon as a "continuum of transcendence," where teachings from Scripture are always more or less tied to their original situation but can never be entirely divorced from that historical setting.[20] They correctly suggest that "most biblical passages stand somewhere between the two extremes on the continuum of transcendence, often because some aspects of their teaching are essentially transcendent while others are circumstantially contingent."[21]

In coining our own terminology, we might refer to this as the "relevance continuum," a sliding scale along the lines of which individual texts or elements within texts can be assessed in terms of their degree of relevance for application today. Evaluation of the relevance of a given passage may be a matter of determining whether a text is relevant for today, but often the issue is more nuanced; it is a matter of deciding *to what degree* and *in what manner* the text is relevant. In this, the categories of cultural and situational relevance, literary dimension, theological

---

19. On gender-related matters, see the discussions in Andreas J. Köstenberger with David W. Jones, *God, Marriage, and Family: Restoring the Biblical Foundation*, 2nd ed. (Wheaton: Crossway, 2010); Andreas J. Köstenberger and Margaret E. Köstenberger, *God's Design for Man and Woman: A Biblical-Theological Survey* (Wheaton: Crossway, 2014); and Andreas J. Köstenberger and Thomas R. Schreiner, eds., *Women in the Church: An Analysis and Application of 1 Timothy 2:9–15*, 3rd ed. (Wheaton: Crossway, 2016).

20. David R. Bauer and Robert A. Traina, *Inductive Bible Study: A Comprehensive Guide to the Practice of Hermeneutics* (Grand Rapids: Baker, 2011), 294.

21. Ibid.

discontinuity, and salvation-historical progression provide helpful filters through which relevance is assessed. But ultimately, evaluation is a highly nuanced process that requires significant thought and wisdom.

Determining Legitimacy in Application

As suggested earlier, not all applications of the text are necessarily legitimate applications. While there may be multiple ways in which the Word of God can be appropriated at a given point, these variations are not unlimited.[22] Any particular application of the text must be in sync with the interpretation of the text; there must be consistency between interpretation and application. Consider as an example the oft-quoted passage Philippians 4:13: "I am able to do all things through Him who strengthens me." While there may be a variety of scenarios in which the believer today can appropriate Paul's statement as his or her own, expecting supernatural support to endure trials and to find contentment in distress, any particular application of this text ought to be in line with the interpretation of the text, that is, what Paul intended for his original audience to understand and expect through his own testimony and experience.

Just as there are multiple ways in which this text can be legitimately applied, so there are numerous ways in which God's people frequently misapply this text. For example, we'd contend that believers who appropriate this text with an expectation that God will supernaturally supply physical strength in athletic competition are misappropriating Scripture. Paul would never have intended to communicate such a promise, and God is under no obligation to accede to an erroneous expectation. However, believers today who experience trials for bearing faithful testimony to Christ and who suffer hardship and persecutions in the name of Christ can expect the same supernatural endurance to persevere as experienced by Paul. Just as Paul affirmed that he learned the "secret of being content" in whatever the circumstances (Phil 4:12), so believers

---

22. Vanhoozer observes that the plurality of perspectives and the cumulative voice of multiple generations in the church "may be needed to mine the treasures of biblical significance." See Vanhoozer, *Is There a Meaning in This Text?*, 424. However, he correctly warns that "the plurality of interpretations should not be confused with a disordered pluralism; not all readings are equally legitimate" (ibid.).

today can do the same, even as their experiences may not exactly match those of Paul.

The main point in determining legitimacy in application is that there must be sensible parallels between what the text *meant* and what it *means* today. The application of the text ought to be anchored in the underlying principles related to its interpretation. Put another way, the parallel tracks of interpretation and application must be drawn together by points of parallel connectivity, that is, corresponding elements that link application back to the interpretation of the text. While Philippians 4:13 may look good on a football jersey, we'd suggest that the link between interpretation and application at this point has been stretched too far—the correspondence between application (receiving physical strength and athletic endurance for victory in a football game) and interpretation (Paul's expectation that God supplies supernatural endurance to live faithfully in the face of persecution) is ultimately found wanting. While we imagine that Paul, too, might be a football fan (or would he?), this kind of appropriation is not what he intended—the link between interpretation and application is stretched too far, and therefore the application is illegitimate.

It may help at this point to consider an illustration already alluded to in the previous paragraph. Although the analogy is imperfect, one might imagine the correspondence between interpretation and application through the picture of parallel rails tied together by cords like the way rail-ties link train rails. These cords are the connecting elements that link interpretation to application in a truly corresponding, parallel fashion. The goal for the reader is to draw clear parallels between past meaning and present significance. In so doing, you'll be better able to make the case for legitimate application as determined through well positioned points of connectivity. These, in turn, keep the corresponding rails of interpretation and application in parallel harmony.

As you envision cords linking interpretation to application, recognize that these cords may be relatively short and tight or they may be flexible and rather extended. In other words, in many cases the most immediate application of the text is the one that most readily corresponds to the intended meaning of the text in its ancient, historical setting. However, there's a sense in which application may be quite extended and distant from interpretation in terms of culture, context, and scenario yet still correspond in a legitimately parallel fashion. In either case, when extending the application of the text from its interpretation, the cords connecting the two must remain intact, retaining a sense of congruity between interpretation and application. If the application of a text becomes so distant or incongruent from interpretation that the cord breaks, then the application is no longer sensible, connected, and legitimate—any parallel between interpretation and application has dissolved, and one must wonder if there's any sense remaining in which a given "application" is drawn legitimately from the authoritative Word.

Figure 13.1: The Parallel Rails with Varying Degrees of Legitimacy

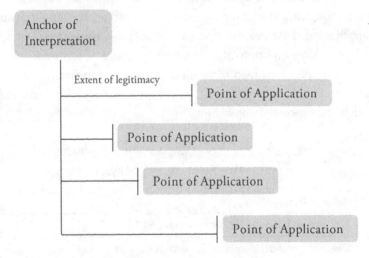

The conscientious pursuit of legitimacy in application is a virtuous goal. It is possible to misappropriate the Word of God, even after proper interpretation is achieved. However, the above illustration suggests that legitimacy may be rather stretched and application yet remain valid. Application is inherently less objective than interpretation, and for any given text there are degrees to which certain points of application may or may not be legitimate. Therefore, it's possible that parallels between interpretation and application may be more or less distant and that the cords attaching the two can be stretched and extended, though they shouldn't be broken.

Because of this, it may help to think in terms of degrees of legitimacy; some applications are closer to the intent of the original author while others are further extended. Yet we don't want to overstate the point; determining legitimacy in application is rooted in objective intention. While it is proper to refer to degrees of legitimacy in application, we nonetheless seek to avoid misappropriation of the Word of God, knowing that ultimately our goal is to apply Scripture with integrity and precision.

The process of finding legitimate parallels between interpretation and application generally involves five steps. These steps are not necessarily sequential, but they do work in concert with one another, assisting the thoughtful reader through the process of determining legitimacy in application. One feature that carries through these steps is that of inquiry—asking questions that speak to the issue of legitimacy. Just as interpretive questions help to facilitate the transition from observation to interpretation, so questions of legitimacy guide and direct the reader through the process of application.

Table 13.2 — Five Steps for Finding Parallels between Interpretation and Application	
1.	Discover how the original author intended his original audience to apply the written text.
2.	Distinguish between "knowing" texts and "doing" texts.
3.	Distill the underlying principles within the text.
4.	Determine the appropriate boundaries of what the text can and cannot mean for today.
5.	Develop potential scenarios in which the text can be applied today.

Step 1: Discover the way the original author intended his original audience to apply the written text. Ask: "How did the author intend the original audience to apply the text?" Our first step is to understand application as it would have been understood by the original audience. The first recipients would have understood the meaning of the text in their day as immediate—there was no distinction between "us" and "them" for the original audience. Many of the challenges we face in application would have been non-issues in their day, including the issues of relevance dealt with earlier in this chapter. The goal is to understand intended application in the "then and there," apart from matters of relevance, prior to determining legitimate parallels to the "here and now." If we're going to discern legitimate parallels in our context, then we must first understand intended application in the original readers' context.

Step 2: Distinguish between "knowing" texts and "doing" texts. Ask: "Does this text primarily relate to the original audience knowing something or doing something?" Dividing the application of Scripture in its original context into either "knowing texts" or "doing texts" may be an oversimplification, but it's still helpful.[23] Simply put, there are some texts that inherently speak to the issue of *knowing* something (variously called cognitive, declarative, propositional, or informational), and other texts that inherently speak to the matter of *doing* something (their ethical or practical dimension).

In many biblical texts, the author sought to instruct and *inform* his reader concerning God, humanity, or some aspect of God's redemptive plan for humanity. In these texts, the author wanted his original audience to receive knowledge—an element of truth to be appropriated by the mind more so than practiced through tangible activity.

In other cases the primary thrust was action based—the original author wanted the original recipients of the text to *do* something. Therefore, as we work through the process of determining legitimate

---

23. Both kinds of texts are represented in the words of 2 Tim 3:16–17, "All Scripture is inspired by God and is profitable for teaching, for rebuking, for correcting, for training in righteousness, so that the man of God may be complete, equipped for every good work." It is certainly true that instruction which transforms the mind also transforms behavior. In some sense the two function hand in hand.

application, it's helpful to discern whether the primary thrust of application for the original audience pertained to knowing something or doing something. Legitimate application in our day will typically follow suit.[24]

Step 3: Distill the underlying principles within the text. Ask: "What is the core teaching in this text?" In order to draw legitimate parallels between interpretation and application, you must discover the underlying principles within a given text. Underlying principles provide the link between interpretation and application that keep the two in parallel synchronization. But what are the underlying principles? How do they relate to application, and how do you "distill" these underlying principles from the text?[25]

Distilling the underlying principles within a given text essentially involves the reader in separating of the core message of the text from its historically particular origin. This obviously requires some level of discernment. However, underlying principles aren't mysterious or hidden—they typically involve nothing more than a distilled version of interpretation. In other words, by removing (or perhaps better, "looking beyond") the cultural and situational background of the text, you typically find the underlying principle, the theological or practical core of what God wanted his people to know or to do.

Relating this to the preceding step, it's important to remember that not all underlying principles are directly linked to the "doing" of something. Some texts are inherently more oriented toward the revelation of *knowledge*—texts related to the *knowing* of something about God or his program of redemption. In these texts, the underlying principle may be inherently linked to the revelation of knowledge, to the self-disclosure

---

24. Speech act theory distinguishes between three types of speech act: (1) *locutionary* (the linguistic dimension of a given utterance, i.e., what a given speaker or writer is actually saying); (2) *illocutionary* (the type of utterance, e.g., a command, offer, or promise); and (3) *perlocutionary* (the utterance's psychological effect on its recipients, e.g., hope, reassurance, or dread). According to speech act theory, utterances frequently have a performative function. Speech act theory was pioneered by J. L. Austin (*How to Do Things with Words* [Oxford: Oxford University Press, 1962]). It was further developed by John Seale ("A Taxonomy of Illocutionary Acts," in, *Language, Mind, and Knowledge*, ed. K. Günderson, Minneapolis Studies in the Philosophy of Science 7 [University of Minneapolis Press, 1975], 344–69) and has been appropriated by evangelical scholars such as Kevin Vanhoozer (*Is There a Meaning in This Text?*) and many others.

25. We're adopting the term "distill" from Plummer, *40 Questions about Interpreting the Bible*, 171.

of God through his word. Conversely, many texts are inherently oriented toward *practice*, toward the expectation that God's people ought to *do* something. The underlying principles in these Scriptures are readily made for application. If God wanted his people to do something in the ancient context of Scripture, then the underlying principle will usually suggest that we do something in our own contemporary context. Similarly, if God wanted an ancient audience to know something by divine self-disclosure, then he likely desires all of his people from that point forward to know something about himself through that Word. Throughout Scripture there are underlying principles, some more related to knowing, others inherently related to doing, but all reflecting God's revelation to humanity—what he was saying to them and what he is saying to us. In distilling the underlying principles of the text, you must therefore discern between two alternative paths by which Scripture might be relevant for today: (1) the appropriation of knowledge; and (2) the application of practice.

Step 4: Determine the appropriate boundaries of what the text can and cannot mean for today. Ask: "How far can this underlying principle be stretched in applying it to a new context?" With an understanding of the core underlying principles of the text in mind, the next step is to determine the appropriate boundaries of what the text can and cannot mean for today. This requires some probing into potential scenarios in which the text can be applied today (our next step in the list; but remember, these steps aren't necessarily sequential). Thinking in terms of our parallel rails, to what extent can we stretch an underlying principle connecting these rails before the cord breaks? Where's the line drawn between an appropriate application and one that loses all sensible connection to the original author and audience? After all, underlying principles are reflected by an author's purpose and what he expected them to do or understand in the original context of Scripture. The underlying principle within the text then acts as a safeguard against misappropriation. When application is no longer a reflection of the underlying principle, then it has lost its link to legitimacy.

Step 5: Develop potential scenarios in which the text can be applied today. Ask: *"In what way can I envision this text being applied today?"* This is the tangible step by which the reader envisions scenarios in which a contemporary audience might apply the text in a legitimate manner. Due to the transmittable (or transferable) nature of application, multiple settings and situations are certainly valid. Therefore, developed scenarios for application ought to be varied, yet specific. As one envisions possible options for valid application, there's a sense in which one begins to articulate how this text *might* relate to us today.

An Example: 1 Corinthians 8

Consider the process of discerning and developing legitimate application through the frequently quoted precept, "Knowledge puffs up, but love edifies" (1 Cor 8:1b NKJV). Following the five steps outlined earlier, you might come to a very different perspective on application than is often assumed with this particular verse.

Step 1: Discover the manner in which the original author intended his original audience to apply the written text. Ask: "How did the author intend the original audience to apply the text?"

How did Paul intend his original audience (the church at Corinth) to apply the precept, "Knowledge puffs up but love edifies"? The function of this statement in Scripture is contextually particular, even if its wording has relevance outside of the contextual boundaries of Paul's original utterance.[26] An interpretation of the passage reveals that the knowledge of which Paul speaks is the knowledge that "an idol is nothing in the world" and that "there is no God but one" (1 Cor 8:4). Those who had *this* knowledge were compelling those *without* such knowledge to participate in activities ("eating food offered to idols," v. 4, and "dining in an idol's temple," v. 10) that caused their weak conscience to be defiled (v. 7).

---

26. This is especially true if these words are not original with Paul, perhaps reflecting a proverb or saying that Paul adopts for his own use in the letter. However, we're primarily interested in applying the statement in the context of the inspired sense in which Paul uses these words in his letter to the church at Corinth.

In wounding their weak consciences, those with "knowledge" were sinning against their brothers and, in turn, sinning against Christ (v. 12). Paul's exhortation to the strong—to those with such knowledge—was to limit the exercise of their liberty, even if this meant that they would "never again eat meat" (v. 13). The point of Paul's argument in 1 Corinthians 8:1–13 is that *love* ought to take precedence over the exercise of *liberty*, even to the extent of *limiting* one's liberty for the sake of others. The statement in 1 Corinthians 8:1b is an introductory summary of this point; the intended application was for the strong in conscience to limit their liberties—an act of humility—and by doing so, to build up the weaker brother by their act of love.

Step 2: Distinguish between "knowing" texts and "doing" texts. Ask: "Does this text primarily relate to the original audience knowing something or doing something?"

Is this precept inherently oriented toward the *knowing* of something or to the *doing* of something? While Paul must convince his audience of the merits of his argument through logical discourse, the intention of this discourse is to effect tangible outcomes. In other words, he wants his audience to *do* something, to change their behavior and their actions. He wants his audience to understand what it is they are doing and why they need to change their behavior, but it is ultimately their behavior that he expects to change.

Step 3: Distill the underlying principles within the text. Ask: "What is the core teaching in this text?"

What is the core teaching, the underlying principle in this text? In twenty-first-century North American contexts, we don't deal with issues related to food offered to idols or dining in an idol's temple (unless something is going on in the grocer's market of which we were not aware!). Yet the underlying principle isn't bound by the cultural, situational context of Paul's day. Peeling away the situational context, you discover that the underlying principle relates to the issue of Christian liberty, and even more specifically, the exercise of restraint as a practice of love.

The underlying principle can therefore be stated as follows: the exercise of Christian love must take precedence over the exercise of Christian liberty.[27]

> *Step 4: Determine the appropriate boundaries of what the text can and cannot mean for today. Ask: "How far can this underlying principle be stretched in applying it to a new context?"*

In keeping with the spirit of the underlying principle, where should we set the boundaries for legitimate application? There may be numerous scenarios in which some Christians have the liberty and strength of conscience to participate in certain disputable matters, whereas others do not. But the principle of love limiting liberty is primarily relational and not dependent on the actual disputable matter. The underlying principle is easily transferred and applied to various contemporary scenarios.

As long as the precept "Knowledge puffs up, but love edifies" is applied to situations in which Christians with a "stronger" conscience lovingly and willingly limit the exercise of their freedom for the sake of others, then the cord is intact no matter what the issue at hand. However, there are multiple ways in which this text is commonly used where the underlying principle is breached, where the cord is snapped, where we suppose that Paul would say, "I never meant for this to ever be applied *that* way"! For example, it's common for readers to assume that this saying pits knowledge against love, supposing that knowledge refers to academic knowledge, book smarts and advanced degrees, while love that edifies speaks of doing the work of ministry, of loving on people rather than spending time in the books.

As educators, we cringe at the notion of students being counseled against the pursuit of higher education based on a misappropriation of this statement, the general idea being that going to seminary will make

---

27. To elaborate, the principle suggests that those with "knowledge" should take heed not to consider their own interests in the exercise of liberty; rather, they must first consider the effect that the exercise of liberty has upon those without such "knowledge." Note that it is not *general* pride or arrogance Paul is addressing here but a specific scenario in which a certain kind of knowledge causes believers to flaunt their Christian liberty rather than bearing with those who haven't yet attained the same kind of knowledge. In other words, the knowledge is legitimate, but Paul's concern is to urge believers to balance this knowledge with a considerate attitude toward others.

one inevitably conceited, "puffed up" with head knowledge, while what God ideally seeks are those who will build up the church through love. By implication, one should bypass academic training and get into ministry right now—after all, "Knowledge puffs up, but love edifies"! We'd suggest that such an application is misguided and illegitimate. It has lost all connection with Paul's intended meaning and has thus failed to be accurate or "meaningful" in the true sense of the word. Other potential misapplications exist when these words are used to support misguided approaches to child-raising, counseling, and discipleship.

Step 5: Develop potential scenarios in which the text can be applied today. Ask: "In what manner can I envision this text being applied today?"

What are some possible scenarios in which this text can be applied today? To answer this question, you simply need to do a little brainstorming to develop real-world scenarios that fall in line with the underlying principle in the text. In reference to the statement, "Knowledge puffs up, but love edifies," any application ought to center on the core issue of love calling for restraint in the exercise of Christian liberty. This may be applied to numerous disputable matters in the realm of Christian engagement with our present society; you could brainstorm the possibilities, or draw from your own experience.

I (Al) recall a situation as a young believer where I was exposed to an older, more mature believer who had come out of a gambling background. As a young man, I had never been exposed to the darker side of gambling or the use of playing cards in that setting. I simply had no conscientious objection to the use of playing cards in home gatherings. In fact, I had fond memories of my grandparents coming over to our house when I was a child to play cards with my parents. However, this older, more mature believer had by his background attached a stigma to playing cards, which for him was very real. For this man, whose conscience was weak (on this matter—he was not spiritually immature or weak in general or in other matters), using playing cards would have been sin. For me, a proper application of "Knowledge puffs up, but love edifies," was to limit the exercise of my freedom for the sake of my brother in Christ. Playing cards was not sinful for me, but to compel or tempt him to do the same would have been sin: sin against him, and sin against Christ. I had "knowledge" that playing cards was "nothing" and not inherently sinful. But rather than exercise that liberty while in relationship to that other believer, I practiced restraint and in this act of love was able to build up my brother rather than tear him down.

To give but one more example, I (Andreas) was saved out of a background in which playing keyboards in a rock band was a major part of my college life. Later on, as a new believer after my conversion to Christ, a friend took me to a restaurant where loud rock music was playing over the speakers. At once the music evoked associations with my past prior to my conversion. I asked my friend if we could go to another restaurant instead, and he graciously agreed. To make matters worse, the music played at the second restaurant was much the same as that played in the first. Again, we left. Fortunately, we eventually found a non-offensive location. My friend at that time displayed remarkable patience with me whose conscience was weak at the time. I have since come to realize that there's nothing intrinsically offensive in that kind of music. A new context, but the same principle, and many such scenarios could be developed through a multitude of modern contexts.

Developing Teaching Points in Application

In answering the programmatic question, "How might this text relate to us today?" we have thus far dealt with the important hermeneutical issues of evaluating relevance and determining legitimacy. These inductive steps provide the necessary legwork in determining how and whether Scripture relates to a contemporary Christian audience. However, it's helpful to bring this stage of application to completion by articulating a clear response to our question. This is accomplished through the development of "teaching points." Teaching points are clear, concise statements that summarize what God's Word is teaching *us* at any particular point in Scripture. They reflect the underlying principles in a text, extending the timeless and transcendent principle to our current context. Our goal is therefore to develop sensible teaching points that accurately reflect an eternally relevant and exegetically legitimate application of Scripture.

Guided by the preceding work of evaluating relevance and determining legitimacy, we can develop teaching points by asking and answering either of the following two questions: (1) "What does God want his people to know through this text?" or (2) "What does God want his people to do through this text?" Notice that the question is not "What *did* God want?" but "What *does* God want?" Asking the question in the present tense will help you to articulate teaching points that reflect an eternally relevant, transcendent principle transferred to a modern context.

A teaching point for application shouldn't be confused with a teaching outline or "big idea" in the arena of homiletics. Teaching points comprise the summary of what Scripture teaches at a particular point or in a particular literary unit. A teaching point is a statement articulating God's revelation for the sake of contemporary, practical application or theological appropriation. Once understood, teaching points can serve as the basis for outlines, propositional questions, and "big ideas" in sermon preparation, but their purpose is not the organization of the text for sermon delivery. Rather, they function as a means of articulating legitimate application of the Scriptures for today.

Developing Teaching Points

What, then, might such teaching points look like, and how are they developed? The process begins with interpretation and subsequently moves to the distilled underlying principle. From this underlying principle, contextualized teaching points can then be developed. Let's again use our example from 1 Corinthians 8, "Knowledge puffs up, but love edifies."

Interpretation. Taking the text through the rigors of interpretation, we understand that Paul's message to a particular segment of the church at Corinth was this: "Don't allow your knowledge that 'food offered up to idols is nothing' become a stumbling block for those who don't have such knowledge.[28] Rather, cautiously limit the exercise of your freedom by not eating food that may have been offered up to idols. To limit one's freedom requires humility, and restraint is an act of humility. But by limiting your freedom, you demonstrate love for your brother, building him up rather than tearing him down. Such is the way of Christ."

The above summary is admittedly rather lengthy, but it accurately conveys the application as Paul intended it for his original audience. Summarizing the teaching of Scripture in its original context will often require a few sentences, perhaps even a paragraph. Also, note that our focus extends beyond the summary saying in verse 1, embracing the entire literary unit (1 Cor 8:1–13). Teaching points are not limited to verses or sentences; remember, meaning is usually conveyed beyond the sentence level. In this case, our teaching point extends throughout the whole unit of 1 Corinthians 8:1–13, which is summarized in Paul's opening statement, "Knowledge puffs up, but love edifies."

The Underlying Principle. Moving now to the distilled, underlying principle, we look beyond the situational, cultural context reflected in the letter to the Corinthians. As noted earlier, the underlying principle is love limiting liberty, the general premise that as believers relate to one another in the church, the exercise of Christian love must take precedence over the exercise of Christian liberty. Starting from this, the teaching point will simply be a modern, contextualized version of the underlying principle. You might state the teaching point of 1 Corinthians 8:1, and to some extent the whole passage of 1 Corinthians 8:1–13, in this manner: "Within the community of the church, and in reference to disputable matters, believers who have the freedom of conscience to participate in certain activities ought to consider first the effect this may have on their brothers and sisters who don't have the same freedom of conscience. If the exercise of Christian liberty, whether in reference to food, drink, entertainment, associations, affiliations, or anything else, results in another person stumbling into sin, then the loving thing to do

---

28. Knowledge in this context may be understood as freedom of conscience.

is to refrain from the exercise of one's freedom for the sake of the 'weaker' brother or sister."

Ideally, we should be able to abridge this statement even further so that it can be easily adapted to more specific contexts. Keep in mind that there's no one "right" way to state a teaching point; there's definitely some flexibility. Perhaps another way of stating the teaching point of 1 Corinthians 8:1–13 is as follows: "Those with liberty in reference to disputable matters ought to refrain from the practice of their liberty for the sake of those without such liberty. Doing so demonstrates love; not doing so demonstrates pride."

Contextualized Teaching Points. Moving from the articulation of the underlying principle to a contextualized teaching point often requires a specific, real-world situation.[29] On a recent trip to biblical Turkey, I (Al) was impressed with an example that fits our underlying principle and subsequent teaching point well. As our tour group visited sites such as Pergamum, Laodicea, and Ephesus, we were often greeted in gift shops with Turkish charms and pendants, the most common of which was the "blue evil eye." Based in centuries-old superstition, the talisman is shaped like a circle, is blue on the outside, and has the image of an eye in the middle. It is said to ward off evil, but for some in our group, the talisman was simply a representation of evil. Others, however, were quick to purchase these as souvenirs, looking to bring a bit of Turkish culture home (let's hope they were not made in China!). At least one person in the group was quite offended at how others regarded these talismans so lightly. Perhaps we might consider this example as just one more manifestation of a disputable matter which for some believers is a cause for stumbling while others have knowledge that such talisman souvenirs are "nothing." To apply the teaching point to this context, we might suggest that those who have the "knowledge that the blue evil eye is nothing" refrain from purchasing them as souvenirs, knowing that

---

29. A generalized teaching point and a distilled underlying principle are virtually one and the same. However, in phrasing an underlying principle, the goal is to leave it devoid of situational context, whether ancient or modern, as much as possible. With teaching points, specific application can be adapted to suit the modern context of twenty-first-century believers.

the practice of such liberty might cause others to stumble. Doing so is a manifestation of selfless love, knowing that the edification of others trumps the right to practice to one's own liberty.

To give but one more example, I (Andreas) have often observed that many, even Christian, tourists have pictures of their smiling faces taken in front of the Roman Coliseum (and then splash them proudly on social media). I have often thought that this seems rather insensitive to the fact that this site witnessed the gruesome spectacle of Christians being fed alive to lions in the arena, with pagan audiences looking on and cheering as Christians went to their death. How can anyone, much less believers, be oblivious to the symbolism conveyed by posing in front of such a site? The lesson, once again, is that without necessarily meaning to, we may offend others who attach a certain amount of significance to a given act, site, or object. This calls for greater sensitivity and for love limiting its exercise of liberty so as not to cause offense, even unintentionally.

Final Thoughts

Developing a methodical process in application may seem burdensome and unnecessary. After all, doesn't Scripture simply implore us to be "doers of the word and not hearers only" (Jas 1:22)? Yet we have discovered through this chapter that answering the question, "How might this text relate to us today?" is not a simple process. Appropriating an ancient, situational, and literarily diverse book of divine revelation to a contemporary context requires careful analysis. We always ought to have good reason for why we apply Scripture in one particular way or another. If we can't reasonably justify the manner and degree to which we apply a given text, we should reevaluate our application. As demonstrated in this chapter, hard work and careful thinking are as important in application as they are in interpretation. In some sense, application requires even more effort; in application, we must combine discernment with the acquisition of knowledge. We're again reminded of the words of Kevin Vanhoozer: "discerning significance . . . is a matter of wisdom."[30]

---

30. Vanhoozer, *Is There a Meaning in This Text?*, 423.

Haphazard thinking at the investigative level of application will result in the misappropriation of God's Word at the personal, devotional level. However, there's nothing haphazard when following a methodical, inductive approach to Bible study. Through the evaluation of relevance, the determination of legitimacy, and the development of teaching points, any segment of Scripture can speak with clarity and precision as the Word of God to the people of God today.

14

Appropriating the Meaning
Living Out the Text in Our World

By following a methodical approach to Bible study, the preceding chapters have laid the groundwork for an acquisition of biblical knowledge, the fuel that feeds spiritual transformation and growth. However, in an age where information is plentiful, we're reminded that God's desire is not that his people simply *know* the truth, but that the truth of his Word *transforms* his people. The groundwork for personalized application is absolutely necessary. When the Word of God is mishandled at the levels of interpretation and evaluation, misappropriation logically follows. But let's not be deceived into thinking that the journey ends with an understanding of what the Word meant to *the original readers* or even what it means to *us* today. Spiritual transformation is ultimately *personal* transformation, an active knowledge of what the text means for *me* today.

The Role of the Holy Spirit

If observation requires hard work, and interpretation requires sharp thinking, then it's equally true that application requires illuminated wisdom. In the preceding chapter, we dealt with the role of wisdom in discerning matters of relevance and legitimacy. Yet until now we've said little about *illumination*, the vital role of the Holy Spirit in the inductive process. As we turn our attention to the personal appropriation of God's Word, there's no more fitting place to discuss the role of the Holy Spirit.

Most believers come to the Bible expecting that God will speak to them there, that the Holy Spirit may even "illumine" their minds so as to better know the truth. This is an understandable expectation; after all, shouldn't a divinely inspired text require a divinely illumined interpreter? However, there are common misconceptions regarding what this divine illumination entails. In what sense does the Holy Spirit open the interpreter's eyes to the truth, turning on the lights in the mind of the believer?

Many assume that illumination is God's provision of supernatural interpretive insight, the occasional "Aha!" moment where the baffled reader finally understands what the text is saying. Others might view illumination as the Spirit's enablement to "perceive facts and judge the plausibility of arguments with greater clarity."[1] Still others see illumination as an exegetical safeguard, God's means of rectifying the distortion of truth. Some even suggest that the Spirit's role in interpretation is so absolute that the Spirit-filled believer needs no other tool but illumination in Bible study. Although these approaches reflect different degrees and emphases in the work of the Spirit, they have one thing in common: a primary focus on divine enablement to accurately *interpret* the Bible.

While the Holy Spirit is certainly capable of providing interpretive insight, we'd suggest that illumination has more to do with *appropriation* than interpretation. This doesn't mean that God never provides illumined clarity in the process of interpretation or that he cannot steer the Spirit-filled believer away from erroneous conclusions. However, the normative procedure for interpretation requires hard work and study—albeit enhanced by sanctified common sense—and those who neglect hard work and study do so to their own detriment. God the Holy Spirit can illumine the mind to exegetical truth, but we shouldn't expect this to take place as a normative substitute for exegetical spadework. Illumination can quicken the mind, but it is the heart that God is ultimately after—your affections, your volition, and your resolve to obey in unconditional trust what he commands.[2]

---

1. Robert L. Plummer, *40 Questions about Interpreting the Bible* (Grand Rapids: Kregel, 2010), 146.
2. For Old Testament examples of obedient faith in action, see the "cloud of witnesses" paraded in the "Hall of Faith" in Hebrews 11 (cf. Heb 12:1).

Scripture provides some insight into the work of illumination, although there's little that speaks directly to Bible study. Most Scripture references that hint at illumination focus on the Spirit's role in bringing the knowledge of truth to a darkened mind. It's in this sense that Scripture speaks of divine enablement to discern the truth (1 Cor 2:14; 2 Cor 3:13–16; Matt 13:11–16; Luke 24:44–45).[3] But we're concerned with the Spirit's work in relation to hermeneutics, the divine enablement that assists the reader in understanding the Word of God. The term "illumination" is absent from Scripture, but the concept can be inferred. Illumination is not revelation. Illumination is not a simple spark of interpretive insight. But Scripture does speak of divine enablement to discern the truth of the gospel in God's revelation, to understand that the Scriptures point to Christ.

We'd also suggest that this sets the believer on a trajectory by which the Word *means* something to the believer—to the one whose eyes have been opened to the truth of the gospel—that it doesn't mean to the unbeliever. A scholar in ancient Near Eastern literature may understand all there is to know about Old Testament historical background yet have a mind that is darkened to the spiritual truth revealed in the text. A linguist may understand the grammar and syntax of the original languages yet without the divine spark of illumination bypass the truth even as she parses Greek or Hebrew grammar. Illumination is not divine enlightenment as to the exegetical meaning of the text but rather a matter of divine enablement to find something truly meaningful in the text in appropriating it to one's life.[4]

What's more, not only does illumination enable the interpreter to understand and apply biblical truth, it also helps overcome spiritual opposition in the context of the spiritual warfare that engulfs the entire

---

3. First Corinthians 2:10–16 is frequently cited as a proof-text for the doctrine of illumination. However, this passage doesn't address Bible study *per se*. Rather, it speaks to the origin of Paul's message (i.e., the Spirit) and the manner through which its truth is discerned (i.e., by the Spirit). See David E. Garland, *1 Corinthians*, BECNT (Grand Rapids: Baker, 2003), 98–103.

4. Duvall and Hays surmise that, "When it comes to biblical interpretation, the Spirit appears to work little in the cognitive dimension, more in the area of discerning truth, and most in the area of application." We agree that biblically and experientially, the Holy Spirit illumines the Spirit-filled interpreter primarily in the realm of personal application. See J. Scott Duvall and J. Daniel Hays, *Grasping God's Word*, 3rd ed. (Grand Rapids: Zondervan, 2012), 228.

cosmos ever since Satan first cast doubt on the veracity of God's Word.[5] Thus not only is the Spirit active in Bible interpretation and application, but Satan is active as well, seeking to keep people in spiritual bondage, blindness, and darkness, so they are kept from grasping the glorious truth of the gospel of forgiveness and salvation in Christ.[6] In this way, Satan seeks to distort the truthfulness of God's Word, whether keeping people from reading the Bible altogether or seeking to thwart their accurate understanding of it or at least keeping them from applying the truth they have come to know. If Satan is active against us, we are equally confident that God the Holy Spirit is active for us, opening the truth of the Word so that we might stand firm against the "tactics of the Devil" (Eph 6:11).

Appropriating the Truth

Appropriating the truth of God's Word doesn't lend itself to a rigid methodical process. To place too much emphasis on procedure would seem counter to the spiritual enlightenment that "hears" the Word speak; it would seem to snuff out the divine spark that drives us to action. So please bear with us as we examine the process of moving from what the text means to *us* to what it means to *me*.

On one hand, personalizing relevant, legitimate teaching points derived from Scripture requires little more than a shift in pronouns, describing the message of the text in first-person singular ("me," "my," and "I") rather than first-person plural language ("us," "our," and "we"). The hard analytical work of evaluation and discernment is accomplished, and now we simply take that message and apply it personally.

However, internalizing the Word of God still requires some kind of process. Knowing that a biblical characterization of applied truth sees little difference between the community and the individual, we strive not to overanalyze or overemphasize this transition. Yet in terms of inductive study, the focus culminates in the individual—for most, *inductive* study is *personal* study.

---

5. Genesis 3:1, 4–5.
6. Cf., e.g., 2 Cor 4:3–6; 10:3–5.

Therefore, in personalizing the meaning of the text, there are three practical points of distinction in moving from *general* to *personal* application: (1) personal assessment, (2) reflective meditation, and (3) individual appropriation.[7]

Figure 14.1: Moving from General to Personal Application

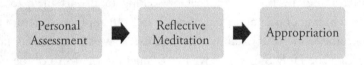

Personal Assessment

As interpreters, we're vitally concerned with knowing the content of Scripture. It is the Bible that speaks; clearly, we must know the *content* of the message! But we must also realize that communication is two-sided; after all, the Bible speaks to *me*, personally. In order to appropriate the Word of God, I must understand myself having come face to face with the Word of God. Personal application requires knowledge of Scripture and knowledge of self.

James describes the law (and by extension, the Bible) as a mirror (Jas 1:22–25). To look into a mirror but not see oneself is shortsighted and blind. Certainly, the Scriptures reveal what is in a person. But personal assessment also requires openness before the authority of Scripture. It requires honest inventory, an open, humble assessment of where we stand in the face of interpreted truth.

While attitude is essential, are there any practical helps in performing personal assessment? We'd suggest performing a personal inventory assessment at this stage of application. In the context of inductive study, such an assessment focuses on matching a specific text with your own corresponding life situation. As with most steps of inductive study, it's worth taking the time to write this out on paper (or a screen) and develop

---

7. We are using the term "appropriation" to refer to the internal, active reception of God's Word in the life of the believer.

a list of teaching points from the text in conjunction with the parallel circumstances of your own context.

While there may be situations in Scripture that don't parallel our own, more often a personal assessment reveals comparable situations where teaching points speak into the circumstances of one's own life and where the original context finds a parallel with my context.

Much searching goes into inductive Bible study. But too often students of Scripture fail to search themselves to know where they stand before the Word of God. It goes without saying that even a little time spent doing personal inventory pays rich spiritual dividends, especially when joined with the hard work of observation and interpretation. Effectual life change doesn't occur in the knowing of facts but in the Spirit-charged conviction that brings those facts to bear on myself.

Reflective Meditation

Assessing your own personal situation in light of the teachings of Scripture is itself introspective. In this sense, steps 1 and 2 are hardly distinct. However, in *personal assessment* the emphasis is on an honest and humble search of your own heart. In *reflective meditation* we're primarily concerned with the content of Scripture rather than personal inventory. In the process of study, it's all too easy to lose touch with the devotional side of reading—prayer, reflection, and meditation. While these are ideally companions throughout the whole process of inductive study, we realize that this balance is difficult to maintain. So at this point we encourage a dedicated dose of reflective meditation.

If there's any biblical treatise on the merits and value of Scripture, it is Psalm 119. In all the wonder of this wisdom psalm, there's no instruction on *how* to study the Bible. There's no inductive plan, no exegetical arrangement, no analysis of context and content. There is, however, an emphasis on meditation, the permeating presence of Scripture in the mind of the psalmist. While we stress the importance of careful and methodical Bible study, it's clear what Scripture itself stresses. The psalmist doesn't celebrate exegetical process, but he does celebrate the Word and its ability to effect change from the mind to the heart. With the psalmist, our heart cry when studying Scripture should be this:

> Search me, God, and know my heart;
> test me and know my concerns.
> See if there is any offensive way in me;
> lead me in the everlasting way. (Ps 139:23–24)

This humble and contrite spirit, in turn, is undergirded by a deep, heart-felt longing for God and his presence:

> As a deer longs for streams of water,
> so I long for You, God.
> I thirst for God, the living God.
> Deep calls to deep . . . (Ps 42:1–2, 7)

Truly, it is fear of and reverence for God that is the proper disposition for anyone seeking to encounter God face to face in his Word:

> This is the LORD's declaration.
> I will look favorably on this kind of person:
> one who is humble, submissive in spirit,
> and trembles at My word. (Isa 66:2)

The goal of meditation is not accuracy in interpretation or legitimacy in application. Rather, the goal of meditation is to hear what God is saying through the text on a personal, spiritual level. It is to perceive what *God* is saying through the text. This is not to suggest that careful interpretation has no role in meditative reading. The integrity of Scripture's voice is bound by the safeguards of interpretation. *Scripture shouldn't mean something on the personal, spiritual level that is not supported at the exegetical level.* However, we'd suggest that a meditative reading is not only bound by interpretation, to the contrary, it is bolstered by it. In a wondrous display of grace, God often speaks through his Word even when interpretive precision is lacking. If the Word has power to speak in spite of sloppy interpretation, how much more will it speak with power through a fully discovered, accurately interpreted text?

Individual Appropriation

Individual appropriation is the transformative stage in application, a matter of becoming "doers of the word and not hearers only" (Jas 1:22). However, appropriation isn't simply a matter of us doing what the text says. It also involves what the text is doing *to us*; that is, the text is performing the work of spiritual transformation in the heart and mind of the reader. If personal assessment requires honest inventory, and if meditation requires perceptive reading, then appropriation requires a submissive posture. Honest self-assessment, along with perceptive reading (hearing the Word), precedes the submissive act of appropriation.

As the reader submits to the text, she also submits to God. Much of application can be described as an obligation to holiness—behavior and activities that honor God in the daily routine of life. Yet the term "appropriation" implies a greater work, the act of transformation and the development of Christian character. In this we ought to think of application in broader terms than simply doing what the Bible tells us to do. The study of Scripture results in a holistic transformation of our minds into conformity with Christ.

Recently, I (Al) caught my five-year-old son doing something he was not supposed to do. His response to my discipline seemed less than genuine: "But I don't know how to be good!" In return, I responded, "This should be simple; just do what I tell you to do!" In my mind, the transition from hearing to doing should have been easy, but upon further reflection I realized that my son had experienced the same principle Paul mused over nearly 2,000 years earlier: "When I want to do what is good, evil is with me" (Rom 7:21).

Paul understood that obedience without transformation is a hopeless struggle. Yet sometimes we have that very same attitude toward application. Our "go to" verse for this chapter, "Be doers of the Word and not hearers only," seems simple enough. Just apply what the text tells you to do! But without transformation, application ultimately falls short. For this reason, we see the goal of inductive study as appropriation, the internal, active reception of God's Word in the life of the believer. Appropriation embraces the personal application of "knowing" and "doing" texts. Through inductive study, Scripture speaks in a transformative way, meeting us even when we don't know "how to be good."

Practically Speaking

The idea of personal transformation through the appropriation of Scripture seems admirable, but are there any other practical steps to getting there? Yes and no. Obviously, it's hard to put personal transformation on a desktop or to strategize with pen and paper. Yet we do find that writing out devotional summaries of Scripture helps to clarify and refine what God is already writing on our hearts. Devotional summaries are simply personalized reflections on the teaching points of the text. While we avoid the first-person singular throughout most of the inductive process, here we are intentional on emphasizing personal commitments. A devotional summary mirrors the teaching points of the text with devotional points for personal application. These "devotional points" are reframed to begin with "I will" statements, often followed by contextualized scenarios reflecting our own concrete circumstances. They are specific, measurable points of personal application derived from the text itself.

Devotional summaries tend to reflect points of application on an individual's spiritual journey. You might read a particular passage of Scripture ten years after engaging in an initial study and find that because your life circumstances have shifted, so has the way in which Scripture now speaks to you. It's not that the *interpretation* of the text has changed; nor has a shift occurred with regard to *relevance* and *legitimacy*—in fact, the teaching points remain the same. However, over the course of time, life inevitably moves forward. Devotional points will reflect the new circumstances and context of a personal, ever-changing life. Relationships change, settings shift, and with this, God's Word speaks to us anew.

Teaching Points and Devotional Points

At this juncture, it may help to illustrate the difference between *teaching points* and *devotional points*. For the sake of illustration, we'll use an obscure legal text that nonetheless has a clear underlying principle:

"If you build a new house, make a railing around your roof, so that you don't bring bloodguilt on your house if someone falls from it" (Deut 22:8).[8] Although this is an obscure law text, it is easy to find parallels to our own situation. For the ancient Israelite, this was a practical civil law. Because it was common for people to spend time on their roofs, especially on summer evenings, it was important that they also build a wall around their rooftop to keep guests and family from falling off.

While in North America it is rare to have flattop roofs, it's still quite easy to find legitimate parallels based on the practical underlying principle. Possible parallels include railings around porches, fencing around swimming pools, covers over swimming pools, leashes on dogs, car seats for children, seat belts for adults, life jackets on a boat, and a multitude of additional safety measures adopted in modern industry (many applications of this principle are today manifest in modern legal code). The principle is rather straightforward, yet the potential for variety in teaching points is considerable.

However, in appropriating the principle in this text, we must shift from general statements of how this applies to *us* to specific statements detailing how this applies to *me*. In doing so, the practical nature of the teaching point should remain intact—in shifting to appropriation, we shouldn't spiritualize the text. We're not dealing with setting up railings around our *heart*, or building walls of protection from *sin*. But we do find personal, measurable application quite straightforward.

Consider an application related to car seats for children. One of the many legitimate teaching points derived from this ancient Israelite law is the following: "Those who own cars and transport children in cars ought to put them in age-appropriate car seats." With the arrival of children, this "law" took on new, personalized significance. I (Al) remember bringing my firstborn home for the first time from the hospital. It was also the first time I had ever used an infant's car seat. I had no idea how to install the carrier, so I took special measures to have it put in properly.

8. Due to the clear yet distinct transference between ancient and modern contexts, this verse is frequently cited as an example for applying underlying principles from Old Testament law. See Daniel M. Doriani, *Putting the Truth to Work: The Theory and Practice of Biblical Application* (Phillipsburg, NJ: P&R, 2001), 241–43; and Duvall and Hays, *Grasping God's Word*, 372.

As a father, the weight of responsibility now rested on my shoulders. Of course, it was not just that I was applying an obscure law text from the Old Testament. The state of Virginia has its own laws to "assist" me in taking responsibility.

But interestingly, a few years later, while traveling abroad with my family, I faced a situation where I was no longer obligated by Virginia state child safety laws to place my toddler in a car seat. This is where the teaching point, "Those who own cars and transport children in cars ought to put them in age appropriate car seats," took on new significance in personal appropriation: "I will place my son in a car seat even though I'm not bound by law to do so. I choose to take responsibility for his welfare and safety, knowing that neglecting such safety measures would make me guilty of negligence if an accident were to occur."

While this devotional point may seem less than spiritual, it is legitimate. Keep in mind that not every teaching point in Scripture is overtly spiritual. But in this case, both the teaching point and the personalized devotional point reflect a godly attitude toward a practical issue. In fact, truth is often intensely practical, and there is no legitimate dichotomy between Bible knowledge and application. The adage that some are "so heavenly-minded as to be of no earthly good" is misleading. Look at the wisdom literature, especially the book of Proverbs. Or read the book of James. At the heart of application is wisdom, the skill to live life in the light of God's revealed truth. If anything is true, it's worth knowing, and if it's worth knowing, it's also worth applying.

Final Thoughts

In arguing the case for methodical, progressive Bible study, we've stressed that application follows interpretation. In our unit on application, we've presented a linear approach where one step proceeds from the other, culminating in appropriation. However, we realize that in practice we can't help but personalize the text as soon as we read it; to do so is only natural. Understanding Scripture generates an almost instantaneous response in the heart and mind of the Spirit-filled believer.[9] In some sense, this is the way it should be. What is more, Scripture itself affirms that we must put our knowledge into practice. While, methodologically, it may be helpful to separate interpretation and application, in Scripture the two are ultimately inseparable.

An honest approach to application will therefore recognize that interpretation and application often overlap. Daniel Doriani describes this as the "permeable barrier" between meaning and application.[10] Although application cannot occur without interpretation, and although interpretation logically precedes application, the two are often integrated without boundary in theory and in practice. To overemphasize the distinction between them may in fact be detrimental to the health of the church. Should we think that God wants a hard and fast line to be drawn between interpretation and application? We don't think so. Scripture itself testifies that to know God is to obey him, and to know Scripture is to do what it says.

---

9. Doriani, *Putting the Truth to Work*, 22–23.
10. Ibid.

15

Doing Theology

The Outflow of an Inductive Approach to Scripture

W hat is the goal of inductive Bible study? Where does it end? Does it finish with simply doing the Word of God? Or is it a matter of knowing the Word of God? The answer is actually both. Interpretation leads to application, and application involves both the "knowing" and the "doing" of the interpreted Word. As demonstrated in the previous chapter, each text of Scripture, when studied inductively, ought to result in the personal appropriation of God's Word in heart, mind, and action. But is there more? Is there another channel that flows from the reservoir of interpretation—the cumulative effect of the interpreted Word of God? What is the result of methodical Bible study when conducted over an extended period of time and applied to the whole Word of God? We'd suggest that the result is *theology*—the outflow of a lifetime of inductive Bible study.

Knowing the Word of God requires more than knowing the individual parts of Scripture. No matter how well-honed our interpretation of individual parts, the parts must be tied to the whole. After all, God has revealed himself through the metanarrative cased in the whole canon of Scripture. Understanding the Bible demands a *synthetic* approach, one that appreciates the whole council of God in the Scriptures. *Theology is that synthetic approach to Scripture, the correlation of individually observed, interpreted, and applied texts.* Although the term "theology" seems intimidating, conjuring thoughts of long-bearded men in ivory towers, at its core it is really nothing more than the correlation of interpreted Scripture, the end game of inductive Bible study.

We've studied the theory, procedure, and benefit of correlation in two previous chapters. In chapter 9 we explored interpretive correlation, the process by which Scripture is interpreted by Scripture, allowing the whole to inform the exegetical interpretation of the parts. In chapter 11 we studied thematic correlation, an inductive approach to the synthetic interpretation of biblical motifs. In each of these interpretive ventures, the primary goal rests in the interpretation of individual parts, represented either within the literary unit or by the thematic motif. Yet there's another, final phase of correlation in the inductive method that stems from the cumulative observation, interpretation, and application of all biblical texts—theology.

The basic concept of correlation is generally uniform; correlation is simply comparing Scripture with Scripture, albeit with some level of synthetic analysis between texts. As the natural outflow of inductive study, the final phase of correlation involves the synthesis of Scripture in regard to major biblical themes and doctrines. It essentially involves the unpacking and organization of the whole message of Scripture. It's the outworking of a lifetime of inductive study, but it's not an unintentional byproduct. Through a synthetic understanding of the whole message of Scripture, judgments are rendered on how texts compare and relate to one another theologically. In the development of theology, we find ourselves involved in the methodical and intentional final phase of inductive study.

Basic Approaches to Doing Theology

Ideally, all Christian theology is derived from the interpretation of Scripture. However, there are different approaches to how theology is done. The greatest line of distinction lies between biblical theology and systematic theology. *Biblical theology* approaches the Bible on its own terms, deriving theological categories from the interests and terminology of the biblical writers. *Systematic theology*, on the other hand, arranges its structure around the interests of the community of faith—that is, the church. Biblical theology reflects the historical context of *Scripture*, while systematic theology reflects the historical and contemporary interests of the *church*. Biblical theology tends to reflect and adapt to the literary diversity in Scripture, while systematic theology tends to flatten the literary topography of the text. But perhaps the greatest line of distinction between the two relates to how the theological message of the text is synthesized into a framework of categories. Biblical theology works within the framework of theological categories presented in the Bible, while systematic theology builds a framework for doctrine around categories not directly reflected in the biblical text.[1]

This short comparison of biblical and systematic theology may sound disparaging toward the systematic approach, but we really don't intend to diminish its value—the truth is that systematic theology and its logical framework of doctrine is very necessary for the church. It provides believers with answers to the pressing theological questions of their day, even as those questions shift from one period and community to the next. Following logical categories of interest, the church benefits from the work of others who have wrestled with theological questions in earlier generations, reaping the harvest of their cumulative study of the Scriptures.

What is more, through the systematic approach new believers are taught by a list of doctrines and corresponding support references what to believe about God, man, sin, and salvation. They receive guidance into the deep mysteries related to the work of Christ and the redemption that his substitutionary atonement provides. Systematic theology provides structure for exploring the divine—whether by way of the attributes of God or the triune nature of his being. Through systematic theology believers are guided in the realm of theological truth without having to do all the work of correlation themselves—after all, how could a person new to the Bible be expected to synthesize the teachings of Scripture by Scripture? It requires time to develop biblical literacy, to understand the

---

1. For a concise treatment evaluating the history, interests, and primary distinctions between biblical and systematic theology, see D. A. Carson, "Systematic Theology and Biblical Theology," in *New Dictionary of Biblical Theology: Exploring the Unity and Diversity of Scripture*, ed. T. Desmond Alexander et al. (Downers Grove: InterVarsity, 2000), 89–104.

relationship between interpreted parts, to reach the culminating step of inductive study. Yet over time, we begin to realize where those doctrines come from and how they are developed. We see that theology is based on the interpreted text. As we involve ourselves in the study of Scripture, we begin to make our own judgments regarding the teachings of Scripture—in a sense, we begin to "do" theology on our own.

The Case for Biblical Theology

In following the path of inductive Bible study, what approach to theology best reflects an inductive approach? We would suggest that, in principle, biblical theology best fits the inductive method. This is not to infer that systematic theology is a "lesser" approach—but it is more inherently *deductive*. There's a place for systematic theology in the life of the church. Neither biblical nor systematic theology is inherently right or wrong. But when we speak of theological correlation as the outflow of inductive Bible study, biblical theology is the natural result.

In describing biblical theology, it may help to list the ways in which it reflects an inductive approach to the study of Scripture. Consider the following characteristics of biblical theology.

Biblical Theology Is Framed by Categories Found in the Bible

Biblical theology is framed by the natural historical, literary, and theological boundaries represented in the Bible.[2] This is most easily demonstrated in theologies related to individual books (a theology of Romans), authors (a theology of Paul), or collections (a theology of the letters to Timothy and Titus). But biblical theology can also be built around historical periods or literary genres (a theology of wisdom literature). The variations possible within biblical theology are as diverse as the canon itself. For example, you can draw out a theology of the eighth-century prophets (centering on a historical period) or develop

---

2. Systematic theology is built around categories not directly represented by the historical, literary, or theological structure of the Bible. In other words, the Bible is not structured around books or literary units that teach systematic doctrines (such as a book on Pneumatology).

a theology of the Minor Prophets (building theology around a literary collection). The diverse categories possible within biblical theology naturally reflect the historical, literary, and theological aspects of Scripture. While biblical theology must ultimately accommodate the teachings of the whole canon of Scripture, it begins by performing theological correlation in cohesive segments of Scripture. Such an approach embraces the historical, literary, and theological diversity in the Bible while also validating its essential continuity.[3]

Biblical Theology Is Built upon Motifs Presented in Scripture

Whereas systematic theology is concerned with questions of orthodoxy (questions and concerns developed through the course of church history—past or present), biblical theology is concerned with the motifs presented within the canonical text (questions and concerns developed through the course of biblical history). Consider the study of the doctrine of God. Systematic theology lists and defines the characteristics of God (e.g., holiness, goodness, immanence), considers the attributes of God (e.g., omniscience, omnipotence, omnipresence), and explores the mysteries of the triune nature of God (co-equal and co-eternal in nature, subordination within the Godhead, etc.). Yet never in a systematic theology class will students find God described as a "divine warrior," even though this is one of the prominent motifs describing God in the Old *and* New Testaments.[4] Although the councils defending church orthodoxy never argued the case for God as divine warrior, the biblical text goes to great lengths describing God as a warrior who protects and defends his people while waging war against his enemies. The prophets implored people to depend upon the divine warrior to protect their interests and they warned them to fear the warrior who would wage battle against his enemies. The narrative of Scripture plays out the drama of God functioning as divine warrior, leading even to the final battles waged in the apocalypse of Revelation. This is an organic depiction of God revealed

---

3. Systematic theology tends to focus on the entire Bible rather than on segments of the Bible.

4. See Tremper Longman III and Daniel G. Reid, *God Is a Warrior* (Grand Rapids: Zondervan, 1995).

throughout the biblical narrative. Grounded in the history of real events, the biblical record presents God as a warrior who destroys—but also as the one who saves. It is a description of God based in a theological motif very much at the heart of the biblical story.

Biblical-theological motifs represent the interests of the biblical writers. These interests are as diverse as Scripture itself. They reflect the cultural and situational contexts of their day yet communicate biblical truths with timeless consistency. Among the wonders of biblical theology is the diversity of means and richness of imagery by which truth is revealed through Scripture. God is not described in the Bible only as a divine warrior. He is also presented as a loving father, a jilted husband, a roaring lion, a caring shepherd, and a mighty king. In addition, there is a great diversity of motifs presented in Scripture that deal with topics other than the person of God. Some motifs embody the human condition, while others consist of elements within the grand scheme of redemption. A few are cerebral, while others are practical. Some motifs are confined to specific books, while others reflect the concerns of the whole canon of Scripture.

The number of channels through which the Bible teaches truth is quite astonishing. Consider, for example, a selection of topics drawn from the InterVarsity Press New Studies in Biblical Theology series. There is a book detailing a theology of repentance, another covering a theology of possessions, one assessing a theology of race, and yet another tracing a theology of incarnation.[5] Metaphors also represent theological motifs, and so the series contains volumes ranging from the motif of spiritual adultery to the motif of being Christ's slave.[6] Other titles are more specific to individual books of the Bible. For example, the series includes *Father, Son, and Spirit: The Trinity and John's Gospel; The Cross from a Distance: Atonement in Mark's Gospel;* and *Now My Eyes Have Seen You: Images of*

---

5. Mark J. Boda, *'Return to Me': A Biblical Theology of Repentance* (Downers Grove: InterVarsity, 2015); Craig L. Blomberg, *Neither Poverty nor Riches: A Biblical Theology of Possessions* (Downers Grove: InterVarsity, 2000); J. Daniel Hays, *From Every People and Nation: A Biblical Theology of Race* (Downers Grove: InterVarsity, 2003); Graham Cole, *The God who Became Human: A Biblical Theology of Incarnation* (Downers Grove: InterVarsity, 2013).

6. Raymond C. Ortlund Jr., *God's Unfaithful Wife: A Biblical Theology of Spiritual Adultery* (Downers Grove: InterVarsity, 1996); Murray J. Harris, *Slave of Christ: A New Testament Metaphor for Total Devotion to Christ* (Downers Grove: InterVarsity, 2001).

Creation and Evil in the Book of Job.[7] There are literally dozens of legitimate biblical-theological motifs threaded throughout the pages of Scripture.

Biblical Theology Is Developed by Working Upward from the Text

Biblical theology begins by asking questions related to the text: what were the original authors of Scripture interested in communicating to their original audience? What questions about God, man, and reality were they seeking to address? What issues were they most interested in resolving? By exploring *their* questions rather than *our* questions, biblical theology inherently lends itself to an inductive methodology.[8]

Consider the question of the destiny of the unevangelized. What happens to those who never had the chance to hear the gospel? What about infants, children, and those with severe mental disability? As much as we may be interested in clear, explicit answers to these questions, there's no place in Scripture where the biblical writers provide a propositional treatise answering these most pressing questions.[9] Sure, the prophets answered the question about who God is (Yahweh v. Baal), and Paul brought clarity to the question of food offered up to idols (1 Corinthians 8), but what about the so-called age of accountability? It would seem to be a pressing question, but for whatever reason it is not a point of interest among the biblical writers.

By necessity, systematic theology takes a deductive approach to answering questions related to the destiny of the unevangelized and infants. It comes to the text from the outside looking for answers to these vital questions. This doesn't negate the importance of finding answers to these questions or the confidence that we might have in answering them deductively. Our point is simply that these were not the theological

---

7. Andreas J. Köstenberger and Scott R. Swain, *Father, Son, and Spirit: The Trinity and John's Gospel* (Downers Grove: InterVarsity, 2008); Peter G. Bolt, *The Cross from a Distance: Atonement in Mark's Gospel* (Downers Grove: InterVarsity, 2005); Robert Fyall, *Now My Eyes Have Seen You: Images of Creation and Evil in the Book of Job* (Downers Grove: InterVarsity, 2002).

8. Systematic theology tends to develop out of logical deduction, addressing questions centered outside of the primary interests of the biblical writers.

9. For an exploration of the issue and proposed answers to the questions, see Gabriel Fackre, Ronald H. Nash, and John Sanders, *What About Those Who Have Never Heard? Three Views on the Destiny of the Unevangelized* (Downers Grove, IL: InterVarsity, 1995).

questions being raised by the biblical authors in their historical, situational settings. Biblical theology, rather than looking *to* the text for answers to questions, draws both the questions and the answers *from* the text of Scripture.[10] Biblical theology works upward from the text, exploring those issues that represent the interests of the biblical writers, rather than downward, finding in the text answers to questions that the biblical writers were never asking.

Biblical Theology Embraces the Theological Tension Reflected by the Text

Biblical theology recognizes the diversity of contexts in Scripture, whether historical, literary, or theological. Set within the unfolding drama of revelation history, biblical theology recognizes movement in relationship and agenda between covenants and situational contexts throughout Scripture. This can be illustrated by the stark difference between Isaiah's message in the late eighth century BC and Jeremiah's parallel message in the early sixth century BC. Isaiah proclaimed that God would deliver Zion from the impending threat of the Assyrians if only she were to trust in him to act as divine warrior. Jeremiah proclaimed that God would *not* deliver Zion from Babylon—God had already determined that Nebuchadnezzar would act as his servant to bring judgment upon his people. Ironically, in Jeremiah the false prophets proclaimed that God would not allow Zion to fall—their message was similar to that of Isaiah 120 years earlier! In developing a theology of Zion, biblical theology embraces the tension between Isaiah's message (God *will* deliver this city) and Jeremiah's message (God will *not* deliver this city). It fully recognizes that the reversal in theological message stems from a shift in circumstances. There is no reason to resolve this tension given the situationally dynamic nature of Scripture.[11]

---

10. That is, biblical theology is built upon sound exegesis of individual passages: it is predicated upon the exegetical principle (see chapter 2).

11. Systematic theology has a tendency to reject (or remedy) the tension revealed by a progressive text. This is seen in the historical interests of orthodoxy as the church has sought clarity on issues ranging from the sovereignty of God to the extent of the atonement and beyond. Theological dogma is uncomfortable with unresolved tension within the text—biblical theology, on the other hand, embraces it.

Another example of contextual flexibility in biblical theology involves the "Day of the Lord" motif in Scripture. Depending upon the context, the Day of the Lord may refer to God's judgment upon Israel or God's judgment meted out against the Gentile nations. In other cases, the Day of the Lord is a positive reflection of God's activity, resulting in the ultimate restoration of Israel. Sometimes "that day" points to a temporal, situational period of God's activity, while in other contexts it refers to an end-time reality. Ultimately, context determines the nature and timing of God's activity "in that day." Biblical theology recognizes the importance of the "Day of the Lord" as a motif, but it also embraces the inherent flexibility of that term in describing God's involvement and activity in the affairs of this world.[12]

Principles for Doing Theology

Does theological correlation simply happen, or is there a process that provides structure and rules for doing theology? As the outflow of inductive study, the development of biblical-theological conclusions ought to reflect the careful observation of individual passages of Scripture. It assumes the correct interpretation of individual passages, but in addition requires the correct understanding of how individually interpreted passages relate and connect. Moreover, biblical theology reflects the evaluation and appropriation of individual passages.

For example, in developing a biblical theology of marriage and family, one must wrestle with the relevance of biblical texts rooted in ancient cultural practices on a case-by-case basis. How we evaluate those texts influences the development of a biblical theology of marriage and family— our theological conclusions are practical and relevant, not relegated only to the ancient historical context of Scripture. Therefore we recognize that the process of doing theology necessarily involves the whole process of inductive study. Yes, biblical theology ought to flow out of an inductive

---

12. For an overview of the flexibility in the day of the Lord concept, see J. D. Barker, "Day of the Lord," in *Dictionary of the Old Testament Prophets*, ed. Mark J. Boda and J. Gordon McConville (Downers Grove, IL: InterVarsity, 2012), 132–43.

treatment of Scripture, but we should not think that theology develops without significant inductive background and process.[13]

While theology flows out of the observation, interpretation, and application of individual texts, these texts must be synthesized for theology to develop. Because theology develops out of correlation, the same rules that guide interpretive correlation and thematic correlation also apply to the work of doing theology. These include the practical disciplines of thinking categorically and summarizing conclusions as a means to articulating biblical truth.

In addition, as we finalize the process of induction, let's consider a set of guiding principles for doing theology. The following principles are simple yet profound, drawing our attention to the inductive platform upon which theology stands.

Be Intentional

Doing theology involves the intentional pursuit of drawing out connections between related texts. However, an inductive approach demands balance: we must pursue theology intentionally while not forcing the correspondence between texts in an unnatural manner. In the intentional pursuit of correlation, you should strive to discover the natural synthetic relationship between biblical texts.

Be Exegetical

Let's not forget that sound theology, like legitimate application, must find its basis in sound interpretation. Theology is bigger and broader than the interpretation of individual texts, but misinterpreted texts will inevitably lead to erroneous theological conclusions. Therefore, as a basis for doing theology, we agree with Klein, Blomberg, and Hubbard in the premise that "valid theologizing must follow the sound

13. For examples of biblical theology in relation to marriage and family specifically and to God's design for man and woman generally, see Andreas J. Köstenberger (with David W. Jones), *God, Marriage, and Family: Rebuilding the Biblical Foundation*, 2nd ed. (Wheaton: Crossway, 2010); and Andreas J. and Margaret E. Köstenberger, *God's Design for Man and Woman: A Biblical-Theological Survey* (Wheaton: Crossway, 2014); see also the online course based on the latter book available on www.biblemesh.com and www.biblicalfoundations.org.

exegesis of the appropriate biblical texts."[14] An inductive approach requires that exegetical interpretation precede the development and articulation of theological conclusions.

Be Balanced

In the synthesis of related texts, there's a natural tendency for theologians to give differing weight to texts based upon perceived importance. Often, the weight given to particular texts is determined more by theological preunderstanding than by exegetical significance.[15] An inductive approach to theology requires that equal weight and consideration be given to texts when they seem to support opposite sides of a position. Remember, theological tension is common in biblical theology.

Be Sensible

An inductive approach to theology requires the reader to draw legitimate correspondence between the biblical text and theological topics. Even though a passage may seem to speak to a particular topic, this perceived correspondence must be evaluated exegetically. Moreover, the correspondence between related texts must be evaluated as texts are correlated and synthesized. Theology shouldn't be built upon flimsy connections between texts.

Be Thorough

Inductively driven theology is comprehensive in its consideration of relevant texts. Although biblical theology allows for categorical boundaries, including Old and New Testament theology, an honest approach doesn't neglect relevant texts that speak to a given subject. Ultimately, biblical theology is canonical—it will consider theological relationships between all segments of Scripture and will never consciously neglect some texts while actively embracing others.

---

14. William W. Klein, Craig L. Blomberg, and Robert L. Hubbard Jr., *Introduction to Biblical Interpretation*, rev. ed. (Nashville: Thomas Nelson, 2004), 462.
15. Ibid., 385.

Be Practical

An inductive approach to theology naturally incorporates the practical application of Scripture into its theological framework. Biblical theology is in some sense practical theology. It is developed out of an understanding of what Scripture meant to them *and* what it means to us. Therefore, proper theology provides an articulation of what the Bible teaches in terms of knowledge and practice. It is an inherently practical discipline, especially when understood as the final outflow of the inductive process. As Bauer and Traina state, "the goal of biblical study is the development of a biblical theology that may form the basis for Christian faith and life."[16]

Final Thoughts

A survey of biblical theologies (including Old and New Testament theologies) suggests that there are many ways to do biblical theology. Some find in biblical theology a central thematic core which is supported by diverse thematic motifs, while others understand those motifs only as components set within a broader unfolding story.[17] The truth is somewhere in-between. As a theological revelation of God, the Bible presents thematic content about God and his relationship with creation. Yet the Bible is a story—a complex story based in historical events, presented through the pages of a book.

The theology of the Bible flows out of that story—it is the revelation of God in history, the revelation of God through literature. Theology is not just a set of doctrines, nor is it a mere set of motifs. Theology is the *story of God's redemptive relationship with humankind,* revealed to us in a book. It is an intensely practical message, one that impacts every facet of the believer's life, from our way of thinking to our practice of living. As we enter into the story of God's redemption in our own lives, the Scriptures effectively change our whole being.

16. David R. Bauer and Robert A. Traina, *Inductive Bible Study: A Comprehensive Guide to the Practice of Hermeneutics* (Grand Rapids: Baker, 2011), 341.

17. Jeannine K. Brown, *Scripture as Communication: Introducing Biblical Hermeneutics* (Grand Rapids: Baker, 2007), 229–30.

The heart of this book has been to equip you to appreciate, comprehend, and understand the message of that story revealed through the pages of the Bible more fully. We trust that through the steps of the inductive method, practiced within the framework of the hermeneutical triad, you'll be better equipped for your journey of unpacking that message as you take your place and live out your part in the story of God's redemptive mission. While this story has its roots in eternity past and comes to a climax in the substitutionary death of Jesus Christ, it is not over. As those redeemed by the blood of God's beloved Son, we live out his Word faithfully, laboring until that story finds its ultimate consummation at the return of Jesus Christ.

Glossary

Acrostic: highly structured poetic arrangement where each line of poetry begins with a successive letter of the (Hebrew) alphabet

Apocalyptic literature: a genre of prophetic writing which developed during post-exilic Jewish culture, characterized by visions and symbols revealing future realities and spiritual truth

Autograph: the original manuscript of a scriptural document

Biblical theology: the theology of the Bible in its original historical context as conveyed by the terminology of the biblical writers

Boundary features: elements of a text such as initial or final markers that help the interpreter determine what constitutes a literary unit

Canon: the sixty-six books of the Bible which have been recognized as inspired and authoritative

Chiasm: a thematic "crisscrossing" between adjacent lines of poetry, sometimes occurring in extended passages of prose literature

Common priority fallacy: unwarranted assumption that common meaning of a word will be determinative for any given context

Concordance: a verbal index of all the words in the Bible, listed alphabetically with attendant Scripture references

Correlation: comparing a given Scripture with other passages on the same topic

Dead Sea Scrolls: group of over 900 ancient Hebrew manuscripts that was discovered starting in 1946 but is dated to between the second century BC and the first century AD

Deductive: assumption-based study

Discourse: communication made up of a coherent sequence of phrases or sentences, structured in prose or poetic literature

Discourse analysis: the study of features within textual units that establish the structural components and framework for the communication of meaning in discourse

Dynamic equivalence: free translation or paraphrase

Epistolary literature: the genre consisting of letters, primarily found in the New Testament

Exegesis: the analysis of a text that draws out the interpretation of that text

Exegetical distinction fallacy: unwarranted assumption that writers are always intending heightened theological distinctions between different words

Full semantic range fallacy: unwarranted assumption that a word used in a particular biblical context is in some manner communicating aspects of its entire semantic range (also known as illegitimate totality transfer)

Genre: a category (or kind) of literature that shares common form, style, function, or content

Grammar: the framework or structure of a language (i.e., syntax, morphology, etc.)

Hapax legomenon: a word that only occurs once in the Bible

Hermeneutical triad: the three dimensions of biblical interpretation, namely history, literature, and theology

Hermeneutics: the science and art of biblical interpretation

Homiletics: the art of sermon writing

Illumination: the role of the Holy Spirit in the interpretation of Scripture

Inclusio: the repetition of a word or phrase at the beginning and ending of a literary unit

Inductive: evidence-based study

Inspiration: the role of the Holy Spirit in the writing of Scripture

Koine Greek: the common Greek of the New Testament

Lexical meaning: the meaning of a word as found in a lexicon (or dictionary)

Linguistics: the study of the nature of language

Manuscript: a book or document written by hand

Masoretic manuscript tradition: the text of the Hebrew Bible compiled by the Masoretes, a group of Jewish scribes from the Middle Ages, which comprises the basis for most Old Testament translation

Parallelism: a common feature in Hebrew poetry where successive lines correspond in form or content

Pentateuch: also known as the *torah*; the first five books of the Bible

Pericope: a self-contained unit in narrative literature

Preunderstanding: knowledge an interpreter brings to his or her interpretation of the text.

Root fallacy: unwarranted assumption that a word *means* at the time of writing what it *meant* when it was first coined (also known as etymological fallacy)

Semantics: the area of linguistics concerned with word meaning

Semantic field: a collection of related words (including synonyms and antonyms) within a given language

Semantic field study: study of a cluster of related words

Semantic range: the potential meanings that a given word might convey depending upon contextual usage

Septuagint: the Greek translation of the Hebrew Scriptures originating some 250 years before Christ

Stanza: a group of lines in poetry that convey consistency in form and content

Syntax: the branch of linguistics that analyzes word relationships and arrangements

Textual criticism: a necessary analytical science that seeks to reproduce the most accurate original language text possible based upon available manuscript evidence

Textual variant: differences between biblical manuscripts that can occur by mistake or by intentional redaction at the hand of a copyist

Textus Receptus: Latin for "Received Text," this is the Greek text used by Martin Luther in his original German Luther Bible and by the King James Version translators

Translation theory: the degree of dynamic equivalence applied to the process of translation

Vulgate: Latin version of the Bible translated by Jerome, later made the official Bible of the Roman Catholic Church at the Council of Trent

For Further Study

Alexander, T. Desmond, Brian S. Rosner, D. A. Carson, and Graeme Goldsworthy, eds. *New Dictionary of Biblical Theology.* Downers Grove: InterVarsity, 2000.

Bauer, David R., and Robert A. Traina, *Inductive Bible Study: A Comprehensive Guide to the Practice of Hermeneutics.* Grand Rapids: Baker, 2011.

Beale, G. K. *Handbook on the New Testament Use of the Old Testament.* Grand Rapids: Baker, 2012.

Beale, G. K., and D. A. Carson, eds. *Commentary on the New Testament Use of the Old Testament.* Grand Rapids: Baker, 2007.

Black, David Alan, and David S. Dockery, eds. *Interpreting the New Testament.* Nashville: B&H, 2001.

Brunn, Dave. *One Bible, Many Versions: Are All Translations Created Equal?* Downers Grove: InterVarsity, 2013.

Carson, D. A. *Exegetical Fallacies.* 2nd ed. Grand Rapids: Baker, 1996.

Cotterell, Peter, and Max Turner. *Linguistics and Biblical Interpretation.* Downers Grove: InterVarsity, 1989.

Doriani, Daniel M. *Putting the Truth to Work: The Theory and Practice of Biblical Application.* Phillipsburg, NJ: P&R, 2001.

Fee, Gordon D., and Douglas Stuart. *How to Read the Bible for All Its Worth.* 4th ed. Grand Rapids: Zondervan, 2014.

Hays, J. Daniel, and J. Scott Duvall. *Grasping God's Word.* 3rd ed. Grand Rapids: Zondervan, 2012.

Hendricks, Howard G., and William D. Hendricks. *Living by the Book.* Chicago: Moody, 1991.

Hirsch, E. D. *Validity in Interpretation.* New Haven, CT: Yale University Press, 1967.

Kaiser, Walter C. Jr., Peter H. Davids, F. F. Bruce, and Manfred T. Brauch. *Hard Sayings of the Bible.* Downers Grove: InterVarsity, 1996.

Kaiser, Walter C. Jr., and Moisés Silva. *Introduction to Biblical Hermeneutics: The Search for Meaning.* Rev. ed. Grand Rapids: Zondervan, 2007.

Klein, William W., Craig L. Blomberg, and Robert L. Hubbard Jr. *Introduction to Biblical Interpretation.* Rev. ed. Nashville: Thomas Nelson, 2004.

Klein, William W. *Handbook for Personal Bible Study: Enriching Your Experience with God's Word.* The Navigators Reference Library. Colorado Springs: NavPress, 2008.

Köstenberger, Andreas J., and Raymond P. Bouchoc, *The Book Study Concordance of the Greek New Testament.* Nashville: B&H Academic, 2003.

Köstenberger, Andreas J., and David A. Croteau, eds. *Which Bible Translation Should I Use? A Comparison of 4 Major Recent Versions.* Nashville: B&H Academic, 2012.

Köstenberger, Andreas J., L. Scott Kellum, and Charles L. Quarles. *The Cradle, the Cross, and the Crown: An Introduction to the New Testament.* 2nd ed. Nashville: B&H Academic, 2016.

Köstenberger, Andreas J., and Richard D. Patterson. *Invitation to Biblical Interpretation: Exploring the Hermeneutical Triad of History, Literature, and Theology.* Grand Rapids: Kregel, 2011.

Köstenberger, Andreas J., and Richard D. Patterson. *For the Love of God's Word: An Introduction to Biblical Interpretation.* Grand Rapids: Kregel, 2015.

Louw, Johannes P., and Eugene A. Nida. *Greek-English Lexicon of the New Testament Based on Semantic Domains.* 2 vols. New York: United Bible Societies, 1988, 1989.

Merrill, Eugene H., Mark F. Rooker, and Michael A. Grisanti. *The World and the Word: An Introduction to the Old Testament.* Nashville: B&H Academic, 2011.

Olesberg, Lindsay. *The Bible Study Handbook.* Downers Grove: InterVarsity, 2012.

Osborne, Grant R. *The Hermeneutical Spiral: A Comprehensive Introduction to Biblical Interpretation.* Rev. ed. Downers Grove: InterVarsity, 2006.

Plummer, Robert L. *40 Questions About Interpreting the Bible.* Grand Rapids: Kregel, 2010.

Ryken, Leland, James C. Wilhoit, and Tremper Longman III. *Dictionary of Biblical Imagery.* Downers Grove: InterVarsity, 1998.

Sandy, D. Brent. *Plowshares and Pruning Hooks: Rethinking the Language of Biblical Prophecy and Apocalyptic.* Downers Grove: InterVarsity, 2002.

Sandy, D. Brent, and Ronald L. Giese Jr. *Cracking Old Testament Codes: A Guide to Interpreting the Literary Genres of the Old Testament.* Nashville: B&H, 1995.

Schultz, Richard L. *Out of Context: How to Avoid Misinterpreting the Bible.* Grand Rapids: Baker, 2012.

Silva, Moisés, ed. *New International Dictionary of New Testament Theology and Exegesis.* 5 vols. Grand Rapids: Zondervan, 2014.

Traina, Robert A. *Methodical Bible Study.* Grand Rapids: Zondervan, 2002 [1952].

VanGemeren, Willem A., ed. *New International Dictionary of Old Testament Theology & Exegesis.* 5 vols. Grand Rapids: Zondervan, 1997.

Vanhoozer, Kevin J. *Is There a Meaning in This Text? The Bible, the Reader, and the Morality of Literary Knowledge.* Grand Rapids: Zondervan, 1998.

Wegner, Paul D. *The Journey from Texts to Translations: The Origin and Development of the Bible.* Grand Rapids: Baker, 2005.

Zuck, Roy. *Basic Bible Interpretation.* Colorado Springs: Chariot Victor, 1991.

Scripture Index

13 *122, 130*
13:10 *28*
14:6, 20, 26, 39 *162, 164*
15 *206*
15:12, 35 *162, 164*
15:35–50 *229*
15:50–58 *122, 127*
16:20 *10, 41, 295*

2 Corinthians
3:13–16 *330*
4:3–6 *331*
5:17 *229*
5:17–21 *107–8*
5:21 *117*
8:1 *71*
10:3–5 *331*
13:12 *10, 295*

Galatians
1:9 *88*
1:10 *122, 134, 146*
1:14 *244*
2:19–20 *262*
2:20 *260*
3:1–4 *142*
3:19 *122, 131*
3:24 *58–59, 61*
5 *262*
5:1–6 *263*
5:15 *260*
5:16–18 *260*
5:16–25 *122, 127*
5:19 *260*
5:22–26 *259, 262*
6:2 *122, 140*
6:11–15 *263*
6:14 *262*

Ephesians
1 *133*
1–3 *133*

1:7 *68*
2:8–9 *248*
2:13 *68*
3:1–9 *210*
3:20–21 *162, 164*
4 *132*
4:1 *133, 164*
4:1, 17 *162*
4–6 *133*
4:11–12 *122, 130*
4:11–16 *133*
4:13–16 *122, 130*
4:17 *122, 133*
6:5–9 *309*
6:10 *162, 164*
6:11 *331*
6:23–24 *162, 164*

Philippians
2:1–2 *135*
2:1–4 *135*
2:1–11 *122*
2:3–4 *135*
2:4 *136*
2:5 *135*
2:6 *106*
2:6–11 *106, 122, 135, 138*
2:7 *106*
3:1 *162, 164*
3:2–10 *174, 176*
4:8 *162, 164*
4:12 *311*
4:13 *311–12*

Colossians
1:14 *67–68*
1:15 *225–26*
1:15–20 *122, 138, 225*
1:18 *225, 226*
1:20 *68*
1:25–27 *210*

2:8 *244*
2:11–15 *263*
2:14 *262*
2:20–3:11 *263*
3:1 *122, 134*
3:1–11 *228*
3:9 *263*
3:10 *228–29*

1 Thessalonians
4:13–15 *146*
5:16–22 *122, 138*
5:26 *10, 295*

2 Thessalonians
2:15 *244*
3:6 *244*

1 Timothy
1:2, 4, 5 *244*
1:3 *244*
1:10 *244*
1:18 *244*
2:1–7 *98*
2:2 *98*
2:5–6 *122, 138*
2:7 *244*
2:8–12 *98*
2:8–15 *83, 93–98*
2:9 *98*
2:9–15 *95*
2:11–12 *96, 97*
2:11–15 *228*
2:12 *244*
2:13 *96*
2:13–14 *97*
2:14 *97*
2:15 *96–98, 248*
3:1–7 *98*
3:2 *31*
3:8–13 *98*
3:16 *122, 138*

Name Index

Subject Index